STUDIES IN THEORETICAL AND APPLIED
ECONOMICS
General editor:
B. T. BAYLISS

THE MOTOR INDUSTRY: AN ECONOMIC SURVEY

D. G. RHYS
Lecturer in Economics at University College, Cardiff

LONDON
BUTTERWORTHS

THE BUTTERWORTH GROUP

ENGLAND

Butterworth & Co (Publishers) Ltd
London: 88 Kingsway, WC2B 6AB

AUSTRALIA

Butterworth & Co (Australia) Ltd
Sydney: 586 Pacific Highway, Chatswood, NSW 2067
Melbourne: 343 Little Collins Street, 3000
Brisbane: 240 Queen Street, 4000

CANADA

Butterworth & Co (Canada) Ltd
Toronto: 14 Curity Avenue, 374

NEW ZEALAND

Butterworth & Co (New Zealand) Ltd
Wellington: 26–28 Waring Taylor Street, 1

SOUTH AFRICA

Butterworth & Co (South Africa) (Pty) Ltd
Durban: 152–154 Gale Street

First published in 1972

© D. G. Rhys, 1972

ISBN 0 408 70356 3

Printed in England by
C. Tinling & Co. Ltd, London and Prescot

PREFACE

In this volume I have attempted to illustrate and explain the development and structure of the motor industry and to show how the industry fits in with the economist's theory of the firm.

The international character of the industry can only be expected to develop further during the coming decades and it is for this reason that much space has been devoted to the motor industry abroad and to the various aspects of motor vehicle exporting. An understanding of the nature of foreign competition and foreign markets should help to put the British industry's position in the world's motor industry in perspective, and to show that traditional arguments concerning Britain's export performance need questioning.

Labour relations in the industry has also been singled out for particular attention in order to illustrate that good or poor labour relations depend upon a wide variety of factors and that there is no simple remedy for strike proneness. It has been deemed worth stating that although harmonious labour relations depend upon initiatives from both sides of industry, the onus of responsibility in the final analysis rests upon management.

Particular attention has been paid to all aspects of the commercial vehicle industry if only to illustrate that the British motor industry contains the business acumen and expertise to satisfy most of the needs of the market, especially in terms of the nature of the product and where price and quality is concerned. The fact that American owned companies use the United Kingdom as their major non-American manufacturing sector is both cause and effect where the strength of the commercial vehicle sector is concerned.

The interesting and pertinent facts concerning the development of the British motor industry from the earliest days and up to World War II are commented upon. In many ways the post-war history of motor manufacturing is a continuation and culmination of trends already discernible in the 1920s and 1930s.

The nature of competition in the industry is dealt with at length, as are the crucial areas covered by the chapters on the demand for and the supply of the products of the motor industry. Here, as in most instances, an attempt has been made to utilise and discuss available statistical and econometric data in a way

PREFACE

which can be easily followed by the layman. This has been the aim wherever economic analysis of a technical nature is utilised.

Finally, a word of acknowledgement. It would be invidious of me to single out any individual, but I must express my gratitude to Mr. George Maxcy of the Economics Department, University of Hull, for giving me such help and encouragement, and also to the many people connected with the motor industry for their time, care, and attention.

D. G. Rhys

University College, Cardiff

CONTENTS

CONTENTS

1

THE EARLY DAYS

The motor car was invented by everybody and nobody. The cars produced by Emile Levassor, Karl Benz, and even Etienne Lenoir of Paris, who can be credited with building the first petrol-engined carriages in 1862, were only a synthesis of earlier inventions.

The wheel is found on carved pictures dating from 3500–4000 B.C., while the differential gear was almost certainly known to the Chinese as early as 2000 B.C., but forgotten until re-invented by millwrights in the fourteenth century. Early in the fourteenth century Rudolph Ackermann developed a front-wheel layout for carriages on which today's car steering is based. In the seventeenth century Christian Huyghens suggested the internal combustion engine, the central principle suggested being explosions inside a cylinder, and in the same century Robert Hooke invented a universal joint, a mechanism for transmitting energy around corners which is a crucial feature of powered road vehicles. Farish and Cecil built an engine worked by the explosion of hydrogen gas in 1820, and in 1838 Barnett was running one powered by coal gas. Around the same time, Michael Faraday invented the generator which would provide the electricity for the lamps invented by Joseph Swan which would light the way for road vehicles.

During the nineteenth century the invention of the necessary components went on apace. Mackenzie patented a clutch in 1865 and Emile Levassor derived from it the car clutch for his Panhard-Levassor cars. In 1869 Markus produced his petrol-engined car, which seems to have been forgotten, and in 1872 George Brayton sought a patent for an engine using oil instead of gas. Everyone knows, however, that in 1885 Karl Benz developed an automobile.

In turn, many devices were invented but never put into production. Dunlop, for instance, is credited with inventing the pneumatic tyre in 1888, but he had to fight the claim of Robert Thompson's patent filed in 1867. Benz's car got its fuel mixture by drawing air over the surface of petrol in the tank; a more advanced carburettor similar to those used today was invented by Wilhelm Maybach, another German. The Marquis de Dion, however, developed a rear suspension system so successfully that it remained the main form of suspension for racing cars until the early 1960s and is still used in many production cars, for example, the Rover 2000.

One of the outstanding inventors of the car was Frederick Lanchester. It is suggested that of 36 major car components Lanchester invented 18, including the disc brake. By the 1920s most major items had been invented; however, the process continues. In the inter-war period Dr. Ferdinand Porsche developed torsion-bar suspension. Charles Kettering's 'self starter' of 1912 became popularised, therefore making it possible to start a car without risking life and limb. The 1920s saw the arrival of four-wheel braking with hydraulic systems replacing less reliable mechanical ones. The 1920s also saw the appearance of integral construction, which gradually replaced the chassis where car production was concerned. The cars of the 1920s embodied and continued the technical progress of an earlier age. In 1934 Citroen synthesised these new developments with a car of front-wheel drive, independent suspension and springing by means of torsion bars, removable cylinder liners and an integral chassis-less construction. The 1930s brought the development of automatic gear changing, with different designs being produced by Daimler in the U.K. and the General Motors Corporation in the U.S.A. World War II brought the development of four-wheel drive vehicles of great versatility. Technical progress has been rapid since 1945 with added refinements. Better braking, simplified automatic gear changing, more precise steering and suspension, and new types of engine, such as the turbine and rotary piston have been some of the developments taking place. Future progress lies in the direction of completely new power sources, either steam generated or electric, plus ways and means of preventing smoke emission and general pollution from the internal combustion engine.

THE ORIGINS AND DEVELOPMENT OF THE MOTOR INDUSTRY

STEAM PROPULSION

The development of the culmination of the inventions of centuries has been rapid. The production of viable motor vehicles powered by internal combustion engines stems from the last decade of the nineteenth century. Steam propelled vehicles have a longer history. The Jesuit Ferdinand Verbist produced a model steam car around 1665–1680 and there is reason to suppose that the 'fire cart' was known to the Chinese long before this. The first full size steam 'automobile' was produced by Joseph Cugnot in France around 1769, with a larger design appearing in 1771. In 1801 Robert Trevithick built a steam road vehicle and Peugeot in France produced a similar vehicle in 1828, but utilising a differential gear and steering of an advanced design. It was at this time that Gurney and Hancock started to construct really road-worthy steam carriages and made attempts to use steam transport as a commercial proposition. The problem of using coal to 'stoke the fire' prompted designers to toy with the idea of using liquid fuel in place of coal. In 1868 Joseph Ravel in France produced a steam car with liquid fuel.

Other paths of investigations led away from steam. Isaac de Rivoz, a Swiss, propelled a carriage in the spring of 1804 by exploding hydrogen and air inside a cylinder—the manifestation of Huyghens's idea and crude 'engine' of 1673. In 1860 Lenoir patented a two-stroke internal-combustion engine which powered the world's first automobile, in the accepted sense of the word, in 1862–1863. In 1876 Otto designed a practical four-stroke engine although he built no cars. Between 1869 and 1890 Markus built two single cylinder cars using crude petrol engines. Had Markus followed up his far sighted ideas he would have become the father of the modern automobile.

In 1883–1864 Delanore–Deboutteville built a two-cylinder car, but this design was not followed-up either. The year 1885 was a turning point, with Karl Benz and Gottlieb Daimler, quite independently of each other, producing viable automobile designs which were developed into marketable commodities, as distinct from 'one-off' inventor's curiosities. But it was France and not Germany, which became the cradle of the automobile. Daimler's patent rights were bought by Edourd Sarazin for the firm Perrin, Panhard and Cie in 1887. Sarazin died and his widow married Emile Levassor who took over the patents and founded the concern of Panhard and Levassor. It was this firm that brought the petrol motor car into being; their first car left the factory in 1890 and with it the modern motor car and automobile industry was born. Regular Panhard production commenced in 1891.

The steam car still held a leading position and the electric model was in serious contention. However, the electric car needed frequent recharging and the petrol car had come to stay as a viable transport method. Steam cars had a long life, with Stanley and White steamers being produced up until just after World War I.

THE BEGINNINGS OF MASS-PRODUCTION

European road transport was well organised before the first railways were laid. This was of great benefit to Europe's first car designers. In the United States, the railways preceded the roads, so no trunk road routes existed and the roads were totally unsuited to motor cars. Consequently the American pioneers concentrated on producing very light cars, the production of which was suited to bicycle makers who had the necessary machinery and technical knowledge. Other pioneers stemmed from the horse-drawn carriage business, notably Studebaker and Durandt. It is ironic, in the light of subsequent developments, that European cars were much larger and more powerful than American ones, but only light cars could traverse the mud tracks that passed as roads in the U.S.A. at that time.

This difference had a tremendous economic significance far transcending the mere differences in design. While the European car industry's pattern was one of hand building by individual designers, the building of cars in the U.S.A. had an industrial look about it from the beginning. This followed from the situation facing the bicycle industry. A decline in the demand for bicycles forced the leading makers and their component suppliers to make motor cars and to make them in large numbers and at low prices. The light car necessitated by American road conditions was eminently suitable to production by bicycle makers.

In the U.S.A. the Selden patent, and in the U.K. H. J. Lawson's British Motor Syndicate, attempted to monopolise or at least to centralise the production of motor cars. Both attempts failed because of financial failure, technical developments and the force of law.

Between 1885 and 1900 the birth of the motor car as we know it today took place. Initially designs were of light, rickety, horseless carriages, but by 1901 these were out of date. From being merely a converted horse-drawn carriage the car had become in less than 20 years a vehicle conceived solely as an 'automobile'. It was only the bonds of tradition—which still exist—which dictated similarities with the horse-drawn carriage.

During World War I, car factories were turned over to the mass-production of war materials. So in 1918 many car factories had technical knowledge of large-scale production. Also, the war had shown the possible uses of motorised transport and the failure of the horse—the 'favourite' of the 'governing classes', ever eager to crush the new upstart by taxation and legislation. Engineers brought technical logic to the arbitrary designs and chaotic production methods of the self-taught pioneers of the motor car. Similarly, finance moved in with the investment needed for the mass-production necessary to satisfy the large post-war demand for mechanised transport. The motor industry was born and mass-production replaced hand-built production. The inter-war years saw a division between the cars from the conveyor belts of mass-production and those from the work-shops of smaller manufacturers. The depression of 1929 destroyed many of the latter type of enterprise, most of which were technically brilliant but financially weak. The large-scale production of cars using moving conveyors and mechanisation began in the U.S.A., and the Model T Ford of 1908–1927 was the embodiment of this. In 1913 Ford made 100 000 Model Ts, in 1914 the figure was 200 000, reaching the million mark by 1919. Manufacturing had reached levels demanding substantial capital investment, but at the same time promised dividends large enough to attract investors.

In 1910 Ford sold 600 cars in the U.K. and in 1911 the Ford Motor Company (England) Ltd. was incorporated. By 1914 Ford produced more vehicles than any other company in Britain and prices ranged from £125 to £135 which was below anything charged by other British firms for comparable products. By 1918 Ford was making 12 000 vehicles a year at its Manchester factory. For various reasons the Ford Company's fortunes declined in the British market in the 1920s only to recover in the 1930s. It will be seen later that in many ways Ford has been a predominant force in the British motor industry. Early dominance was replaced by decline in the 1920s, but in the 1930s a process of advance and consolidation was begun which was still evident in 1971. What then of the early development of the British motor industry?

THE BIRTH OF AN INDUSTRY

No precise date can, of course, be given for the establishment of the British motor industry. As in all engineering activities, the industry was preceded by a long period of experimentation and development. Almost a century of such experimentation and development occurred in the case of the motor industry, from Trevithick's steam road vehicle of 1801 (probably the first mechanically propelled road vehicle used in the U.K.) through Gurney and Hancock's steam carriages in the 1830s and Anderson's electric road vehicle of 1839, culminating in Butler's production of a motor vehicle powered by an internal combustion engine in 1888. It was the petrol spark-ignition engine which represented the technological breakthrough as regards the development of the 'self-powered' road vehicle.

The early development of the internal combustion engine, however, took place on the Continent of Europe. This form of engine was invented in France in 1860 by Lenoir, and the first 'motor' car was produced by him in 1862. It was in Germany that the motor vehicle was first produced in any quantity, although the centre of activity soon moved to France. The German pioneers were Otto, Benz and Daimler, the latter producing a petrol driven car in 1887. Thereafter a rapid succession of virtually independently conceived inventions proceeded to appear in the U.K., Italy and the U.S.A. between 1888 and 1894 from men such as Butler, Bianchi and Elwood-Haynes.

The main impetus to the development of the U.K. industry came in 1896 when the 'Locomotives on Highways Act' repealed the restrictive 'Red Flag' legislation of 1865. This legislation imposed a theoretical speed limit of 14 m.p.h. but 12 m.p.h. was the maximum permitted. After the turn of the century this was raised to 20 m.p.h. for some vehicles and continued as such until 1930. The legislation of 1865 may have had a discouraging effect on inventors, but more probably retarded the development of the industry. After all, self-propelled vehicles were restricted to walking speeds and could therefore be outpaced by horse-driven carriages.

However, there was not quite the same stultifying effect on the development of steam-powered goods vehicles. Obviously it was advantageous to dispatch as much merchandise traffic as possible by railway, but some journeys necessitated the use of roads. Light loads were carried by horse-drawn vehicles, but the steam-powered mobile traction engine which appeared in 1856 was used for heavier traffic.

By 1865 a large number (about 100) of traction engine builders were in existence, firms such as Aveling and Porter, Foster and Fowler, the latter producing its last traction engine in 1944. The early models could haul loads of around 5 tons and the later heavy types loads of up to 100 tons. It was not until the early 1890s with the development of light, liquid-fuelled steam engines and the appearance of the petrol engine that the lorry-type vehicle appeared to rival the traction engine and the horse. The heavy coal-fuelled steam lorry did not appear until 1897, from the factories of Thornycroft and Leyland. It would appear then that, apart from the traction engine, the development of self-powered goods vehicles was impeded by the legislation of 1865. In addition, it must be remembered that while roads in Britain were good, they were not really suitable for bearing heavy loads.

THE EMERGENCE OF THE MAJOR PRODUCERS

Following the Act of 1896, the engineering ideas of F. W. Lanchester, Herbert Austin and J. H. Knight were put into production. Before 1896 no British car had been produced: the first car to be made on any scale in the U.K. appeared in 1896. This was the German Daimler, built under licence by the Daimler Motor Co., a subsidiary of the British Motor Syndicate (BMS). This was quickly followed in the same year by the public companies, Lanchester, Riley, Rover and Triumph. The BMS attempted to gain a patent monopoly in the new industry but a Court decision in 1901 prevented this. Therefore the path remained open to continued free entry into the new motor industry.

It was Henry Ford in the U.S.A. who laid the foundation of motor vehicle manufacture as it is known today. The principle of mass-production is very old and was widely applied by the early nineteenth century. Ford took things one stage further with the introduction of the moving production line and mechanical handling. The idea was based on the meat handling techniques used in Chicago slaughter-houses. Ford was the first manufacturer to introduce standardisation into the industry. He was also the first to introduce special purpose machines and the first to use outside component suppliers on any scale. Ford's ideas on the large scale manufacture of standardised vehicles were formulated by 1903 and came to fruition in 1908 with the introduction of the Model T*.

In 1911 the U.K. had its first experience of relatively capital intensive

* Fifteen million were made between 1908 and 1927 at steadily decreasing prices.

mass-production of motor vehicles when the Ford Company began to assemble and partially manufacture the Model T at Old Trafford, Manchester. This was the first really inexpensive vehicle produced in the U.K. In the same year, Wolseley, Morris, Austin, Singer and Rover all introduced low price motor cars, with outputs ranging between 1000 and 3000. So by 1911 high volume and consequently lower-priced motor cars were being produced, but at the same time this increased the capital needs of the firms in the industry. As a result, engineering skill alone was no longer sufficient a resource for establishing a motor manufacturing firm; business acumen and access to capital were becoming more important.

Even after 1911, however, successful entry into the industry was not impossible, only more difficult. In the early years, before 1911, it was a simple matter to enter the industry. A knowledge of engineering methods allied to modest sums of capital was sufficient to establish a vehicle producing firm. General engineering firms such as Wolseley and Leyland, or firms engaged in cycle manufacture such as Rover, Dennis and Humber were therefore well suited to motor vehicle production. Nevertheless, the industry expanded much more slowly than the American motor industry.

In the U.S.A. the engineering industry as a whole had evolved a system of standardised part-interchangeability allied to the great use of subcontracting. None of these features were particularly evident in the British engineering industry at the turn of the century. Consequently British vehicle manufacturers endeavoured to make all their own parts and components. Obviously this added to the capital requirements of the vehicle builders. The need for it was greater than it would have been if outside component producers, with their own capital equipment, had existed.

Standardisation and sub-contracting allowed the American manufacturer to use his capital on establishing his vehicle assembly capacity and at the same time he was able to purchase low-cost parts and components produced by outside specialists with relatively long production runs. Vehicle production expanded rapidly and consequently prices were quite low. In the U.K. each firm produced a small number of cars and at high prices. This restricted the total vehicle market; and it was not until the appearance of the Austin Seven in 1921 that a really cheap car existed. This development extended the industry's sales by vastly increasing the public to which motoring was possible.

As entry was easy in the early days before World War I it was only to be expected that commercial failure was common-place. Many firms failed to keep up with the rapid technical advances made in these years or succumbed to the great competition from other producers. All this was to be expected within a new industry, but the development of the industry as a whole suffered from the absence of an efficient components industry. One British producer who had a policy of purchasing from outside suppliers—William Morris—had to turn to the U.S.A. in 1914 when no British producer was found who could make sufficient quantities of standardised parts to satisfy his increased needs. The differences in volume were reflected by differences in costs and prices. In 1914 Morris purchased complete engine units from the Continental Motor Manufacturing Co. of Detroit for $85 (£17 14s. 2d.), on the basis of an initial production run of 2500 in the first year building up to 5000 units in each subsequent year. The lowest price quoted by a U.K. manufacturer—White and Poppe, the Coventry engine makers—was double this. The chassis of the Morris car incorporated Belgian made components. In the immediate post-war period the only factory in the U.K. capable of meeting Morris's engine requirements was owned by Hotchkiss et Cie, a French company*.

The birth pains of the British industry is illustrated by the number of firms entering and leaving the industry. Up to 1913, 198 different makes of British cars had entered the market, of which 103 quickly disappeared†. In the same period, about 150 different makes of commercial vehicles had entered the industry of which about 130 had disappeared. Taking the industry as a whole, the Society of Motor Manufacturers and Traders (SMMT) data shows total British vehicle production in 1913 at 34 000; perhaps 25 000 were cars. In France 45 000 cars were produced, whereas the American figure was 462 000 cars and 23 000 other vehicles. The development of the American industry was startling. As early as 1902 it had passed the 'experimental' stage with vehicle production estimated at 9000 units produced by over 100 firms. In 1904 about 120 firms produced 22 830 vehicles, using 57 firms for supplies of components. In 1913 there were almost 300 vehicle producers supplied by almost 1000 component makers.

Two main reasons account for this situation. Firstly, by the turn of the century, American per capita income was significantly greater than British or French levels. Indeed some studies suggest that this

* Sir Miles Thomas, *Out on a Wing: an autobiography*, Michael Joseph, London (1964).
† *Motor Vehicles: A Report on the Industry*, Political and Economic Planning, London (1950).

was so as early as 1840*. Secondly, as mentioned earlier†, the method
of production and the industrial structure was different. In the early
years the European car industry's structure was that of hand-made
vehicles produced by individual designers. In the United States, the
production of cars had an industrial air about it from the start. A
decline in the market for bicycles had forced the main producers and
their component suppliers to seek new markets and some turned to
making cars and to making them in large numbers and at low prices.
By 1902 the Oldsmobile was being mass produced. The American car
itself was smaller, lighter and therefore cheaper in terms of direct
costs than the typical European car. This was partly because roads in
the United States were so poor that heavy vehicles would become
bogged down and partly because the American car was aimed at a
mass market instead of being the plaything of the rich. In short, high
per capita purchasing power allied to low cost products and production
methods meant the establishment of a large industry.

WORLD WAR I: THE INCREASE IN POTENTIAL CAPACITY

World War I severely curtailed the production, sale and development
of cars in Europe. This allowed the U.S.A. to attain dominance in the
world's markets. Consequently the American motor industry's growth
was unchecked by World War I. Car sales in the domestic market also
advanced following upon the increased prosperity the war brought to
the American economy.

A further result of the war was the extension it made to the productive
capacity in the British economy, the motor industry included. Those
vehicle manufacturers producing munitions and military vehicles
particularly benefitted. For instance, the Associated Equipment Company (AEC) in 1914 was one of the most sophisticated and experienced
manufacturers of goods vehicles in the country. Consequently the
War Department used AEC to produce 40% of its total requirements
for military trucks, and at its peak AEC's annual production was
about 4000 vehicles. For the time this was a vast figure. It was made
possible by the use of a moving-track assembly line which was put
into full operation in 1915. This form of sophisticated production
process was virtually unknown in British car production—apart from

* See R. E. Gallman, 'Gross National Product in the United States, 1834–
1909', also 'Output, Employment and Productivity in the United States after
1800', *Studies in Income and Wealth*, Vol. 30, National Bureau of Economic
Research: Columbia University Press, New York (1966).
† Page 4.

Ford's—let alone in commercial vehicle manufacture. This efficient method of production was expanded and developed during the war, leaving the firm with greatly increased capacity when peace came. Leyland Motors produced almost 6000 vehicles for the War Office during World War I, the largest total being 1694 produced in 1916. For Leyland the war years were a period of considerable expansion under government direction. By 1918 the company had doubled their workforce and trebled their pre-war capacity for vehicle production.

Apart from the increased potential capacity, World War I saw another important and far reaching event. This was the imposition in 1915 of the McKenna duty of 33⅓% *ad valorem* on the landed cost of imported cars. This duty practically removed foreign competition from the British domestic market. This McKenna duty was absorbed into the general tariff structure in 1931. (It remained at its original level until 1956 when it was reduced to 30% to be followed by further reductions in the 1960s. In 1972 the rate on cars falls to 11% compared with 22% on commercial vehicles, the latter being omitted from the Kennedy Round of GATT negotiations on tariff reductions.)

1918–1939: THE CONCENTRATION OF PRODUCTION

After World War I, the pent-up demand for vehicles led to an increase in the number of producers. In 1919 and 1920, 40 new car producers appeared, another 46 entering the industry between 1921 and 1925. In addition, over 30 firms entered the commercial vehicle industry. The inter-war period, however, was one of keen competition in the motor industry and instability in the economy generally. This resulted in either the merging of firms or in the complete elimination of particular producers. Elimination could either mean the liquidation of a manufacturer or the closure of the vehicle building sections of a large combine. The effect of the 1922 slump was severe; for instance, the £1 share of a well established firm like Leyland could be purchased for 2s. 3d., the firm making a loss on the year's trading of £1 million. Other producers were less able to weather the storm; the number of companies wound-up between 1921 and 1925 exceeded 150. The inter-war period shows a continuous decline in the number of firms making road vehicles (*Table 1.1*).

Although a significant number of car and commercial vehicle producers remained, the number of manufacturers gave no indication of the degree of concentration. *The Economist* for 19 October 1929 stated that 75% of the industry's car output was produced by Morris,

Table 1.1

Year	No. of vehicle producers	Predominantly cars
1922	196	96
1929	119	41
1939	74	33

Austin and Singer. The dominant car producers were Morris and Austin and the commercial vehicle industry was dominated by Ford and Morris, although their output consisted almost entirely of lighter vehicles. In 1939, the 33 car firms listed included producers owned or controlled by other car firms. The Rootes Group consisted of three producers, the Nuffield Organisation four, the Birmingham Small Arms Company (BSA) three firms, and Rolls-Royce two. So by 1939 the degree of concentration in the industry was not adequately reflected by simply listing the total number of companies in the industry. On the car side only about twenty independent firms remained and in the commercial vehicle industry there were about 35 independent firms operating in 1939.

The outbreak of war in 1939 saw 90% of car output in the hands of the 'Big Six'—Nuffield, Ford, Austin, Vauxhall, Rootes and Standard. Another 8% was produced by Rover, Singer, BSA and Jaguar. Over 70% of the commercial vehicles produced were accounted for by Nuffield, Ford and Vauxhall; another 10% was represented by the output of Rootes and Austin. The largest of the heavy-vehicle producers was Leyland followed by Albion, Guy and AEC. In the market for goods vehicles of over 5 tons payload and for buses, these firms accounted for about 50% of sales and almost all the remainder was accounted for by the other heavy vehicle builders as the car producing firms were almost completely excluded from this market. The advent of the heavy-oil (diesel) engine as the most efficient motive unit for heavy vehicles allowed a number of firms to enter the market in the 1930s. Atkinson and Foden, already established as steam-vehicle producers, ERF and Seddon all entered the diesel commercial vehicle industry during this period.

One of the most remarkable features of the period 1929 to 1939 was the change in the relative importance of different firms. In 1932 Ford began producing at its Dagenham plant. One of the key factors determining this location was the excellent facilities it offered for shipping raw materials into the plant and completed vehicles out to export markets. In 1928 the small ailing producer of quality cars,

Vauxhall, was purchased by General Motors. Both these American firms grew in relative importance as car producers during the decade, with Vauxhall developing from a minor producer to become one of the 'Big Six'. Standard and Rootes also grew in relative importance. On the commercial vehicle side the most significant entrants at the lighter end were Rootes (through its purchase of Commer Cars, Karrier and Sunbeam) and Vauxhall, whose Bedford trucks dominated the lorry market by 1939.

Further developments in the 1930s saw increased emphasis on quality and variety and less on price competition. *The Economist* for 21 October 1933 commented on the fact that between 1929 and 1934 the number of models produced by the 10 largest firms increased from 46 to 64. By 1939 the total was in excess of 80. However, the effects of this on production costs is not at all clear. Intuitively one would expect this to reflect a movement away from cost-cutting standardisation towards expensive fragmentation and small production runs. However, the SMMT index of car prices gives no sign of increased prices during the late 1930s, although a previous downward trend was not maintained. Between 1924 and 1934 the index fell from 100 to 52; between 1934 and 1938 it remained virtually stable reaching 49 in 1938. The same pattern is repeated for commercial vehicles. The index falling from 100 in 1924 to 62 in 1934, and in 1939 prices were virtually the same at 61. Notwithstanding this, one is still able to contend that British car prices and costs were too high. Firstly, further standardisation would have continued to lower the index in the late 1930s. Secondly, the percentage price changes depicted in the index tell us nothing concerning the absolute price level. In 1938 the price and cost of production of an average British car was something in excess of 30% what it was in the U.S.A. Small production runs meant high cost production for component makers and car assemblers alike.

Although material prices were somewhat higher in the U.K. than in the U.S.A., steel being around 10% more expensive, the main reason for high cost production in the U.K. was more fundamental. In 1935, each car worker in the U.K. produced 2·86 units per year, compared with 8·76 in the U.S.A.[*] This difference was probably a function of the different number of vehicles and parts produced by each firm, and the degree of standardisation within individual firms. In 1939 the three leading models in the U.S.A. accounted for 54% of total sales compared with 27% in the U.K.[*] In the U.K. components

---

[*] L. Rostas, *Comparative Productivity in British and American Industry*, National Institute of Economic and Social Research, Occasional Paper, No. 13, pp. 63,171 (1948).

Table 1.2

Year	Cars	Commercial vehicles	Total
1922	—	—	73 000
1929	182 000	56 000	238 000

industry, physical productivity per head was only 50% of the American level. Given the importance of bought-out components in the total production costs of a typical car—around 70% in 1938—inefficiency and high cost component production meant high cost vehicles. Of course the vehicle producers were partly to blame for this. Excessive product variation imposed small high-cost production runs on the component producer. On the other hand component producers could have used their influence to encourage parts standardisation on the part of their customers by stressing the cost savings forthcoming; furthermore, some component producers were inefficient *per se*.

To summarise the inter-war period: with the restoration of peace in 1918 the industry quickly resumed its progress and new producers still entered the industry. Competition from established firms, especially Morris, and the effects of the severe slump of 1921–1922 had seen many firms leave the industry by 1925. Nevertheless, total production expanded greatly in the 1920s (*Table 1.2*).

It was the 1920s which saw the motor industry mature from one

Table 1.3

THE REDUCTION IN PRICE 1920–1929

	Morris			
	Cowley		Oxford	
Year	(4 st.)	(2 st.)	(4 st.)	(2 st.)
1920	£525	£465	£540	£535
1921	£475	£375	£565	£510
1922	£341	£299	£446	£415
1923	£255	£225	£355	£330
1929	£199		£285	

	Austin		Morris
Year	Austin 7	Austin 12	Minor Tourer
1923	£225	£450–£480	—
1929	£135	£275–£309	£125

composed of a large number of small firms with a high mortality rate, to one composed of a few large firms with a much lower mortality rate. During this decade the components industry began to develop and this helped the small firms as well as the large. Any external economies of scale, however, were not sufficiently large to insulate the small firm from the effects of the mass-production techniques introduced by Austin and Morris. The small-scale producer was quite unable to profitably match the low prices of Morris and Austin. The period 1925–1929 saw the SMMT price index fall from 100 to 75 which was largely a result of the adoption of more efficient U.S. flow-line production techniques by Austin and Morris. Both the increased volume and the introduction of smaller, cheaper cars markedly reduced the prices of their products (*Table 1.3*).

The 1930s saw the emergence of the American firms, Ford and Vauxhall, as major producers. The process of consolidation of output into fewer hands continued. Nevertheless, this still left British costs and prices rather high compared with American ones*.

THE DEPRESSION: ITS EFFECT ON THE BRITISH MOTOR INDUSTRY

Another feature of the 1930s was that the great depression affected the British motor industry much less than was the case in the other main producing countries. Comparing the 1929 level of production with that in the worst year of the depression (1932) the picture emerges shown in *Table 1.4*, where the 1932 figures are shown as a proportion of the 1929 figures.

Table 1.4

PRODUCTION IN THE MOTOR INDUSTRY
IN 1929 AND 1932 (1929 = 100)

Country	1929	1932 Cars	1932 Commercial vehicles	Total vehicles
United Kingdom	100	87	91	88
United States	100	24	26	25
Germany	100	38	21	33
France	100	64	64	64

* A 1938 Chevrolet cost just over £160 in the U.S.A. at the then current exchange rate, compared with around £200 for a typical British 12 h.p. saloon.

To interpret these figures as evidence of the basic strength of the British car market and industry would, however, be a mistake. For instance, the British car market and industry were less developed than those in France and the U.S.A. (*Table 1.5*). The 'Return to Gold' policy had restricted aggregate income and demand in the British economy throughout the 1920s and indeed the detrimental effects of this were felt throughout the 1930s. Nevertheless, the spread of the motoring habit to the middle classes and the emergence of cheaper cars favourably affected the industry during the 1930s.

Table 1.5

PRODUCTION OF VEHICLES IN 1929

Country	Cars	Commercial vehicles	Total
United Kingdom	182 347	56 458	238 805
United States	4 455 178	881 909	5 337 087
Germany	116 700	39 300	156 000
France	211 000	42 000	253 000

That the 'resilience' of the British motor industry in the 1930s cannot be fully explained by its relative lack of development in the 1920s is shown by the German position. The German car industry was no more highly developed than the British, yet it suffered a much more grievous blow during the great depression. In the U.K. during the early 1930s the decline in per capita real income was relatively small compared with the other countries shown. The underlying strength of the U.K. market was shown by the fact that after 1932 in the case of cars and 1933 for commercial vehicles, production was greater than that prevailing in 1929. The recovery in the United States and France was much slower and 1929 output figures were not repeated until after World War II. More specifically, the United States and France had to wait until 1949—in the case of French cars, 1950—to reach the heights of 1929. Germany's experience was closer to that of Britain's, for although the slump had had a disastrous effect on the motor industry, the 1929 production level was surpassed in 1934, the situation being greatly helped by Nazi commercial policy.

Perhaps the final factor cushioning the effects of the slump on the British motor industry was the existence of the very cheap small car on the British market. Customers suffering a decline in income did not necessarily leave the market altogether; rather, they 'traded down' to the car they now could afford. The British motor industry, more than any other in Europe, or of course America, catered for the really low incomed customer. The small car of 10 h.p. or less became responsible for over 50% of total home sales after 1932, whereas up to that time over 50% of sales were of cars of 11 h.p. and above. The really small cars of 8 h.p. or less showed a steady increase from 16% of total home sales in 1927 to 30% in 1938; but the dramatic evidence of 'trading-down' was in the 9–10 h.p. class. This became the most important size of car and its development almost exactly mirrored the decline of the car of 13 h.p. and above after 1930. Between 1929 and 1931 Ford and Morris introduced small cars priced at £125 or less. This increased the range of vehicles available to the low income earners in a way which was unique in Europe. Consequently when the slump came, the relatively small decline in British real income allied with the availability of a range of cars of 10 h.p. and below, some of which were extremely cheap, helped to reduce its impact. Underlying all this was the fact that the post 1928 period was one of keen prices and low profit margins, especially in the low horse power sector. This was merely a symptom of the competitive pressure which the main firms sought to impose on their rivals; a competitive pressure which led to the industry's early recovery in the general depression of the early 1930s and its success in selling an increasing output volume. This increased competition also led to annual model changes in the 1930s, normally in the early autumn. This tended to reinforce the seasonal pattern of demand* which therefore led to increasingly severe annual fluctuations in output and employment. The first firm to really break with the tradition of annual 'face lifts' was Morris after the introduction of the Morris Ten in 1935. The announcement that cars were to be manufactured over a period of years without significant outward change allowed Morris to experience a smoother production flow, which had beneficial effects on the costs of both the component suppliers and the car producer. In addition, it gave more regular employment. This meant that the seasonal fluctuation in demand was not aggravated by a change-over in car models.

The outbreak of World War II in 1939 brought great changes. Car production fell to extremely small levels but commercial vehicles increased to record volumes due to military and war effort demands. Also, vehicle producers used their existing capacity plus new capacity to produce a wide range of war goods. Much of the extra capacity—machines and buildings—was retained after the war. This allowed the industry to expand production to levels well in excess of pre-war.

* Car demand is higher in the spring and summer and lower in the autumn and winter.

2

THE POST-WAR DEVELOPMENT
OF THE MOTOR CAR INDUSTRY

In this chapter, the development of the car assembly side of the motor industry from 1945 to the present day is analysed. The main features of this period are threefold. Firstly, the continued concentration of car production into fewer and fewer hands; secondly, the progressive strengthening of American influence in the industry; and thirdly, the rapid growth in output. A number of other features are also of considerable significance, such as the increased export orientation of the industry and changing patterns of location following from the Government's regional policies, and these will be discussed later.

THE CONCENTRATION OF PRODUCTION

CONCENTRATION IN THE PERIOD 1945–1960

At the end of the war there were just over 20 firms involved in motor car production. However, in 1947 most of the total output of 287 000 cars was produced by the same six groups which had come to the fore during the 1930s. The situation is summarised in *Table 2.1*, which shows that the dominance achieved by the large producers in the 1930s was maintained in the post-war period. Apart from Rover, Singer and Jaguar, each specialist producer only made a very small number of cars. Nevertheless, firms such as Rolls-Royce/Bentley, BSA (Daimler and Lanchester) and Armstrong-Siddeley (Hawker-

Table 2.1

MARKET SHARES OF BRITISH MANUFACTURERS IN 1947

Manufacturer	Share (%)
The 'Big Six'	
Nuffield	20·9
Austin	19·2
Ford	15·4
Standard	13·2
Vauxhall	11·2
Rootes	10·9
Total	90·8
Others (mainly specialist producers)	
Rover	2·7
Singer	2·1
Jaguar	1·6
Total	6·4
All others (including Rolls-Royce, BSA, Alvis, Jowett, Armstrong-Siddeley, Allard, Healey, Morgan, etc.)	2·8

Siddeley Group) were quite significant in the market for high price and quality executive saloons.

Even given the high degree of concentration, the industry was not yet in a position of equilibrium as regards the number of firms. Small producers were forced out of the industry as were Lea-Francis and Jowett in 1954, and Singer Motors was saved from bankruptcy in 1955 when it was purchased by Rootes (Singer's decline had been dramatic, for in 1929 it was the third largest producer in the country, but had lost ground in the 1930s). On the other hand, firms continued to enter the specialist side of the industry, for instance the Bristol Aeroplane Company in 1947 and Lotus in 1953. This side of the market continues to see the demise of some firms and the emergence of others. Their life span tends to be short but some survive producing cars in very small volumes either complete or in kit form. The only new entrant of any note in the post-war period has been Lotus Cars. This concern was a 'backyard' enterprise in 1953 but in 1968 the firm went 'public'. The company owns a new and efficient plant near Norwich from where it is hoped to produce 8000 vehicles a year by 1973.

Although firms have entered or left the industry, the main structural development has been the merging or absorption of existing firms.

The first major example of this in the car industry was the creation of
the British Motor Corporation in 1952 by the merging of Austin and
Nuffield. This was the third, and this time successful, attempt to
merge the two companies. In 1924, Sir Herbert Austin wanted a
merger between his company, the Morris organisation, and Wolseley
Motors Ltd. (then controlled by the Vickers Group). Although Austin
was quite willing to give William Morris managerial control, Morris
wanted to preserve his freedom of action and turned down Austin's
advances, although as a sequel he purchased Wolseley in 1927. Austin
was within a hair's breadth from selling out to General Motors in
1925, but the American concern felt the selling price too great and
Austin's management too weak. So Austin and Morris continued as
independent firms until 1948 when merger was again mooted and
again dropped. By 1952, however, William Morris (by then Lord
Nuffield) felt that a merger was highly desirable in order to create an
organisation which could compete successfully with the Americans
and the newly awakening European industry in world markets. On a
more personal note, Nuffield's change of attitude to merger was
perhaps partly due to the fact that he had finally settled the top management structure of his group. He had also already decided to retire
(which he did in 1954) and as a result his own personal desire for
'freedom of action' was no longer a factor, having decided to hand
over the reins of power. In 1952 the 'Big Six' consequently became the
'Big Five', a situation which was to continue until the early 1960s.
By 1954 the industry's output of 769 000 cars was distributed as
shown in *Table 2.2*.

Table 2.2

MARKET SHARES OF BRITISH
MANUFACTURERS IN 1954

Manufacturer	Share (%)
The 'Big Five'	
BMC	38
Ford	27
Standard	11
Rootes	11
Vauxhall	9
Total	96
Others	
Jaguar and Rover	3·2
All others	0·8

Source: *L'Argus*.

Comparing the position in 1954 with that in 1947 a number of points emerge. (1) The mass-producers increased their market dominance at the expense of the specialists. (2) BMC's market share compared with that of Nuffield and Austin combined had declined by 2%. However, this was purely temporary and BMC came to regard 40% as its normal or 'rightful' share of the market even though it did fluctuate between 38% and 42% over the period 1952 to 1965. (3) Ford had considerably improved its position. This it did at the expense of all other producers apart from Rootes and Jaguar. (4) GMC's British subsidiary was still a relatively small firm and by 1954 it was the smallest of the mass producers on the car side. The fact that the U.K. was the only important motor car producing nation where Ford was larger than GMC was a particular irritant to Vauxhall's American masters.

Following the formation of BMC in 1952 and the demise of Jowett and Singer as independent entities, the process of concentration into fewer hands came to a halt. The 1950s was a period of quite spectacular growth in the output of motor cars. Output increased from just over half a million cars in 1950 to 1·3 million in 1960—a compound growth rate of almost 15% a year. This growth in production was only achieved by increases in productive capacity, especially by BMC, Ford and Vauxhall, some of it in new geographical locations, notably Merseyside and South Wales. The general buoyancy of the market helped firms to expand, but even so, not all producers prospered. Hawker-Siddeley's motor car subsidiary, Armstrong-Siddeley, slipped into the red during the late 1950s and production ceased in 1960. For a small-scale producer, Armstrong-Siddeley was very highly integrated, making its own engines, gearboxes and various components. The capital-outlay involved could not be covered by the volume produced or the prices charged. Expensive metal bodies were also used which added to the costs of the product. The demise of this well-established specialist producer showed that even under favourable overall market conditions competition could still lead to the decline of some firms. In a nutshell, the high performance but keenly priced products produced by Jaguar had captured over 70% of the market for large high quality saloons, leaving very little for other firms such as Armstrong-Siddeley. Hardship, however, was not only confined to the specialists; the general prosperity of the motor industry during the late 1950s was not shared by either Standard-Triumph or Vauxhall, but their difficulties stemmed from quite separate problems.

Standard-Triumph's annual car production during the 1950s varied between 60 000 and around 85 000 units. This meant that by the late 1950s Standard-Triumph was a small-scale car producer, given the overall growth of the car industry. The firm's relative lack of interest as regards car production was probably due mainly to its agricultural-tractor interests. Standard-Triumph was responsible for the production and marketing of Harry Ferguson's tractor designs; this gave the firm a stable market and adequate financial rewards. Consequently car production was regarded as a bonus which added to the steady returns provided by the tractor division. However, in 1957 Massey-Harris of Canada purchased the Ferguson tractor interests. It soon became plain that the new Massey-Ferguson group wanted its own production capacity, and with this aim in view Massey-Ferguson attempted to gain control of Standard-Triumph through the activities of nominees acting in the Stock Market. This attempted 'back-door' take-over was condemned by nearly all financial opinion so Massey-Ferguson made a formal bid. In the event, this bid was defeated. Following this episode, the relationship between the two organisations was not conducive to good or efficient commercial relations. Consequently Standard-Triumph's tractor plant was sold to Massey-Ferguson which also made itself independent of Standard-Triumph, as regards the supply of diesel engines, by purchasing Perkins Diesel of Peterborough.

The effect of all this on Standard-Triumph was severe. The organisation was momentarily financially sound due to the proceeds from the sale of plant to Masseys, *but* commercially the firm was vulnerable. Firstly, the firm was now entirely dependent on its car production activities. Secondly, it was heavily dependent on outside suppliers. As regards the first point, the firm's output volume was too small to achieve the efficient or low cost use of the available capacity. To produce a profitable but competitively priced product needed an output volume which was nearer firm and plant optima. As a result, a new design was rushed into production before it was fully developed and the consequence was adverse publicity concerning the new Triumph Herald's performance and quality, which of course reduced sales. As regards the second point, much of the proceeds from the Massey-Ferguson purchase went on trying to quickly create a group which was as highly integrated as its competitors. A large number of independent producers were purchased for relatively high prices in the effort to achieve this; notable amongst these was the foundry and general engineering works of Beans Industries and the car body makers Mulliners. The disruption and upheaval caused by the attempt to revive car output on the one hand and the desire to establish a new integrated organisation on the other, was considerable, and 1961 saw the firm on the verge of bankruptcy. The result was absorption by the

Lancashire based commercial-vehicle producer Leyland Motors.

Vauxhall's problems were rather different. From the 1954 market shares data (*Table 2.2*) it is seen that Vauxhall's car production in the U.K. was relatively small, with a wide gap developing between BMC and Ford on the one hand, and the other mass-producers on the other. If Vauxhall was to become a predominantly car producing firm rather than a commercial vehicle firm and comparable in size to Ford or BMC, then significant investment was needed. Vauxhall's output patterns during the 1950s are shown in *Table 2.3*.

Table 2.3

VAUXHALL: PRODUCTION OF VEHICLES 1950–1960

Year	Cars	Commercial vehicles	Turnover (£ million)
1950	47 025	40 429	32
1951	35 374	42 503	36
1952	35 640	43 522	45
1953	61 606	48 535	59
1954	70 115	60 836	67
1955	75 634	67 933	76
1956	61 463	62 180	72
1957	91 444	58 783	76
1958	119 177	55 439	95
1959	157 365	88 720	130
1960	145 742	106 284	136

Source: Vauxhall Motors.

Until 1956 Vauxhall's car production was quite small, considering that total British car output in 1956 was over 707 000. In addition, up to 1956 Vauxhall was as much a commercial vehicle producer as a car manufacturer. During 1956 GMC realised that its British subsidiary had fallen behind in the British car market. A crash programme of capital investment and general expansion was hence embarked upon which was completed by May 1958. During this period of two years an expansion took place which would normally have been phased over a longer period of time. As a result net losses of over £1 million after tax were made in 1957 and only a small net profit in 1958. This was because of the need to borrow resources from the American parent in order to finance investment. Only a firm backed by a giant industrial grouping could have afforded to embark upon such a large investment programme over such a short time period. This expansion programme gave Vauxhall a car producing capacity of around 160 000 units a year, which was still significantly below the output of Ford or BMC. Consequently between 1960 and 1964 a new car producing complex was built at a new location—Ellesmere Port on Merseyside. This increased the car making capacity to about 250 000 units a year. This was still small compared with BMC and Ford, although proportionally Vauxhall had grown faster than either of these organisations (*Table 2.4*).

Table 2.4

CARS PRODUCED AND MARKET SHARES

Firm	1954	Share (%)	1964	Share (%)	1967	Share (%)
BMC	290 030	38	720 000	39	539 219	35
Ford	204 150	27	525 000	28	440 711	28
Vauxhall	72 600	9	236 000	13	196 877	13

In 1954 Vauxhall produced only about 25% as many cars as BMC and just over one-third as many as Ford. This had improved to almost a third as many as BMC and almost 50% of Ford's output by 1964. By 1967 when the car market was being squeezed by government measures to curb consumer demand Vauxhall's position had further improved *vis à vis* BMC. Taking the 1964 figures as better indicators of car making capacity Vauxhall is still dwarfed by BMC and Ford. This is despite its efforts to improve its relative position through both capacity expansion and the introduction of new products.

Overall then, after the formation of BMC in 1952 very little appeared to happen to increase the concentration of the motor industry's output into fewer hands. Between 1954 and 1960, for instance, relative market shares did not alter significantly. This tended to hide some underlying weaknesses, notably the positions of Standard-Triumph, Rootes, and even Vauxhall, in the industry. The latter firm however due to its GMC percentage and its very strong and profitable position in the commercial vehicle market was in no danger of leaving the industry. The 1960s were nevertheless to be years of significant change which resulted in the emergence of the British motor car assembly industry in its final form.

A DECADE OF CHANGE 1960–1970

Further concentration of the industry during the 1960s took on the form of both vertical and horizontal integration. As regards vertical mergers the main considerations were twofold. Firstly, integration to improve the planning of production schedules, and secondly, to reduce production costs by increasing efficiency and abolishing the value added by independent component makers. This contrasted with the vertical integration which took place during the early 1950s when the overriding motivation was the protection of components and materials, especially motor car bodies. The most notable merger was that between Pressed Steel and BMC in 1965, which for the first time enabled BMC to become self-sufficient in motor car body production. The Fisher and Ludlow organisation, purchased in 1953 together with body making capacity formerly owned by Nuffield, was unable to satisfy much more than 50% of BMC's needs in 1965. In addition, Pressed Steel produced bodies for other manufacturers, notably Jaguar, Rover, Rolls-Royce and Rootes and their interests were guaranteed under the BMC–Pressed Steel merger terms. Rootes' American parent, Chrysler, found this reliance on outside suppliers anathema to American practice however, especially since a finished body can represent 40% of the costs of a completed car. In order to gain greater control over production and costs, Rootes in 1966 purchased the Pressed Steel plant at Linwood from BMC. Nevertheless, some of Rootes' car body requirements were still met by the Pressed Steel Fisher organisation as late as 1970.

Although vertical mergers have taken place, and will most certainly continue to occur, the significant developments in the 1960s concern horizontal integration. In many cases the merger was defensive, as between Leyland and British Motor Holdings. In other instances the merger was offensive, such as Chrysler's purchase of Rootes to gain a foothold in Britain in particular and Europe in general. Such mergers reinforced the post-war pattern of production which was towards increased standardisation. There has been a reduction in the number of different models. In many instances they have been replaced by slight variations in a single model of motor car. Parts and components have also been standardised to a certain extent. However, the motor industry's 'Standardisation Committee' set up in 1948 still feels that much more can be done here, and this is certainly the view of the large component producers such as Lucas and Lockheed. Despite such standardisation, competition is still fierce in the motor industry and following the lull in the 1950s new and significant mergers occurred in the 1960s.

In 1961 the ailing Standard-Triumph company was purchased by the fiercely competitive and ambitious Leyland Motors Corporation. The late chairman of Leyland, Sir Henry Spurier, realised as early as

1945 that a motor company's survival depended upon (1) exports and (2) growth. He realised that Europe's motor industry would become concentrated into fewer hands because of the economics of the industry —large scale production with highly capital-intensive methods. From the beginning Spurier intended that Leyland would be one of the survivors and also a large scale firm. In 1945 this far-sighted but ambitious aim would have appeared no more than wishful thinking on Leyland's part: a company centred on Lancashire with the capacity to make about 5000 heavy commercial vehicles a year. Leyland's phenomenal growth will be discussed in Chapter 4, but suffice it to say that with the purchase of West Yorkshire Foundries in 1945 the company began a development which ended in it becoming the U.K.'s largest vehicle producer. Further component makers and important commercial vehicle makers were purchased in the 1950s, but its entry into the car industry came in 1961.

In 1960 Jaguar's need for extra capacity and diversification was partly satisfied by its purchase of BSA's vehicle producing subsidiaries. The company purchased the Daimler cars subsidiary, and the Transport Vehicles (Daimler) concern which produced bus chassis and components. This was followed in 1961 with the acquisition of the assets and goodwill of the Guy Motors Company of Wolverhampton. This firm had gone into liquidation, but its range of heavy trucks and buses together with its Sunbeam Trolleybus subsidiary gave Jaguar a stronger footing in the commercial vehicle market, as well as holding out the possibility of cost cutting integration with Daimler buses. Further purchases followed in 1963 and 1964 when Coventry Climax engines and the Meadows engine plant were purchased respectively.

Leyland was active in the commercial vehicle field during these years, purchasing its most powerful competitor in the heavy vehicle field in 1962. The purchase of Associated Commercial Vehicles made Leyland second only to Daimler-Benz in the European heavy vehicle industry. A share exchange with the nationalised Transport Holding Company gave Leyland a minority shareholding in Bristol Commercial Vehicles.

The most significant development on the car side during these years was Chrysler's entry into the British industry. Chrysler was the one American firm without a significant holding in the European motor industry. Its policy was geared to rectifying this situation, and the first development was the purchase of the commercially vulnerable Simca concern in France in 1963. In 1964 Chrysler purchased the majority of Rootes' capital but only a minority of the equity. This saved the company from extinction. The company had been brought to this position by a severe strike at its Acton components plant in 1961, by an ageing range of vehicles, and some some internal problems. Links were strengthened in 1965 when Chrysler sold its Dodge truck subsidiary to Rootes. The company's fortunes, however, continued to decline and recovery required a further massive injection of capital from Chrysler. Not surprisingly the Americans wished to control the way the money was spent. Consequently, in 1967 Chrysler purchased a majority holding in Rootes' equity. The company's fortunes revived in 1968 but subsequently its trading position still gave Chrysler cause for concern. The American company was faced with further calls for expenditure before Rootes became fully competitive. With Chrysler buying Rootes, over 50% of the U.K. motor industry's unit output comes from American controlled firms.

Following its purchase of Pressed Steel, BMC absorbed the Jaguar Group in 1966. BMC's need was to strengthen its large-car and truck range while Jaguar was in need of more capital to finance research and development. BMC's move into the executive car range was countered by Leyland's purchase of Rover cars in 1967. This added to Leyland's range of cars and commercial vehicles thereby strengthening its position in home and foreign markets. At the same time Rover was given greater financial backing. Rover had itself purchased the Alvis company in 1965. BMC's move was highly defensive for during this period its total car production fell from over 720 000 units in 1964 to just over 600 000 in 1966. The percentage decline was much greater than that of its nearest rival Ford. However, Leyland contrived to hold its car output remarkably steady and its purchase of Rover was part of its general offensive to become a major car producer.

The main features in the British motor industry during the 1960s, apart from the activities of the American firms, was the continual commercial and financial improvement of Leyland and the rapid decline of BMC after 1965. Even the Jaguar–BMC merger and the subsequent creation of British Motor Holdings (BMH) in December 1966 failed to reverse this rapid downward trend.

In January 1968 Leyland Motors and BMH merged to create the British Leyland Motors Corporation (BLMC). Tentative plans were made for merger in 1966 and 1967, but on both occasions they fell through because Leyland would have then been the junior partner. This was not consistent with Leyland's grand design to become the largest vehicle producer in the U.K. and ultimately Europe. However, 1967 was disastrous for BMH—an overall loss of £3·28 million was made, despite profitable workings by Jaguar and Pressed Steel

Fisher. BMC's share of total car production had fallen from its 'customary' 40% to 34% in 1966, and to 35% in 1967. These annual figures did not show the true magnitude of the fall, for during the last months of 1967 BMC's share of car production was under 30%. The firm faced a general market collapse, its share of the medium-weight van market falling from 30% to 20%, and its share of the market for lorries of over 2 tons from 20% to 10%. While BMH's profits slipped from £27 million in 1960 to a loss of £3·28 million in 1967, Leyland increased its profits from £9·16 million to £18 million over the same period.

This had important implications for the market valuation of the two companies. By the beginning of 1967 the nominal share capital of LMC stood at £70 million which compared with BMH's £64 million. However, LMC's shares were undervalued in the market so it was not until the middle of 1967 that BMH's losses and LMC's profits brought the market valuation of the two companies' equity into almost perfect equality. Following the devaluation of the pound in November Donald Stokes, LMC's managing director, immediately announced plans to reduce export prices. This conveyed LMC's market preparedness to the stock market, with the result that LMC's share prices advanced ahead of BMH's. The result was that Leyland was in a position to make a successful take-over bid for BMH. To avoid any acrimony which a take-over may have caused, agreed merger terms were worked out. Quite clearly, however, Leyland was the chief partner, with Donald Stokes becoming the chief executive. Leyland's philosophy of an integrated company with executive powers in the hands of one man responsible to the board prevailed over the BMH belief in an essentially committee-controlled federation. In effect Leyland had grown from a concern producing 5000 commercial vehicles a year to a firm producing a wide variety of vehicles with a total annual productive capacity of about 1·25 million vehicles a year in just over 20 years.

The story of BMC since 1960 sums up a tragic commercial failure by an industrial giant. It is true that Leyland made a record profit of £18 million in 1967 but this figure had been achieved by BMC as early as 1954. The 1950s saw BMC advance steadily with net investment, increasing capacity and profits. In 1960 BMC made a record profit of £27 million. Since then the commercial and financial edge became blunted. Management was excellent on the technical side but extremely weak as regards marketing. Labour relations were poor, often due to a rather lax attitude towards labour relations on the part of the company. No systematic attempt was made to eliminate the friction creating piece-rate payments system, in favour of a time-rate plus bonuses method of payment. Much of BMC's plant was old and inefficient. Furthermore, BMC was left with too many and often too small plants which were a legacy of the separate Austin and Nuffield empires. No effort was really made to rationalise production through the closure of inefficient plants. Some of BMC's models were too old and mechanically outdated, and no modern medium-sized saloon car existed to compete with the products of Ford. The dealer network was also a legacy of pre-BMC days, with little attempt to concentrate sales through fewer but more efficient distributors and retailers. The retention of Nuffield and Austin dealerships when the only difference in the product was in the radiator grill and badge was somewhat absurd. A more rational distinction would have been between model types if separation was thought necessary. In short, BMC became an organisation producing some, but not enough, first-rate products. It was run by a management which contained many weaknesses and, perhaps most of all, was not quite sure how to efficiently market the product once it was made. For instance, it was not unkown for the company to announce a new car before factories were geared-up for trouble free, high volume production. This created long waiting lists. In turn this led to the loss of goodwill both because the advertised product was unavailable and then when it did arrive many teething troubles remained to be cured.

The merger movement was not quite completed in 1968 for in 1969 Reliant cars announced the acquisition of Bond. Both firms specialised in the production of three-wheel cars and high performance sports saloons. Both firms used glass-fibre construction in bodybuilding and Reliant had established a significant export trade by helping countries with limited markets to establish motor industries. The use of glass-fibre obviated the use of expensive capital equipment which required large volume production for successful amortisation. Reliant's need for extra capacity was satisfied by the spare capacity existing in the Bond factory. Total annual productive capacity was around 20 000 units a year.

The U.K. motor assembly industry had during the 1960s taken on its final domestic form. Some specialist makers may come and go, but the large volume producers have been reduced to the irreducible minimum 'Big Four'. Any future developments will be in the sphere of links between British firms, probably BLMC, and foreign producers. This could mean outright merger or merely the joint production of certain components. As regards the components industry, further concentration is likely amongst British firms and between

U.K. and foreign firms. In addition, component makers could face a
certain degree of foreign competition on the domestic front.

THE AMERICAN INFLUENCE

The pre-war period had ended with the Ford Motor Company
confirming its position as one of the U.K.'s major motor manufacturers.
Furthermore, GMC had entered the British industry. This it had done
by purchasing Vauxhall cars and by establishing truck assembly and
eventually truck manufacturing facilities. Chrysler remained outside
the British car industry but had commenced commercial vehicle
production at Kew, London, in 1933, although some American components were used until 1952. The proportion of total vehicle production accounted for by the two American car producers, immediately
before and after World War II, is shown in *Table 2.5*.

Table 2.5

PERCENTAGE OF TOTAL PRODUCTION

Firm	Cars		Commercial vehicles	
	1938	*1947*	*1938*	*1947*
Ford	17·8	15·4	20·0	22·9
Vauxhall-Bedford	10·1	11·2	24·6	20·3
Total	27·9	26·6	44·6	43·2

Adapted from *Motor Vehicles: A Report on the Industry*, Political and Economic Planning,
p. 26.

During this period just over one-quarter of total car production was
accounted for by the American firms, a significant but not an over-
whelming proportion. The domination of the commercial vehicle
market was much greater. This was due to the commercial foresight
and productive efficiency of the American firms in producing light,
cheap, and reliable trucks for carrying payloads of less than five tons.
    The post-war period has been one of greatly increased market
penetration by Vauxhall and Ford, especially the latter. The process
is summarised in *Table 2.6*.
    A number of interesting points emerge from *Tables 2.5* and *2.6*.
Between 1938 and 1967 the market share held by Vauxhall (and
indeed Rootes) remained remarkably constant. On the other hand
Ford shows a very great advance, both in percentage terms and

especially in absolute volume. The increased market penetration of the American firms between 1938 and 1966 was due entirely to the growth of the Ford Motor Company. Between 1965 and 1968 two points

Table 2.6

PERCENTAGE OF TOTAL CAR PRODUCTION

Firm	1954	1963	1966	1967	1970
Ford	27	31	29	28	29
Vauxhall	9	10	11	13	10
Rootes*	11	11	11	12	12
Total	37	52	51	53	51

* Chrysler assumed control in 1967.

emerge: (1) Vauxhall increased its market share to record levels due to the success of its small-medium saloon, the Viva; (2) over 50% of domestic production was accounted for by American firms following Chrysler's final take-over of Rootes in 1967. By 1970 Vauxhall had experienced a relative decline but the second point was still valid.

So far the discussion has concerned the share of total production supplied by American-controlled firms. This does not necessarily reflect their share of the domestic market, as the proportion of output exported tends to vary from firm to firm. The share of the domestic market held by different firms over recent years is shown in *Table 2.7*.

Table 2.7

PERCENTAGE SHARE OF THE DOMESTIC CAR MARKET

Firm	1965	1966	1967	1970
Ford	26	26	25·5	26·5
Vauxhall	12	11	12·5	10·0
Rootes	12	12	12·5	10·5

Quite clearly from a comparison of *Tables 2.6* and *2.7* it emerges that Ford exported a larger percentage of its output than either Rootes or Vauxhall. Furthermore the figures for 1970 reflect the fact that imported models accounted for a record 14·3% of the British market.

The relative advance of the American firms had as its main corollary the relative deterioration in BMC's market penetration. In addition, Standard-Triumph suffered a dramatic fall in its market share. From

13·2% in 1947 it had fallen to less than half of this in 1961. However, under Leyland's guidance the organisation's fortunes recovered so that by 1968 it held over 9% of the market. Nevertheless, the most significant feature of the U.K. motor industry in the post-war period was Ford's growth and BMC's relative decline.

Before 1952 Nuffield and Austin normally accounted for just over 40% of total production. Initially, this state of affairs continued with the formation of BMC. A market share of about 40% was regarded as a sign that BMC continued to be commercially prosperous. In 1964, with BMC accounting for 40% of total car production, the company made goodly profits from record output. There was, however, no 'natural law' governing BMC's market penetration and the following years saw a marked and serious decline in the company's fortunes. BMC's share of total production fell to between 34% and 35% in 1966 and 1967, and a further reduction to just in excess of 30% occurred during the last months of 1967. The reasons for this were discussed earlier* and it was suggested that a large number of problems came to a head at the same time. Between 1964 and 1969 total car production declined, but BMC's decline was proportionately greater. With the creation of BLMC the output of BMC cars increased from the low point of 540 000 cars in 1967 to 633 753 in 1969. However, BLMC as a whole only accounted for just over 40% of total output. In other words, BMC's market share had fallen well below 40%. Furthermore, in 1964 the total share of car production accounted for by BMC, Jaguar, Rover and Leyland was just on 50%. So clearly BLMC would not have restored its full commercial or competitive position until it had increased its market share by around 10%. This reflected the competitive advance of the American controlled firms, notably Ford and Vauxhall.

Ford and Vauxhall have developed in much the same way, although in direct contrast to the other main motor car producers. Vauxhall grew entirely through its own expansion and not by purchasing other vehicle or component makers. Ford's development has been similar although a few acquisitions were made, the most notable of which was the purchase of Briggs Motor Bodies in 1953.

Vauxhall was an established, if not very successful, motor company when it was bought by GMC in 1928. Since it had concentrated on large expensive cars, GMC was forced to start afresh to establish a motor company able to satisfy the needs of the mass market. GMC's commercial vehicle venture was based entirely on the company's own efforts, no other manufacturers being absorbed.

* Page 28.

Ford was a very early entry into the British industry; production of the Model T had commenced at the Old Trafford (Manchester) factory in 1911. The growth in the British car market meant that the company needed extra capacity, and a new location was sought. The Dagenham area was chosen mainly because of the possibilities it gave for further expansion and also the ease with which a river-side site could be used to import raw materials and export the finished product. When the Dagenham plant was opened in 1931 it was the most highly integrated plant in Europe, with its own foundry and smelting facilities*, together with special jetties equipped with mechanised loading and unloading systems. The plant was geographically isolated from any other main location of the motor industry. In effect this meant that the company was not competing with other high-wage industries for the available labour. The work force was highly efficient but subject to strict discipline. Consequently although working hours were shorter and rates of pay were higher than those offered by other motor manufacturers at the time, labour costs per unit of output were the lowest in the industry.

Ironically, Ford was forced to seek expansion elsewhere after the war, even though one of Dagenham's original advantages was the room it provided for plant extension. The Government, however, wished to see the motor industry confer benefits to new areas. This is mainly why Ford's first piece of post-war expansion in 1949 was at Langley.

The ownership structure of the two companies differed markedly for a number of years. Initially the Ford Motor Company of Great Britain's equity was equally divided between U.S. Ford and British private investors. However in 1960 U.S. Ford successfully bid for all the outstanding equity. Since 1928 Vauxhall's equity has been wholly owned by GMC, although debentures are privately held by British investors.

Originally the Rootes Group had evolved from a series of mergers. Chrysler bought the firm as a going concern serving the mass market. Since 1967 the majority of the equity has been in Chrysler's hands although some is still held by outside interests.

Although both Ford and Vauxhall have grown largely from a single stem, BMC's position was quite the opposite. Created initially from a merger of two British companies, the process of further acquisitions was continued throughout the 1950s and 1960s culminat-

* These narrowly missed nationalisation in 1950; however, in official eyes the prospect of American badwill just offset the desire for an 'all embracing' state steel complex.

ing in 1968, when, to all intents and purposes, British Motor Holdings was absorbed by the Leyland Motors Corporation. The market share held by BMC and its successors has remained at around 40% of total production. This has reflected both the relative decline in the position of the British owned motor industry *vis à vis* the American controlled sector, and also that BMC had had to absorb other firms merely to maintain its current position. Now that the industry is in its final domestic form BLMC must protect its market position through its own expansion, for there is no other course open. In addition, the group needs to increase its market share if all the constituent parts are to be restored to their former pre-eminence.

THE GROWTH IN OUTPUT

World War II brought car output to a virtual halt, but the output of commercial vehicles increased to meet the demands of the war effort. At the same time motor manufacturers increased their productive capacity to produce a wide range of military goods. Much of the new buildings and machinery was retained after 1945, thereby allowing the industry to expand production beyond pre-war levels.

Taking 1937 as the year of highest pre-war car and total vehicle production as a base, it is clear that the motor car industry soon re-established itself. In fact by 1949 car output exceeded the 1937 figure quite considerably. In the immediate post-war period, commercial vehicle output was maintained at the record breaking wartime levels, but by 1948 the highest wartime figure had been passed. In 1949 over 200 000 units were produced and this milestone was exceeded by another in 1950 when a quarter of a million commercial vehicles were made. Consequently by 1950 car production was over 30% greater than it was in 1937 while commercial vehicle growth had been even more spectacular, the 1950 output level being more than 100% greater than the highest pre-war level.

Post-war expansion was achieved in the face of great difficulty. On the car side, factories had to be changed back from war work to car production. This was not always easy and generally took time. Vehicle output was hampered by a steel shortage, especially where sheet steel was concerned. Although this badly affected the production of car, van, and bus bodies, commercial vehicle chassis production was not so badly affected as sheet steel was not used. The general steel shortage became acute in 1951 and 1952. This had a number of effects. Firstly, a drop in car and commercial vehicle production. Secondly, the purchase of body building firms by car makers anxious to protect body supplies. Thirdly, the demise of firms like Jowett because of a shortage of car bodies. This situation was aggravated by restrictive measures such as changes in purchase tax, hire purchase conditions, and fuel tax. Production recovered in 1953 to reach a short-run peak in 1955.

Figure 2.1

ANNUAL PRODUCTION OF CARS AND COMMERCIAL VEHICLES (1000s)

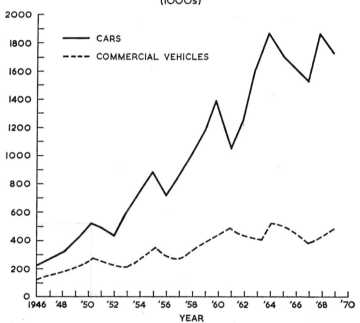

The post-war pattern of production for cars and commercial vehicles is shown in *Figure 2.1*. The peaks and troughs show a similar pattern but the commercial vehicle production trough is always lagged. It follows the car trough by a period of between one and two years. Annual data suggests that the peaks are, except for 1961, reached simultaneously in both sectors. Monthly data, however, suggests a time lag for commercial vehicles here as well; it is a shorter but noticeable lag of about nine months.

Apart from the steel shortage of 1951 to 1952 every trough has been largely induced by government measures to curb demand. Even the period 1951 to 1952 saw the usual restrictions on hire purchase repayment periods with increased minimum deposits, increased purchase tax, and higher fuel duties. Indeed, 1952 saw the introduction of hire purchase controls for the first time, following the imposition of purchase tax on commercial vehicles for the first time in 1950.

The main periods of increasing and decreasing fiscal and monetary restraint were as depicted in *Table 2.8.*

Table 2.8

THE POST-WAR PATTERN OF MONETARY
RESTRAINT

Year	Increasing restraint	Decreasing restraint
1950–1952	×	
1953–1954		×
1955–1956	×	
1957–1958	Partial Easing	
1959–1965		×*
1966–1971	×†	

* Some restrictions were reimposed between 1960 and April 1962.
† Particularly severe restraint, with some *short-term* easing on hire purchase initial deposits.

The pattern of production summarises the general economic climate as reflected in monetary and fiscal policy. Sometimes a recovery, as in 1953, preceded the removal of some restriction, such as hire purchase measures, but reflects a significant drop in others, such as a fall in purchase tax. Only in 1965 did a production downturn precede the imposition of both hire purchase and purchase tax restrictive measures. The strength of commercial vehicle production after the car downturn in 1960 can be explained by the continuing buoyancy in the commercial vehicle market after the abolition of purchase tax on commercial vehicles in April 1959, and an extremely vigorous export effort which reached a temporary peak in 1961.

Broadly speaking then, the British motor industry enjoyed a period of almost uninterrupted growth from 1946 to 1955. It was not until the period 1954–1955 that the underlying domestic excess demand for cars, caused by the war and the export-drive, was satisfied. In 1954 and 1955 almost one million new cars were registered on the home market and this largely mopped-up the backlog of unsatisfied demand. The year 1956, however, brought the first real setback when the credit squeeze, import restrictions abroad, and the Suez crisis caused a severe fall in British production. The registration of new cars and commercial vehicles fell by 20% and 3% respectively and exports fell by 14% and 8% respectively. Production recovered in 1957 to reach a new peak in 1960. Thereupon new credit restrictions were imposed, with output falling in 1961. Recovery followed in 1962 and a particularly strong boom, generated initially by a relaxation of controls and basically supported by an upsurge in real per capita national income, lasted from 1962 to 1964. Although a downturn occurred in 1965 severe restrictions were not imposed until 1966 and these were reinforced throughout the rest of the decade especially after the devaluation of sterling in November 1967. The fall in production between 1965 and 1968 had been the longest and most severe reverse the industry had suffered since the war. Restrictions aimed at making a success of devaluation through restraining home consumer demand and stimulating exports hit the motor industry's domestic market very severely. Although exports exceeded their 1967 level they were not sufficient to offset the fall in domestic sales. The need for a strong home market to both reduce unit costs and to support low export prices is always put forward by the motor industry, although the export orientation of firms like Bedford or Volkswagen almost reverses this argument. This is returned to in a later chapter but a few points are worth mentioning at this stage concerning the home and foreign markets of the motor industry.

EXPORTS AND THE HOME MARKET*

Before World War II there was no concerted export drive on the post-war scale on the part of the major car producers. The best pre-war year for exports was 1937 when 14% of car production and 22% of commercial vehicles were sold abroad. In absolute terms, 78 000 cars and 21 000 commercial vehicles were exported. Although the government had planned that traditional industries such as cotton and shipbuilding should lead the post-war export drive in search of much-needed foreign exchange, it soon became obvious that such industries could not produce the necessary results. However, the newer industries could and one of the most marketable commodities was motor vehicles. The industry vigorously expanded exports in a seller's market to dollar and European markets, as well as to the more traditional Commonwealth markets. As we will see later, there were a number of factors helping

* For a fuller discussion, see Chapter 11.

the industry, such as the general dollar shortage which hit American exports and the need for the European motor industries to recover from the ravages of war. The result was that in 1950 the U.K. displaced the U.S.A. as the world's leading exporter of motor cars although it was not until 1960 that it also became the leading commercial vehicles exporter. In 1950, the U.K. sold 75% of car production and 60% of commercial vehicle production overseas. In addition, the U.K. motor industry accounted for 52% of world trade in motor vehicles, compared with less than 15% in 1937. Since the early 1950s the U.K. has lost ground to her European competitors on the export front and many of the initial advantages held have been squandered (*Table 2.9*).

Table 2.9

CAR PRODUCTION (1000S) AND EXPORTS (%) 1964–1969

Year	U.K.		Germany		France	
	Prod.	Exports	Prod.	Exports	Prod.	Expor
1964	1 868	36	2 650	51	1 390	32
1965	1 722	36	2 734	52	1 423	34
1966	1 604	35	2 830	52	1 286	28
1967	1 552	32	2 296	59	1 777	31
1969	1 717	45	3 313	57	2 168	36

A number of points emerge. The U.K. motor industry's post-war production pattern differs greatly from pre-war due to the importance of exports. As a result a set-back in export markets will now have a much greater effect on total production. The corollary of this is that fluctuations in home demand need not have the same effect as pre-war due to the importance of production for abroad. German exports rose rapidly after 1950, while between 1950 and 1953 British exports fell. This was partly due to import restrictions in the important Australian market. In fact, the 1950 level of exports was not exceeded until 1957, having been hit once more in 1956 by import controls in Australia. German exports continued to increase and in 1956 they exceeded British car exports for the first time. It was not until 1967 that the level of German exports actually fell below the level of a previous year; this contrasts sharply with the fluctuating nature of British car exports (*Figure 2.2*). British car exports have continued to fall behind those of the aggressively competitive German industry; in addition French exports exceeded the U.K.'s for the first time in 1967, and the Italians narrowed the gap. Although in absolute terms the motor industry is the U.K.'s largest exporter, one is forced to suggest that it could have

Figure 2.2

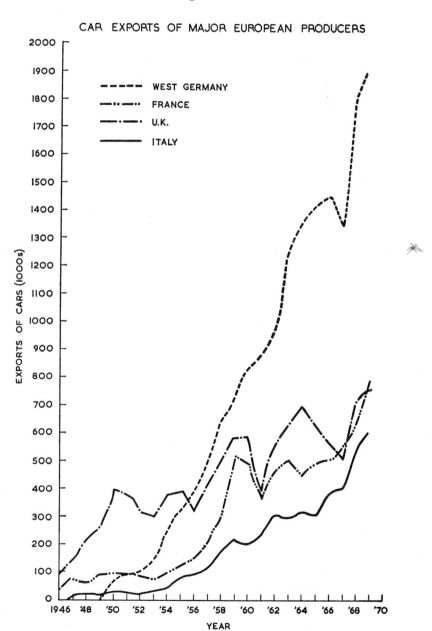

CAR EXPORTS OF MAJOR EUROPEAN PRODUCERS

Figure 2.3

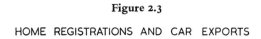

HOME REGISTRATIONS AND CAR EXPORTS

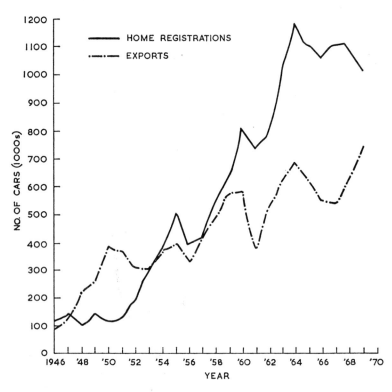

done even better. Aggressive sales methods by the Europeans backed by excellent sales and service organisations in export markets has not been emulated by the British car industry. The success of the British commercial vehicle industry in this respect is reflected by their pre-eminence; the car industry could have been in a similar position if more attention had been paid to the entire marketing concept. This does not simply refer to advertising, but covers the entire commercial outlook of the firm. This includes meeting delivery dates, quality control, the adequacy of the sales and service organisation, the avoidance of over-dependence on a few export markets, and so on.

The immediate post-war concentration on export markets had repercussions on the home market. Government pressure to export as much production as possible meant that demand exceeded supply in the domestic sector. Due to the domestic needs of industry and commerce the commercial vehicle export targets were set lower than that for cars, so as early as 1946 domestic registrations exceeded the highest pre-war level. However, on the car side the 1937 peak for home registrations was double the annual totals prevailing between 1946 and 1951. Indeed, the 1937 figure was not exceeded until 1954. The pent-up consumer and business demand for replacement and for new car ownership had various repercussions. In short, the post-war market was one of long waiting lists, a frustrated motoring public and high second-hand prices which at times were double the list price for new cars. This was despite very high levels of purchase tax on cars. Between 1940 and 1951 it was $33\frac{1}{3}\%$ and between 1951 and 1953 this rose to $66\frac{2}{3}\%$. The demand for car ownership was such that the British car population in 1948 already exceeded the pre-war figure. After 1953 more cars flowed onto the home market, and the upsurge in registrations during 1954 and 1955 satisfied most of the excess demand. Much of that remaining was temporarily postponed in 1956 with the credit squeeze but the upsurge in production and home registrations during the period 1957 to 1960 saw the last traces of post-war excess demand disappear. In 1959 the seasonal autumn fall in demand occurred. By 1960 the growth in the motor industry's domestic market became dependent on real disposable income, access to credit, purchase tax levels, and any variation in the vehicle replacement cycle.

LOCATION

The post-war period saw significant changes in the location of the motor industry. Until the late 1950s most expansion took place in the traditional home of the motor car industry, the West Midlands and the Home Counties. The government's location policy, however, such as it was, did manage to persuade the motor industry to establish integrated assembly plants in new locations, sometimes with disastrous results for the firm concerned.

The early days of motor car production saw the existence of a widely scattered industry, but even then a high degree of concentration was discernable in the West Midlands and in Scotland. The Scottish industry soon withered and died due to a lack of business finance, local components industry, and a sizeable local market which could afford the costs of motoring. The West Midlands experience was quite the contrary as the light engineering traditions and local wealth were conducive to the successful establishment of a motor car industry. Indeed, in the early development of the industry it was quite a widely held view that Wolverhampton-Birmingham-Coventry was the only area suitable for the establishment of new motor firms.

That this was not necessarily so was shown by William Morris who established his motor manufacturing business during 1912–1913 in Oxford, away from the engineering environment of the West Midlands. Probably the main reason for the success of this location was Morris's decision to concentrate on assembly and to purchase components from outside specialists. Any transport costs involved were more than offset by the external economies Morris enjoyed by purchasing from firms reaping significant internal economies through specialisation. By concentrating on assembly Morris did not need to establish his own metal machining capacity. To have done so at Oxford would have been expensive and probably inefficient when compared with the real costs of carrying out such activities in the traditional engineering areas in the West Midlands or Lancashire. Given his method of production Morris's choice was correct, for his assembly costs were lower than they would have been in the West Midlands. His employees earned much more than the average wage for the area, but labour costs were relatively low compared with those in the West Midlands. In addition the quality of his labour was always excellent. As the firm grew it attracted first-class labour from other districts, even from as far afield as South Wales. His value of output was always such that his outside suppliers could reap economies and pass them on in lower costs. In short, Oxford was a good location, yet outside the West Midlands.

Being in the West Midlands itself was not a guarantee of success. During the first years of the 1920s Wolverhampton was third only to Birmingham and Coventry as the most important location of the motor industry. By the end of the 1930s however, not one car firm remained—Sunbeam, Clyno, Star, Briton and AJS had all closed down. The only firms that remained were Guy Motors, the commercial vehicle producer, and Sunbeam's trolley-bus factory. The exact reason for this debacle is not clear. Clyno and Star were purchased by Guy Motors. The cars made by the three firms were large and expensive and during the depression of the 1920s their sales collapsed. Much the same can be said concerning Sunbeam, while AJS concentrated on motor-cycle production in its other Midland's factories. Clyno also tried to compete directly with Morris in terms of price and product, but did not produce a sufficient volume to do so profitably.

The heavy commercial vehicle industry has tended to localise in the Lancashire–North Cheshire area. The heavy industry and metal engineering tradition of the area were the roots of the industry. In many instances heavy commercial vehicle producers began their existence by producing steam-powered coal-fired road tractors.

Apart from the odd exception the car industry tended to locate itself in the West Midlands. The first change came in the late 1920s when there was a southward movement to London and the Home Counties. This was associated with the large-scale flow-production techniques which came to the fore in the 1920s. With such a production process the need for traditional engineering skills was greatly reduced. The manufacturing process became one of the repetitive production of single items which were assembled into complete components or sub-assemblies and then in turn incorporated or assembled into complete cars. As motor-car assembly in general became a semi-skilled process the industry became more footloose with respect to localisation. It would be wrong to say that it could now be located anywhere, but it was faced with a greater choice than previously. As long as the new location had some advantages, any disadvantages caused by moving away from traditional craft areas could be overcome. William Morris's early conversion to motor car assembly as distinct from complete manufacture on one site, showed the wisdom of this.

An associated movement during the 1920s and 1930s was the emergence of Lancashire as a centre of the motor components industry. This was partly associated with the decline of the cotton industry, which freed factory buildings and labour. The requirements of war added to the growth of the Home Counties and Lancashire as centres connected with the motor industry, a process reinforced by the wartime 'shadow factories' built by or eventually purchased by the motor firms in these areas.

The second main change in location patterns occurred after 1960. This was greatly influenced by government policy towards areas of above-average unemployment, hence the movement of firms connected with the motor industry to South Wales, Scotland and especially Merseyside.

A survey in 1962 showed that the industry was highly concentrated in a few areas. *Table 2.10* shows the percentage of the industry's total labour force employed in these areas.

Since 1962 the proportions changed in favour of Lancashire (because of the new Merseyside assembly and components complex), Scotland and South Wales. The later situation is shown in column two in *Table 2.10*.

The location pattern of the motor industry hence falls into three

Table 2.10

PERCENTAGE OF TOTAL LABOUR FORCE

Area	1962*	1967†
Midlands (Mainly Coventry and Birmingham)	36	40·4
London and South East (Mainly Dagenham and Langley)	20	34·1
East and South (including Luton, Oxford and Cowley)	21	
Lancashire	8·4	12·9

Sources: * *Ministry of Labour Gazette* (March 1962) and † *Motor Industry Statistics*, 1959–1968, NEDO: H.M.S.O. (1969.)

distinct phases: pre-1914, the inter-war period, and the changes which occurred in the 1960s. It would be useful to look at these in a little more detail.

PRE-1914

The period which saw the establishment of the motor industry before 1914 was one which confirmed that the West Midlands had many locational advantages from the motor industry's point of view. The area had relatively easy access to all parts of the U.K., produced a plethora of industrial products and contained numerous light engineering firms, and as a corollary of this possessed a pool of skilled labour in industries which had skills relevant to the motor industry such as upholstery, precision engineering, toolmaking and cycle production. The area was the first to see the establishment of assembly industries and specialist component makers. As a result of all this, the area had a strong locational attraction for the production of components and quality vehicles; after all, the motor vehicle was a piece of high quality engineering until the mass produced Model T came on the scene. The relative importance of the region however, declined with the southward drift of assembly plants and firms plus the movement to Lancashire of many component plants and firms.

1918–1939

The period 1918–1939 saw the adoption of mass-production assembly techniques, pioneered in the U.K. in 1911 with Ford's 'Model T'. This weakened the locational pull of the West Midland's pool of skilled labour. Mass-production called for large numbers of non-skilled and semi-skilled workers. As it happened the mass market area of London and the South East, in close proximity to potential export markets in Europe, also had such labour available. Of course this type of labour was cheaper than the skilled labour force in the West Midlands. Vauxhall at Luton, Ford at Dagenham and Morris at Oxford, all had access to a labour force where trade union organisation was weak. In addition, none of these firms were faced with competition from other large-scale or highly paid industries in these respective areas. In short, adequate supplies of labour suitable to the demands of the new productive processes were available. Large markets for mass produced cars were also close by. The mass-production processes using long mechanised production lines required extensive plants, which also required plenty of land; in fact cheap land was readily available and more existed which would satisfy future expansion needs. Of great importance to the suitability of these southern locations was that components were available from the near-by Midlands and London areas.

Ford in particular wished to control the quality and availability of steel supplies. The decision to produce its own steel for castings and bodies required the importation of iron ore and coal. The riverside site at Dagenham was perfect for this and for the easy export of completed products.

The assembly plants were gradually followed southwards by various component firms. These could be new independent firms or subsidiaries of the assembly plants (e.g. GMC's AC-Delco subsidiary) or extensions to existing Midland's firms. For instance, an independent bodybuilder, Pressed Steel, established plants at Cowley (Oxford) and Swindon. By 1935 three of the 'Big Six' car assembly firms were producing most of their output outside the West Midlands, i.e. Ford, Vauxhall and Nuffield.

Lancashire contained a variety of engineering trades, some stemming from the manufacture of textile machinery, others from farm machinery, and others from shipbuilding. Ford had commenced its U.K. operations in Manchester, where the Model T came off the production lines as early as 1911. Sir William Lyons of Jaguar began production of side-cars and car bodies in Blackpool. Leyland Motors' birth-place was at Leyland, now the centre of a whole complex of factories producing chassis and components. Atkinson commercial vehicles, steam-powered and then diesel-engined, are produced near Preston while Crossley Motors had their plants near Manchester. The commercial vehicle producers had a complex of specialist bodybuilders establishing themselves around them, such as Northern Counties coach works and Massey Brothers. Decline of the cotton industry resulted in a wide variety of trades supplying components to the motor industry moving into vacated premises. The main centres were Burnley, Chapel-en-le-Frith, St. Helens, Speke and Manchester. The products made included tyres, brake linings, vehicle springs and various electrical components.

During the inter-war period and immediately after World War II, a variety of vehicle producers took over plants in new locations. The need was for expansion and the availability of vacant factories, government factories, or 'shadow factories', allowed firms to boost production in the shortest possible time. Ford established plants at Langley, Basildon and Doncaster (subsequently the Doncaster plant was sold to International Harvester, a tractor producer). Nuffield expanded capacity at Abingdon and Cowley, while Vauxhall moved its truck plant to nearby Dunstable. Leyland took over fresh capacity in Preston plus the Albion and Scammel concerns in Glasgow and Watford respectively. Components factories were established in South Wales by Nuffield, with later expansion by BMC, Lucas, Dunlop, Smiths and Guest, Keen & Nettlefold. Ford acquired capacity in Leamington Spa and the Briggs Body plants at Dagenham, Romford and Southampton. AEC purchased component and bodybuilding plants in Leeds, while Simms established capacity at Bath. The Rootes group, by acquiring the Tilling Stevens-Vulcan commercial vehicle firm, acquired assembly and components capacity at Luton and Maidstone.

POST-1960

It was not until the 1960s that the third major locational change occurred. After 1960 a number of assembly and components plants were established in areas away from the West Midlands and the South East. The new developing markets in the West and North, plus the newly established steel mills at Newport in South Wales and Ravenscraig in Scotland, may have had a minor role to play, but the real reason for the new locations has been Government policy. The provision of Government subsidies, grants and loans under various Local Employment Acts, plus the permissive powers of the Board of Trade with respect to Industrial Development Certificates, were used to persuade the industry to move to areas of relatively high unemployment. Further measures during the 1960s such as favourable capital and depreciation allowances, as well as extra rebates in respect of Selective Employment Tax, have been used to try to maintain the motor firms net investment in their new locations in the development areas.

The new locations of the motor industry were Merseyside and Scotland for major assembly plants plus the establishment of components factories in South Wales. Merseyside became a new major location. Ford established a fully integrated car and light van plant at Halewood near Liverpool, with an annual capacity in excess of 250 000 units. The Vauxhall plant at Ellesmere Port produces components as well as cars and light vans. Here again the productive capacity for vehicles exceeds 200 000 units a year. Leyland expanded the components and body plant of Standard-Triumph at Speke near Liverpool. Lucas built major plants near Manchester. Liverpool provides an outlet for exports while the Shotton strip mill in North Wales supplies body materials. Lancashire and Yorkshire provide a large market for the finished product. Other components are also available nearby in Lancashire, Yorkshire or down the M6 Motorway in the West Midlands.

In Scotland the Rootes group established a fully integrated car plant at Linwood in Renfrewshire. On an adjacent site Pressed Steel established a car body plant geared primarily to meet Rootes' needs. BMC transferred all their tractor and truck production to Bathgate, around which a number of commercial vehicle bodybuilders established themselves. The main locational advantages were the existence of available labour supplies and the steel strip mill at Ravenscraig. However, the locations caused problems for both firms. BMC had to transport all necessary components from either Lancashire or the Midlands and then transport the finished product south again. This, allied to a collapse in BMC's larger-truck's market, had led to severe annual losses on their Bathgate operations. Labour unrest at both Bathgate and Linwood, plus the need to train labour to the needs of mass production, had also contributed to the situation. Again, the Rootes cars produced at Linwood did not sell in sufficient volume to allow either very profitable levels of plant utilisation or to persuade the labour force that its jobs were secure. Subsequently the Rootes group transferred most of its body needs to Linwood;

in addition, other car models were made on the Imp lines.

South Wales did not have the same influx by the motor industry as either Merseyside or Scotland. A new BMC car body pressings and radiator plant was established at Llanelli, adjacent to the existing 'Nuffield' plant. Rover established a major factory at Cardiff for the production of major components and sub-assemblies. This was intended as a Land-Rover assembly plant but the location may have been expensive. Paradoxically, although Welsh steel is used in nearly all vehicle bodies, the Land-Rover uses an aluminium and steel construction made only in the West Midlands! Consequently the need to transport bodies to South Wales and then probably back again would have been costly. The existence of local sheet steel and export facilities did not induce the entry of new assembly plants, but the available pool of labour attracted many components plants. The good communications with the West Midlands and the South East make South Wales a good centre for such plants. Other major plants established were the Dunlop–Semtex brake plant at Brynmawr and the large Ford components and sub-assembly plant in Swansea. The establishment of Ford's at Swansea contains a moral for all development areas as it showed the need for a locality to 'sell' its advantages on the market. A major industry may be induced to move to a location, which it did not even consider, by active lobbying on the part of that location. The plant Ford now occupy was one of the largest government 'advance factories' built. It was built initially for Pressed Steel's venture into domestic washing machines. This venture, despite subsequent help from John Bloom of Rolls-Razor fame, was never profitable and the plant became vacant. A number of Swansea businessmen were quite close acquaintances of Sir Patrick Hennessey the chairman of Ford, and they brought the existence of the vacant plant to Hennessey's attention. After careful consideration, Ford decided that the plant was eminently suitable. It was modern, with room for expansion and a pool of skilled labour available. Most of those employed were not part of the unemployed as many were employed by the National Coal Board (NCB). The higher wages and better conditions in new industries has left the NCB with a shortage of miners, and this is one of the paradoxes which reflects itself in a social cost of regional policy.

The locations of the 1960s have in some cases proved disastrous, but this should not be over-emphasised. Merseyside and South Wales appear to be good locations, although some labour unrest caused by the new unfamiliar working patterns, together with traditional absenteeism, has been detrimental. These, however, should be short term problems*, and should not be over-emphasised. In addition, the 'old' locations such as the West Midlands and the South East have certain economic drawbacks; labour tends to be scarce and land expensive, therefore expansion is difficult. From the country's point of view a thrusting motor industry bidding labour away from other employers is not just a case of sound micro-economic resource re-allocation. It creates as well a dose of 'demand shift' inflation which can lead to all the harmful paraphernalia of 'stop-go'. Expansion in the new areas avoids this, areas which in the motorway age are on the doorstep of the facilities provided by the West Midlands and the South East. A case in point is that Rover found it extremely expensive to expand at Solihull when the new Land-Rover plant was established there instead of in Cardiff. Initially the labour they managed to attract was from the bottom of the labour market barrel. The result was high training costs followed by absenteeism and a strike epidemic. From the point of the West Midlands as a whole, especially Coventry, the danger is that they will become over-dependent on one industry. Admittedly any unemployment is likely to be seasonal or govern-ment induced, i.e. frictional. It is hoped, however, that within the area itself the motor industry will expand elsewhere and new types of industry come into the area†.

The new locations have received an injection of new dynamic growth from the motor industry. It is not pure gain of course, the established industries could lose their existing labour to the high wages in the car factories, but this should be countered by greater efficiency on their part. Labour-intensive industries could suffer if they have to increase wages too quickly, that is before increases occurred in productivity. This for instance could harm the commercial vehicle specialists and bodybuilders in Lancashire and North Cheshire. The net effect though, from the point of view of the growth and per capita incomes of these areas, has been highly beneficial.

* Economic Development Committee for the Motor Industry, *Regional Policy and the Motor Industry*, NEDO: H.M.S.O., p. 3 (1969). The conclusion here was that regional locations had not been disadvantageous.
† *Financial Times*, Survey on The Midlands (24 March 1969).

3

THE STRUCTURE OF THE
MOTOR INDUSTRY: 1 CARS

In micro-economics an industry is defined by a homogeneous product produced by a number of individual but virtually identical firms. When one attempts to define an industry in practice, however, matters become a little more complex. The straightforward solution of grouping together all firms making the same product or service begs the question of how to define what constitutes the same product or service.

Obviously, for firms to be grouped together in an industry there must be some common denominator. The problem is that there are a number of criteria (or denominators) for grouping firms into separate industries. One possibility is to group firms together according to common processes employed, although this could mean that motor manufacturers differing in the degree to which they were integrated were placed in different industries. Again, the grouping could be made on the basis of firms using the same raw materials, or alternatively on firms producing a product with identical physical characteristics. It is likely that different sets of firms will be obtained depending on which of these criteria are used. Yet another set of firms is likely if we use as a definition of an industry those firms producing goods which are close substitutes, although defining an industry in terms of the cross elasticity★ of demand can lead to problems not the least of which is where to

★ The cross elasticity of demand is the:

$$\frac{\text{Percentage change in the amount of } X \text{ demanded}}{\text{Percentage change in the price of } Y.}$$

draw the line between successive measurements of cross-elasticity, thereby deciding which goods are close substitutes and therefore the 'same' and which are 'different', that is, those which are not close substitutes.

The U.K. has its own Standard Industrial Classification (SIC) which is further divided into Minimum List Headings which are themselves broken down into further sub-divisions. These measures are used in official statistics and are defined in terms of establishments primarily engaged in producing a product or group of products that are related by technical process or raw materials used in manufacture; in other words, the definition of an industry is on the supply side. For example, small commercial vehicles and motor cars may be made by the same technical process so on the supply side they come from the same industry, but are they used by the same category of consumer for fulfilling a similar need? It is unlikely that the answer would be in the affirmative, therefore on the demand side cars and commercial vehicles are not close substitutes. In short it is impossible to find either a single industrial classification or definition which suits all purposes. So although *a priori* reasoning may help to group firms, empirical studies are crucial in determining correct groupings, for only in this way can it be found which firms or groupings are most closely related.

Although no clear-cut or rigorous definition of an industry can be given, like the elephant we can recognise one when we see it. The motor industry will be defined as comprising of those firms making (and selling) cars and commercial vehicles—not necessarily as the principle product—and their suppliers of parts and components. It would not be realistic to include the suppliers of raw materials, such as ferrous and non-ferrous metals, coal, electricity, and so on, as the products they sell the motor industry are indistinguishable, for the most part, from those sold to other customers. So the boundaries of the industry are largely defined by the large firms and their suppliers; and the products of that industry tend to be the principal products of these large firms. A practical example will clarify this hypothesis. One of the firms in the British motor industry is the Rootes group; in turn, the motor industry produces products such as cars and commercial vehicles, which are the principal products of the Rootes Group, and not central-heating plants which are a minor activity of the same firm. The principal product definition of a firm's position in the nation's industrial make-up is a good working definition, but it is not all embracing. In Germany, for instance, the commercial vehicle division of MAN and Klockner-Humboldt-Deutz are obviously part of the motor industry, but these firms are general-engineering giants the principal products of which would be listed under other industrial headings. In the case of a conglomerate, in many instances no principal product could be determined. However, once the industry is defined by looking at the products of the large dominant firms in that industry these become relatively minor problems, for we are still left with a good working definition of an industry.

Broadly speaking the output of the motor industry can be split into seven headings: cars, commercial vehicles, tractors, special equipment for the construction and civil engineering industry, trailers, and parts and components of all sorts. The seventh category is the very important one of the retail trade in motor vehicles.

In this chapter we will analyse the motor car industry and the activities included in the other categories which are geared to satisfying the needs of the car industry. The next chapter will deal with the structure of the commercial-vehicle industry and the various activities geared to meet this industry's needs, such as trailer production or the production of parts and components.

THE MASS-PRODUCERS

The *Motor* and *Autocar* motor magazines for January 1970 list 30 makes of British cars and about 58 distinct models. If one adds the different engine, gearbox and performance variations available in one basic body shell, plus variations to the body shell itself such as two-doors or four-doors, coupe bodywork, or general trim, then the model variations available exceeded 200. This final display of variety is the way a mass-production industry attempts to cater for all tastes without sacrificing the economies of scale following from long production runs. The total of 30 individual makes was in a sense also misleading,

Table 3.1

UNIT SALES AND MARKET SHARES
OF THE MASS PRODUCERS

Company	Unit sales	%
British-Leyland	818 289	45+
Ford	553 701	31—
Vauxhall	244 819	13+
Rootes	189 102	10+
Others	10 025	1—
Total	1 815 936	100

because the high degree of concentration meant that some producers were responsible for more than one make. The number of independent producers was only 16. Out of this number, four producers accounted for 97% of the total British production of cars. In 1968 the unit sales and market shares of the 16 firms were as shown in *Table 3.1*.

Of the four largest firms, Leyland and Ford each produced over two and a half times as many cars as Vauxhall and Rootes, and account for about three-quarters of the total. The products of all four firms, however, plus prices, production methods and commitment to vehicle production allows us to lump all four firms together as highly competitive mass-producers of cars and commercial vehicles. Each firm has a combined car and commercial vehicle production capacity of over 300 000 units a year. Rootes is the smallest, with a potential car making capacity of about 250 000 units a year and a commercial vehicle capacity of about 50 000 units a year. Vauxhall's capacity is almost 300 000 units a year for cars and over 100 000 units annually for commercial vehicles. Ford's total capacity is over 750 000 motor vehicles a year, and BLMC's total capacity is around $1\frac{1}{4}$ million vehicles a year. Clearly none of the groups were working near to capacity in 1968, the motor industry's best year to date being 1964 when 1 867 640 cars and 464 736 commercial vehicles were made. Nevertheless, the combined car and commercial vehicle output of the smallest of the mass-producers is over 15 times as great as the next largest firm which is Reliant cars of Tamworth owned by the Hodge Group of Cardiff.

The mass-producers mainly compete amongst themselves in the mass market, and the great majority of their output is not directly competitive with that of the specialists. However, BLMC produce sports cars which compete with the products of the specialist sports car producers, and BLMC's 'Specialist Car Division' competes with the luxurious high performance saloons and coupes made by the small-scale producers. In addition, Ford and Vauxhall have attempted, with only limited success, to enter the luxury car market with executive versions of the standard Zodiac and Cresta body-shells and engines. Since Jaguar and Rover were absorbed by larger groups however, and eventually combined in the British-Leyland complex, the vast majority of big, luxurious, high quality saloons and limousines are produced by the large groups. Prior to this the mass-producing groups had only a minority of this market. Although luxury saloons and coupes are still produced by specialist firms and compete to a certain degree with the products of the large groups, the competition is not very close. For instance, the most expensive 'specialist' car made by the big groups in

1969 was the Jaguar 420G which cost a total price of £2686, this compares with the cheapest saloon/coupe made by a small specialist producer which was the Aston Martin DB6 costing £4497.

THE SPECIALIST PRODUCERS

The products of the specialists fall into three categories or narrow markets: (1) ultra-utilitarian cars (2) sports and racing cars (3) high performance and quality saloons, limousines or coupes. All these categories are protected to a certain degree from competition from the mass-producers by some special characteristic or the appeal to exclusiveness. In category (1) the special appeal is through low initial running costs; in the case of categories (2) and (3) it is through high performance, or high price, or both.

The ultra-utilitarian cars are produced by Bond and Reliant, the latter absorbing the former in March 1969. These firms produce three-wheeled vehicles (although Reliant produces a low-priced four-wheeler) which are subject to a lower rate of road tax than four-wheeled cars. Engines are also of small capacity and use relatively little petrol. The car bodies are made of fibreglass which obviates the need for expensive tools and presses and therefore keeps fixed capital costs to the minimum. Consequently although annual production figures for utilitarian vehicles tend to be quite small (13 000 by Reliant and 3000 by Bond), fixed charges are relatively low, as a result prices are very competitive. For instance, the cheapest Mini produced by BLMC in 1969 had a basic list price of £413, whereas the comparable Reliant and Bond three-wheelers were £387 and £410 respectively. The Reliant 'Rebel' four-wheeler cost £433 basic. In other words, although the total number of Minis produced in 1968 totalled 210 203 compared with a total output of utilitarian type vehicles from Bond and Reliant of approximately 3000 and 13 000 respectively, the latter are competitive in basic price. This follows from the methods of production, the cost of the materials involved, and the type of product made. The method of production, by avoiding the need for large capital outlay on body-building capacity, is particularly suited to car and light-van production in developing countries. Reliant's expertise and knowledge has been used by Turkey, Greece and Israel to establish domestic motor industries.

The other two categories cater for vastly different needs with both the sporting and 'conspicuous consumption' urges catered for. Of the 16 independent groups existing in 1970, four were mass-producers;

one was a utilitarian-car maker; five made luxury cars; and seven made sports-type cars. The discrepancy in the totals is accounted for by the fact that the utilitarian-car producer also produces sports cars.

The sports car producers, by purchasing major components such as engines and gearboxes from the mass producers and incorporating them in cheap-to-produce glass-fibre bodies, keep prices surprisingly low. Purchasing from the cheapest source and then controlling internal production costs, both fixed and variable, by using glass-fibre bodies helps to keep overall costs down. Consequently production can be both profitable and competitively priced. Not all small sports-car producers use fibreglass in their products, for instance the Morgan Motor Company of Malvern uses spartan, simple but well-finished metal bodies on steel chassis. This can be a relatively cheap method of production. Another way of keeping prices low is to sell cars in a 'kit' form. The customer by assembling his own car avoids most purchase tax and most factory assembly costs.

The sports car producers are seven in number and range from organisations with quite large and well appointed factories such as Lotus or Reliant, to workshop producers such as TVR of Blackpool, or Elva Courier. Typical output and price data for 1968 are given in *Table 3.2*.

Table 3.2

THE SPORTS CAR PRODUCERS

Car	Price Range (Basic)	Annual Output*
Lotus	£745–£1 718	3 500 (bodies only)
Morgan	£670–£1 155	500
Marcos	£199–£1 500	400
Reliant	£1 232–£1 375	2 000 (approximately)
Bond	£722– £935	1 800
TVR	£1 250	300
Gilbern	£1 500–£1 800	250 (approximately)

* Adapted from *The Times*, Business News (24 June 1968.)

The other two producers of any note in this specialist field are Fairthorpe and Elva. As total production in this sector is only around 6000 cars, compared with the motor industry's total output of almost two million cars, this is clearly a very small segment of the market. This sector has a very good export record considering the size of firms involved—well over 50% of the total output of Morgan, Lotus, TVR and Marcos is exported.

The firms in this market are more affected by restrictive budgetary

C

and monetary measures than they are by the continuing movement towards concentration in the motor industry. Restrictive policies tend to hit luxury or exclusive products particularly hard, due to their high income elasticity of demand. Given the long run growth in incomes, however, young affluent customers would probably continue to react against the conventionality of the mass-produced product by seeking a car with a difference. Hence Lotus's aim of producing 8000 vehicles by 1973, about 3000 of which would be sold at home. On the other hand, these producers face a limit to their expansion. This is caused by the need to preserve the existing production techniques which allow relatively low cost production. A significant expansion would require a drastic overhaul of the methods of production because of the inelastic supply of various factors. A different technique, however, would need annual outputs in excess of 100 000 units a year to maintain current prices. This would be virtually impossible to achieve, so to remain competitive and profitable these specialist producers must remain small.

One or two of the specialists not only buy their major components from the mass-producers, but also have close links in other ways. For instance, Lotus modified Ford engines are used in Ford production cars, and Bond markets its sports coupes through the Triumph distribution and service network. Although these firms are independent financially they rely greatly on the mass-producers for major components. In short, they design and assemble cars but do not really manufacture them.

The third category is the high performance and luxurious saloon and coupe sector. The position is summarised in *Table 3.3*.

Table 3.3*

THE HIGH PERFORMANCE AND QUALITY CAR PRODUCERS

Luxury Cars	Prices (Basic)	Output
AC Cars	£2 400 – £4 245	100–150
Aston Martin	£3 518 – £4 473	700
Bristol	£4 692	150
Jensen	£3 620 – £5 365	600
Rolls-Royce	£6 095 – £10 050	2 000 (approximately)

* Source: *The Times*, Business News (17 June 1968).

AC Cars, Jensen and Bristol all use large American engines but Rolls-Royce and Aston Martin produce their own major components. Indeed, Aston Martin produces its own bodies as well, while Rolls-Royce uses either the products of its Park Ward-Mulliner subsidiary or a more standard product purchased from Pressed Steel. AC Cars and Jensen purchase their bodies from Italy but Bristol buys a fibreglass body shell from Leyland's Park Royal subsidiary. All these manufacturers use either expensive imported components or high cost production methods. For instance, the high degree of integration achieved by Rolls-Royce and Aston Martin means the use of capital intensive methods with small annual production runs. To a certain extent this is offset by the long life of each model and an even longer life for the components used, but even so unit costs must be high.

The break-even point for each manufacturer tends to vary. Jensen and Aston Martin become profitable at an output rate of 12 cars a week. However, AC Cars produce profitably with an output as low as two cars a week and Bristol break even at three cars a week. Rolls-Royce have much more capital tied up in car production and the break-even point is probably in excess of 20 cars a week.

Costs of production tend to be high but demand is limited. Customers are prepared to pay the very high prices charged in order to acquire a distinctive and exclusive product. The product will of course remain distinctive only as long as production levels are low, but while production is low costs remain high. However, any attempt to reduce costs by increasing annual production significantly would probably put the producers in a 'no man's land'. In other words, if output was increased to 4000 units a year* so that price could profitably be reduced to £3500 then the product is no longer exclusive. As a result people's 'tastes' for luxury cars could change with the demand curve shifting downwards. In the long-run the firm may become unprofitable and be forced to leave the industry. Even when the product is exclusive, Bristol just break-even, AC car production is not all that lucrative, and Jensen and Aston Martin cars made losses in 1966–1967, although both were profitable in 1968. Aston Martin in 1965–1966 produced 627 cars, but the economic measures of July 1966 cut demand by 50%. Aston Martin's reaction was a price cut of about £1000 per car which doubled demand. This increase in revenue was more than sufficient to absorb all unit losses and leave a surplus. The price elasticity of demand in the relevant ranges of the demand curve was about five†. The precariousness of these firms, however, was

* With this increase in output the increase in total revenue is greater than the increase in total costs.

† Total revenue increased by about 80% (100% increase in demand minus price cut of 20%); total costs increased by about 62% (at 50% of capacity about 33% of total unit costs are fixed): as a result net revenues increase by over 18%. If most sales are from stock then marginal cost is zero and then the short-run increase in net revenue is about 80%!

shown by the fact that Aston Martin again made losses in 1969–1970.

Although a limited market exists for luxury cars and prices can be set at high levels, nevertheless the financial returns are quite low. Why, therefore, do these firms remain in business when perhaps their resources could be more profitably used elsewhere? The answer is perhaps this. Aston Martin and, until recently at least, Rolls-Royce cars have been made by companies whose main interests lie outside the car industry. Rolls-Royce had traditionally made most of its profits from the sale of aero engines, rather than from Rolls-Royce or Bentley cars★. Aston Martin is part of the David Brown engineering complex. However, this organisation has a large stake in the motor industry in general through its tractor production and the manufacture of gears, gear boxes and other components for the commercial vehicle industry. Although both organisations' car making activities are currently profitable, another consideration in maintaining car output is pure prestige. The cars made by both firms can be regarded as 'advertisements' for the organisations in general. As such they can be regarded as one of the most effective types of advertising in maintaining the high quality image of the firms involved.

Bristol was purchased from the Bristol Aeroplane Company in 1960 by Bristol businessmen. The main reason for the continued existence of the car is the enthusiasm of the two partners (Sir George White and Mr. Anthony Crook) to preserve the name as a going concern.

AC Cars is a small public company which has been profitable since the shares were introduced in 1952. Most of the profits, however, came from the production of invalid carriages and the occasional railbus. Although car production *per se* is profitable, it is not particularly lucrative. Nevertheless, the company has been in the car market since 1907 and, quite simply, wishes to remain in it.

Jensen was sold by the Norcros Industrial Holdings group to a private consortium in 1968. In 1967 the firm made a loss but an

---

★ In 1971 when losses on the aero engine side made the company bankrupt, the car division remained profitable but it only accounted for 5% of total turnover. By the end of 1971 it was being suggested that Rolls-Royce Motors, which was now operated independently from the reconstituted aero engine company Rolls-Royce (1971) would, through the issue of shares to the public, become an independent privately-owned company. Previously the intention was to sell the Rolls-Royce motor division as a going concern to some other domestically-owned producer. With an asset value of £20 million and an annual turnover of £34 million, Rolls-Royce Motors would in itself rank as one of the U.K.'s 300 largest concerns. In 1971 an output of 2300 cars and 3200 diesel engines was reported as producing an 'adequate' return on investment, so clearly even Rolls-Royce Motors was only partly dependent on the car industry as such.

American management consultant improved its position to the break-even point in 1968 and to profitability in 1969. The firm follows the principle recently put forward by U.S. Ford that the future world motor industry would consist of a very few large firms and a few very small ones, with nothing in between. In other words, there is no place for the medium-sized firm which requires a great deal of capital and must compete closely with the giant mass-producers. Up until 1967 Jensen's main activity was sub-contract work, mainly producing large Austin Healey sports cars for BMC. Although other sub-contract work was offered by other producers Jensen decided to concentrate on the production of its own cars. It was then realised what an expensive hobby the production of six Jensen cars a week was; clearly internal costing was poor. One of the first things a small motor producer must do is to control its costs and this is what the American consultant Mr. C. F. Duer did. As costs were controlled and output expanded the break-even point was set at 12 cars a week, but production in 1969–1970 reached 15–20 cars a week. Jensen believed that the small specialist producer could survive profitably in the true luxury class for cars selling between £4000 and £8000, and the firm intended to avail itself of this opportunity.

So like the specialist sports car producers the survival of each firm ranges from profitability on the one hand to sheer enthusiasm and break-even economics at the other. Of the specialists, most luxury car producers are either part of a large industrial group or a smaller industrial or garage group, only Jensen is completely committed to car output. Of the sports car producers the majority are car producers *per se* such as Morgan or Lotus. Gilbern however is controlled by a London based investment company, and Reliant-Bond have their major stake in the three-wheeled vehicle market.

All these producers in categories (2) and (3) will remain small or perish. No producer in a mature car industry has yet succeeded in bridging the gap between small-scale and large volume production. (The first exception to this could be the German BMW* company, but the probability is that eventually BMW will be absorbed by a larger group.) On the other hand, it is unlikely that the mass-producers would successfully invade these very specialised markets. Firstly because the production methods are so different and secondly because the customer wants something different. No doubt the mass-producers could attempt to encroach by producing specially adapted versions of their own standardised products, and this could eliminate some of the specialists but probably not all of them. It appears that the modified mass-produced

* Bayerische Motoren Werke.

car does not satisfy the need for exclusiveness. In addition, competition among the specialists may see the entry of some new firms as the capital requirements are comparatively small, in short competition amongst the specialists could be quite severe.

THE PARTS AND COMPONENTS INDUSTRY

Compared with car production elsewhere in the world, one of the most striking features of the British industry is the fact that over 50% in value of the average British car is bought from outside suppliers. This is compared with from 25% to 40% in Japan, Italy, Germany, France and the United States. Since over 50% of the value of a British car represents bought-out components it means that to a large degree even the large mass-producers confine their manufacturing activities largely to sub-assembly and final assembly work, including body-building and the machining of engines and other major mechanical components such as gearboxes. As a result the supplier takes on a very important role, supplying anything from thousands of tons of sheet steel to tiny rubber seals and nuts and bolts.

There are four main reasons why a car manufacturer may decide to purchase from outside. (1) He may not wish to become involved in an area of technology with which he is unfamiliar. (2) He may not have, or wish to tie-up, the capital needed to establish component-making plant. (3) Many parts are too small a proportion of costs to be worth the trouble of making. (4) The optimum size of plant needed for the production of certain components may be so large that if all economies of scale are to be reaped just one or two firms would be able to meet the needs of an entire industry.

Not all producers have the same 'bought out' content. BMC, for instance, purchased 70% of the value of its vehicles from outside, whereas the Jaguar group purchased 60%*. Even Ford purchase over 50% of a car's value from outside the organisation. The most highly integrated producers in the motor industry are Leyland's bus and truck divisions and the specialist producers Aston Martin cars and Foden heavy vehicles, the bought out content of their products is only around 30% of final unit value.

A product the size of a motor car which is both complex and an assembly of about 3000 totally different parts, offers scope for the participation of numerous different firms in the various stages of its

* *Autocar*, p. 21 (10 August 1967). (This was before BMC purchased Pressed Steel.)

manufacture. In 1967, for instance, BMC spent £320 million purchasing items from 4000 outside suppliers. The total number supplying the car industry as a whole is somewhat greater than this as some suppliers have exclusive contracts with producers other than BMC (or British Leyland). Although a large number of component firms exist, the overall structure of this part of the motor industry does not present a picture of many firms fighting to supply the vehicle producers under conditions akin to those of 'perfect competition'. As the final stages of production are highly concentrated the immense needs of the vehicle producers leads to considerable specialisation and concentration among suppliers. In order to produce efficiently the suppliers were obliged to introduce flow line techniques wherever possible; conversely, the full benefits of such techniques would only be reaped if the market for a particular component was in the hands of just one or two firms.

Typically, out of the total costs of a British mass-produced car costing £1000, anything between £500 and £650 is accounted for by items bought from outside suppliers. The major items are as shown in *Table 3.4*.

Table 3.4

Electrical equipment	£90
Castings and drop forgings	£70
Tyres and wheels	£85
Front suspension assembly	£60
Brakes	£35
Paint	£18
Glass	£22
Upholstery	£18
Miscellaneous iron and steel items	£40
Total	£438

Leaving aside the last category in the table, around 60% to 80% of all bought-out components are accounted for by a small number of major items. Clearly it is of prime importance, where the total costs of the motor firms are concerned, that the suppliers of these items operate with the maximum efficiency. Information received from car firms suggest that between 50% and 65% of total car costs are accounted for by bought-out components, there being some slight differences in the degree of reliance on outside suppliers for certain items. Vauxhall, for instance, purchases most of its electrical components from a subsidiary company AC-Delco. Ford's Autolite associate produces some electrical equipment such as starter motors. Leyland Motors manufacture some electrical items under licence from the United States. Nevertheless, tyres and electrical equipment are still mainly in the hands of outside suppliers, as is the production of the hoard of smaller items such as dashboard instruments, steering gears, fuel pumps, sparking plugs, locks, door handles, seats, windows and so on. Only Ford★ and BMC make carburettors, and even then BMC's SU subsidiary does not satisfy all its needs.

Although the integrated firm buys less components from outside it purchases more raw materials. Obviously the firm with its own body-building and foundry capacity will be performing manufacturing operations which will require adequate raw material supplies. A large outlay would be needed on items such as steel, pig iron, brass, bronze, copper, zinc, aluminium, rubber, wood, PVC, plastics, glass, leather, paint, insulating materials, upholstery, springs, formica and so on. Only Ford in the U.K. has its own blast furnace which mainly produces cast iron, the sheet being bought from outside; the company purchases iron ore, limestone and coal from outside suppliers. The firms supplying basic materials such as limestone, steel, plastics, glass and springs act as suppliers to industry in general; hence they cannot be counted as part of the motor industry. On the other hand the motor industry is either directly or indirectly responsible for a significant proportion of such industries' output, for instance 6% of coal and 5% of electricity is in one way or another taken by the motor industry. Turning now to the structure of each component market.

THE CAR BODY

The most important item of expenditure is the car body. All the four mass-producers own body building capacity. British Leyland, since its purchase of Pressed Steel, is self-sufficient in car bodies. The body-building division of British Leyland is made up of Pressed Steel, Fisher and Ludlow, Morris bodies, Nuffield bodies and Mulliners. All car producing firms in the group used to buy some of their bodies from Pressed Steel. Rootes still do although most needs are satisfied by the firm's own facilities. It was to be expected that Chrysler would wish to make its British subsidiary independent of one of its major competitors for the supply of car bodies. Rootes' own body plant, British Light Steel Pressings was closed in 1968 as being too small and inefficient with no possibility of being able to introduce profitable

─────

★ Ford only makes carburettors for original equipment, so does not compete in the replacement market.

production methods in the rather cramped space available. Ford and Vauxhall produce all their own bodies, Ford through its subsidiary Briggs Motor Bodies. Rolls-Royce, Morgan, and the Swedish firm Volvo purchase a large part of their body requirements from Pressed Steel. No large scale independent body builder now exists, and with all the mass-producers committed to producing their own needs there is no market available for such a firm. There are, however, about a dozen small scale bodybuilders independent of the large groups. These satisfy specialised markets, such as coach-built limousines, convertibles, estate cars, sports cars or hearses. Rolls-Royce's Mulliner-Park Ward subsidiary produces limousines in competition with British Leyland's Vanden Plas subsidiary. BSA's Carbodies subsidiaries specialise in taxi bodies on BMC chassis. Convertibles are made by firms such as Crayford Engineering and so on.

ELECTRICAL EQUIPMENT

The second most expensive item of expenditure is electrical equipment. The Monopolies Commission's report on the supply of electrical equipment for road vehicles published in December 1962 distinguishes between eight classes of equipment. The principal suppliers were Lucas, Chloride, Smiths and Champion. The report suggested that the proportion of total vehicle costs made up of electrical equipment in a family $1\frac{1}{2}$ litre saloon was between 5% and 10%. The vehicle producers themselves only produce a limited number of electrical components. Ford's Autolite subsidiary makes ignitions, dynamos and windscreen motors. GMC's AC-Delco subsidiary produces some instruments but mainly concentrates on fuel pumps, oil filters, ignition coils and distributors, horns and sparking plugs*. AC-Delco's customers include car and commercial vehicle producers other than Vauxhall-Bedford, and Leyland Motors produce starter motors and dynamos for heavy vehicles under licence from the Leceneville Corporation of America†. The one supplier which produces almost a complete range of products —featuring in six out of the eight main classes of electrical equipment— is Joseph Lucas Ltd. The company has a virtual monopoly in the manufacture of key items such as lamps, windscreen motors, dynamos

---

* *The Supply of Electrical Equipment for Mechanically Propelled Land Vehicles*, Monopolies Commission Report, H.M.S.O., p. 118 (1963).

† These are marketed under the Butece label. Production commenced because Lucas supplies constantly lagged behind the demands of CV producers. The quality of Lucas equipment for heavy vehicles had also been questioned.

and ignition coils. Smiths is in a similar position in the production of heaters and instruments. In the case of sparking plugs for initial equipment, Champion supplies over 70% of the vehicle producers demands. However, in the electrical equipment field the dominant firm is Lucas. Because it has a monopoly in some fields the company is in a strong position to win original equipment business in related fields where it faces competition, notably in the markets for batteries, ignition coils, distributors and windscreen wipers.

TYRES AND WHEELS

From *Table 3.4* we can see that Tyres and Wheels are the third largest cost item. All tyres are bought by vehicle manufacturers from outside producers. There are about twelve independent companies producing tyres in the U.K., but six[*] account for the vast majority of sales to the car producers. Published evidence on market shares is now rather dated[†], but the broad picture is that almost 60% of car tyres sold as original equipment come from the factories of Dunlop; the rest is shared by Avon, Firestone, Goodyear, Pirelli and Michelin. Apart from Dunlop the only British firm is Avon; Michelin is French, Pirelli Italian and the others are American. In 1970 Pirelli and Dunlop expressed their intention to merge, which was effected in January 1971. The only vehicle producer making car wheels is Ford through its subsidiary, Kelsey-Hayes Wheel Company. The other vehicle producers obtain wheels from three main sources: Dunlop, Rubery Owen and Joseph Sankey, the last being a Guest, Keen and Nettlefold (GKN) concern. Dunlop and GKN have introduced an element of market sharing, Dunlop mainly concentrating on cars and GKN concentrating mainly on the commercial vehicle market. Although in the tyre and wheel field the vehicle producers have a wide choice of suppliers they have tended to buy from a limited number of suppliers. This has allowed suppliers to tool-up with expensive equipment in the knowledge that they possess a market of a size sufficient to absorb the large volume of goods produced. This in turn confers external economies on the vehicle producer.

---

[*] Dunlop, Michelin, Avon, Pirelli, Firestone, Goodyear.
[†] Monopolies and Restrictive Practices Commission, *Report on the Supply and Export of Pneumatic Tyres*, H.M.S.O., p. 38 (1955).

OTHER COMPONENTS

As regards the front suspension, a number of firms supply the complete front axle assembly—such as Alford and Alder and Rubery Owen. The former is a member of BLMC. At the same time a number of firms specialise in particular items, such as Armstrong Patents or Girlings (Lucas) in shock absorbers. In addition it is usual for the large vehicle producers to make some of the equipment needed but to buy-in specialised components and then assemble the completed unit.

The only major vehicle producer without its own foundry facilities for casting cylinder blocks, cylinder heads, rear axle castings, pistons, etc., is Vauxhall. For some types of specialised castings the large firms tend to purchase from the many foundries scattered around the U.K. These are foundries geared to the needs of the industry in general but they are also able to meet the requirements of the vehicle producers. The one firm which tends to supply all its own casting needs is Foden, the producer of heavy vehicles. The large car producers rely greatly on the Birmid Group and GKN, two firms which specialise in supplying the motor industry.

The other main items of expenditure are on brakes and forgings. The former item comes from two sources, Automotive Products' Lockheed Division and Lucas's Girling subsidiary. As regards forgings, a large number of companies are in a position to supply the motor industry, but in practice most of the industry's business is given to Guest, Keen and Nettlefold. GKN's Garrington subsidiary is the largest forging organisation in Europe, producing a vast number of items such as crankshafts, connecting rods, half shafts, etc., for the motor industry. Garringtons formed the basis of GKN Forgings Ltd. a division which now includes three other firms purchased by GKN in 1963. These were Ambrose Shadlow & Co., Ltd., Smethwick Drop Forgings, Ltd., and Smiths Stamping Works (Coventry) Ltd.

GKN's sales in 1968 reached £433·5 million, 42·8% of which was to the U.K. motor industry alone. The Group probably makes more of a motor car than any outside supplier, accounting for about 15% of total vehicle costs. As well as forgings, the organisation makes the majority of bumpers used in British cars, this item being produced by the Joseph Sankey and Pyrene subsidiaries. In addition, Sankey make wheels and truck cabs for Leylands as well as producing their own vehicle—the FV 432 Armoured Personnel Carrier for the British Army. Another subdivision of GKN is GKN Castings Ltd. Its main location is the batch of foundries in the West Midlands, but other foundries are located in Cwmbran and Rochester. Other activities include producing transmissions, transmission components and bearings. The large step into the transmissions sector came in 1966 by the purchase of Birfield Ltd. This organisation had a very large stake in the motor industry through its various subsidiaries, namely Hardy Spicer, Laycock Engineering, and Salisbury Transmissions. All the transmission activities have been grouped into GKN Birfield Transmissions, which is responsible for most of the transmission components in the U.K. This was quite remarkable when one realised that it was not until 1956, with the purchase of Blade Research and Development Ltd. (BRD), that GKN first entered the transmissions side of the motor industry. Ironically, BRD was established to produce propeller shafts in order to provide an alternative source of supply to the virtual monopolist Hardy Spicer. In 1967, GKN moved into the production of bearings through the acquisition of Vandervell Products Ltd.

From 1963 onwards GKN's already considerable involvement in the motor industry was greatly increased through the acquisition of many independent companies. It became GKN's policy to increase its participation in the motor industry as it was felt that this was the only major industry capable of absorbing their vast output. After 1963 the emphasis shifted from individual companies to the single central organisation, hence the emphasis on operating-divisions.

The dependence of GKN on the motor industry was matched by the motor producers' dependence on GKN, despite an inevitable difference in emphasis. Indeed, while the motor industry depends on over 5000 independent outside suppliers, in value terms the vehicle producers' expenditure is concentrated on a few major items from a few major firms. Probably six suppliers—Lucas, Smiths, Dunlop, GKN, Birmid and Automotive Products—account for about 50% of the car firms' expenditures on bought-out parts and components. The other 50% is distributed among a vast number of other suppliers. Very few of these items would cost the car maker more than £10, the majority of the products would be nuts, bolts, cloth, glass, washers, wire and so on. However, although these items are a relatively insignificant proportion of total costs nevertheless most of the suppliers would be highly dependent on production for the motor industry. In addition, most of the items would be essential to the correct functioning and assembly of a motor vehicle—hence the motor industry's vulnerability to strikes in the most obscure small-scale producer's factory.

Summing up here, although the dependence of different vehicle producers on outside suppliers varies due to different degrees of integration, the broad picture is now basically similar, especially following BMC's purchase of Pressed Steel. The most significant differences amongst the Big Four follows from the fact that Vauxhall is the only major producer without its own foundries, while Ford is the only producer with its own blast furnaces*. So although no two producers are identical in their dependence on outside suppliers, the table at the beginning of the chapter is a fair reflection of the material and component expenditures of the integrated firm and the contribution of various components to the total unit costs of car production.

THE OVERALL PICTURE

THE BRITISH MOTOR INDUSTRY

The present state of the British motor industry is one of a high degree of concentration, a situation which is repeated in all other major vehicle producing countries. The situation in the U.K. for 1967 is summarised in *Table 3.5*.

Table 3.5

PERCENTAGE OF MARKET SHARES

Manufacturer	Cars	Commercial vehicles
BMC	34·8	27·8
Jaguar	1·4	0·7
Leyland	7·9	6·2
Rover	2·7	8·1
Total BLMC	46·8	42·8
Ford	28·4	24·4
Rootes	11·7	7·6
Vauxhall	12·7	23·2
Others	0·4	2·0
Total	100·0	100·0

Source: SMMT.

Therefore four major groups account for over 99% of car production and 98% of commercial vehicle production in volume terms. The role of the remaining producers is mainly one of production for specialist and/or limited markets, such as very expensive cars, and

* Traditionally Ford has the lowest bought-out content of any mass-producer and makes more materials, parts, and components, than its competitors.

heavy commercial vehicles. As we will see in a later chapter, it is in the latter field that independent producers still play their most significant part. Heavy commercial vehicles are almost always designed to meet individual requirements, or at the very least they incorporate individual modifications to meet particular customer-requirements. The result of this is that production is on a jobbing or batch basis, and the sacrifice of economies of scale are less significant than it would be with the mass production of light vans or cars for two reasons. Firstly, the method of production is less capital intensive, and the machinery used is normally multi-purpose instead of being designed to do one repetitive task. Secondly, customers are prepared to pay for quality and individual production. That is, they are prepared to pay prices which cover the high average costs of production—which is the premium for quality and individual treatment. The one heavy vehicle producer which has moved away from batch production is Seddon Diesel of Oldham; this firm supplies standard models at very competitive prices.

Such outstanding differences in the method of production almost places the specialist car and commercial vehicle producers in a separate industry to that of the Big Four and their suppliers. However, the differences in product have diminished during the 1960s. The mass-producers of cars or commercial vehicles have attempted to enter the lucrative specialist markets, especially on the commercial vehicle side, by introducing models that attempt to woo the customers of the specialist producers. As yet the attempt has been unsuccessful. Nevertheless the 'fringe' competition between the mass-producers and the specialists can be expected to increase. Indeed in the case of Reliant cars and Seddon commercial vehicles the specialists are attacking the markets of the mass-producers.

The degree of vertical integration varies in detail from firm to firm, but basically the degree of integration is not large. Each of the Big Four is heavily dependent on outside suppliers and independent retail outlets. The main movement towards increased vertical integration during the post-war period has been the purchase of independent bodybuilders by the vehicle producers. All the significant suppliers, Fisher and Ludlow, Briggs, Mulliners and Pressed Steel were absorbed by the large vehicle-building groups. Ford, Vauxhall and Leyland also produce some of their own electrical equipment, but only GMC's AC-Delco subsidiary can be said to hold a major portion of the market for electrical goods. So the small degree of vertical integration in the industry gives an important role to the outside suppliers, some of which are almost as large as the vehicle builders themselves, for instance Dunlop, Lucas* and GKN. As these firms (plus one or two others) are responsible for a high proportion of the total unit costs of a car, it is imperative that their production methods are of the most efficient or least-cost variety. Allied to this the supplier must be fully geared to meeting all the likely demands of the vehicle producer, otherwise expensive bottlenecks would occur in the assembly process.

This last point is of equal relevence to all the industry's suppliers who vary in size and in dependence on the motor industry. Many small-size suppliers specialise in the mass-production of the vast number of vital items—big and small—required by the motor industry. Although their individual share in the total cost of a vehicle is small, much depends on their efficiency. It is essential that costs are kept to a minimum and that they are geared to meeting all the needs of the vehicle builders. The Industrial Reconstruction Corporation (IRC) was alive to this need, and their promotion of horizontal integration between the three major—but relatively small—British producers of ball-bearings was a reflection of this. The establishment of a U.K.-owned ball and roller bearing group based on the 1969 merger of Ransomes and Marles, Hoffman Manufacturing and Pollard Ball & Roller Bearing was fully supported by the IRC and British Leyland. The main arguments in favour of such a grouping were: (1) greater standardisation of product leading to longer production runs and therefore lower costs, and (2) the creation of a secure British owned firm in a key sector for industry in general. The IRC took financial control of Hoffman and then gave financial backing to Ransomes to bid for Pollards in the face of strong competition from the Swedish SKF (Skefco) group.

So British car producers are dependent on the efficient running of thousands of firms if their own assembly plants are to be given the chance of running at maximum efficiency. In fact, many suppliers were unable to meet the requirements of the car firms† when the latter were running at optimum production levels. For instance, when the old BMC division of BLMC produced at a long-run rate of 93% of scheduled output (about 80% of actual capacity) component shortages appeared. Most of the large firms like Lucas, Dunlop and GKN have the capacity to meet BMC's needs when the latter produces at 100% of schedule, plus the capacity to keep pace with the vehicle

---

* In 1969 Lucas's pre-tax profits were £18 million on a turnover of over £300 million compared with BLMC's profits of just under £30 million on a turnover of almost £1000 million.

† *The Sunday Times*, Business News (12 January 1969).

producers planned expansion★. This arises from the regular contact of supplier and assembler regarding future production forecasts. However, a large number of suppliers have been unable to keep pace with existing production levels quite apart from meeting any planned expansion. The firms which constantly fell behind and thereby caused production holdups at BLMC have been dropped and their business was transferred to firms which showed themselves able to match any BMC output level. At the same time BMC started to reverse its former policy of one supplier per component per model, preferably British-owned†. Dunlop and Girlings lost their monopoly of tyre and brake supplies respectively in late 1968. Furthermore, if a British supplier proved unreliable with no domestic alternative available the group made it clear that it would purchase abroad. In some cases it proved difficult to break a monopoly position, for instance, that of Lucas for many electrical components. However, the Corporation attempted to minimise the impact of strikes in a supplier's factory by seeking to minimise the number of crucial monopoly suppliers in the way Ford has done since 1945‡.

If BLMC really wanted to ensure control over its supply sources then integration would be required. The American industry has greater control over its final assembly schedules through establishing its own component production units or by taking-over major suppliers. Ford and Vauxhall are more integrated than BMC which has traditionally relied on outside suppliers, although BLMC is in some areas more integrated, for example, it produces its own radiators and some of its own carburettors. While control of supplies is an attraction, there is the drawback posed by expense. For instance, in the case of BLMC over 60% of components are bought outside. Lucas, Dunlop, Smiths, GKN and Automotive Products represent the backbone of outside suppliers with total earnings from the motor industry in the region of £400 million. This cash-flow is generated by capital intensive plant and equipment which the motor firms would have to either purchase or establish themselves in order to produce their own components§.

★ Lucas finds it difficult to keep abreast of the demand for commercial vehicle components, *The Sunday Times* (15 March 1970).

† *The Supply of Electrical Equipment for Mechanically Propelled Land Vehicles*, Monopolies Commission Report, H.M.S.O., p. 251 (1963); *The Sunday Times*, Business News (12 January 1969).

‡ *The Supply of Electrical Equipment* Monopolies Commission Report, H.M.S.O., pp. 248 and 249 (1963).

§ Lucas in the U.K. and Bosch in Germany are unusual in being major independent entities in the electrical field with their own technical expertise. The usual position is ownership by vehicle firms or mere sub-contracting.

In the U.K.'s case this may not be the best answer. After all, the main component producers supply the entire motor industry and not just one firm. As a result they have the opportunity of producing at a lower cost than the motor manufacturers.

THE AMERICAN MOTOR INDUSTRY

In the U.S.A. motor production is more integrated vertically and horizontally than it is in the U.K. The American market is dominated by the three domestic giants, GMC, Ford and Chrysler, one medium-sized firm, American Motors, and the dominant importer Volkswagen. The giant firms produce more of the components entering into the final product than do their U.K. counterparts. The average proportion of an American car's ex-works value which is bought-out is much less than 50% compared with significantly more than 50% in the U.K. The reasons for this structural difference are twofold. The larger size of the American market makes the manufacture of their own components economically viable. The volume of cars produced is large enough to allow a single firm to gain most, if not all, of the economies of scale available at each stage of production. This eliminates the cost advantages of vertical disintegration, as existing in the U.K. This factor justifies vertical integration, but it is not the main historical reason for the creation of a vertically integrated industry. This second factor was the convictions of the two great founders of the industry, Henry Ford and William Durant (of GMC). They both believed in a high degree of corporate self-sufficiency. Ford expanded 'backwards' into the production of components and semi-finished materials in order to control production and assembly costs more effectively. Durant believed in buying an interest in his suppliers, but GMC is less vertically integrated than Ford. This follows from a policy decision in the 1920s when General Motors decided to limit its activities to the production of those components and materials where the bulk of the industry's output was sold to the car industry. So General Motors has not followed Ford into steel, plastic or glass manufacture where the motor industry is only one among many customers. As regards components overall, however, General Motors produces more of its requirements than Ford, usually in specialised divisions that grew out of suppliers acquired by the group (the same type of policy as that of GKN in the U.K.).

Despite a higher degree of concentration than exists in the U.K., the American car and commercial vehicle producers still buy from a large number of outside suppliers. The Big Three of GMC, Ford and

Chrysler buy from 62 000 independent firms*. However, there are no monopoly suppliers as in the U.K., and all suppliers know that inefficiency on their part would lead to a switch in purchasing either to another outsider or to internal production on the part of the vehicle producer. This is a much more real threat in the U.S. than the U.K. due to the difference in output volume. In the U.S. 'inside' production at high volumes by least-cost production methods is always possible whereas it is not in the U.K. The American firms' practice of encouraging competition in price and quality between outside suppliers and between outside suppliers and their own manufacturing divisions often leads to purchases being split between different suppliers. In this respect American practice is akin to continental Europe's, rather than Britain's. Although the U.K. industry itself is moving towards a multi-supplier position where it can, in certain fields, such as those dominated by Lucas or Smiths, this is very difficult as there is little room for a second supplier.

THE EUROPEAN MOTOR INDUSTRY

On the Continent vertical integration is usual, but for a different reason. Here it is a result of necessity rather than choice. Historically the growth of an independent components industry lagged so far behind the growth of a vehicle manufacturing industry that vehicle firms had no alternative but to make a large proportion of their own parts and components. As a general statement this point is valid, but it must be made clear that there is no 'typical' European country or car maker. In practice the two opposite extremes of the European pale are provided by Sweden and Italy.

The Swedish motor industry consists of two medium-sized vehicle builders Volvo and Saab-Scania. Both firms produce quality cars at a medium price and both firms produce quality built medium and heavy commercial vehicles. Due to the relatively low levels of production neither firm could afford to produce its own parts and has to buy them from outside sources.

Significantly, their largest single source of supply is the U.K.: about 10% of the ex-works price of a Volvo car or a Scania truck consists of British parts and materials. Specific items include Hardy-Spicer propeller-shafts for Volvo and a new Triumph engine for Saab. However, following the experience of strike-interrupted suppliers

* *The Economist*, Supplement on Cars and their Components, p. x (23 October 1965).

Table 3.6

	1967	1966	1965
Cars	193 976	173 499	181 755
Commercial vehicles	20 584	26 411	23 818

Source: The Association of Swedish Automative Manufacturers and Wholesalers.

from the U.K. the Swedes now buy from more than one source.

In Italy Fiat has a tradition of self-sufficiency which was reinforced during the post-war expansion, especially during its rapid growth in the 1960s. Fiat makes the majority of the components it uses and also has the most elaborate establishment for metal making and shaping of any motor manufacturer in the world. This gives Fiat very great control over cost and quality at all stages of the metal-making and shaping process. The other Italian companies are all medium sized. In practice the presence of Fiat in an overwhelmingly dominant position had put Lancia, Innocenti and state-owned Alfa-Romeo in a difficult position. They were too small to efficiently produce their own components but at the same time they had to compete in the domestic market with a fully integrated giant. The result was that their costs were greater than they might otherwise have been. This follows because virtually no independent components industry exists in Italy, for without Fiat's custom sufficiently long or large production runs were impossible. Consequently the medium-sized firms have to buy components from Germany, France and the U.K. The tariff barrier has inflated the cost of such components in the past, consequently the abolition of tariff barriers in the European Economic Community allowed these firms to acquire components at a cost more in keeping with those faced by Fiat.

The French motor industry is supplied by over 500 component companies with the average size of firm being small to medium, i.e. less than £1 million turnover and fewer than 200 employees. There are however some giant concerns, for instance Chausson supplies all the radiators for French vehicles, Jaeger over 70% of the instruments, Ferodo all clutches, and Michelin has over two-thirds of the tyre market. The French vehicle builders normally seek at least two suppliers per item such as Marchal and AC-Delco for sparking plugs, Paris Rhone and Ducellier for dynamos and starters. Unlike the U.K. components industry, however, very few producers supply more than one car producer, in other words, each vehicle builder will have a different pair of suppliers to his competitors.

The resulting fragmentation of the components industry, while insuring alternative sources of supply, often leads to high cost production. The supplier's market is frequently limited to one vehicle firm, but this hides further limitations. The French vehicle makers are bold technical innovators while at the same time specifying conflicting technical requirements for different cars in their range of vehicles. Low car prices allied to technical innovation can only occur if there is some rationalisation of individual models or, failing this, the use of common components. At present only Simca, under Chrysler's influence, is fully conversant with this need in its efforts to acquire efficiently made and therefore low cost components.

In Germany the use of a 'cascade' turnover tax for many years had encouraged car makers to purchase components from firms they themselves control, thereby avoiding the tax. At the same time firms have not wanted to become too wide-reaching in order to avoid the odium attached to cartels in Germany. As a result, German car makers have nurtured a large number of independent suppliers. Quality has been controlled because outside suppliers are in fact subcontractors. They produce items whose design and quality was determined by the car makers and rigidly inspected by them at all stages of production. Costs are kept to the minimum by firms buying each part from only a very small number of suppliers. Where costs are sacrificed to ensuring a wide range of alternative sources the product is sold more on quality than price anyway—this is certainly the case with Mercedes-Benz cars and commercial vehicles. The American firms Ford (Taunus) and GMC's Adam Opel tend to be more integrated than German owned ones. However some monopolist component makers exist: Solex produces 98% of the carburettors, nearly all the toughened-glass is sold by a co-operative cartel of four firms and Bosch produces the majority of the electrical items. These virtual monopolists normally insist on a guaranteed minimum production run of four weeks for any item, if necessary at the vehicle maker's own cost. This means that vehicle producers normally hold large stocks and the component producers have long low cost production runs. This sort of insurance is far heavier than most U.K. companies are prepared to pay for, even though they suffer from recurrent shortages and bottle-necks.

THE JAPANESE MOTOR INDUSTRY

The Japanese situation is more akin to Italy's than to anyone else's, but it has many distinctive features of its own. The Japanese motor producer exercises very tight control over his suppliers. The vehicle builder and his bank are the centre of a firmly controlled complex of enterprises. The motor company itself may appear less highly integrated than its American or European equivalent—adding $33\frac{1}{3}\%$ to the value of its output compared with 50% elsewhere (apart from the U.K.). Nevertheless, many of the parts used come from either a subsidiary company or a small independent firm dependent on the vehicle builder for orders. Without these orders the small firm cannot find financial credit. Consequently a large vehicle producer such as Toyota helps its 300 odd suppliers to acquire adequate finance from their banks; in all cases suppliers enlist the help of the vehicle builder to obtain credit.

Compared with the U.K. or the U.S.A., there are relatively few independent component suppliers. The total number of 350 is in turn mainly made up of small to medium firms, although the 21 producers with over 2000 employees each supplied a third of their respective markets in 1968. However, the particularly Japanese characteristic of this part of the industry is found outside this inner ring of companies. For outside those firms which are highly integrated with the vehicle producers there are thousands of small sub-contractors. The Japanese industrial census* listed 8000 firms with less than 10 employees and between 20 000 and 30 000 with fewer than four employees.

These tiny producers give the main manufacturers (1) flexibility and (2) cheap labour. The vehicle builders' main contractors can always reduce the amount of sub-contracting in poor times thereby protecting their own output volume. In addition it is suspected that the labour employed by these very small enterprises is paid substantially less than the men employed directly by the motor companies who are now paid on almost European scales plus some expensive fringe benefits.

The Japanese government and vehicle builders are together urging the component suppliers to integrate their production and to amalgamate. It is not the intention to help establish monopoly suppliers on the Lucas model but to establish two integrated groups of components makers. Each one will supply one or other of the two giant vehicle builders Toyota and Nissan. In addition, because the smaller vehicle firms such as Honda, Toyo Kogyo and Mitsubishi tended to buy their components from the same pool of suppliers as the two giants, there is no question of further component complexes being established around these smaller motor firms. On the other side of the coin, if two groups of component suppliers were established their increased size and efficiency would give them the financial strength to face the two giant

* *The Sunday Times* (9 March 1969).

car firms on equal terms, thereby safeguarding a source of components to Mitsubishi and Company which was financially independent of Nissan and Toyota. At the same time the smaller vehicle producers would be able to purchase efficiently produced low cost items.

In short then, because over 50% of the cost of a Japanese car is made up of bought-out parts, the vehicle industry must nurture a secure and efficient components sector. The component makers themselves are being constantly urged to introduce the most efficient techniques available in order to lower costs to the minimum.

THE INTERNATIONAL NATURE OF THE MOTOR INDUSTRY

Turning away from the relationship between supplier and motor manufacturer to the most significant feature on the side of the ownership of vehicle builders.

The motor car industry in the U.K. and Germany shows that the concentration of ownership extends beyond national boundaries. In the U.K. in 1967 and 1968 over 53% of the cars produced came from American owned firms. A similar situation exists in Germany as well as in many countries with newly established motor industries, such as Australia. The firms normally involved are GMC and Ford, for Chrysler being for a number of years in a rather unsatisfactory trading position, had little capital or time to establish foreign subsidiaries. However, when Chrysler improved its competitive position it attempted to emulate its American rivals. It purchased ailing European firms such as Rootes in the U.K., Simca in France and Barrieros in Spain. Because these firms were ailing Chrysler had to inject a great deal of capital into them in an effort to make them viable. For instance, the accumulated losses of the Rootes group made between 1964 and 1970 were almost £20 million. As well as a strong stake in the vehicle assembly industry, the Americans are strongly entrenched in the components field. Borg-Warner is one of two market leaders in the automatic transmission field, AC-Delco, Champion Sparking Plugs, Chloride batteries, Goodyear, U.S. Royal and Firestone tyres, Butec electrical equipment: these firms are all subsidiaries of American parents. In addition all the giant body presses used in the U.K. motor industry although built by Vickers are of American design.

In the U.K. this American pressure was one of the reasons why British Leyland was created. Indeed the revolution in the organisation of the British-owned motor industry is the other main feature of the present overall situation.

The merger between Leyland and BMC showed the situation in its true light. Leyland having expanded from its Lancashire citadel had imposed hegemony over the British-owned sector of the motor industry. For eight months after the merger in January 1968 Sir Donald Stokes of Leyland and Sir George Harriman were officially 'twin monarchs'. This period ended with the retirement of Harriman and his elevation to the non-executive position of President. This move reflected a new management structure on the one hand and the re-organisation of the company into seven operating divisions on the other.

The integration of the straggling BMC-Leyland empire into separate but coherent units was a pre-requisite to the creation of an efficient enterprise. The establishment of divisions was the only way to bring order to BMC's diverse operations. The two key sectors concerning the overall prosperity and survival of BLMC as a giant vehicle-producer were (1) the volume car and light commercial vehicle sector and (2) the specialist car division. BMC cars make up the former while Triumph, Jaguar and Rover make up the latter. The other divisions are headed by the large-truck and bus sector, followed by the Foundry and general engineering division, the Construction Equipment division and the Overseas Division.

This new streamlined organisation was still faced with the need to rationalise its production and sales policy before it could work with any degree of smoothness. First of all it was faced with the need to close-down much old and crammed plant which was a legacy of BMC's reluctance to rationalise. The second great need was to rationalise the retail side. This was a great weakness of the U.K. motor industry in general but of BMC in particular. The company was strong on the technical side but weak where production and marketing were concerned. Marketing developments were quickly discernible. The old idea of 'badge-engineering'—where an identical car was sold under Austin, Morris, Wolseley, Riley and MG labels—tended to disappear. Instead, three distinct model ranges were planned, with retail outlets concentrating on one or the other. The range to be sold under the Austin label would consist of technically advanced vehicles, such as the front wheel drive Austin Maxi. The second popular range would be marketed under the Morris name, and these would be technically simple motor cars. This range would compete with cars like the Ford Cortina which are relatively large in comparison to the price paid. The third set of dealers would handle the specialist cars, such as Jaguar, Triumph and Rover. So model rationalisation would be accompanied by changes on the retail side. Moreover, these changes would hide further rationalisation, for although BLMC has four times as many dealers as Ford, Ford sells more cars per retail outlet. The larger turn-over per dealer allowed better sales and service facilities plus lower prices. In other words, Ford dealers have been able to offer much better 'trade-in' values than BMC's dealers. Only when the problems on the production and retail side had been solved would BLMC be truly efficient. This pre-supposes that a third main problem, that of labour-management relations, had already been overcome.

Such then is the present situation in the British motor industry. The industry must work efficiently and successfully because of its important effects on the economy. In terms of employment, the industry reached a peak in 1966 of 497 500 employees, over 400 000 of whom were located in the South, West Midlands and North East. This represented over $5\frac{1}{2}\%$ of the employees in all manufacturing industry. As the figure for 1959 was just over 380 000 the average annual growth rate over the period 1959 to 1966 was over $3\frac{1}{2}\%$ with the increase in unit production being just over $3\frac{3}{4}\%$ a year. In terms of industrial production the total current and capital direct and indirect requirements of the motor industry account for some 10·6% of industrial production*. Hence although fluctuations in the economy have significant effects on the motor industry, the industry in turn has a large effect on the economy.

* Economic Development Committee for the Motor Industry, *The Effects of Government Economic Policy on the Motor Industry*, NEDO: H.M.S.O., p. 8 (1968).

4

THE STRUCTURE OF THE MOTOR INDUSTRY: 2 COMMERCIAL VEHICLES

In the early post-war period the producers of commercial vehicles were split into two quite distinct categories: mass-producers and specialists. The first section consisted of the mass-production of fairly standardised products which in turn could be split into three categories. Firstly, light vans with a carrying capacity of less than 15 cwt. largely based on passenger car designs. Secondly, medium-sized vans and pick-up trucks of between 15 cwt. and 25 cwt. carrying capacity. Finally, trucks and large vans of over one ton capacity. In the early post-war period nearly all mass-produced vehicles in the third category were either small or medium sized, with payload* limited to five tons or below. As this sector of the commercial vehicle industry lent itself to the production of standardised products in large numbers it was dominated by the mass-producing car firms. Of the 155 000 commercial vehicles produced in 1947 the mass-producing car makers accounted for about 124 000.

The other main section consisted of specialist and heavy vehicle builders. Not all the specialists made heavy vehicles, that is, the maximum size of vehicle as laid down by the 'Construction and Use Regulations' that could be built on two, three, or four axles. Some specialists concentrated on the light and medium-weight ranges, and as a result they faced some competition from the mass-producers. How-

* The weight of goods that could be legally carried.

ever, in the early post-war period up to about 1953 these firms faced little competition from the mass-producers in the medium-weight range of between five and eight tons payload. Firms such as Guy, Seddon, Dodge, Jensen, Vulcan, Albion, Thornycroft and Dennis tended to concentrate on the light- to medium-weight market. The traditional heavy vehicle producers numbered six, and these were, Foden, ERF, Atkinson, Scammell, AEC and Leyland. It is interesting to note that most of Leyland's output consisted of heavy buses and coaches and medium-heavy goods vehicles. As regards the market for heavy goods vehicles, Leyland was one firm among many and in no sense did it dominate this particular sector of the specialist vehicle producers' market.

THE VEHICLE BUILDERS

Table 4.1 shows the commercial vehicle industry as it looked in 1947. As can be seen from the table, the mass-producers accounted for just

Table 4.1

THE COMMERCIAL VEHICLE INDUSTRY IN 1947

Firm	No. produced (approx.)	Market shares (%)
Mass producers		
Nuffield	21 200	13·6
Austin	22 300	14·3
Ford	36 000	22·9
Bedford	32 000	20·3
Rootes	12 500	7·9
Others	5 000	4·3
Total	129 000	83·3
Specialist producers		
Leyland	3 400	2·2
AEC★ (ACV)	4 500	2·9
Albion	2 000	1·3
Dennis	1 400	0·9
Thornycroft	1 600	1·0
Scammell	1 100	0·7
Guy	3 750	2·4
Others	8 200	5·3
Total	25 950	16·7

★ Including Crossley and Maudslay bought in 1948.

over 80% of production and the specialists for just over 16%. However, by 1954 the position had changed quite dramatically from the specialists' point of view (*Table 4.2*).

Table 4.2

THE COMMERCIAL VEHICLE INDUSTRY IN 1954

Firm	No. produced (approx.)	Market shares (%)
Mass producers		
BMC (Nuffield–Austin)	94 000	35
Bedford	58 000	21
Ford	42 000	15
Land-Rover	25 000	9
Rootes	24 000	9
Total	243 000	89
Specialist producers		
Leyland	10 000	4
ACV (AEC)	5 000	2
Others	12 000	5
Total	27 000	11·0

The share of the market held by BMC, Bedford, Ford and Rootes remained almost constant at 80%, but the inclusion of Rover, a new entrant into the CV field in 1948, increased the mass-producers' market share to almost 90%. Leyland and ACV improved their relative positions slightly, but the market share of all the other specialists was halved. The early 1950s saw the start of the process whereby the mass-producers moved up the weight scale to produce larger and larger vehicles. As a result many specialist producers of light and medium-weight vehicles came under increasing commercial pressure from the cheaper mass-produced products of the car firms. Consequently a number of firms left the industry either through bankruptcy, merger, or the concentration of activities on other lines. For instance, Vulcan was absorbed by the Rootes group, and Jensen withdrew from the CV market to concentrate on cars. The firms which remained tended to phase-out the manufacture of light and medium vehicles to concentrate on heavier products. Here they came up against competition from the well-entrenched and established heavy vehicle makers such as Foden, ERF, Atkinson, AEC and Leyland.

Firms like Guy, Dennis, Seddon and Dodge found the competition extremely severe and the first three's financial position became precarious compared with the prosperity of the early post-war period. Seddon had pioneered the small diesel powered truck, but during the early 1950s BMC, Ford and Bedford introduced their own diesel engines, while Rootes introduced Perkins-engined products. Only Dodge prospered in the specialist sector left outside that held by the heavy vehicle builders. This Chrysler subsidiary kept costs to the minimum by purchasing keenly priced components from efficient producers, and utilised assembly methods which avoided over-capitalisation but yet economised on labour. This resulted in the production of a relatively standardised range of vehicles which was assembled with great care by more labour intensive methods than those employed by the mass producers. The combination of relatively low costs and prices on the one hand and quality and more individual specifications on the other allowed the firm to profitably produce around 5000 vehicles a year during the 1950s. Albion Motors had foreseen the encroachment by the mass-producers and had at the height of its fortunes sold-out to Leyland. The combined output of the two firms of nearly 10 000 units a year allowed the group to remain in the medium weight sector as well as in the heavy vehicle market. The skilful interchange of components and the mechanisation of production through methods which avoided the introduction of expensive capital items controlled fixed costs as well as variable costs. Some firms which found it difficult to find new markets, while at the same time were highly integrated and faced with expensive fixed cost items, were in a perilous position. Guy never recovered and went into liquidation. Dennis Brothers has continually sought to recover past prosperity. Consequently years of loss making have been mixed with years of small profits. Only Seddon, of the smaller producers in the medium-weight sector, remained a prosperous entity, but only after initial uncertainty and small profits.

The heavy vehicle producers, faced with a steadily growing market, prospered during the 1950s. Even with the dominance of ACV and Leyland in this sector, the small firms ERF, Foden, Atkinson and latterly, Seddon, did well. The tendency for Leyland and ACV to bring a degree of standardisation to their products meant that customers requiring a high degree of individuality in the vehicle they purchased tended to favour the custom-built products of Foden, ERF and Atkinson. Despite claims by the mass producers, and to a lesser extent Leyland-AEC, to be able to satisfy all individual needs it was only the heavy vehicle specialists who could supply an entirely custom-built product. The amount of capital utilised by the mass-producers, and to a lesser extent Leyland, necessitated larger and more standardised production runs.

The specialist market has seen many changes, mainly caused by the mass-producers making larger and larger vehicles. The requirements of custom building however, meant that mass-production techniques could not be profitably used. Consequently it was not in the interests of the mass-producers to use their plant and equipment for the manufacture of highly individualistic vehicles. Therefore the heavy vehicle builders had a safe and secure market as long as their costs did not become markedly different to those experienced by the mass producers. In such an event the customer could judge that the cost differential was not adequately covered by the quality difference. The importance of the industry's independent supplier is obvious here and this will be discussed later.

The 1960s saw changes in the commercial vehicle industry which often, but not always, mirrored changes in the car side. ACV after a spate of take-overs in the late 1940s, waited until 1962 before it made a further acquisition, when it purchased Transport Equipment from the Thornycroft group. The most significant development in the industry came with the ACV–Leyland merger, which was sandwiched by Leyland's acquisition of Standard-Triumph and Rover Cars. Jaguar cars established a CV group in the 1960s through its purchase of Daimler and Guy Motors respectively. This was followed by the BMC–Jaguar merger and then of course came the creation of BLMC. Leyland's tentacles also spread into the specialist firms with minority shareholdings in Foden and Atkinson*. In addition, Leyland purchased a minority holding in the state owned bus producer, Bristol Commercial Vehicles, which grew to 50% in 1970. Further developments occurred as a consequence of the Chrysler–Rootes merger when the Dodge CV interests were integrated with those of Rootes.

PEACEFUL CO-EXISTENCE: THE SPECIALISTS AND THE MASS-PRODUCERS

As in the car industry, the commercial vehicle sector is composed of giant groups on the one hand and small specialists on the other.

* Following the purchase of Atkinson by Seddon Diesel in 1971, British Leyland's share of Seddon's equity was 4·7% plus 19·8% of the convertible loan stock issued in respect of the merger, which came from its 19·8% holding in Atkinson. In September 1971 British Leyland sold both its stake in Seddon and its 26·8% holding of Foden's equity in order to improve its cash position and to find resources for investing in its own automotive products.

One of the giants however—BLMC, was established around a specialist CV producer. The special characteristics of both the product and the market were recognised when British Leyland established the Truck and Bus Division. This established specialist production alongside mass-production, although the different products came from separate plants with different production methods.

The present structure of the commercial vehicle industry is summarised in *Table 4.3* for the years 1968 and 1969.

Table 4.3

THE COMMERCIAL VEHICLE INDUSTRY IN 1968 AND 1969

Firm	No. produced (1968)	Firm	No. produced (1969)
BMC★	105 195	British Leyland	
Ford	108 017	Austin/Morris Division	59 985
Rootes–Dodge (Chrysler U.K.)	27 066	Truck and Bus Division	125 021
Bedford	97 222	*Total*	185 406
Daimler–Guy★	2 621	Chrysler (U.K.)	31 909
Rover★	36 694	Ford	137 029
Leyland★	23 854	Vauxhall–Bedford	102 524
Atkinson	1 196	Atkinson	1 028
Bristol	766	Bristol	854
Others	6 555	Others	6 970

★ British Leyland Companies.

In volume terms the industry is dominated by light-and medium-weight vans and pickups, and the mass produced trucks and buses manufactured by the car making groups. When the specialist and heavy CV divisions of these groups are added, for instance Leyland and Daimler-Guy, the dominance becomes much greater. However the small-scale specialist producers such as Atkinson, Seddon and Bristol still produce over 8000 vehicles a year and they account for about 30% of the market for goods vehicles over 20 tons gross weight, that is about 14 tons payload.

Although over 70% of the vehicles made by the mass-producers are either light- and medium-weight vans or light lorries below six tons payload, these firms have now entered the heavy vehicle market. Throughout the 1950s and 1960s the Rootes group, followed by Bedford, Ford and BMC, moved gradually into markets traditionally left to the specialist producers. The Rootes group tended to be the first to 'climb up the ladder' as it was itself attempting to avoid the competition of its bigger rivals.

Although BMC normally produced the largest number of vehicles, much of its total consisted of car-derivatives, such as mini-vans or medium-weight vans and pick-ups. In the light-van sector BMC tended to hold just over 50% of the market, and until 1967 was also predominant in the medium van sector, with over 30% of the market; in 1968 however, Ford's new range of vehicles had reduced this by 10%. This was an unprecedented reverse even in the highly competitive CV industry. In the market for trucks, buses and vans of over two tons payload, Bedford has been the traditional leader with about 24% of the market. However, in recent years Ford has thrust itself to the front with 25% of sales. At the same time BMC, with a disastrously poor new range of medium-weight trucks, found its share of the market falling, from 20% in 1965 to 10% in 1967, a decline exactly equal to Ford's improvement. In the field for the lightest trucks of between one and a half tons and four tons payload, BMC has between 55% and 65% of total sales, which only emphasises the total collapse in its market for larger trucks between 1965 and 1967. Leyland and Rootes-Dodge each hold about 17% of the market with the remaining 10% satisfied by the specialists and imports.

The market for trucks of over 16 tons has, however, been dominated by Leyland, Guy and the specialists, with the mass producers holding just over 5% of sales.

All this serves to show the high degree of competition in the industry, the extent to which each of the mass-producers is dominant in one sector or another, and the mass producers' overall weakness in the market for larger vehicles. Until 1967 the light- and medium-van market was dominated by a battle between BMC and Ford, with BMC in the forefront. After 1967 BMC lost ground to Ford in the medium-van and pick-up market although still dominating the light van sector. The medium-truck market, that covering vehicles of from two tons to eight tons payload, was dominated by Bedford until 1967 with Ford and BMC contesting second place. Subsequently Ford displaced Bedford from market leadership. Ford's success bears analysis. It began in 1963 with three separate measures: the establishment of a Special Vehicles Division; the appointment of a Director of Commercial Vehicles; the re-organisation of the CV truck and sales network. On this foundation was laid a new and successful range of vehicles in 1965 and 1966. In 1966 and 1968 Ford's total CV production exceeded that of BMC the traditional market leader, which reinforced Ford's new pre-eminence in particular sectors of the CV market.

THE FRAGMENTED MARKET FOR COMMERCIAL VEHICLES

In the same way as the car market is divided between different sectors in terms of car size, with various sectors showing different growth characteristics, the CV market is split-up between different payload categories or seating capacities, as in the case of buses. The three main tasks undertaken by vehicles reduce roughly to the retailing, wholesaling and haulage functions. Small and medium vans and pick-ups predominate in the first sector; the second function is done by medium vans, pick-ups and trucks of up to about 10 tons payload; the third function is done by the largest vehicles of over 10 tons payload and up to the maximum size of 32 tons gross, that is over 20 tons payload.

Over the period 1958–1969 the registration of commercial vehicles by unladen weight was as is shown in *Table 4.4.*

Table 4.4

NO. OF VEHICLES (1000s)

Vehicle	1958	1959	1960	1961	1962	1963	1964	1965	1966	1967	1969
Up to 16 cwt.	55	52	62	72	67	64	67	67	65	68	70
16 to 30 cwt.	67	78	88	77	65	75	86	87	81	79	80
$1\frac{1}{2}$ to 3 tons	27	28	32	28	25	25	25	25	24	20	22
3 to 6 tons	25	35	44	43	35	40	46	43	45	40	44
Over 6 tons	3	3	5	6	6	8	11	13	17	20	23
Total Goods	177	196	231	226	198	212	235	235	232	227	239
Passenger vehicles	5	6	7	7	6	6	6	7	7	7	7
Total	182	202	238	233	204	218	241	242	239	234	246

Over this period the peak in registrations occurred in 1965 but in effect registrations have remained fairly static since 1960. The two lightest categories typically cover around 66% of all new goods vehicle registrations. Perhaps the most noticeable feature is the increased importance of the over six tons group which accounted for 9% of registrations in 1969 compared with less than 2% in 1958. At the same time the medium-sized goods vehicles of $1\frac{1}{2}$ to 3 tons have declined over the period from over 15% to less than 9%. The registration of buses and coaches have remained pretty stable in absolute and percentage terms over the entire period.

From the individual manufacturers point of view it means that the market for light and medium vans and pick-ups has held steady, mainly to the advantage of BMC and Ford. The decline in the $1\frac{1}{2}$ to 3 ton sector hit BMC very hard, for this was the only part of the truck market where the company was a market leader; it held over 50% of new sales here. The growth in the larger vehicle categories has helped Bedford and Ford; Ford's new dominance had been aided both by its overall relative improvement and by its relative improvement in the faster growing sectors of the domestic CV market. In addition, Leyland, Guy and the specialist producers have benefited from the growth in the over six tons category. Some evidence for this could be found in the output figures of some of the smaller producers (*Table 4.5*).

Table 4.5

APPROXIMATE OUTPUT FIGURES

Firm	1960	1968	1971*
Atkinson	800	1 196	1 800
Seddon	900	2 000	3 000
Guy	750	2 000	2 500
ERF	650	1 500	2 000

* Approximate capacity.

The present-day structure of the CV manufacturing industry is one of dominance by vehicles produced by mass-production techniques, whether they be light vans or full-sized lorry chassis. At the same time there is a significant and growing market open to the makers of heavy batch and custom built vehicles, whether they be small independent producers or the specialist vehicle plants of larger groupings.

THE PARTS AND COMPONENTS INDUSTRY

As in the case of motor cars, the CV industry shows a high degree of vertical disintegration, with many materials, parts and components purchased from independent outside suppliers. Significantly, the bought-out content of non car-derivative vehicles produced by the large groups is lower than that of a car. For instance, compared with a bought-out content of over 60% in the case of cars, only 50% of the total costs of a BMC truck is made up of bought-out items. This situation is duplicated in the case of Ford, Bedford and Rootes. Nevertheless, the specialist CV makers, like most of the specialist car makers,

D

are highly dependent on outside suppliers. The main activity of the vehicle builders is one of assembly; manufacture being carried out by other independent firms. In the case of firms like Atkinson and ERF, some 85% of total costs are made up of outside purchases. Other specialists, such as Dennis and Foden are more highly integrated and the latter is probably the most highly integrated firm in the U.K. motor industry, with a bought out content as low as 20% of total costs.

In some cases outside suppliers supply all the CV industry but in other instances they have to compete with the more highly integrated vehicle producers, some of whom supply items to other CV makers.

In the case of electrical equipment, tyres and wheels, front suspension assemblies, castings, brakes and forgings, the CV market is largely supplied by the same firms that supply items for car production, although some differences do exist.

THE SUPPLY OF ELECTRICAL EQUIPMENT

In the case of electrical equipment, Leyland in 1967 broke Joseph Lucas' monopoly in heavy duty alternators and starter motors by making its own Butec brand under licence from the U.S.A. During the period 1967–1969 Butec was in a position to supply 75% of AEC's requirements and 50% of Leyland's own needs. Until 1968 there was rigorous competition in the important market for diesel engine fuel pumps and injection equipment between CAV-Lucas on the one hand and Simms Industries on the other. Over the period 1960–1967 Simms came under severe pressure from Lucas when the latter produced new types of equipment at roughly one quarter the cost of the Simms product. In addition, Simms fortunes were tied very much to the CV market, whereas CAV with the financial backing of the Lucas empire, could hedge through its activities in the aircraft and car fields. Consequently the smaller firm's position deteriorated and in 1968 it was absorbed by Lucas. In retrospect the Leyland organisation admitted that it was mistaken in allowing this take-over which created a monopoly in fuel pumps. The only viable alternative source of supply is from Bosch in Germany.

Thus for most classes of electrical equipment the CV industry is supplied by the same firms as the car industry, with just a few exceptions. Butec has already been mentioned as a supplier peculiar to the CV market; in addition, Clayton Dewandre is a far more significant supplier on the CV side. This is especially so in the supply of heaters where they and Key-Leather have undercut Smiths, the market leader.

Similarly in the market for stop and tail-lamps Lucas has lost business to Butler and also to Flexible Lamps. In fact Lucas and Smiths have faced significant price competition in the CV market and have lost business to these firms and to AC-Delco and Clear Hooters. The CV producers have as a general policy the aim of keeping two suppliers for each item in order to help maintain price competition. However, the vehicle builders' customers often specify the type and make of equipment which can militate against the policy of trying to keep two suppliers. Often the customer specifies a particular make of equipment after being subject to intensive canvassing by the supplier of the equipment—Lucas has been very active here.

An obvious problem in supplier-vehicle manufacturer relationships, and one which often leads to supply difficulties, is that heavy vehicle builders often require special non-standard items of equipment delivered in relatively small quantities. Clearly firms like Lucas, Smiths and AC-Delco which are geared to large-scale production are not really suited to satisfying this type of business. Where firms are committed to standardisation it is sometimes difficult to meet orders for small quantities of special items on time. In fact, a certain divergence of interest exists here. Because the standardised items made by many suppliers, especially in the electrical equipment field, are geared to the car market they are not always suited to the needs of CV operators who require stronger heavy duty equipment. The need for more reliable equipment, as well as questions of delayed delivery, was the main motivation behind Leyland's decision to supply some of its own electrical equipment needs. So the vehicle builder often has to supply custom-built vehicles with non-standard equipment if he is to meet the customers' requirements, whereas the component producer would prefer to supply standardised equipment. Obviously the latter situation allows cost advantages to both the supplier and the CV builder, but from the vehicle builders point of view cost reductions are of no account if they result in inferior products which do not meet the customers' needs and which could result in a reduction in demand.

THE SUPPLY OF OTHER COMPONENTS

Tyres and wheels are purchased from the same firms as supply the car industry, with the addition of Rubery Owen as a supplier of wheels. In addition Sankeys and Dunlop have come to an arrangement whereby the former would concentrate on the CV industry leaving Dunlop the car and car-derivative CV market.

Brakes are purchased from Lucas, Automotive Products, Clayton Dewandre and Westinghouse, which are also the car industry's main suppliers. Much the same situation exists where the supply of front assemblies, forgings and castings are concerned. However, Leyland and Fodens produce their own iron, steel and aluminium castings in their ferrous and non-ferrous foundries. Fodens is one of the few specialists to produce the major proportion of its requirements for units such as gearboxes, clutches, steering gears and cabs. Although the company does not own forging facilities it undertakes nearly all its own machining. Only Leyland in the heavy vehicle sector is as highly integrated as Fodens. Dennis however, carries out much of its own machining as well as producing a large range of units such as gearboxes, axles and steering gears. No firm produces its own forgings, and these are purchased from outside suppliers such as Kirkstall Forge, GKN and other firms in the West Midlands, the former being highly dependent on the CV industry. Front assemblies are produced by the BLMC subsidiaries Alford and Adler, and Newton Bennet, and also by Kirkstall Forge, Rubery Owen, Eaton Manufacturing Co., GKN and Moss Gears. In addition, some car and CV makers produce either the complete axles and steering gears or just certain components. The small specialists Foden, Dennis, Bristol and Daimler-Guy, produce most of their requirements in these areas.

It appears then that, as one would expect, many of the firms supplying the car industry also supply the CV side. In some cases there are different suppliers involved and some instances of firms being more significant as suppliers to the CV industry than they are to the car sector. There are some very important bought-out items, however, which are peculiar to the CV industry, items which the car producers make for themselves. Involved here are the purchases of gearboxes, diesel engines, axles, transmissions and chassis frames from outside sources.

DIESEL ENGINES: A CASE STUDY IN COMPETITION

Engines are bought from four main sources: Perkins Diesel Engines, Gardner Engines Ltd., The Cummins Engine Company and Rolls-Royce. In terms of output volumes, Perkins is the world's largest producer of diesel engines and out of a total annual output of around 600 000 units about 200 000 are for automotive uses. Customers include Bedford, Ford, BMC, Rootes, Shelvoke and Drewry, Dennis, ERF, Atkinson, Seddon, Dodge and Bristol in the U.K. and Chrysler, Saviem, White and International Harvester abroad. The growth of the company was a post-war phenomenon based on the firm belief that diesel engines could be successfully used in small and medium vehicles as well as in large ones. The pioneering work in the use of diesel engines in small trucks was undertaken by Seddon, and the success of this company in exploiting new fields attracted the mass-producers into the market. Until the early 1950s no mass-producer made its own diesel engines although Nuffield made a Swiss Saurer unit under licence. Consequently the mass-producers, and some of the specialists, turned to Perkins to supply their needs. Although eventually the mass-producers made their own diesel engines, many of their customers still preferred to use a Perkins engine in their vehicles. As a result, Perkins units power a whole range of vehicles from the 1·7 litre engine of 42 b.h.p. powering medium-sized vans of around 1 ton payload, to the 8½ litre V8 unit of 185 b.h.p. in trucks of up to 30 tons gross vehicle weight (g.v.w.). Perkins can number amongst its customers the majority of specialist firms and all the mass-producers, even though the latter often produce engines which are directly competitive. The firms most dependent on Perkins are Rootes-Dodge, Dennis, Shelvoke and Drewry, and Seddon, although all firms apart from Foden, Leyland, AEC, Albion and Scammell buy some engines from Perkins.

The company was purchased by Massey-Ferguson of Canada in 1959 at a time when it was emerging from a difficult financial period and when it was still in the middle of a production re-organisation. Massey-Ferguson for its part wished to terminate its dependence on Standard-Triumph for its supplies of diesel engines. This was following an unsuccessful 'undercover' take-over bid in 1958 for Standards by Massey-Ferguson which had generated a degree of ill-will between the two companies. As a result the merger between Massey-Ferguson and Perkins admirably suited the two companies involved.

Until 1966 the Perkins engines powered vehicles of between 2 and 20 tons gross vehicle weight. Where larger vehicles were concerned the independent supplier traditionally used was Gardner of Manchester. The size and power of engine ranged from 3·8 litres to 10·45 litres giving from 60 b.h.p. to 150 b.h.p., although until the early 1960s the company's most powerful lorry engine was rated at 125 b.h.p. Until 1964 the heaviest vehicles in normal use allowed on British roads were of 24 tons g.v.w. so the Gardner engine gave adequate power. Only the specialist producers used Gardner engines as until the mid-1960s the mass-producers did not make vehicles of sufficient size to warrant the use of such engines and firms such as Leyland and AEC used their own engines exclusively. As a result it was left to the likes of Foden, ERF, Atkinson and Guy on the goods side and Dennis, Daimler,

Bristol and Guy on the bus side to buy Gardner products. Gardner's market then, on the automotive side, was mainly in sales to the heavy vehicle specialists. Gardner engines were used in goods vehicles of between 16 and 24 tons gross vehicle weight and in large buses and coaches. The company places emphasis on very high quality with each engine meticulously assembled by hand utilising expensive materials. Consequently output volumes are small, being around 5000 engines a year. On all counts the retail price is increased, being from £200 to £300 more than equivalent AEC and Leyland engines. However, the very durable, efficient and reliable product which results persuades buyers that it is cheaper to use in the long run. Another factor is that the various capital investment grants and allowances available to CV buyers reduces the difference in net costs even further.

The decision to allow heavier vehicles on U.K. roads was made in 1964. The amendment to the 'Construction and Use' regulations allowed the use of vehicles of up to 32 tons gross vehicle weight. These larger vehicles required engines of between 170 and 225 b.h.p. to give them sufficient power, which was a requirement that Gardner was unable to meet until 1966. This initial demand for more powerful engines plus a long drawn out strike at Gardner's in 1964, intensified the company's inability to meet all the demands of operators and vehicle builders. It must be explained that Gardner engines typically experienced excess demand but the company always refused to sacrifice high standards of workmanship to the higher volume of output which the market required. As a result of these factors the American Cummins concern was given the opportunity to enter the British market.

Table 4.6 shows that the ratio of payload to gross vehicle weight increases as the size of the vehicle increases; consequently many operators were eager to avail themselves of the opportunity to use

Table 4.6

SIZE AGAINST COST

Type of Vehicle	Miles per week	Payload as % of total weight	Operating costs per mile
Morris Mini ¼ ton	200	27	27½p
Ford Transit 1½ tons	300	53	6p
Bedford KD 10 tons	400	68	2p
Bedford KM 16 tons	600	73	1p
Leyland Beaver 32 tons	1 000	83	½p

Adapted from *Commercial Motor* and *Motor Transport* cost tables.

larger vehicles. Leyland, Guy and the heavy vehicle specialists were eager to satisfy this new demand. Leyland produced engines of sufficient power to meet the new operating conditions resulting from the amendment to the 'Construction and Use' regulations, the increase in the speed limit in 1964 for vehicles of over three tons unladen from 30 m.p.h. to 40 m.p.h. and the dawn of long-distance high speed motoring as produced by the Motorway system. The small specialists, however, were reluctant to become dependent on their largest competitor for engine supplies, but finding no suitable engine produced by Gardner or Perkins, they were obliged to purchase from Cummins.

In terms of sales value Cummins is the world's leading diesel engine producer. For instance, in 1968 total sales amounted to £153 million compared with about £120 million in the case of Perkins. Measured in output volume, Cummins made about 70 000 units in 1968, which is significantly lower than Perkins' figure or British Ford's volume which amounts to over 100 000 units a year.

Cummins opened its British operations by establishing a manufacturing plant at Shotts, Lanarkshire, in 1957. Output consisted of high powered engines for automotive, marine, and civil construction purposes. Typically, over 80% of output is exported mainly to Scandanavia and the Commonwealth, especially Canada. The difficulty the company experienced in breaking into the European market can be judged by the failure of the Shotts operation to earn profits until 1964. Cummins was induced to establish itself in Europe for a number of reasons. The market for diesel engines was larger in Europe than in the U.S.A., especially before the mid 1960s. Also diesel engine production is relatively labour intensive which makes diesel manufacture very expensive in the U.S.A. Manufacturing in the U.K. specifically gave Cummins the advantage—such as it was—of Commonwealth preference, as well as access to a very strong domestic CV industry.

In 1965 Cummins undertook considerable expansion in the U.K. by establishing two factories in Darlington, one for the manufacture of diesel engines and the other for the manufacture of engine components and the assembly of engines from imported parts. In 1964 Cummins was virtually the sole independent source of very powerful diesel engines available to the specialist makers. As a result Cummins began selling quite significant numbers of 'in line' engines built at Shotts to Atkinson, Dennis, ERF, Foden, Guy, Norde as well as to old established customers in the Leyland group, such as Scammell and Thornycroft. The 'V type' engines built at Darlington were sold to Dennis, Dodge, Daimler and Ford★.

★ 'In line' and 'V type' refers to the cylinder block configuration.

An alternative source of supply of very powerful diesels was the Rolls-Royce diesel engine division at Shrewsbury. However, between 1950 (when the division was formed) and 1966, engine sales to CV builders were small; indeed, in the early 1960s Rolls-Royce lost much of its market to Cummins. It appeared that the Rolls-Royce product was more expensive than competing designs whilst failing to offer any great advantage in thermal efficiency or reliability. The fact that Cummins was able to offer lighter, cheaper and more efficient units induced Rolls-Royce to introduce a new range of engines in 1966. These were technically good and competitive in price with the products of other engine producers. As a result they cornered a significant share of the market and gave the specialist producers another viable alternative source of supply.

These are the main sources of engine supply but certainly not the only ones available. It is possible for the small specialist to purchase units from firms such as Rushton and Hornsby or English Electric-Dorman. Another source of supply would be from foreign producers of CVs, such as Scania in Sweden or Deutz or MAN★ in Germany. As long as the sales and service network existed operators could be induced to buy a MAN engined vehicle from say ERF or Atkinson. If the operator was not prepared to do this, perhaps because of unfamiliarity with the product or because he felt the import duty did not make it worthwhile, then the specialist producer must rely on existing domestic sources. At present there is no disadvantage in this as substantial competition exists between engine sellers which keeps costs and prices down. At the same time the specialist producer has a viable alternative to Leyland-AEC for their crucial engine-supplies.

Just a word is needed on the competitive nature of the diesel engine market. Cummins moved very quickly into the market in 1964 and established a large British sales and management organisation. This was soon followed by the full operation of the Darlington factories, one of which was initially jointly-owned with Chrysler. Despite some initial success, Cummins' market share fell. This was due to the prompt, if slightly late, reaction of British producers and the slightly inferior product Cummins produced in terms of fuel efficiency, noise and cost. The Darlington plants manufactured engines of between 140 b.h.p. and 185 b.h.p. and assembled units of between 200 and 265 b.h.p. The 'smaller' engines were made by the Chrysler-Cummins plant which had a capacity of 30 000 units a year, one-third of which it was assumed would be required by Rootes-Dodge and the remainder being sold through Cummins International or the U.K. sales and service organisa-

★ Maschinenfabrik Augsburg–Nürnburg A.G.

tion. However, Perkins retaliated with a more powerful engine which proved very popular. Rootes-Dodge, Guy and Ford, in the light of consumer preference, had to change their policy of offering the Cummins unit as standard with Perkins engines offered as an optional alternative; this situation was in fact reversed★. A further agreement between Jaguar and Cummins to jointly produce engines was never implemented; the few Cummins engines used in Daimler buses were units assembled from either German or American made Cummins parts. Gardner and Perkins engines proved much more popular with operators interested in fuel efficiency, and firms like Seddon and Dennis did not offer the Cummins engine at all, their sales revival being based mainly on Perkins engined vehicles. As regards the 'larger' engines, fuel-economy conscious U.K. operators found the new Perkins and Gardner engines of around 180 b.h.p. more reliable, more efficient, and quite adequate to power vehicles of up to 32 tons gross. In 1970 Gardner's position was further strengthened by the emergence of 250 b.h.p. units. If operators found these inadequate they tended to specify the new Rolls-Royce unit or even Leyland or AEC powered vehicles from the specialists. The largest haulage vehicles produced by Leyland-AEC used their own engines exclusively.

The American company overreached itself in the U.K. Its vast London-based management organisation was drastically reduced in size in 1968. In addition, Chrysler found itself with a white elephant in Darlington with the sales of Cummins engined trucks falling to a trickle. As a result it sold its interests to Cummins. In 1969 Darlington's production volume was only 65% of capacity; and 70% of production was exported, mainly to the U.S.A., Canada and Mexico. Although the medium duty engines of between 140 and 185 b.h.p. made at Darlington had failed to penetrate the U.K. market, it is only fair to point out that one of the reasons for the establishment of the Darlington complex was to establish the world-wide source of supply for such engines in the U.K. As a result any increased market penetration abroad means extra exports for the U.K. Nevertheless, the prompt reaction of Perkins (in particular), Gardner and Rolls-Royce to the threat to their large domestic market had left Cummins with a smaller share of the U.K. market and greater production losses than it anticipated. The small specialist producers and the other users of the diesel engines produced by the independent suppliers, benefited greatly from the increased choice available with even Gardner encouraged to increase its volume of production.

★ In 1969 only 2% of Dodge vehicles supplied to British customers had Cummins engines.

GEARBOXES, AXLES AND FRAMES

Turning from engines to the supply of other major components. In a
CV, even more so than in the case of cars, the gearbox is a crucial
piece of equipment, for to give acceptable acceleration whilst carrying
various loads and yet conserving fuel requires a complex but efficient
gearbox. Unfortunately, in the U.K. gearbox makers have modified
their products after and not before changes in operating specifications
occur. They have not anticipated foreseeable new requirements. The
British makers of CV gearboxes, AEC, Leyland and David Brown have
only moved slowly to meet operators requirements. In the design of
gearboxes it would appear that American and Continental producers
have tended to be more alert than their U.K. rivals. This, for instance,
allowed Turner Engineering of Wolverhampton to capture a large
slice of the market with products built under licence from the American
firms of Clarke and Fuller. Even Leyland offers the American Wilson
design—built under licence—as an alternative to its own products. All
CV makers, not only the heavy vehicle producers, offer bought-out
gearboxes purchased from a wide variety of sources. Apart from those
already mentioned the list includes GMC's Allison division, Volvo,
Voith, and SRM of Sweden, and ZF from Germany. The gearboxes
used in heavy CVs can be very expensive—a price of £200–300 is not
unusual—so maximum efficiency and quality control is required on the
part of these manufacturers if the price of heavy vehicles is not to
become prohibitive. Firms such as Bristol, Daimler, Guy, Foden and
Dennis are in a position to supply most of their own needs for gearboxes and transmission, but the likes of Seddon, ERF and Atkinson are
entirely dependent on outside suppliers.

    There are a number of independent axle producers, the largest
being the American owned Eaton Axle Company and the British firm
Kirkstall Forge based in Leeds. The other significant suppliers of
vehicle and trailer axles are Rubery Owen, York Trailers, Moss Gears
and the GKN subsidiary Salisbury Transmissions. In addition, a quite
separate axle market exists where specialist firms convert the basic two-
axled CV as produced by the vehicle producer into a three-axled
vehicle. One or more of these 'chassis conversion firms' are often given
official approval by a particular vehicle builder, normally one of the
CV mass producers. The main firms in this market are All Wheel
Drive Ltd., County Commercial Cars, Unipower, Primrose Third
Axle Co., and the Reynolds-Boughton concern. Other producers
include Henry Boys and Sons, Mayfair Garages (Tamworth) Ltd.,

North Derbyshire Engineering, Sparshott and Sons, York Trailers, and Eaton Axles. In other words, the size of firm is typically small scale with very low overheads, and this is important as competition keeps prices keen with individual output volumes relatively small. Consequently the low overheads involved allow profitable operation in a highly competitive market where production runs are quite small. A few firms such as Eaton and Unipower are larger and more capital intensive, presumably the output volume being sufficient to reduce unit costs to a profitable level.

If transmission units are not made by the vehicle builder they are normally purchased from GKN, David Brown, Eaton or Kirkstall Forge.

Unlike the vast majority of cars, which are of integral chassis-less construction, nearly all vehicles above the car derivative category utilise a chassis frame. All manufacturers use chassis frames made by Rubery Owen, one of the closest approximations to a monopoly supplier in the CV industry. However, Dorman Long supplies some of the industry's requirements and would be a potential alternative source of supply if the market leader attempted to exercise monopoly powers. Some buses are made of a chassis-less construction, the 'running' units being installed in a strengthened body. Although this is the predominant type of bus design abroad, the majority of British buses and coaches are made of traditional design incorporating a separate chassis. This takes us nicely into the important field of CV body, cab, and trailer production to which we turn below.

PECULIARITIES OF THE CV PARTS AND COMPONENTS INDUSTRY

It is evident that although many of the CV suppliers are also suppliers to the car industry, there are some distinguishing features on the CV side. For instance, in the case of brake and electrical equipment suppliers there are some firms supplying the CV market which do not participate in the market for car components. Again, no important car producer is dependent on outside suppliers for such important items as engines or gearboxes, although Rover does use a GMC design and many of the specialist producers buy items from the mass producers. The existence of independent suppliers of engines and gearboxes is largely a phenomenon peculiar to the CV side of the industry. A further point is that many of these large items of equipment are not only supplied to the specialist CV producers, but also to firms such as Rootes-Dodge which are for instance highly dependent on outside producers for engine supplies.

THE COMPLEX WORLD OF THE COMMERCIAL VEHICLE BODYBUILDER

Many commercial vehicles leave the factories in chassis-cab form without a fully made-up body. This is generally true for light, medium and heavy trucks and for buses and coaches, and a large number of medium-weight vans and pick-up trucks are not fitted with bodies when they leave the factory. On the other hand, all car derivative vehicles and those medium-weight vehicles of integral construction are produced as complete vehicles with bodies made by the vehicle producer.

In the case of some medium-weight vans and with trucks and buses the customer can make a separate contract with a bodybuilder of his own choice. In practice this often means that the operator will buy a complete vehicle from the retail dealer, the latter having ordered a complete vehicle for 'off the peg' sale. However, the operator if he wishes can make his own arrangements in this respect.

Many CV bodies are made by the vehicle builders. All car derivatives and many medium-sized vans and pick-ups are bodied by the vehicle manufacturer. Most of these are complete body shells of integral construction although some are built on sub-frames. In addition, most manufacturers produce metal or wooden bodies for their larger CV ranges, Rootes and Ford have their own facilities as do Seddon and ERF among the specialists. About 450 concerns are engaged in producing goods vehicle bodies, ranging from state-owned concerns such as Star Bodies and Richard Thomas and Baldwin, vehicle manufacturers such as Dennis, Seddon or Scammell, to 'back yard' and small-garage proprietors. The typical size of firm is small with no marked concentration of ownership or output. The market is extremely competitive with vehicle owners being presented with keenly priced alternatives, especially from the small firms with low overheads. As many 'one-off' products are required by operators production runs are often quite small, although the product and the process of manufacture may be comparatively simple. In some cases a standardised product is possible, as in the case of flat platform bodies for trucks, which allows longer production runs but at the same time the need for expensive productive equipment remains small. Highly specialised products such as tankers, refrigerated vans and so on require rather more capital intensive production methods. Even so, final assembly is still relatively labour intensive. Most CV goods bodies are constructed by fitting panels of varying materials to a basic framework.

This is in direct contrast to the capital intensive manufacture and assembly of a few basic pressings as in the car industry.

The bodybuilders serve varying markets with some relying on local custom and others serving a region, while a few have a national market. In some instances the vehicle manufacturer will issue a list of 'approved' bodybuilders, and this of course helps to establish a firm nationally. As relatively little capital is needed to establish a CV body plant or workshop there is easy entry. The industry is also foot-loose and widespread, being either located near the customer or near the vehicle producer. Large concentrations of bodybuilders are found in areas adjacent to the CV plants, for example near the specialist producers in Cheshire and Lancashire, and near the producers in the West Midlands and the Luton–Dunstable area. Often a vehicle is delivered to a nearby bodybuilder from the vehicle factory and then delivered complete to a distributor or direct to a customer.

THE PROLIFERATION OF THE SMALL FIRM

The continued survival of so many firms is due to a number of factors. For instance, the product is often extremely simple, requiring little expensive equipment or 'know how'. Also there are thousands of separate customers each requiring his own particular product. In addition, the materials used are conducive to the survival of small firms, as body-construction on wooden frames or the use of fibreglass is well within the capabilities of the small firm. The 'one-off' nature of much of the business militates against the growth of large firms using techniques and equipment geared to long production runs. Also the ubiquitous nature of bodybuilding implies that contact with customer or manufacturer is important, obviously strong local or regional attachments make for the survival of many producers. Finally, the great variety of bodies required by customers allows both for specialisation and the survival of a large number of firms.

THE PRODUCTION OF BUS BODIES

The bus body market is rather different to that for lorry and van bodies for a number of reasons. Most significant perhaps is the fact that the number of firms in the industry has fallen greatly, from over 100 in 1945 to around 20 by 1970. Of the survivors, only 10 were of any great significance.

During the early years of CV production and until the early 1920s bus chassis were little more than modified goods vehicle chassis. This state of affairs prompted the Birmingham and Midland Motor Omnibus Company ('Midland Red') to begin manufacturing vehicles of its own design in 1924. In this way the company acquired vehicles which fully met bus operating requirements*. The corollary of this was that until 1924 any small bodybuilder could produce a typical bus body, a body which was of relatively unsophisticated design. However, from the mid-1920s bus designs improved, vehicles became larger, and operators required more sophisticated bodywork. As a result, many bodybuilders found bus body production beyond their resources. Many small independent operators however, purchased vehicles with locally produced bodies, a state of affairs lasting until the mid-1930s, by which time competition from firms which had grown relatively large had made serious inroads into the local producers' markets. With the growth of large territorial bus companies, normally owned by the Thomas Tilling or British Electric Traction groups, plus the emergence of large municipal fleets, operators were able to place quite large contracts with the bodybuilder. The firms winning these orders were those with sufficient capacity, with mechanised production techniques, and the right product. After the initial contracts such firms were able to consolidate their position by further capacity expansion to meet new and repeat orders. Often these larger firms making standardised units worked in close contact with a chassis builder, an example of this in pre-war days was Duple bodies designed specially for the Bedford company.

The decline of the small producer was hastened by World War II and the resulting material shortages. A scheme introduced by the government in 1941 placed the building of 'utility' bus bodies under government control which effectively excluded small producers from the controlled market. Only the larger firms had the facilities to meet the need for long production runs produced with maximum efficiency. As a result, many of the firms excluded from the wartime market never returned to the industry, despite the post-war excess demand for bus bodies, although some small firms utilised their resources by doing overdue repair and maintenance work.

The early post-war period was marked by material shortages, steel allocations, and production and export targets for the entire motor

* The company ceased making its own vehicles in 1970. The company was always at the forefront of technical development, producing products with a 'Midland Red' produced diesel engine and other components. The difficulty of recruiting suitable workmen in a 'car city' led to production ceasing.

industry. Material allocations were normally based on some previous production or export performance and the period 1937–1939 was usually used as a norm. Firms leaving the bodybuilding industry during World War II could, as a result, theoretically have returned; however, they were given no official encouragement to do so, the government ministries preferring to deal with larger producers. Some firms nevertheless were induced to enter the industry for the first time. They were attracted by the excess demand for bodies resulting both from the wartime backlog and by the post-war increase in demand for transport facilities which meant an increased demand for buses. With varying periods of delay these new entrants were given material allocations, the most crucial being the steel quota they were allowed. These new firms sold on a local, regional, and national basis. Some were small scale producers, others subsidiaries of larger organisations. One feature was the entry of firms associated with aircraft production and general engineering, such as Scottish Aviation, Saunders-Roe, and Welsh Metal Industries. These firms judged that they could apply their existing knowledge, production methods, and techniques, to large scale bus-body production. The post-war period saw technological changes with, for instance, the gradual introduction of metal frames in place of wood. This allowed greater use of batch or mass-production final assembly from mass produced parts. As the all-metal body became increasingly popular, firms were obliged to tool-up with the equipment required to produce such units in the most efficient way. As a result the smaller firm could not undertake the capital investment needed and gradually left the market. So despite a short-term increase in the number of bus-body builders the pre-war trend towards fewer and larger firms soon re-emerged. The result was the fall in bus-body producers from over 100 in the immediate post-war period to less than 20 in 1970. Of these 20 only about 10 were of significance. Furthermore, the market for double decker bus bodies is dominated by just seven producers.

Apart from the technological reasons for the decline in the number of producers, another factor was the decline in the annual demand for bus bodies. This occurred when the pent-up demand caused by wartime and post-war backlogs had been satisfied.

The extent of the backlog caused by the war depended largely on the operators' replacement cycle. As vehicles became stronger and more reliable their lifetime increased. During the 1920s and early 1930s between 4 years and 6 years was the normal lifetime depending on the conditions of operation. During the 1930s the life-cycle increased, and about 12 years was the usual figure by 1939. As an average figure for the service bus operators, 12 years was a reasonable figure, but it must be remembered that coaches were replaced on a cycle of 1 to 12 years. The actual figure depended on the nature of the work done and the type of owner. Assuming a 12 year life-cycle for vehicles before scrapping, as distinct from resale, the six year gap (1939–1945) would have meant that 50% of buses in use at the end of the war should have been replaced. However, some bus production did occur between 1939–1945. During this period total production for the home market equalled about 1½ years total registrations pre-war. As a result perhaps between 35% and 40% of bus fleets were in need of replacement, although in some cases the position was worse. For instance, 50% of London's fleet in 1946 was in need of replacement. Consequently the manufacturing capacity owned by chassis and body builders had to meet this pent-up demand as well as the normal annual replacement demand which amounted to about 8½% of the total bus population. In addition, there was a growth in net demand of about 5% a year over the early post-war period generated by the increased demand for bus passenger miles. From the data on new registrations of motor vehicles it would appear that the backlog of demand was not finally cleared until 1952 (*Table 4.7*).

Table 4.7

REGISTRATION OF HACKNEYS
1946–1953

Year	Registrations
1946	3 946
1947	7 614
1948	9 843
1949	12 351
1950	11 333
1951	7 759
1952	5 388
1953	5 012

One thing is obvious, the post-war demand for buses was not as high as one may have expected, given the shortage of buses during the war. Using the 1939 figure of almost 7000 new bus registrations and comparing this with the trickle of wartime supplies, it would appear to indicate a pent-up demand for 36 000 buses for replacement alone. However, between 1947 and 1951 only 14 000 of this backlog was worked off before the market appeared to have settled down once again. Using this crude approach, and using our assumptions concerning life-cycles, about 22 000 vehicles were not replaced. Nevertheless between 1946 and 1950 the total bus population increased from 105 000 to 139 500, which indicates a number of things. Firstly, the life-cycle of buses continued to lengthen because of vehicle improvement, and during the 1950s it hit a peak of about 20 years although by 1970 it had fallen to 15 years. Secondly, and allied to the first point, many operators re-bodied existing chassis; this eased the pressure on the vehicle builder but increased that on the bodybuilder. Thirdly, many of the vehicles replaced were replaced by larger vehicles, so the real shortfall was less than 22 000 vehicles. Consequently a pent-up demand of 36 000 would appear to be an overestimate, the real demand being in the region of 14 000 vehicles.

Between 1952 and 1959 new annual registrations remained fairly constant at between 5000 and 5500 vehicles a year. Between 1950 and 1954 however, the bus population fell from 139 500 to 110 000, and it continued to fall until 1959 when it reached 94 000. In other words it was during the 1950s, especially between 1950 and 1954, that vehicles were scrapped without replacement. The combination of a constant level of new registrations and a falling bus population meant a fall in the average age of vehicles used, as well as the use of larger buses. The evidence of a large volume of vehicle scrapping in the 1950s rather than the 1940s fits in with the probability that our original figure for pent-up demand was too high.

The excess demand of around 14 000 vehicles over the period 1947 to 1951 was still enough to put strain on the bodybuilding industry, especially as sheet steel was in such short supply. Although the smaller firms benefited from a seller's market, it was the larger producers who benefited most. Firms such as Duple, Park Royal, Eastern Coach Works and Metro-Cammell Weyman were helped by their pre-war and wartime experience of producing standardised products in large numbers. Consequently they were well suited both to satisfy the large available market and at a low real cost. As resources were so scarce, their efficient use was all important. As a result, the large firms tended to receive preferential treatment in the allocation of materials. Most of the smaller firms had concentrated on the relatively small type of body; only a few had made large bodies for single- or double-decker vehicles. In addition, the trend in favour of metal frames, which required more capital than did wood-based output, hastened the demise of the small-volume producer. These factors meant that the position of the small producer was a precarious one.

After the immediate post-war period other factors tended to add to the tendency towards concentration. The link between large operators and the bodybuilder became stronger. The British Electric Traction group, for example, tended to design a standard body for use by its many subsidiaries. The manufacture of the product was contracted out to firms having the facilities to tool-up for long production runs at low cost. Since many smaller operators sold out to the large groups the small bodybuilders' market tended to contract further.

The total market open to the bus body builder was smaller than that available to the firm making goods bodies. For instance between 1958 and 1967 the total number of buses registered yearly in the U.K. was between 5000 and 7000. However the market for the goods body builder grew from 120 000 units a year to around 170 000 units over the same period. Obviously the bus market could support fewer bus body makers than was the case on the goods body side. Furthermore it would appear that economies of scale are more easily reaped on the bus side. The largest bus body makers such as ECW, MCW, Duple, and Park Royal produce between 700 and 2000 units a year. As the market is dominated by these firms the typical size of firm is medium to large in relation to the total market size. The typical goods body firm is small, the medium to large firms probably only accounting for about 10% of the total market.

As far as one can estimate, over 75% of the bus and coach body market is in the hands of the six firms Park Royal, Eastern Coach Works, Duple, Metro-Cammell Weyman, Plaxton, and Marshall*. All these firms are either members of larger groups or are concerned with activities outside bodybuilding. Duple is a subsidiary of the Capitarium group, having remained independent until 1970. Park Royal and ECW are subsidiaries of Leyland although the state owned National Bus Company has a substantial shareholding in both. MCW is a part of the Vickers group, and Marshall is a general engineering company. The Plaxton company is mainly concerned with bus body building but it is also engaged in civil construction work. Nearly all the remaining significant business is done by the Lancashire firms East Lancashire–Neepsend, a member of the John Brown Group, Northern Counties-Massey, and Penine Ltd., a subsidiary of Seddon. The remaining producers of any note are Alexanders of Falkirk and Strachan (Coachbuilders) Ltd. The remaining firms have very small markets and in the main they produce bodies for works buses or mini-buses.

The rather specialised luxury coach market is dominated by only

* In 1971 the six became the seven again when Duple sold its Willowbrook division to an independent purchaser.

two firms, Duple and Plaxton, both firms producing about 1500 units a year. Competition in this sector has gradually eliminated the other manufacturers, a process which culminated in Plaxton's takeover of Harringtons in 1966. Although this sector of the market is a growing one, other British firms have found difficulty in entering the market; for instance, major producers such as MCW and Park Royal made only a short-lived effort to enter this sector in the period 1967–1968. The only competition to the two established firms came in 1970 from imported products. For example, Alfred Mossley a major vehicle distributor, took advantage of the European Free Trade Association to import partly assembled bodies from Portugal. Whether such a venture became a long-run venture depended of course on the degree of market penetration achieved. In turn this was partly a function of price and also the strong fashion element in this sector of the CV industry which induces firms to buy a distinctive product.

Other firms, notably ECW and Park Royal, supply less luxurious coaches to vehicle operators. These are used both for tours and excursions and for long distance express services. Another type of product is the 'dual service' vehicle which is used on both long distance express routes and on shorter stage-services.

Many bodybuilders purchase body frames from Metal Sections Ltd., a Tube Investment Company, although some firms produce their own requirements. Metal Sections and some bodybuilders, notably Duple and Plaxton, established a significant export business, especially in the sale of body-kits to be assembled into complete bodies by the importing nation.

MCW, Park Royal and Plaxton are also vehicle manufacturers in their own right, producing buses of integral construction. These firms produce specially strengthened bodies which do not require a normal chassis, the 'running units' such as engines and gearboxes are then fitted directly into the bodywork.

The goods and bus body industries are extremely varied and extremely competitive. The bulk of the business is in the hands of independent producers, except in the case of car derivative CVs and medium weight vans and pick-ups. There is a greater degree of market concentration on the bus side in comparison to that prevailing in the goods body sector and it is possible that further concentration will occur. In the period 1966–1970 Plaxton purchased two other bodybuilders, Northern Counties absorbed Massey, and ECW came into the same ownership as Park Royal-Roe. In addition, Duple after being constantly surrounded by take over or merger rumours, was eventually purchased by Capitarium in 1970.

This is usually a separate operation to bodybuilding as only car derivatives invariably have one-piece cabs and bodies. Medium-weight vans and pick-ups, for instance, are often supplied in the chassis-cab form which is also usual in the case of light, medium, and heavy trucks.

The cabs of medium-weight vans and pick-ups are made by the vehicle producer. BMC, Rootes, Ford and Bedford supply all their own needs, although both BMC and Rootes used to buy-out from Pressed Steel. Leyland, Guy and many of the specialists, however, still buy-out, but some of the specialists integrate their own cab and chassis production.

The cabs made by independent producers and vehicle builders are made in a variety of materials, utilising plastic, fibreglass, wood or steel. The manufacture of steel cabs readily gives rise to economies of scale as expensive tools and dies are needed if cab-pressings are to be produced in the most efficient way. Consequently the production of steel cabs necessitates a large market if it is to be carried out by least cost methods. The economic use of steel cabs is only made by a large scale CV producer or a large scale independent bodybuilder with a large market. This requirement is borne out in practice. The large scale producers BMC, Rootes, Ford and Bedford produce their own requirements whereas the independent producers Sankeys and Motor Panels produce steel cabs for a number of different producers, thereby passing on their own internal economies as external economies to their customers.

The tooling costs for metal steel cabs has been estimated at £1 400 000, for aluminium cabs at £630 000, for reinforced plastic using 'matched dyes' at £150 000 and £25 000 for 'open-mould' production in plastic★. Based on the 1963 price and cost structure it was estimated that the maximum volume at which a 'matched dye' moulded reinforced plastics cab could be made at a lower real cost than steel was 45 450 units, or 9090 a year based on an amortisation period for tooling costs of five years. A hand lay-up mould would produce a maximum output of 21 979 more cheaply than steel, or 4396 units a year on a five year amortisation period. In 1969, both Ford and Bedford produced over 45 000 trucks, BMC about 20 000 and Rootes about 15 000; consequently steel appears to be a viable and efficient

★ 'Owen-Carning Fibreglas', report summarised in *Motor Transport* (8 November 1963).

proposition for these firms as regards cab production. As Leyland produces about 16 000 goods vehicles a year, its decision to place a contract with Sankeys for the latter to manufacture a steel cab for Leyland's exclusive use appears justified on economic grounds. However, firms such as Guy and Seddon, producing 2000 to 3000 vehicles a year, Foden producing 2000, Atkinson, Dennis and ERF around 1750 a year, would take between 20 years and about 50 years to amortise tooling costs on the same basis as their large competitors! Obviously expensive body presses would be under-utilised during any given year, with sub-optimum high cost production as the result. It is evident that the use of glass-fibre bodies by Scammell, ERF, Foden, Atkinson and Dennis, produced by simple hand lay-up moulds, is the most efficient method for the volumes concerned.

Thus how does one evaluate the policy followed by Guy, Seddon and Dodge, and to a lesser extent by Scammell, Foden and ERF, to buy steel cabs? In effect here is an interesting example of vertical disintegration, for all these manufacturers purchased from the one source. Motor Panels utilises the same basic pressings to produce cabs for Guy, Seddon, Scammell, ERF and Foden. The Dodge product is different. The total production of vehicles using the common cab approached the 6000 a year mark in 1970. It may have been better to use matched dye methods to produce a plastic unit, but the point is that the sharing of a common design is the only way for small specialist producers to purchase a steel cab at reasonable cost. The only alternative is to produce a glass-fibred product, as many of the specialists in fact do. Dodge had hoped to produce over 10 000 units a year of its post 1966 truck range, but a number of factors, such as the use of a Cummins engine (which put-off many customers), meant that the target was not reached. However, 10 000 units would make steel cab production an economic proposition and as the Dodge product has some pressings common to the Seddon-Guy cab, Motor Panels is able to produce at near optimum levels.

Some of the specialists also make steel cabs for road vehicles and for 'off the road' dumper trucks. These are normally constructed by hand using individual steel sheets riveted to a wooden or metal frame. They are not constructed by welding together large metal pressings made by expensive equipment.

It would appear that vehicle cabs are typically made by the vehicle producers, as only Leyland and Dodge of the larger concerns purchase from independent suppliers. The specialist producers buy their pressed steel cabs from outside sources but glass-fibre, wooden and some sheet steel cabs are internally made. In one or two cases plastic cabs are bought-out; Scammell, for instance, buys from Thomas Plastics and Dennis buys complicated front mouldings from outside. In terms of material costs steel is the cheapest form of cab production, for every £100 spent on steel, £120 would be spent on aluminium, £128 on reinforced plastics made from matched dyes, and £163 using open moulds. However, the tooling costs for plastics are much lower, so where low volumes are involved plastics is the best material to use. Indeed, as tooling costs for plastics are so low there may not be the same reluctance to introduce design improvements which involve tooling costs. Furthermore, production in plastics could mean that new bodies from the design stage are put into production faster than in instances where metal is used. The time involved in designing and tooling up is less than a year compared with two to three years for steel. So in some respects production in plastic has an advantage. On the other hand some manufacturers and operators feel that steel cabs are intrinsically better than those made in other materials.

TRAILER PRODUCTION

There are two distinct types of product manufactured in this sector of the motor industry: (1) the full-trailers which can be towed behind ordinary lorries and (2) semi-trailers which are pulled by a specially designed towing vehicle called the 'motive unit' or the 'road tractor'. This latter combination is called an 'articulated vehicle' or 'artic'. The 1960s was a decade of rapid growth in the use of motive units and semi-trailers, a development which was accounted for by four main reasons.

Firstly, there was the overall increase in the demand for transport facilities needed to carry the products of a growing economy. The economics of transport being what it is meant that most of this increased traffic was carried by road mainly because of the lower carrying costs and flexibility of the road vehicle.

Secondly, the revision of the Construction and Use regulations for road vehicles in 1964 allowed an increase in the maximum lengths and gross weights of vehicles. In fact the greatest increase in permitted payloads was allowed in the case of articulated vehicles. Whereas before 1964 the largest 'rigid' vehicle and 'artics' carried largely the same payload, after 1964 the maximum artic payload was around 22 tons as compared with less than 19 tons for a rigid eight wheeled vehicle. The larger the payload the lower the operating costs per ton mile, so many operators wishing to purchase maximum size vehicles would naturally turn to 'artics'.

Thirdly, articulation provided greater flexibility and efficiency in the use of expensive motive units. The use of more than one trailer with each motive unit allowed greater vehicle utilisation and with little wasted time spent in loading and unloading; while one trailer was being loaded or unloaded the motive unit returned to use immediately with a previously loaded semi-trailer.

Fourthly, the continuing increase in international trade has led to the development of 'roll-on, roll-off' ferries on the one hand and containerisation on the other. In both cases the most economic use is made of expensive tractive units by keeping them on the road instead of idle aboard ship. Consequently the ferries typically transport the loaded trailer on its own and the container ships only carry containers. In the latter case the most common container used for international trade is 40 feet long with a carrying capacity of 30 tons*. In 1968 the Construction and Use regulations were altered to allow the carriage of 40 feet containers on British roads, and the only vehicles allowed to do this were artics. Even then, however, the gross vehicle weight was still limited to 32 tons which meant that such containers could not be carried fully laden on U.K. roads. Hence the pressures exerted in 1970–1971 to increase gross vehicle weight limits to 44 tons† and even to 56 tons.

In the U.K. in contrast to the Continent, the trend towards trailers only applied to semi-trailers. This was because the use of 'full' or 'draw-bar trailers' in the U.K. meant the double manning of the motive unit. It was obviously more efficient from the operators point of view to use semi-trailers, although from the vehicle producers point of view the draw-bar trailer does not pose such severe technical problems. In 1970 some of the archaic legislation applying to full-trailers was amended so as to allow single manning.

Taking 1960 as a starting point, output of trailers and semi-trailers almost doubled by 1967 from 19 610 units to 37 777, and by 1969 the figure was 46 966. Figures for semi-trailers are available separately from 1963 and show a rapid increase in volume between 1963 and 1965 (*Table 4.8*).

At the same time there was an increase in demand for motive units. For instance, in 1950 the total was less than 1000 a year with semi-trailer

---

* Other standard containers are 20 and 30 feet long.

† Doubt is expressed as to whether such containers ever carry their theoretical maximum load. Problems of packing normally mean that the effective payload is rarely over 26 tons.

Table 4.8

OUTPUT OF SEMI-TRAILERS

Year	Export	Home	Total
1963	671	8 376	9 047
1964	865	11 436	12 301
1965	866	15 752	16 618
1966	791	15 686	16 477
1967	799	15 994	16 793
1968	876	20 462	21 338
1969	1 225	24 093	25 318

Source: *The Motor Industry of Great Britain*, SMMT Year-book, Table 12, p. 24 (1970).

production being of much the same order, but during the 1960s the position had changed greatly (*Table 4.9*).

Table 4.9

OUTPUT OF MOTIVE UNITS

Year	Output	Exports
1963	8 392	
1964	12 168	
1967	15 190	1 256
1969	16 710	1 631

Sources: SMMT Yearbooks 1964, 1965, 1968 and 1970.

A further breakdown between tractors for the heaviest artics of over 26 tons gross and those below is also available (*Table 4.10*).

Table 4.10

Output	1967	1969
Rigid vehicles for 20 tons gross and over	3 803	4 387
Motive Units for 26 tons gross and over	5 739	7 589
Motive Units for below 26 tons	9 451	9 131

Source: SMMT.

It is evident that the vast majority of really heavy road vehicles currently produced are articulated units, rather than three- or four-axled rigid vehicles. From what we said earlier concerning the advantages of artics this is only to be expected. A further point is the relatively small export percentage for motive units, less than 10%, compared with almost 18% for large rigid vehicles. At the same time less than 5% of semi-trailers are exported. Both figures are characteristic of a rather poor export performance but can be explained by the fact that the U.K. has in the past sold most vehicles in markets not sophisticated enough to make the best use of trailers. This is gradually changing as more attention is paid to Europe and some existing markets become more sophisticated.

Following spectacular growth in 1965, the first full year of the new operating conditions, the slow-down in economic activity and the effects of this on the growth in the volume of road traffic resulted in a levelling off of trailer production. However, once the economy accelerated the demand for semi-trailers tended to grow. In addition, the future growth in output could be greater in the short-term than that called for by the increased economic growth rate. For one thing the Construction and Use regulations will probably be altered at some time in the future to allow road trains of up to between 36 and 40 tons gross. This is likely despite the Ministry of Transport's decision in 1970 not to allow larger vehicles in the immediate future. If the latter figure is achieved then British operating conditions would be largely similar to the rest of Europe, something which the 1964 measures aimed to create but failed.

The growth in container traffic will also no doubt continue. As the standard sizes are 20 feet to 40 feet long, this will mean increased demand for special trailers to carry containers. Interestingly, most of the trailer firms also produce containers. A further important point is that the movement towards greater use of 'artics' is by no means complete. The ratio of semi-trailers to tractors in the U.K. in 1969 was 1·3:1 which is low compared with foreign conditions. This implies that greater use can be made of the motive units which in turn implies a need for more trailers. Although the output of trailers was double that of motive units between 1967 and 1969, the more important semi-trailer to tractor ratio for home deliveries was only 1·1:1. There is in other words a large potential growth in the demand for semi-trailers if operators find ways to make the most efficient use of their motive units. Basically this entails having more trailers per tractor. In short, given these factors it could mean a short-term period of growth for semi-trailers of 20% a year broadly equivalent to the 1963–1965 conditions. After this short term boom it is likely that the demand for trailers would be governed by the growth in the demand for transport facilities and by replacement demand.

One big question-mark is posed by the existence of roll-on roll-off methods of transportation on the one hand and container ships on the other. In the first case semi-trailers are used on road and sea, therefore roughly at least two trailers are needed per motive unit. If containers are used then only one semi-trailer is needed but two containers. The more dominant does the former method of transport become the greater the new demand for trailers and vice versa. On the other hand as most containers are made by trailer manufacturers their total business is unlikely to be harmed either way although individual firms may suffer.

There are a large number of varied producers of trailers. Of the vehicle producers only Scammell and ERF produce their own trailers although Foden manufacture some under licence from an independent producer. Competition between producers is intense with rather small profit margins. Consequently profitable production depends upon either a large turnover to spread fixed costs or on low overheads. As a result the trailer industry is tending to polarise itself into two types of producer—the firms which are very large in relation to the market and the very small. There are only a few public companies exclusively or mainly engaged in trailer production*. The main ones are Crane-Freuhauf Trailers and York Trailers. In 1968 the former absorbed the one other significant publicly-owned trailer maker, namely Boden Trailers of Oldham. These three concerns had been the market leaders since 1964 and in 1966 it was estimated that these three firms shared half the market between them†. In terms of relative size there was little difference between the three concerns involved although York may have been marginally the largest. However, the state of the market in the middle and late 1960s was such that market leadership simply devolved on the firm with the biggest production capacity. In 1966 Boden made 2500 trailers compared with 2200 in 1965; further expansion increased capacity to 4000 units a year in 1967 and 5000 in 1968. It is not known whether these final output levels were in fact achieved given the levelling off of the market in 1967. Nevertheless it appeared that York, Crane-Freuhauf and Boden produced about 8000 trailers between them in 1966, which would be roughly 50% of total output. Since 1968, when Crane-Freuhauf purchased Boden, the combine had become a clear market leader, with York Trailers in second place. Despite their market dominance, these two firms cannot

* Peak Trailers went public in 1968. In 1966 this caravan firm entered the semi-trailer market and trailers accounted for £500 000 of the £1·9 million turnover in 1967.

† *Financial Times* (18 June 1966) and *The Sunday Times* (11 September 1966).

claim anything like a monopoly or utilise any monopoly power. There are other quite powerful and well established firms in the market such as Scammell, Merriworth, Dyson, British Trailer, Carrimore, Northern Trailers, Hands, Highway, Tasker, Pitt, Brockhouse, Rubery Owen and Thompson. Scammell's market is mainly that for the lighter type of trailer capable of carrying loads of from 7 to 12 tons. In volume terms, Scammell's output is similar to York's, so three firms account for about 60% of total output. Other smaller firms include Fox, Interconsult, King, M and G, Morgan, Murfitt, Peak and Scottish Aviation.

Some firms such as Dyson and Taskers tended to concentrate on producing trailers for super heavy loads of up to 100 tons. Such weights exceed the Construction and Use regulations but are permitted under the 'Authorisation of Special Types' ordinances. The competitive nature of the industry is exemplified by the fact that an old established firm such as Taskers went into liquidation in 1968 and only remained in business as part of a larger combine. The vulnerable firms are within the group of companies which produce at volumes well below that achieved by York or Scammell, but none the less have invested more heavily in capital intensive methods than very small firms such as Fox or King. Firms continually leave and enter the industry; two new entrants in 1970 partly offset the three firms leaving the industry.

Trailer makers in the U.S.A. have a very large domestic market for very large semi-trailers. Consequently American firms had much more experience of producing large semi-trailers than did U.K. firms. Their methods of production also tended to be more efficient and more sophisticated, partly reflecting the size of the market but also reflecting more enterprising and efficient management techniques. The size of the American producers can be exemplified in an extreme form by the Freuhauf Corporation which produces around 30% of all the world's trailers.

A number of U.K. firms have forged transatlantic links to draw upon the engineering knowledge and research of giant American and Canadian firms. For instance, Crane trailers of Norfolk concluded an agreement with Freuhauf in 1961 which gave the U.S. firm a one-third holding in the total equity of Crane-Freuhauf. Again, York Trailers is a wholly owned subsidiary of the York transport equipment group of Toronto. The need for large trailers became acute after 1964 and the firms with transatlantic links were often at an advantage in being able to utilise existing U.S. designs which were tailor-made for the new conditions. In 1965, although the output of semi-trailers increased by one-third, firms such as York and Crane-Freuhauf grew by 60%*. Other firms quickly forged links with American firms in an attempt to improve their competitive position and to make up for lost time. Consequently Thompsons of Bilston began producing trailers of U.S. Trailmobile design in 1967 and Merriworth offered U.S. Multiwheeler products until they left the industry in 1971. On the other hand, Boden's expansion had kept pace with York and Crane's between 1963 and 1968, and the company had quickly emerged from obscurity to challenge for the market leadership. The firm's all-British designs showed that foresight and domestic ingenuity could compare with foreign experience and expertise given a management of sufficient quality and dynamism.

The rapid growth of the industry can be shown by three factors. Firstly, the rapid emergence of new firms from obscurity to quite large scale turnover and output. Secondly, the rapid increase in turnover of successful companies. Thirdly, the entry of new firms into a market which already supported over twenty firms.

The three market leaders in the period 1964 to 1968 were all relatively new entrants to the U.K. semi-trailer market. Although Cranes was an old established firm it was not until 1961 that it became a significant force in the industry. This followed the opening of a new factory for the large-scale production of trailers and the association with Freuhauf. These two events marked the emergence of what was virtually a 'new' company. Boden only began producing semi-trailers in 1961, and 1964 marked the beginning of the company's real growth. York trailers first established itself in the U.K. in 1956, since which time the child had outgrown the parent. The firm is the largest European producer of semi-trailers and trailer axles with production being undertaken in the U.K. and in Holland. York's 'fifth wheel couplings' are in addition fitted to about 45% of all British motive units, with most of the remainder supplied by Scammell. The growth of these three firms together with the long term dominance of Scammell has resulted in a few firms emerging above the general mass. The market leaders tended to grow at least *pro rata* with the demand for the product and this left less than 40% of the total market to be shared by around twenty producers.

The rapid growth in this sector of the CV industry was reflected by the improvement in the financial position of the three public concerns dependent on trailer manufacture. Between 1962 and 1966 Crane-Freuhauf's profits increased tenfold from £53 000 to £569 000 with profits tripling between 1965 and 1966. Boden trailers also experienced

* *Financial Times* (18 June 1966).

rapid profits' growth when an independent company; for example, a very rapid rise of from £54 000 to £340 000 occurred during the three financial years 1963–1964 to 1965–1966. However, in the financial year 1966–1967 profits fell to £154 000 compared with a target of around £450 000. This reflected an over-optimistic expansion into the container industry and a downturn in the economic growth rate. This reduced the growth rate of Boden's sales at a time when the company had increased capacity on the understanding that past growth trends were to be maintained. By 1967–1968 the company's fortunes had recovered to a pre-tax profit of around £300 000 by which time the company had been absorbed by Crane-Freuhauf. For a brief period Mr. Bill Boden, the company's founder, became managing director of the new group. The increase in company profits reflected the increased demand for trailers, a feature which was reflected in turnover figures. For instance, between their establishment in 1956–1957 to the boom in demand in 1965–1966 York Trailer's turnover had increased more than tenfold from £351 000 to £3 800 000. Subsequently a steady but less spectacular growth in sales has been evident; in 1969 turnover had increased to £7 300 000, with a further increase of 38% in 1970 to £10 100 000. In terms of profitability, York's record figure of £481 700 achieved in 1966 was not surpassed until 1970 when £856 000 was earned. In the interim, profits were less than £200 000 in 1968, although recovering to just over £400 000 in 1969. Only in 1970 did output increase sufficiently to enjoy the full benefits of increased efficiency stemming from the increased scale of operations made possible by new capacity. It was evident that until 1970 the sub-optimal operation of York's enlarged capacity was a prime cause of the concern's reduced profitability. The new plant at Northallerton was geared to produce containers, container vans, and trailers in large volumes.

The growth in demand allowed other firms, such as Scammell, to expand capacity, and it also induced new firms, such as Thompsons, to enter the market. As supply expanded to meet the increased demand, the profit earned per unit of output tended to fall, although the tendency has been for the aggregate profits of the successful and expanding firms to continue to increase as their scale of output increased. However, it is unlikely that the industry will continue to support the same number of medium-sized firms as it does at present. Only the largest firms and the smallest will be able to spread fixed costs sufficiently to enable them to operate profitably in an industry typified by keen price competition. Firms such as Dyson specialising on trailers built to carry loads of up to 300 tons and costing up to £70 000 apiece should survive because of the specialist nature of the business involved; also because many of these specialist units are for export. Nevertheless, the need to keep costs and prices down in the more generalised sectors of the industry induces both operator and manufacturer to accept greater standardisation. The result has been that the more standard-lines are for the first time being batch produced. This is especially so in the case of the medium-sized firms; for example, Pitt Trailers ceased making 'one-off' special trailers in 1965 in order to concentrate on a standard range of 14 models*.

With the tendency towards larger and larger trailers for normal haulage work and the existence of established large scale firms with low unit costs of production, it may become more difficult to enter the industry in the future†. Until 1964 the largest trailers had payloads of up to only around 17 tons, and it would appear that relatively little specialised expertise or capital was needed to establish trailer making capacity. As a result entry into the industry was both easy and free. The larger producers also tended to sell mainly through distributors and dealers but the smaller manufacturers tend to sell direct to the customer. Consequently under conditions of excess demand when the price charged by all producers tended to be the same, the small 'backyard' producer was able to enter the industry and sell direct to the customer by offering quicker delivery. Most of the small low-cost firms perform a useful function in forcing the larger producers to remain efficient. Under the post-1964 operating conditions, however, the demand has tended to be one for larger products and furthermore, regulations concerning safety and permissible payloads became more exacting. In effect this has meant a need for trailers of a more sophisticated construction. If the small firm was unable to find the resources to meet the research and engineering requirements then he was unlikely to be able to keep abreast of the high rate of design development which typified the trailer industry after 1964. These conditions may make the small producers' position more precarious but not impossible. In many cases the sophisticated items required were available from outside suppliers, but the correct use of these components puts the onus on the trailer maker to produce a correctly designed and adequately tested unit.

To what extent do trailer makers rely on outside suppliers? The 'running gear', which accounts for 60% of the value, is normally bought-out. Almost all axles are made by Rubery Owen although some are supplied by both Eaton and York. Wheels are produced by

---

* *Motor Transport* (12 November 1965).
† Although as pointed out earlier firms were still entering the industry in 1970.

Dunlop and GKN's Sankey subsidiary. An interesting event was when York established its own axle making capacity after Rubery Owen introduced its own trailers; evidently York was not prepared to buy from a direct competitor. Only four firms are integrated to any large extent: York, British Trailers, Scammell and Crane-Freuhauf. For instance, they make their own chassis when nearly all the other producers buy fabricated sections from Dorman Long. In addition they produce coupling gear, complete bodies for trailers, containers and accessories such as suspension equipment. A number of other trailer makers, such as Rubery Owen and Thompsons, also produce containers.

Many of the larger firms are improving the depth and scope of their sales and service networks, especially the service side, for good distributors can mean the establishment of goodwill and customer loyalty towards the trailer maker. Perhaps the small firms and larger makers which concentrate on production to the detriment of sales or design facilities will suffer in the long run because of the superior way some larger firms look after their customers. In addition, vehicle operators are firmly of the opinion that the quality of the trailers made by certain firms are superior to those made by their competitors. Clearly more firms can be expected to leave the industry.

Trailer makers are devoting more and more resources to design and market research. The increased use of air suspensions is a result of this and the use of rubber suspensions is another possibility. The latter are made by two private outside suppliers, North Derbyshire Engineering and Metalastik Ltd. New markets remain to be tapped at home by stressing the operating advantage of semi-trailers of all sorts. Another potential market is clearly exports, as the 5% of production sold abroad is not a good performance.

The largest potential market for U.K. makers is Europe, for British trailers are cheaper and lighter than their European equivalents. The market is a large one because European operators are used to using trailers on a large scale. The largest market, however, is inside the European Economic Community where a 22% tariff is imposed against the products of the U.K. producer. As a result the largest short term business would come from selling trailer components and equipment and from establishing production facilities within the EEC. As European hauliers travel such long distances, a large sales and service network would have to be established. Although this would be an expensive short-term commitment in terms of capital investment the cost should be more than offset by the long term flow of benefits accruing to the trailer maker.

THE OVERALL PICTURE

This then is the CV industry and its main sources of supply. In many respects this industry can be treated as quite separate to the car industry —for instance, as we shall later see on the sales and service side, many CV specialists sell direct to the customer rather than use a sales and service network. Again, although the demand for all vehicles in the final analysis depends upon national income, more specifically changes in domestic CV demand depend upon changes in investment, while car demand is more closely linked to changes in consumer expenditure★. Other differences are to be found in the export performances of both sectors of the motor industry and in the way the nature of the product and the nature of consumer demand often renders economic a quite different method of production to that prevailing on the car side. Furthermore, the motor car is required to satisfy a final demand whereas a CV is an investment good which is wanted to meet the demand for passenger-miles in the case of buses, or to meet the demand for ton-miles and other transport facilities as determined by the demand for final goods where load carriers are concerned. Later chapters will look at some of these points more fully.

The specialist CV producer tends to satisfy a different market to the specialist car maker. The latter depends either upon high income customers, ostentation, or the demand for high performance, in other words on individuals with 'peculiarities' of taste or income. The specialist's customer requires the vehicle for peculiar conditions, that is long distance heavy duty work which necessitates maximum reliability plus low running costs. Mass-produced vehicles are not always able to meet this function. It is purely a question of function and not one of customer characteristics which determines the demand for specialist vehicles.

A final point is to note how the specialist CV makers are situated in locations quite distinct from those of the volume producers of cars. The roots of many such CV firms lay in heavy engineering and boiler making, hence the location of many firms in North Cheshire, Lancashire and Glasgow. The exceptions can all be simply explained. AEC is situated in the London area because of its origins as the bus manufacturing subsidiary of the main London bus operator. In the same way Bristol Commercial Vehicles and BMMO in Birmingham are

★ Over the period 1946–1969 the R^2 (coefficient of determination) for the relationship between CV demand and changes in investment and consumer expenditures was 0·89 and 0·69 respectively, that for cars 0·48 and 0·92.

offshoots of bus operating combines. Dennis Brothers in Guildford was originally a manufacturer of cycles and lawn mowers, and during the nineteenth century the largest potential market for these products tended to be in the home counties. Scammell of Watford was founded by a family with a military background who lived in the area. The proprietors saw the role which very heavy vehicles could play in the armed forces and established a firm able to meet this requirement. Guy Motors is the last relic of the once thriving motor industry established in Wolverhampton. Unfortunately the company concentrated too long on making specialist light weight vehicles, a market which was invaded by the mass producers between 1950 and 1957, and a heavy vehicle range was introduced too late to save the firm's fortunes. Production was relatively capital intensive as there was a need both to save labour and to increase labour productivity in an area where motor industry wages were governed by the car plants in 'nearby' Longbridge.

E

5

THE OVERSEAS MOTOR
INDUSTRIES: EUROPE AND
NORTH AMERICA

During the early post-war period (1946–1954) the world's motor vehicle markets were dominated by British and American producers. The main European manufacturers were, during this period, recovering from the physical damage to plant and equipment caused by World War II and up to 1950 the majority of vehicles they produced were sold on the domestic market. The year 1950 represents a turning point in the market strategy of the European producers, but this had little effect on American or British firms in world markets. In 1950 West Germany's motor industry came back into international trade, soon to be followed by France and Italy. Between 1950 and 1955 these firms sold largely in the European market and the expansion of this market allowed each country's industry to grow without harming the other countries' trade.

In 1955, however, Germany began selling vigorously on a world scale and it is from this date that—as we will see in a later chapter—that the export dominance of the U.K. industry went into decline; furthermore, it marks the beginning of a rapid growth in the size and scale of overseas car production. Between 1954 and 1956 the German and French industries began their period of rapid growth. Italy's period of rapid expansion occurred somewhat later, with 1959 and 1960 marking the beginning of the significant increase in output of both cars and commercial vehicles. Japan's transformation from a small-scale vehicle producing nation to a very large one can be traced from 1960, although the emergence of Japan as a large producer of cars began later in 1963.

The 1960s also saw the emergence of the motor industry in a number of other countries. Complete motor vehicles are manufactured in Sweden, Australia and Spain, but although the Australian industry is the largest of these, only Sweden supports a domestically owned motor industry. The large motor industries in Spain and Australia are composed of foreign owned or supported manufacturers, GMC being dominant in Australia and the Fiat licencee Seat in Spain. In Eastern Europe, Czechoslovakia has its own motor industry, and East Germany has established an industry based upon plants formerly owned by West German firms; for instance, Wartburg vehicles are built in a former DKW plant and largely to DKW designs. Other East European countries such as Poland and Rumania endeavoured to establish their own industries, and of course the U.S.S.R. has substantial car and commercial vehicle making capacity.

Although a number of countries have their own motor industries, the significant ones are small in number. Apart from the U.S.A. and Canada, the main motor industries are in the U.K., West Germany, France, Italy, Japan, Sweden and Australia. In the future, Spain and the U.S.S.R. may become significant producers, with vehicles of domestic design being produced on a large scale by financially secure firms. Other countries such as Mexico, Argentina, Brazil, South Africa, Holland and Austria may become significant in the very long run. Only a few of these countries, however, will have a domestically-owned motor industry which is also capable of designing its own individual products.

In the case of commercial vehicles the large American and European motor industries are again dominant, although some smaller nations have quite significant CV industries which are almost totally independent of foreign links. These firms are found in Sweden, Belgium, Holland, Switzerland and Austria in Western Europe, and Czechoslovakia, Hungary, Poland, East Germany, Rumania and the U.S.S.R. The Spanish industry, although partly dependent on foreign expertise or capital, manufactures vehicles which are largely designed in Spain; notable here are Chrysler-Barrieros and ENASA. Outside Europe, and apart from the U.S.A. and Japan, only Communist China has an independent motor industry, but details of this are hard to come by.

This chapter concerns itself with the main vehicle producing countries of the world: the United States and Canada, Germany, Italy and France. In the following chapter an analysis will be made of the one remaining major producing country, Japan, and also of those countries where the motor industry is smaller, but is, or is likely to become, a significant force.

THE UNITED STATES AND CANADA

First and foremost among the motor industries of the world is that of the United States. In terms of sheer volume, financial strength, and development, the American industry is dominant. Its total output accounts for almost 50% of world vehicle production per year (*Table 5.1*).

Table 5.1

UNITED STATES VEHICLE PRODUCTION

Year	Cars	Commercial vehicles	Total
1945	69 532	655 683	725 215
1950	6 665 863	1 337 193	8 003 056
1960	6 674 796	1 194 475	7 869 271
1965	9 305 561	1 751 805	11 057 366
1967	7 436 764	1 539 462	8 976 226
1969	8 224 327	1 980 719	10 205 046

Adapted from SMMT Yearbooks 1968 (Table 22) and 1970 (p. 35).

THE DEVELOPMENT OF THE UNITED STATES MOTOR INDUSTRY

The United States motor industry developed early, and on the supply side the introduction of large-scale techniques produced economies of scale and low unit costs. On the demand side the growth of national income meant that a large mass-market existed. Indeed, as early as 1840 American per capita income may have exceeded that in the U.K.[*] The relatively wealthy American worker was able to afford a low-cost automobile. Hence the American manufacturers began to find a mass-market before World War I, although it was the period 1920–1929 and 1934–1941 which saw the real spread of motoring to the masses.

In Europe only the higher income groups were able to afford the costs of motoring before 1939, although the mass-market began to appear in the U.K. between 1933 and 1939. It was not until the early

[*] R. E. Gallman, 'Output, Employment and Productivity in the United States after 1800', *Studies in Income and Wealth*, Vol. 30, pp. 3–8, National Bureau of Economic Research, Columbia University Press, New York (1966).

1950s that the mass-market in the U.K. and Continental Europe really emerged. Cars became more plentiful, after the post-war shortage, and improved production techniques on the one hand and growing national income on the other meant that car prices remained lower than pre-war in real terms but the average wage-level was far higher. This brought the possibility of car ownership to millions of new homes. In the case of the U.K. the total number of cars in use in 1950 was 2 307 379, but by 1960 this had grown to 5 650 461 and by 1967 to 10 554 193. This was an increase of almost 450% in 17 years; in the U.S.A. in the same period the vehicle population grew by rather less than 100%, although in absolute numbers the increase was of course vast.

The early development of the U.S. motor market and vehicle industry has meant that its post-war growth has been smaller than that in the other main producing nations. Between 1950 and 1965 the production of the U.S. car industry increased from 6 665 863 to 9 305 561 or just over 30%. At the same time U.K. production increased from 522 515 to 1 722 045 or over 200%. This latter figure was typical for Western Europe over this period. This early development was reflected in the low growth rate of output which in turn reflected a high car density and a market mainly dependent on re-placement demand. In 1958 there were almost 320 cars per 1000 Americans compared with less than 140 in Sweden, less than 100 in the U.K. and France, just over 50 in Germany, and almost 30 in Italy. By 1967 the U.S. figure had grown to over 400 per 1000 people compared with just over 250 in Sweden, just over 200 in France, just under 200 in the U.K. and Germany, and almost 150 in Italy. Obviously the scope for growth was and is greater in the non–American markets. In addition, there is a great difference between the U.S.A. and the rest of the world as regards the ratio of replacement sales to sales to new owners. This relationship reflects, among other things, the age and structure of the vehicle population, historical sales patterns, and the relative levels of vehicle density. Of every 10 cars sold in the U.S.A. in 1967, 7 replaced scrapped vehicles; in the U.K. and Italy the figures were 3·5 and 2 out of 10 respectively.

THE STRUCTURE OF THE UNITED STATES MOTOR INDUSTRY: THE 'BIG THREE'

Turning now to the structure of the industry. In 1969 the bulk of American car production was accounted for by the three giant firms

General Motors, Ford and Chrysler. There was also one medium-sized firm, American Motors, and one small firm, Checker Cabs. *Table 5.2* shows the output of these firms in the years 1965, 1967 and 1969.

Table 5.2

UNITED STATES CAR PRODUCTION

Firm	1969	1967	1965
American Motors	242 898	229 057	346 367
Checker Cabs	5 417	5 822	6 136
Chrysler	1 392 526	1 363 696	1 467 553
Ford	2 163 138	1 696 224	2 565 776
General Motors	4 420 348	4 117 840	4 949 395
Total	8 224 327	7 412 639	9 335 227

Source: *American Automobile Manufacturers Association Yearbook 1970.*

Over 97% of U.S. car production is accounted for by the three giant firms (compared with 91% in 1954). Of over 2000 American car firms competition has eliminated all but five firms. During the early 1950s the last four independent producers, Nash, Hudson, Studebaker and Packard, formed themselves into two groups, with Nash-Hudson becoming American Motors in 1954 and Studebaker and Packard joining forces in the same year, both groups initially made over 200 000 units a year. Previously, in 1953, Kaiser and Willys were amalgamated, but car production was phased out in favour of the Willys Jeep. In 1970 Kaiser-Willys was absorbed by American Motors. The latter concern attempted to increase its market share in the 1950s by seeking-out its own niche. The result was the 'compact' car of 1959–1960 which was introduced by the U.S. car firms to combat the growing volume of imports. The compact allowed the smaller firms to prosper alongside the giants. This was mainly because Studebaker and American Motors had tended to produce smaller cars than the giants during the late 1950s so the whole market moved in their favour when the Big Three introduced compacts backed by a massive marketing campaign. These smaller cars largely eliminated the demand for imported saloons; only Volkswagen was able to survive the holocaust of 1961 and to increase sales. The market for British and French cars was particularly badly hit. The period 1961 to 1964 was one of modest prosperity for American Motors although Studebaker was less success-ful—the latter only made 60 000 cars in 1963. Gradually GMC and Ford increased the size of their compacts which eventually meant a

major retooling in the car plants in order to manufacture the completely new bodyshells required. Typically some body dies are worn
out on making 250 000 units but others will produce up to 4 million
units at a maximum rate of 2 million a year. At GMC's output levels
such dies and tools are often fully amortised within two years and
similarly for Ford. American Motors, however, would require an
amortisation period of around 10 years in some cases. As a result the
small firms merely replaced the body dies which were worn-out after
producing 250 000 to 500 000 units. This allowed 'face lifts' to be made
but within the context of continuing the same basic body design,
because to produce a completely new body would require huge
investments in new machines, tools and dies, when the existing
equipment was still efficient and not fully paid-off. However, American
Motors' products became 'last year's models' when the new cars
appeared from GMC, Ford and Chrysler, and in addition the market
turned in favour of larger cars. As a result American Motors' market
declined between 1964 and 1967, and Studebaker's collapsed completely.

In 1967 imports of cars into the U.S.A. amounted to over 1 million
units, and discounting those produced by American firms in Canada,
imports from Western Europe and Japan amounted to almost 700 000
units. These small European cars, selling in most instances for below
$2000, were much smaller than any then current American car. Even
the cheapest compact exceeded $2000 and had a body and engine which
was large by European standards. Because of these differences in the
nature and price of the product, American firms stayed clear of the
sub-compact market, apart from importing vehicles from their
subsidiaries abroad. American firms calculated that the optimum
level of output for a single sub-compact model was around 750 000
units a year. This pre-supposed that the new engine which would be
required and some body panels could be interchanged with other
models, as optimum engine manufacture was over one million a year
and that for some body parts was over two million.

In 1970 the U.S. producers demonstrated that they believed that the
market which foreign producers had established was large enough to
justify tooling-up for a new small car. Although optimum production
was still around 750 000 units, U.S. firms are used to making profits at
levels of output equal to 50% of capacity, hence the renewed attraction of the small car market for American producers. Their first move
was to produce a sub-compact model, the first of which was introduced by Ford in 1969. This vehicle, called the 'Maverick' sold for
around $2000 and had a break-even annual output volume of about

100 000 a year. However, the most significant developments occurred in 1970 when GMC and Ford introduced cars of European size and specification, such as the Ford 'Pinto'. The break-even output for these completely new vehicles was around 400 000 units a year. The large firms have committed themselves to model-lives of between 5 and 10 years for these small cars, much longer than is usual in the U.S. car market. Such a policy should help American Motors which was the first to enter the small car market with the 'Gremlin' in 1969.

THE DOMINANCE OF GENERAL MOTORS

The U.S. motor car industry is thus highly concentrated in the hands of three firms. In terms of output, GMC and Ford typically account for over 80%, and GMC alone accounts for over 50%. Ford lost its market leadership during the inter-war period, largely because the firm remained too wedded to its Model T policy, that is, to producing a very limited range of standardised products. GMC's approach was to extend its range of cars in an effort to satisfy as many individual needs as possible. The result was a significant increase in GMC's output and market share at the expense of Ford. Nevertheless, during the 1930s both Ford and Chrysler were extremely efficiently run and presented stiff competition to GMC; the latter however, remained market leader with around 45% of the market.

From 1945 to 1960 GMC traditionally held between 44% and 48% of U.S. car output. During the early 1950s Chrysler entered a period of decline which allowed Ford to increase its lead over Chrysler in terms of market penetration. For instance, in 1954 Ford's share of the market was 25% compared with Chrysler's 20%, whereas in 1953 Chrysler accounted for 22% of output. The main beneficiary of Chrysler's decline was GMC, which increased its market share from as low as 44% to in excess of 50%.

During the 1960s GMC began to regard its normal market share as being between 50% and 55%, the higher figure being achieved when either Ford or Chrysler produced an unsuccessful range of cars. For instance, during the late 1950s and until 1962 Chrysler was in a difficult marketing and financial position with its share of the U.S. market falling to 12% in 1959 and 10% by 1962. Ford retained a relatively constant market share, although some decline occurred between 1958 and 1960 when the unsuccessful range of 'Edsel' cars was introduced, but its position recovered between 1960 and 1962 with the success of the compact cars. GMC's share increased to 55% during this time because of the various troubles which faced Ford and especially Chrysler. However, between 1962 and 1967 Chrysler had a dramatic recovery with its market share increasing to 18%. This was due to renewed emphasis on Chrysler's traditional virtues of reliability and good engineering. Between 1960 and 1970 for the first time since before the war, GMC was faced with two efficient and thrusting competitors. Even so, it was able to retain over 50% of the market.

Between 1962 and 1970 Ford and Chrysler improved their position in the lower price brackets and together accounted for 55% of total sales and output. But, in the middle and upper ranges GMC's Buick, Oldsmobile, Pontiac and Cadillac divisions, had a disproportionate share of total sales. Typically these divisions of GMC held 80% of the middle and upper ranges of the market. In terms of output, GMC produced over 2 million vehicles of this type, whereas the combined output of Chrysler and Ford in this area was 700 000 cars.

Obviously the U.S. car industry is highly concentrated, and such is the dominance of GMC that the Senate has a permanent committee scrutinising its activities. Both the U.S. administration and legislature are in a perpetual quandary over GMC's monolithic structure. In a country committed to preserving free enterprise competition the prospect of a monopolist in the motor industry does not pose an attractive proposition. Hence the continual threat to divide GMC into two or more separate firms roughly equal in financial strength and output capacity to Ford and Chrysler. GMC for its part owes its dominance largely to its own efficiency in meeting the needs of the consumer, in producing at minimum cost and being as competitive as its rivals and generally more so. The possible bankruptcy of Chrysler or Ford would therefore do GMC no good at all, as this would almost certainly mean the separation of the organisation into separate undertakings. Hence the rumours that during the low-water mark of Chrysler's fortunes between 1960 and 1962 GMC was itself purchasing Chrysler automobiles from the showrooms. (On the same lines Fiat injected 'gifts' of capital into Lancia during the mid-1960s; no financial control was involved although it was quite possible that Lancia had given an undertaking not to sell-out to a foreign firm, or at least to a U.S. one.)

THE RETAIL NETWORK

To consolidate the manufacture of eight to nine million cars, the U.S. motor industry has a large and efficient marketing organisation.

Although no resale price maintenance existed to protect dealers, their profits over the period 1961–1964 were similar to the protected U.K. motor trade, at about 2% on sales and 25% on capital. The efficiency of the 1960s was a consequence of the low profits of the 1950s when the sale of new cars was relatively low. Hence greater efforts were made by manufacturers and dealers to make selling cars more efficient and profitable.

The most effective way to increase profits was to cut the number of dealers; this increased the turnover per dealer which in turn allowed dealers to hold a larger stock of new and used vehicles. In 1964 it was calculated that 33 000 franchised new-car dealers existed compared with 41 000 in 1955, with a consequent increase in average sales from $800 000 to $1 140 000, or 226 new cars instead of 175, plus other items. Over this period only Chrysler increased the number of its outlets in order to provide a wider and better national coverage than it possessed immediately after its period of commercial decline. Chrysler now has about 6200 outlets compared with 7700 for Ford and GMC's 13 700. The remainder are split between American Motors and the importers. The car producers sell different makes of car through different dealer chains, for example, Ford dealers divide between the Ford and Lincoln-Mercury divisions, and Chrysler between Chrysler-Plymouth and Dodge, similarly for GMC. Exclusive dealing is the rule, while dealers selling competing products is the exception.

In the U.K. the distributor establishes his own retail dealer chains and little material help is given to the dealers by the car makers. In the U.S.A. the distributor is almost non-existent and the car producer deals directly with the dealer; in addition, the car producers give material help to the dealer. Only importers use distributors which is a way to overcome the problem of both finding and controlling the retailers. In the U.K. the process of reducing the number of outlets only began in the late 1960s. The need for this was shown by the fact that the average number of cars sold per outlet was only about 115. A reduction took place and by 1970 the 11 000 outlets of 1965 had been reduced to 10 000, but much remains to be done as was shown by the fact that each Ford outlet on average sold four times as many vehicles as British Leyland.

VOLKSWAGEN IN THE U.S.A.

Finally a word about Volkswagen in the U.S.A. On the supply side Volkswagen now sells over 500 000 cars in the U.S.A. This makes the firm the fourth largest car supplier on the U.S. market, smaller than the three giants but larger than American Motors. The American and German markets take over 70% of all VW production and the American market accounts for over 60% of all VW exports; in 1970 the total exceeded 560 000 units. The firm is therefore highly dependent on the American market and also vulnerable to any erosion of its sales; hence the alarming importance of VW's temporary fall in U.S. exports of 12% in 1968. The VW sales franchise is highly prized in the U.S.A. The flexibility and independence which VW gives its outlets leads to profits of 4% of turnover per dealer, double the U.S. norm. VW attempts to maximise dealer coverage rather than dealer size, so although on average more cars are sold annually per dealer than by any native make (422, against 365 for Chevrolet) there are few very large dealers. As profit margins are *not* calculated on the basis of a large turnover, small VW dealers do well.

THE COMMERCIAL VEHICLE INDUSTRY

As in most countries there are more commercial vehicle makers than car makers in the U.S.A. As well as the large car firms the American CV industry consists of vehicle-making subsidiaries of large engineering combines and independent specialist producers. The production picture of the industry in 1967 and 1969 is shown in *Table 5.3*.

Table 5.3

UNITED STATES COMMERCIAL VEHICLE PRODUCTION

| Firm | Output Figures | |
	1967	1969
GMC Chevrolet	549 665	684 708
GMC Truck & Coach Division	130 659	150 209
Chrysler (Dodge)	141 865	165 133
Ford	452 253	658 557
International Harvester	167 940	161 080
Four-wheel Drive	1 251	1 403
Kaiser-Jeep	116 744	93 160
Mack	16 634	23 473
White	24 664	31 516
Others	9 402	11 480
Total	1 611 077	1 980 719

Unlike the car industry, the independent commercial vehicle producers account for about 20% of total CV output. Although Ford and GMC are clearly the largest producers, output is less concentrated in the hands of the giant producers than it is with cars. In fact, the third largest producer in the field in 1967 was International Harvester with Chrysler in fourth place, quite closely followed by Kaiser-Jeep.

Most of Chevrolet's and Ford's output consists of light trucks. In 1968 Ford overtook Chevrolet in this sector to become market leader. The majority of these vehicles are now used for pleasure purposes. A market survey by Ford revealed that 65% of all light trucks—or 1 600 000 units—were used for pleasure or personal purposes, rather than for commercial use*. Chrysler's main sales are also in the light truck category. The three car giants account for about 90% of the light truck market, leaving just 9% to the smaller companies, such as International Harvester or Willys-Jeep. The latter firm is mainly concerned with the production of light four-wheel drive CVs or pick-ups, designed for use in arduous conditions.

In the field of larger vehicles the market leaders are International Harvester and GMC's Truck and Coach Division, the latter having a near monopoly of U.S. bus production. The former concern is a giant producer of agricultural and construction machinery of all sorts. Consequently enterprises using International Harvester tractors or bulldozers will for reasons of standardisation, use International trucks as well. International's main market is in the light to medium-heavy sector. As regards the heaviest type of vehicles the market leader is GMC with White, Ford, and Mack, close behind. Other producers of heavy vehicles include Chrysler, Freightliner Corporation, International Harvester, and Pacific Car & Foundry. Other highly specialised trucks such as large four-wheel drive vehicles or fire engines are made by Marmon Herrington, Four Wheel Drive, and La France. The bus market is dominated by GMC but a few vehicles are made by Mack and White, and by specialist bus producers such as Flxible and Twin-Coach.

Because of the low cost of petrol and the high cost of labour, American operators have tended to use high-speed petrol engined vehicles, the greater fuel consumption being offset by greater mileage per day, i.e. greater labour productivity. However, the improved design of diesel engines and the extremely high fuel consumption of large petrol engines has meant that where heavy duty vehicles of approximately $11\frac{1}{2}$ tons gross and over are concerned, the diesel engine has become the usual source of motive power since the early

* *Time* Magazine (11 July 1969).

1960s. For instance, of a total production of 86 704 heavy vehicles in 1963, 52·4% were diesel powered, but in 1968 of 128 448 vehicles 64·5% were diesel powered*. In the medium-weight group of between approximately 6 and 11½ tons gross only 10% of those produced in 1968 were diesel powered. This was a very large market and in 1970 over 350 000 vehicles of this type were produced. The Cummins engine company has estimated that 35% of the vehicles produced in this category in 1975 would be diesel powered. For similarly sized vehicles in the U.K. in 1967 the proportion using diesel engines was equal to about 93% of total production. This illustrates the growth potential facing diesel engine makers in the U.S. market. In the market for heavy duty vehicles the main supplier of diesel engines is Cummins, with over 45% of the market, followed by GMC, Ford, and Mack. A significant foothold has been gained by Perkins, especially in the market for medium-sized vehicles and engines. In this area Perkins is probably the market leader, followed by Cummins. Sales have been made by Perkins to White, Chrysler, International Harvester, and Mack.

Ford, GMC and Chrysler dominate the market for lighter trucks of up to about 6 tons gross, but in the medium-weight sector they face vigorous competition from International Harvester, the market leader. In the heavy vehicle sector GMC, Ford and Chrysler face considerable competition from the efficiently run White concern as well as from International Harvester. In addition, Mack Trucks have staged a commercial recovery after a near bankruptcy in the mid-1960s. Smaller producers such as Kenworth and Marmon Herrington have secure niches in specialised markets. Where bus production is concerned the American situation is very similar to the British with one firm having a near monopoly; in the U.K. that firm is British Leyland and in the U.S.A. it is GMC.

ORGANISATION: INTEGRATION 'PAR EXCELLENCE'

What then of the overall structure of the motor industry in the U.S.A.? We have discussed the degree of integration of the car makers elsewhere†. Briefly, the American car firms tend to be very highly integrated with very much less than 50% of the ex-works price of a car being accounted for by outside purchases. Of course the proportion and

* *Motor Truck Facts 1969*, Automobile Manufacturers Association, Detroit (1970).

† Chapter 3, pp. 71–72.

character of components bought-out varies from firm to firm. American Motors make very few of their own components apart from bodies. As a general rule the larger the firm the smaller the bought-out content. Ford and GMC have very similar bought-out contents, Chrysler is rather more dependent on outside suppliers, and American Motors is very much so. Despite the high general level of integration, no motor firm makes its own tyres, and their component divisions have only a small share of the replacement market for components. Consequently the independent component industry is still very large. In addition the independent suppliers meet most of the needs of those independent commercial vehicle producers whose scale of production does not lend to the efficient production of components. Despite their high degree of integration the three giant firms draw upon 62 000 suppliers of components, semi-finished goods and raw materials. Some of these suppliers are themselves industrial giants such as Chloride, Borg Warner*, Cummins, Bendix, Champion and Eaton. Other firms supply industry in general as well as the motor industry in particular, firms such as Du Pont supplying plastics and paint or General Electric supplying electrical equipment. Such firms are so large that the demands of the motor industry, great as they are, contribute only a relatively small part of their total turnover.

There are no monopoly suppliers, the nearest being Borg and Beck with perhaps half the clutch market, and although in the CV industry neither Cummins engines nor Eaton axles face significant domestic competition, the vehicle builders themselves offer strong competition, as do foreign firms such as Perkins. Any inefficiency on the part of the supplier would lead to the items being made by the car producers— firms which often have markets sufficiently large to make such a move worthwhile. Indeed the vehicle makers encourage price and quality competition between different outside suppliers and between outside suppliers and their own component making subsidiaries.

The CV industry has its own attendent suppliers on the body-building and trailer side. The small firms use pre-fabricated metal cabs rather than pressed-steel units as their output rarely makes the production of tools and dies an economic proposition. Numerous trailer firms exist but the clear leader has been the Freuhauf Corporation. A number of firms produce bus bodies and some such as Flxible and Twin-Coach produce units of integral construction. Typically, labour-

---

* Borg Warner's experience is typical of that facing many U.S. component firms. When the market for automatic transmissions grew sufficiently, all the car firms found it economic to supply their own needs. Borg-Warner therefore sought markets overseas.

intensive bodybuilding is expensive in the American high wage economy, and capital-intensive methods are used to produce standardised bus and goods vehicle bodies. Nevertheless, some bus operating concerns find it cheaper to have bodies built in Europe from prefabricated parts shipped from America which are then returned to the U.S.A. to have 'running-units' fitted.

THE DIVERSITY OF THE UNITED STATES MOTOR INDUSTRY

Turning from this brief survey of the industry's structure to the range of vehicles produced. On the CV side the range stretches from the small van and pick-up right up to heavy lorries of 40 tons gross. No standardised ranges of vehicles are derived from passenger cars except in the case of pick-up trucks. Most American cars are large by European standards, the smallest is the Ford Pinto, a 'Cortina' size vehicle with European made 1·6 litre and 2·0 litre engines which retails in its basic form for just over $1900. The top end of the range consists of 7 litre vehicles costing over $4000. Also as there are no specialist car producers in the U.S.A.*, the giant producers themselves have specialist divisions producing opulent and sometimes sporting cars. GMC's Cadillac division produces vehicles priced between $5000 and $11 000, and this is matched by Ford's Lincoln division with cars costing between $6000 and $7000. Chrysler's equivalent is produced by the Imperial division at prices similar to Ford's.

The market is divided between low, medium and high class products and prices to satisfy the needs of low, medium and high income groups. The 'low class' cars are priced between about $2000 and $2500, 'medium' up to around $3300, and 'high class' above $3300. Most sales by Ford and Chrysler are made in the 'low class' ranges and although GMC's 'low class' Chevrolet division sells more cars than both Ford and Chrysler individually, GMC sells most of its output in the 'medium' and 'high class'. Here profits are higher in dollar terms as is of course the value of turnover. The large market share held by GMC, Buick, Pontiac, Oldsmobile, and Cadillac divisions, largely explain GMC's fantastic financial strength.

The vast majority of the cars sold in the U.S.A. are priced between $2000 and $4000, and of a total output of eight million cars, less than half a million are priced in excess of $4000. At the 1969 exchange rate

* However there are a large number of firms producing conversions of standard mass produced models, 'fun cars' such as the VW-based 'Beach-Buggy', and 'replicas' of inter-war models.

of \$2·40= £1 this is equivalent to a range of about £830 to £1666. So considering that the average level of earnings in the U.S.A. is roughly three times that in the U.K., American motor cars are very good value for money. Crudely, using British earnings as a basis, this range is equivalent to a British price set between £277 and £555. Furthermore as the American normally receives more car for his money, the American prices worked out on a £ for lb. basis are lower than European levels. In view of these prices it is small wonder that the value of American car sales is so huge, resulting in a high density of car ownership.

In terms of quality it is more difficult to compare American cars with their European rivals. Mechanically the large American car with a low stress engine has often been superior to its European competitors. In terms of road holding and quality of bodywork the European product may have been better. However it is wrong to suppose that American cars are built so as not to last too long, as planned obsolescence is more effect than cause. American cars are so cheap in real terms and depreciation so rapid that it is normally more economic to scrap than to carry out a major overhaul. In the U.S.A. the average life of cars is less than 5 years but the same models are often used abroad for over 10 years. Indeed, in the U.S.A. during World War II average car life was extended from 5·6 to over 9 years.

LOCATION

Finally, the location of the American car industry. The industry has component manufacturing plants scattered across a thousand miles of the mid-west requiring assembly plants not only in Detroit but all over the U.S.A. and in Canada between Lake Huron and Lakes Erie and Ontario. GMC, Ford, and Chrysler, have 21, 16, and 6, car assembly plants respectively, and also own 16, 14 and 12 component manufacturing plants respectively. The optimum annual output of an assembly plant, where all scale economies are reaped, is between 150 000 and 200 000 units, with most of the significant economies already available at the lower figure. In the case of foundry work, 150 000 may be the long run optimum, and for the machining of different parts the optimum varies between 360 000 and 1 250 000 a year depending on the item involved. In the case of body pressings the optimum varies between 250 000 and 2 000 000 units per year. If it is economic to transport some items over long distances and not others, then most of the movements involved are of parts which are small in relation to their value. Consequently, engines, gearboxes, transmission units, and other machined items, are best suited to be sent long distances. Body pressings neatly stacked can also be transported cheaply, but not complete bodies. So in the U.S.A. a Fisher body plant will be situated next door to most GMC assembly plants; similarly, Briggs plants are adjacent to Ford assembly factories. Due to the labour intensity and low capital content of final assembly the U.S. producers moved from labour starved Detroit to green field sites with adequate labour supplies. Hence the wide dispersal of optimum-sized assembly plants rather than the duplication of assembly facilities in Detroit, or in Michigan in general. The long run average cost curve in the motor industry being what it is determines that one press shop producing major body fittings will supply at least ten body and final assembly plants.

THE CANADIAN MOTOR INDUSTRY

The Canadian motor industry produced 720 807 cars and 226 448 commercial vehicles in 1967. The four American firms have plants in Canada with GMC accounting for most of the car output and Ford being the market leader in commercial vehicles. As well as the four American firms, Volvo also assembles cars in Canada at a rate of just over 4000 a year. On the CV side, Willys, White and International all have assembly plants in Canada. Following the Canadian–American trade agreement for cars concluded in 1964, American components and cars are imported duty free into Canada and vice versa. As Canadian labour is slightly cheaper than American, the U.S. car producers shipped components from the low cost large optimum plants in the U.S.A. to the Canadian assembly plants, and often the complete car was sold in the U.S.A. This trend was reinforced by the free trade agreement of 1964. In 1967, 310 000 cars were exported to the U.S.A. out of a total production of 714 084 and total exports were just in excess of 330 000. This illustrates the fact that the Canadian motor industry is really part and parcel of the American industry, not only in terms of ownership and production but also from a marketing point of view. The only other export markets to take four-figure exports were Australia and South Africa, where Commonwealth preference may have been useful.

THE EUROPEAN MOTOR PRODUCERS

Following the ravages of World War II, the European motor industry was faced with a massive task of reconstruction. By the mid-1950s the continental industry was on a sound financial, technical, and marketing footing, and in a position to meet the growing foreign and domestic demand for motor vehicles. From 1945 to 1955 the continental producers concentrated on the domestic and the wider European market, but from 1955 onwards first the Germans, and then the French and Italians, began to sell on a world scale. The vigorous pursuit of export markets plus the rapid annual growth in domestic national product meant a rapid growth firstly in the German and French industries and then, during the 1960s, in the Italian. This process was reflected by the fact that during the period 1953 to 1963 the most dynamic growth points in the continental motor industry were provided by Volkswagen and Renault, whereas the period 1963 to the time of writing in 1971 had been dominated in many ways by Fiat. The respective sizes of the French, German and Italian industries can be gauged by the position summarised in *Table 5.4*.

Table 5.4

TOTAL VEHICLE OUTPUT IN WEST GERMANY, ITALY AND FRANCE

Country	Output by year			
	1946	*1950*	*1960*	*1967*
France				
Cars	30 429	257 292	1 175 301	1 776 502
CVs	65 633	100 260	193 909	233 170
Germany				
Cars	9 962	219 409	1 816 779	2 295 714
CVs	13 916	86 655	238 370	186 605
Italy				
Cars	10 989	101 310	595 907	1 439 211
CVs	17 994	26 537	48 710	103 458

Source: *The Motor Industry of Great Britain*, SMMT (1968).

FRANCE

Taking the French industry first; the bulk of the motor car industry's output is accounted for by four firms: Simca, Peugeot, Renault and

Citroen. There is a tiny specialist sector made up of Matra, Hotchkiss and Sovam, but their total output is less than 1000 units. The development of the various manufacturers between 1960 and 1969 is summarised in *Table 5.5*.

Table 5.5

OUTPUT OF VEHICLES (1000s)

Firm	1960	1967	1969
Renault	449	707	911
Citroen	270	419	426
Peugeot	194	374	440
Simca	211	275	388
Others	8	1	3
Total	1 132	1 776	2 168

Obviously the degree of concentration of output in the French industry is high and in terms of financial and marketing linkages it is higher still. Renault and Peugeot, for instance, have been close partners since 1966 despite maintaining strict financial independence; Renault is a state owned undertaking and Peugeot's finances are dominated by the Peugeot family. Since 1968, however, a number of joint ventures have been undertaken, such as building a joint test track and a new factory for the manufacture of a new engine for common use. Ultimately a complete merger of some description is likely in order to preserve a viable French-owned motor industry. Both the other manufacturers are partly owned by foreign producers. Chrysler owns the major portion of Simca's equity*, while Fiat purchased a 15% stake in Citroen in 1968, and by 1971 the holding was just under 50%. At present the foreign financial control of Simca has not yet been repeated in Citroen's case, due mainly to the hostility of the French government which prevented Fiat purchasing over 50% of Citroen's equity. But Fiat is not just a sleeping partner; in 1969 joint purchasing organisations were established together with Citroen, taking responsibility for the marketing and servicing of Fiat vehicles in certain markets. With the continued development of the EEC, firms on the continent will regard the European market as their domestic market, and not just the area encompassed by particular national boundaries. Fiat is one of the first firms to adjust to the new marketing conditions and its aim to transform itself into a European-based firm explains its

* This concern was established in 1931 and until 1951 all output was based on Fiat designs. Since 1951 the firm's products have been distinctive although Fiat had a minority holding until 1963.

partial take-over of Citroen, a concern in both financial and marketing difficulties. With the gradual acceptance of the European ideal of first, economic and then, political unity gradually changing political opinion in France and elsewhere, the emergence of the European firm should become commonplace. Even before such an eventuality the total absorption of Citroen by Fiat can be envisaged.

THE STRUCTURE OF THE FRENCH MOTOR INDUSTRY

The overall structure of the French industry is similar to the British in as much that French car producers buy a very large proportion of the total value of the average car from outside, about 35%, but it is unlike the British in that fewer main component suppliers are large-scale producers. A few giants do exist, notably Chausson who make all the radiators required by the French motor industry, and Jaeger who supply 70% of all instruments, while Ferodo supply all the clutches used, Michelin has over 66% of the tyre market with Dunlop having most of the rest, Solex and Zenith supply all carburettors, and Saint Gobain and Boussais supply all windows. In the U.K. there are about 400 main component suppliers compared with over 500 in France, and in addition all motor firms purchase from producers whose main activity is outside the motor industry; hence a typical U.K. car firm will have over 4000 suppliers and the situation is much the same elsewhere. However, U.K. firms typically buy over 50% of the value of a car from outside compared with about 35% in France. Although the manufacture of many components and products is concentrated in the hands of one, two, or three firms, there are still many small suppliers left. Of the 540 main suppliers about 440 employ less than 200 people. In the U.K.'s case most main items are produced by giant groups, leaving a myriad of producers to supply small, inexpensive, but still important items.

French car firms in general try to maintain more than one supplier, whereas British firms have encouraged monopolists and it was only in the late 1960s that firms such as British Leyland attempted to foster more than one supplier per item.

Due to the French system of motor taxation, which is based on the cubic capacity of the engine, no large cars are made by the French motor industry. The largest is produced by Citroen and by European standards it can be classed as a medium-large vehicle. Vehicles of similar dimensions are produced by Peugeot, but Simca and Renault produce somewhat smaller cars. Prices range from about £380 to

£1500 and sizes from the 425 c.c. Citroen 2CV to the 2175 c.c. Citroen Pallas. The medium-small and small cars retail for under £650, the medium sized cars from about £600 to £900 and the large Peugeots and Citroens for over £1000 and up to £1500. The vast majority of cars produced in France are in the small and medium-small category, accounting for over 50% of the total in 1967, but with the growth in real incomes the medium car sector is the fastest growing, accounting for over 30% of production in 1967. The prices of French medium and medium-small cars reflect very efficient methods of production and therefore such models pose strong competition in third markets to the products of the British industry. In terms of quality the large cars of Citroen and Peugeot have an enviable reputation. However, at one time some of the smaller French vehicles were not noted for durability or reliability, although after the mid-1960s the popular-car makers greatly improved the quality of their products.

THE COMMERCIAL VEHICLE INDUSTRY

The French car industry enjoyed a period of great prosperity during the 1960s, although of course in a competitive market some firms did better than others. Peugeot and Renault improved their financial and marketing performance mainly at the expense of Citroen, and to a lesser extent Simca. The French CV industry, however, has proved vulnerable to competition emanating from both inside and outside the EEC which is evident from a brief analysis of the French industry. The total volume of output and its distribution between different producers in 1967 and 1969 is shown in *Table 5.6*.

When it is considered that almost 150 000 of the units produced in 1967 were light and medium vans and pick-ups and light trucks then the production of medium to heavy trucks and buses only accounted for something over 83 000 units. The comparable figure in the U.K. was in excess of 180 000.

The output of medium-weight vehicles of between 4 and 12 tons gross weight only reached 26 000. This is the type of vehicle which is used in great numbers in the U.K., and the large market allows the use of large volume low cost techniques of production. In turn the low prices charged allow U.K. producers to develop large markets abroad which in turn adds to the output level and further reduces unit average costs of production. Total U.K. production in this category is not publicised but it is in excess of 100 000 units a year. The significance of French weakness in this sector will be discussed later.

Table 5.6

FRENCH COMMERCIAL VEHICLE OUTPUT

Firm	1967	1969
Berliet	15 132	19 998
Citroen	80 885	80 489
FFSA (Unic)	6 484	8 210
Total	102 501	108 697
Peugeot	31 286	48 361
Renault	70 846	98 108
Saviem	27 785	34 617
Total	129 917	181 086
FAR	115	142
Hotchkiss	286	169
Willeme	158	194
Sovam	252	253
Verney	41	69
Total	233 270	290 610

The period 1950 to 1967 had seen a dramatic fall in the number of independent French CV makers. Firms such as Chenard et Walker disappeared completely, others such as Delahye and Salmson were absorbed by other producers when on the verge of bankruptcy. During the 1950s the most significant development was the creation of the state owned Saviem concern. This was made up of the three private firms of Isobloc, Latil and Somua plus the heavy CV activities of Renault. The entire complex was state owned and Saviem became the heavy and medium CV producer of the Renault organisation. Salmson was added in 1955. Delahye was absorbed by the Hotchkiss concern, a general engineering and machinery organisation with vehicle building interests. However, during the early 1960s both Hotchkiss and Willeme became closely associated with Leyland and ACV respectively. Both these French firms rely to a large extent upon engines, gearboxes, axles, and other components supplied by the U.K. producers. Although Leyland and ACV merged into one combine there is no link of any sort between Hotchkiss and Willeme. It is evident that the market shares held by both firms are minute with total output varying between three and six units a week, and Willeme's financial position has long been precarious. The other small firms Sovam and Verney have rather specialised markets; Verney for instance is the bus building subsidiary of a bus operating combine. FAR produces road tractors, often to foreign designs. Until 1967 Berliet was the only independent French CV producer to bear comparison with firms such as Leyland in the U.K., MAN and Mercedes in Germany, or Scania in Sweden. However, production techniques were both expensive, in that Berliet was a highly integrated and capital intensive concern, and outdated; this, coupled with fluctuations in the French economy which hit investment, and the increased competition from German firms as the EEC's trading barriers were dismantled, and the loss of 'Empire' markets, meant that high cost production could not be offset by higher prices. Consequently between 1962 and 1966 profit as a percentage of turnover fluctuated between 1·3% and 0·03%! The concern needed to invest heavily in new plant and equipment and in developing a new range of products its situation was precarious. As a result it was absorbed by Citroen in 1967.

The 1967 merger between Citroen and Berliet and the subsequent link between Citroen and Fiat meant that the latter controlled over 40% of French CV output. This was partly a result of Fiat selling its interest in Simca cars to Chrysler in 1963, for in exchange Fiat gained control of Simca Industries which included Unic, the third largest French heavy vehicle producer. Unic was closely integrated with Fiat's marketing, design, and production organisations. The integration was two-way, with Unic deriving extra funds and marketing outlets from Fiat, but the latter was able to use Unic's new V8 diesel engine. Consequently Fiat's control of Unic allied to its partial absorption of Citroen placed a large proportion of French CV output under foreign control.

Although financially divorced, Saviem and MAN of Germany have close marketing and technical links. Many of the lighter MAN vehicles use Saviem diesel engines and MAN dealers sell Saviem vehicles. In turn Saviem is weak on the heavy vehicle side, and it has to use MAN engines in its larger vehicles as it does not have a sufficiently powerful engine of its own. Saviem also uses Perkins units.

In terms of ownership only the Peugeot–Renault group remains entirely French, although in terms of technical development and the need to have a complete range of vehicles it is partly dependent on foreigners. The same is true of the remaining independents. Not one French CV firm was able to survive as an independent self-sufficient entity and the future of CV production in France rests upon larger European groupings.

The irony of the weakness displayed by the French CV industry is that due to successful lobbying by Berliet the French government accepted the need to exempt CV's from the 'Kennedy Round' of GATT negotiations to reduce tariffs on industrial goods. The rest of the EEC, afraid of U.K. based competition, readily agreed. But the preserving of a 'protected' French market has not insulated Berliet or the other French producers in the past. While U.K. competitors have been temporarily held at bay, German and especially Italian firms are dominating the French CV industry and market. For not only do these countries have a strong stake in French CV production but direct exports from Germany have reduced the domestic market of French based firms; in 1969 Mercedes Benz held a larger share of the French market for heavy vehicles than either Saviem or Berliet.

The French CV industry is therefore weak for a number of reasons. A heavily protected market gave basically inefficient firms a secure living. Once this protection was removed the technical and economic shortcomings of the producers was evident. Firms like Berliet were fully integrated but could not sell sufficient numbers to profit from the heavy capital expenditure involved. This was partly due to the smaller home market for heavy vehicles, but mainly because of increased German competition in the French market and the failure to make the most of export possibilities. Apart from light vans, French CV producers had almost totally ignored world export markets, relying heavily on sales to former colonies which dropped significantly when independence was granted. Protection did not only lead to high-cost inefficient production, for in addition the technical specification and performance of French CVs often proved inferior to those produced by other European firms. On the marketing side the French were no match for the Germans when it came to establishing sales and service networks throughout the EEC. Hence French and other European road hauliers turned to German, Italian, Dutch and even Swedish manufacturers, to meet their vehicle needs partly because of the efficiency of their sales and after-sales network.

The range of commercial vehicles produced by the French industry, like all the other European industries, is greatly less than the variety of products manufactured by the U.K. industry. As regards small vans, and medium sized vans and pick-ups, the French industry is quite strong, although the medium weight category is small in terms of total production. Consequently the attempt to use mass-production techniques leads either to expensive sub-optimum production or to the manufacture of technically inferior vehicles where an attempt has been made to keep down direct costs. In the market for heavier vehicles the French industry is also weak, often relying upon foreign capital or technology to produce an acceptable vehicle range. In both the heavier and medium-weight category production is under high cost conditions and inefficient, prices are anywhere between 30% and 150% higher than those prevailing in the U.K. for comparable products.

The greatest difference is in the market for medium-weight vehicles. In the U.K. the comparatively early development of the economy meant that a large market for vehicles of between two and four tons payload appeared during the 1930s. Between 1945 and 1955 the market for vehicles of between four and six tons payload expanded rapidly. This process continued until the mid-1960s when the over six tons payload market became extremely large. The early appearance of such markets allowed their exploitation by firms using low cost methods of production. As the customer moved up the weight scale so the mass producing CV maker extended his range to satisfy the new demand. As a result of this process the mass production of eight ton payload vehicles became commonplace in the U.K. during the early 1960s. Furthermore, all the mass producers moved into the heavy vehicle field to satisfy the needs of customers who did not require more expensive specialised vehicles. In short, they moved up the weight scale to meet the early and growing demand for medium weight vehicles.

In Europe it was different. The slower development of industry, and especially retail trade and service chains, meant that the overall demand was smaller. In particular, the wholesale and retail sector where most medium sized vehicles are needed was much smaller and economically weaker on the continent where the small scale firm dominated total turnover. Such concerns did not require, nor indeed could they afford, anything larger than a small van or a car to be used for commercial purposes. As a result the medium sized truck and van market was not large enough to justify investment in large-scale production methods. Consequently any need for medium sized vehicles has been satisfied by small-volume specialist producers, and often these French firms were over capitalised. Hence the satisfaction of the medium weight sector has been left to specialist firms with high cost techniques of production. In practical terms this has meant that despite the 22% tariff barrier U.K. firms make significant sales in the French medium weight commercial vehicle market.

On the component side the CV industry utilises many of the firms supplying the car factories but some differences exist. Over 40% of fuel pumps used in diesel engines are produced by Lucas's French interests, another 25% being made by Bosch. Perkins Diesel supply some diesel engines to Saviem especially for the lighter type of vehicle. If the quality and price of domestic products are not satisfactory CV producers buy abroad—Berliet use German ZF gearboxes made both in West Germany and under licence in France. In some cases, French makers are either forced to buy abroad, as when they purchase MAN or Perkins diesel engines, or to buy from a domestic competitor. In the French industry, for instance, there is no equivalent to the independent diesel engine makers which abound in the U.K. Hence Renault light vans have generally been powered by Peugeot diesels.

The French motor industry buys its wheel requirements from Michelin (50%), Dunlop (42%) and Oliver. Michelin also holds 75% of the CV tyre market and 100% of the market for very heavy vehicles such as dumpers and construction equipment.

As regards bodywork, all car bodies are made by the vehicle producers, although some sub-contracting for particular items occurs. However, as regards van bodies, Chausson produces 36% of the total, thereby supplying most of the needs of Renault and Peugeot, although Citroen produce their own requirements. The Renault Microbus is made by an outside firm Carrier. In the case of larger vehicles delivered from the factory in chassis-cab form there are about 30 independent bodybuilders which are used by both customer and vehicle builder. This is a much smaller number than exists in the U.K., and only three are of any size. Another four firms are of medium size, and all seven both produce for customers and also act as sub-contractors for the manufacture of some parts for complete vehicles made by the CV producers. Five firms supply cabs to the vehicle builders although all the CV firms make some if not most of their own requirements. About 60–70% of the heavy CV makers demand for cabs is satisfied by their own production. The rapid pace of technical development in some sectors of the body market, and the increase in foreign, especially U.K., competition means that firms are tending to specialise, and to modernise their plant for larger output volumes. At the same time they are attempting to obtain regular outlets for their products by supply agreements with vehicle manufacturers. The same process is evident in the U.K. bodybuilding and cab producing sectors.

In general the French heavy CV makers only buy-out cabs in the case of small production runs. In the case of specialised bodies for complete vehicles, manufacturers purchase from the cheapest and most efficient source. In the case of bus bodies, buying out is important. About 99% of total bus production comes from Saviem and Citroen-Berliet, Saviem has about 60% of the market and Berliet 25%. Only Berliet makes all its own bodies, Saviem purchases over 50% of their requirements from Chausson and Citroen uses the independent firms of Heuliez and Grau.

The French trailer industry comprises about 10 firms, again far fewer than exist in the U.K., with the market being dominated by four firms: Coder, Freuhauf, Titan and Trailer. Annual production is now around 5000 units a year compared with over 16 000 in the U.K. No heavy vehicle maker produces trailers in France leaving the market to independent specialists. Unlike the situation in Germany, where operators use loaded lorries to pull 'draw-bar' trailers the French operator is like his U.K. counterpart in preferring tractors and semi-trailers. Many of the running units used by French trailer makers are produced by Rubery Owen in the U.K.

Like the truck and bus making side, the overall structure of the CV industry is not strong. Since the major CV makers are all highly integrated their capital investment is of a high order, but sales are not commensurate, therefore unit costs of production are high. At the same time, the French tradition of integrated production precluded the creation of large independent suppliers of major components whose internal economies of scale would be external to the vehicle builders. One result of this was the disappearance of small independent French producers saddled with high production costs, and often faced with no alternative but to supply most of their own needs themselves. Firms such as Willeme and Hotchkiss unable to meet the financial requirements of producing modern main components, such as engines, were forced to buy abroad. There are no French equivalents of ZF in Germany, Gardner in the U.K., or Voith in Sweden.

Both the French car and CV industries are becoming increasingly integrated with those in other European countries but before the significance of this can be discussed it is necessary to briefly analyse first the West German and then the Italian motor industries.

WEST GERMANY

The West German motor industry in 1971 was the third largest in the world after the U.S.A. and Japan. From 1945 to 1966 the total output of cars grew yearly without interruption from 1293 units to 2 830 050 units. The only setback came in 1967 when car output fell to 2 295 714, but recovery followed swiftly in 1968. Commercial vehicle output also grew steadily, but setbacks were experienced in 1953, and between 1965 and 1967.

CONCENTRATION AND COMPETITION

Like all mature motor industries the German one is highly concentrated, and the process of concentration has operated strongly in the post-war period but the final form of the German motor industry has yet to be achieved. In the late 1960s the German industry was less concentrated than any other major motor industry apart from the Japanese, and the distribution of output in 1969 compared with 1960 is shown in *Table 5.7*.

Table 5.7

GERMAN CAR OUTPUT BY MANUFACTURER (1000s)

Manufacturer	1960	1966	1967	1969
Volkswagen	865	1 460	1 038	1 531
Opel	351	648	540	788
Mercedes–Auto Union	236	192	200	257
Ford	186	291	193	301
Others	237	302	239	315

In many ways the 1969 figures were more representative than 1967's as the latter covered the first post-war downturn in car output. The share of the 'Others' in 1960 was as high as 14%, compared with only 5% in the U.K. and less than 1% in France. Even in 1966 the 'Others' accounted for over 10% of total production compared with 4% in the U.K. In Germany the main producers listed under 'Others' in 1960 were BMW, NSU, Porsche, Borgward and Glas. The output of these firms was varied; for instance, Porsche concentrated on high performance cars as well as undertaking research for and selling 'expertise' to the German motor industry, Borgward made a range of vehicles from very small economy cars to high performance saloons and Glas and BMW made economy cars at one extreme of their range and high performance saloons at the other with nothing in between. NSU produced small cars as well as producing Fiat models.

Of these firms, only NSU and Porsche were financially and commercially sound. Borgward's output in 1960 was 85 500 cars and the firm was trying to compete with much larger competitors. In addition, it was more deeply involved in making components for its cars than was truly economic. The company was more integrated than any British firm at the time, making its own bodies, forgings, and castings, yet its production volumes per model varied between 11 000 a year and

36 000. Obviously high integration allied to low volume was not profitable, especially given the prices it was forced to set for its smaller cars which competed with Volkswagen, and VW made 865 000 'Beetles' in 1960! An earlier marketing decision to concentrate on ultra small cheap cars was a mistake for this market soon disappeared with the growth in German prosperity.

The decline in the market for 'sticking plaster' cars also hit BMW, NSU and Glas. In 1960 BMW was recovering from its year of conflict when the firm was almost absorbed by Mercedes in 1959 which wanted the BMW factories as additions to its CV capacity. Unlike, however, Borgward which went into liquidation in 1961, BMW's future improved. A new range of high performance cars tailored to the needs of younger customers in parts of the car market not exploited by Mercedes allowed the firm to grow at a rapid rate. Although near liquidation in 1960, by 1969 the concern had increased production to almost 150 000 units a year by skilfully exploiting market niches left by other firms. This resulted in BMW selling more cars than Mercedes on the German market although the latter exported sufficient numbers to more than compensate for this. BMW's growth was a result of finding new consumers' wants or of satisfying demands not previously catered for and not to taking sales from Mercedes, at least to any great extent. Together with the increase in output and turnover there was a sharp increase in profitability, from losses in 1959 to a profit of over £20 million in 1969. In 1967 BMW absorbed Glas and most of the latter's vehicle production was phased out. The two Glas factories were wanted in order to produce major components and assemblies thereby freeing more room for assembly in the main BMW plant. This allowed the concern to increase productive capacity to cater for increased demand with the minimum of investment in plant and equipment, although by 1967 net investment was £13 million with another £7 million spent on replacement. With an output volume of 150 000 units a year BMW should reap most of the significant economies of scale to be derived from assembly, however, as an integrated car producer BMW is still a small firm. The optimum size for other activities range from 300 000 units a year to around 2 million units, the largest optima existing in the fields of engine production and certain body pressings. Consequently BMW's production costs must be significantly higher than the minimum possible. To a certain extent this is counteracted by using the one basic body shell over six models and amortising the tools, dies and jigs over a long period. However, when the next generation of vehicles are needed, perhaps in the late 1970s, BMW may still find it difficult to find the funds needed for investment in new tooling. Hence merger with a larger group is a long term probability.

The development of the larger groups during the 1960s as shown by *Table 5.7* shows a gradual concentration of output which the situation in 1969 only highlighted even more. The relative improvement of VW's position *vis à vis* Mercedes over the period 1960–1969 is overstated in the table. This was because by 1966 Mercedes had sold its Auto Union subsidiary to VW. This was motivated by the fact that Auto Union's range of vehicles fitted more easily into VW's production and marketing patterns than into Mercedes-Benz's. The latter firm concentrated on producing large cars of over 1·8 litres incorporating many custom-built and quality features, therefore output was not carried out on a pure mass production basis. Volkswagen, however, is a pure mass-producer and was able to bring its expertise in this field to the production of the small and medium size Auto Union and Audi vehicles. With the proceeds of this sale Mercedes extended its CV producing capacity. Perhaps the most significant feature of German production in the 1960s had been the relatively slight growth of the American owned Ford and Opel (GMC) concerns at the expense of their German rivals. In 1960 their combined output accounted for 31% of total production and in 1966 it was 33% but in 1969 it was less than 33%. In other words, German owned producers had matched the sales and production efforts of the U.S. firms, unlike the situation in the U.K. where the domestic producers' share of total output fell during the 1960s. In terms of shares of the German market the American firms have done much better, mainly improving their position at the expense of VW whose production levels are highly dependent on the U.S. market. Nevertheless, attempts by Ford and especially Opel to capture a larger share of the big car and medium-large markets dominated by Mercedes and BMW have failed completely*. This mirrors the situation in the U.K. where the dominance of Ford and Vauxhall in the market for cars over 1·8 litres has collapsed in the face of competition from the Triumph, Rover and Jaguar factories of BLMC. It would appear that the European market is different to the American. The slightly more affluent European customer is not satisfied with a more luxurious, powerful, or larger car from the mass-producers but prefers the more distinctive product of medium-sized firms such as Mercedes, Opel, Volvo, or BLMC s Rover and Jaguar products.

During the latter part of the 1960s concentration increased. In 1967

---

* In 1967 Opel made just 6000 big cars compared with almost 300 000 of the smaller Kadett model.

BMW absorbed Glas, Borgward disappeared, and in 1969 Volkswagen purchased NSU. At the same time VW's purchase of Auto Union from Mercedes was part of the process which was drawing the two German owned giants into closer contact. Various joint projects in the fields of research, technology, and marketing have been established. As yet no complete financial or technical merger is contemplated but such is the optimum size of a fully integrated car producing complex and such is the expenditure on research, marketing and tooling, that a large German owned grouping of VW, Mercedes and BMW would reap significant economies of scale and quicker amortisation of fixed costs.

At the present time both BMW and Daimler-Benz reap all the significant economies to be gained at the final assembly stage. Both firms, however, concentrate on quality cars and avoid the mass-production of motor vehicles. Consequently the lower and slower output of major components, assemblies and sub-assemblies means that production costs are above the minimum. Nevertheless customers are clearly prepared to pay for the higher fixed production costs as well as the higher direct costs of quality production. This should continue as long as costs do not become grotesquely out of line with those incurred by the mass producers, and this requires the maximum inter-changeability of parts to keep expensive equipment as fully occupied as possible without introducing mass production volumes, and also the use of the same basic components and therefore the same production equipment over very long periods. The successful maintenance of long-lived production runs should insure the financial prosperity of both BMW and Daimler-Benz. At the same time further cost savings would follow from a VW-BMW-Daimler-Benz complex.

VERTICAL INTEGRATION: INDUCEMENTS AND RESTRAINTS

Turning now to the overall structure of the German motor industries. The relationship between vehicle producers and component producers has been shaped by two conflicting factors. Firstly, up to 1968 Germany had a system of a 'cascading' turnover tax* which encouraged car makers, among others, to buy as much as they could from companies they themselves controlled and thus avoid taxation. An independent supplier facing a tax on his turnover would pass some, if not all, of it on to his customers thereby increasing their costs. However, integrated firms avoided tax at this stage and their total tax burden would be lower. This incentive to integration was counter-balanced by a desire

* Replaced by a value added tax in 1968.

to avoid becoming too-octupus like and therefore reminding the public of the cartels of pre-war Germany. Consequently the dominant German owned firms, VW and Daimler-Benz have built up a large number of independent suppliers, many being quite small. Quality is maintained because, following the U.S. pattern, such suppliers are only subcontractors supplying products of a design and quality centrally determined by the car makers and very rigidly inspected by them at all stages of production. Costs are kept down by buying each part from only a few suppliers but even so both VW and Daimler-Benz use over 4000 suppliers. The latter firm adds to its costs by using more suppliers per item than VW but as the firm competes more on quality than price anyway the insurance following from alternative sources of supply appears worthwhile.

The same general policy is followed by Ford and Opel although they produce more of their own parts than the German owned concerns and also keep larger stocks, often capable of sustaining four weeks production. Opel is more highly integrated than any British firm, its cars having a bought-out content of only about 35%.

As elsewhere in Europe there are large near monopolist suppliers of some items. Solex, for instance, supplies 98% of the carburettor market, many of the items made being produced under licence from the British Zenith-Solex concern. A co-operative cartel of four firms dominates the market for toughened-glass. Bosch makes most dynamos, fuel injection equipment and a majority of many other electrical items. Dunlop dominates the disc brake market, while ZF holds much of the market for transmission equipment*.

THE RANGE OF VEHICLES

The German motor industry produces a wider range of vehicles than the French industry, ranging from small economy cars to large high powered saloons. The significant feature of German production compared with output in the other main European countries and Japan is the very small output of cars under 1000 c.c. and the very large market share held by cars over 1500 c.c. This relative picture is summarised in *Table 5.8.*

This reflects the general prosperity of the West German economy with its high per capita income. Customers are able to afford more than

---

* Due to the relative scarcity of firms able to make components in the required quantities German firms are typically more self-reliant than their British counterparts.

Table 5.8

PERCENTAGE OF PRODUCTION BY ENGINE SIZE (1967)

Country	Up to 1000 c.c.	1000 to 1500 c.c.	Over 1500 c.c.
Italy	58	33	9
France	45	37	18
Japan	38	46	16
U.K.	19	58*	23†
West Germany	5	59	36
U.S.A.	0	0	100

* 1000 to 1600 c.c.   † Over 1600 c.c.

basic motoring so a large sector of the market requires large-medium and large cars, mainly from BMW and Daimler-Benz. All of Mercedes' output is in the largest category and most of BMW's. In addition, the large export markets established, by Mercedes in particular, also explain the large proportion of total output accounted for by cars over 1500 c.c. Furthermore, a strong home market exists for such cars. In 1969 Mercedes' domestic customers were faced with a nine months waiting list, indeed, only as output doubled from 100 000 to 200 000 cars between 1959 and 1969 did the waiting list gradually fall from its former level of two years. The continued existence of a waiting list for Mercedes (and indeed BMW) shows the growing market in Germany for large cars costing over £1000. Another factor accounting for the smallness of the total production of cars under 1000 c.c. is that basic motoring needs in Germany are satisfied by cars of between 1000 c.c. and 1300 c.c. which nevertheless are sold at a price equivalent to those charged for cars of less than 1000 c.c. in Italy, and are significantly cheaper than the prices charged for some of the small cars made in the U.K. or France. Given that the expenditure taxes on cars and the dealers' profit margins are now basically similar this reflects the extent of efficient low cost production in Germany.

Prices in Germany for cars between 1000 c.c. and 1500 c.c. are influenced by Volkswagen prices; this firm is either regarded as the market leader or as the firm to beat. The basic VW 'Beetle' being of pre-war design and being basically similar to the early post-war production prototypes, has long paid off its initial design, development, and tooling costs*. It is also produced at an annual rate of over

* In 1971 the VW Beetle overtook the Ford Model T's total output of 15 million made between 1908 and 1927, although it took six years longer to reach this landmark.

F

one million and production is at an optimum level for all the processes involved except for the manufacture of some body panels. The real cost of production is therefore lower than for any other car in Europe. Consequently competitive models produced by Opel and Ford closely follow VW prices, and even given the fact that these firms can utilise previous American research and development allied to the fact that output levels are somewhat lower, the real production costs must be higher than VW's; even so, significant profits are still earned.

The 100 000 or so small cars are all made by the smaller firms, mainly BMW and VW's new subsidiary NSU. The market is a declining one because most Germans can afford a low price Opel or VW. In other words the dual conditions of high per capita income and the availability of low price small medium and medium cars leave only a tiny market for those even cheaper vehicles. Such production may soon disappear completely leaving such demand as remains to be satisfied by small utilitarian Italian and French cars which cost around £350 in the EEC.

Taking into account the tiny home market for small cars the German industry produces a wide and varied range of motor cars. These stretch from the VW 1200 and Opel Kadett up to the range of high performance vehicles of around 2 litres produced by VW's Audi division, Opel and BMW. Above 2 litres a varied range is produced by Daimler-Benz, this covers models from 2 litre diesel-engined taxis to 6·5 litre limousines and high performance coupes. Both Opel and Ford have attempted to widen their share of the large car market, but with little success. BMW has opened new markets in the 2 litre to 2·5 litre range. Prices range from £460 for a Volkswagen 1300 and Opel Kadett small-medium saloon, to £500 to £700 for medium-size VWs, Opels and Fords, and over £1000 for large Opels, BMWs and Mercedes. The Daimler-Benz price list stretches from just over £1000 to in excess of £5000.

The market for German cars can be expected to grow at home and abroad. At home the car density in 1967 was just under 200 cars per 1000 people, compared with almost 250 in Sweden, over 300 in Canada, and over 400 in the U.S.A. The enviable reputation for quality and long life possessed by German cars, backed by ultra-efficient marketing organisations, maintained Germany's position as the world's largest car exporter throughout the 1960s and early 1970s. The continuing excess world demand for Volkswagen, BMW, and Daimler-Benz, cars should insure continued growth. It must, however, be pointed out that the quality of some German vehicles is not good but by and large the general standard is high. The one factor which may cause a decline would be a sharp reversal of German fortunes in the U.S.A. The possibility of continued Japanese expansion in the U.S.A. could lead to a decline in German exports which would be difficult to compensate elsewhere. Another problem may be the emergence of the U.S. car industry's 'sub compacts' backed by a huge sales campaign, these could harm all exporters and perhaps unlike the early 1960s German car exports would not be an exception to the general decline.

COMMERCIAL VEHICLES

Turning from the extremely strong and vigorous German car industry to the German commercial vehicle manufacturers. In the U.K. these producers are either off-shoots of car manufacturing groups or specialised concerns whose main or sole activity is commercial vehicle production. In France most commercial vehicles are made by firms associated with car production. In Germany the situation is not quite the same. It is true that the largest producer of medium to large commercial vehicles, Daimler-Benz, is primarily a vehicle producer, and on both the car and CV side pure mass-production is replaced by quality large-scale output. The other car firms making commercial vehicles are Volkswagen, Opel, and Ford but these are unlike their U.K. counterparts. At the present time the only commercial vehicles made by these firms are either light vans using numerous car components or medium-weight vans and pick-ups again often using car components. No full-size trucks, vans, or buses are produced by these firms, hence the absence of mass produced low cost and low price CVs as produced by Ford, Bedford, Rootes or the BMC range, in the U.K. In Germany, full-size vehicles are either made by Daimler-Benz or by offshoots of large engineering combines.

Until 1967 there were five independent CV firms in Germany; Magirus Deutz which was part of the engineering group Klockner-Humboldt-Deutz; MAN's vehicles and diesel engines are produced by the engineering group of the same name which is in turn a subsidiary of the Gutehoffnungshutte combine; the Rheinstal engineering group brought a theoretically integrated group together in the 1960s comprising of Tempo and Vidal light vans, Hanomag light vans and medium trucks and Henschel heavy vehicles. The state owned Saltzgitter group owned Bussing, and Krupp had its own CV division. All these firms were highly integrated capital intensive manufacturers making their own diesel engines, cabs and running units, although most firms purchased transmission equipment from ZF*. Two small independent companies, Auwarter and Kassbohrer, produced integral buses but most of the running units were bought-out from other vehicle builders or independent component makers. The only firms equivalent to U.K. specialist CV builders were Faun and Kaeble, both made the minimum of components concentrating on the assembly of heavy and super-heavy vehicles.

In 1968 the Saltzgitter group sold to MAN its Bussing subsidiary which had been losing £5 million a year; even more significant was the sale in 1969 of Rheinstal's vehicle interests to Daimler-Benz. 1968 also saw the cessation of CV manufacture by both Krupp and the International Harvester Company. In 1967 Krupp had a vehicle building capacity of over 5000 units a year but only produced 735. International Harvester's performance was even more disastrous in 1967 for the concern was only able to produce and sell 30 vehicles. In the market for vehicles of up to four tons gross weight, the Henschel-Mercedes merger has led to a sharp increase in concentration. This is shown in *Table 5.9*.

Table 5.9

GERMAN COMMERCIAL VEHICLE PRODUCTION IN 1965

Manufacturer	Up to 4 tons	4 to 12 tons	Over 12 tons	Total
Volkswagen	83 444	—	—	83 444
Mercedes	22 245	18 667	17 955	58 867
Ford	19 514	—	—	19 514
Magirus-Deutz	—	4 055	8 226	12 281
MAN	—	3 977	7 903	11 880
Henschel-Hanomag	28 215	279	4 011	32 505
Opel	15 474	—	—	15 474
Others	1 138	1 142	6 500	8 780
Total	170 030	28 120	44 595	242 745

Previously Mercedes, MAN, Deutz and Henschel were of much the same size with a fifth, VW, dominating the market. The merger of Mercedes and Henschel created a much larger grouping which had a range of vehicles which could threaten VW's pre-eminence, and leaving the other two producers in a more vulnerable position. In fact since 1965 this sector of the market has become much more highly concentrated than the table suggests. Much of the Ford output consisted of light lorries, largely assembled from parts made by British

* Zahrradfabrik Friedrichshafen A.G.

Ford. This operation was giving only marginal profits and was phased out. The only commercial vehicles then produced were medium-sized vans. Consequently in 1966 Ford's CV output was only 103 units although this had recovered to 875 by 1967 with the introduction ot German Ford's version of the Transit van. This was a different vehicle to the U.K. model, the only common components being a few body panels and heavy duty axles; clearly a greater degree of integration would have meant lower real costs and prices and perhaps even the production of a superior product. By 1969 it appeared that the German Transit had failed to improve the company's share of German CV production. As a result the German market for vehicles up to four tons is now dominated by just two firms, Mercedes and Volkswagen, with Opel as third with a rather limited range of vehicles. This contrasts strongly with the situation in the U.K. where four highly competitive and efficient CV mass-producers give the British customer a wide choice of vehicles. It would appear that VW is as equally as efficient as British firms and competes strongly with them in foreign markets, but the British producers are able to provide a wider range of vehicles at little extra cost due to the skilful manipulation of a few basic components and body pressings.

In the market for medium-weight trucks *Table 5.9* shows that Mercedes is dominant with over 60% of total output, the only other significant producers being MAN and Magirus-Deutz. Compared with the U.K. producers Ford, Bedford and BMC all the German firms are small scale. Bedford and Ford for instance each produce around 60 000 such vehicles. This explains the readiness of all EEC vehicle producers to support French efforts to exclude CVs from the Kennedy Round of Tariff reductions. Even with a tariff disadvantage of 22% the U.K. mass-producers are competitive in the European market for medium-weight CVs due to the low costs conferred by a volume of 150 000 vehicles a year, as compared with 9000 in France and 28 000 in Germany. In the market for heavy vehicles Mercedes is again the largest firm but somewhat less dominant than in the medium-weight sector, having just over 40% of total production. In the production of heavy vehicles German and U.K. production volumes are very similar, although Mercedes-Benz is clearly the largest heavy vehicle producer in Europe.

The German industry makes a wide range of vehicles but its strength lies in the markets for lighter vehicles at one extreme and for heavier ones at the other. As in France, the West German industry is weak in the medium-weight sector especially in comparison to Britain. For basically similar reasons as the French, no German mass producer makes medium-weight trucks, and no mass-produced light lorries exist. The market for full size vehicles ranging from 2 ton lorries up to 38 ton vehicles is satisfied by CV specialists or, as in the case of Mercedes, by a quality car and CV maker. The vast investment required appears to preclude the mass-producing car firms moving into the CV market with vehicles larger than light and medium weight vans. At the same time none of the quality producers, apart from Mercedes, have the resources or expertise to establish mass production facilities or techniques. It would appear then that the German customer must await the U.K.'s entry into the EEC, or the assembly of U.K. vehicles in Germany, before he is able to purchase a low cost vehicle in the range from 2 to 8 tons payload.

The German CV industry's maximum output was produced in 1964 when the industry manufactured 259 474 units. Between 1964 and 1967 output fell continuously to 186 605 units. In 1964 the U.K. industry made 464 736 units which because of the slow-down in economic growth, plus a fall in exports, fell to 385 106 in 1967.

The significant feature of the German CV industry from the point of view of its overall structure was the high degree of integration of many of the heavy CV makers. For instance, although Mercedes-Benz's CV activities are carried out in three separate plants, nevertheless in terms of the production process they are welded into one modern integrated unit. The main truck assembly plant is at Worth on Rhine (built on the proceeds of Daimler-Benz's share in Auto Union sold to VW), the main bus assembly plant is at Mannheim while most capital intensive components as well as special vehicles are made at Gaggenau. Magirus-Deutz and Henschel make most of their own components as do MAN and Bussing, although they all purchase gearboxes from ZF. As the mass-producers only produce lighter types of CV and most of the heavy vehicle builders are self-sufficient, there is only a limited market for any specialised CV component makers. Consequently small scale assemblers such as Auwarter, Kassbohrer, Faun, and Kaeble have to buy engines from other German CV makers or from abroad. Krupp, in an attempt to put its CV activities on a profitable basis, concluded an agreement with Cummins to produce engines both for its own use and for sale to other producers, thereby providing such firms with an alternative supply source to that provided by the existing vehicle producers. The high degree of integration has led to expensive vehicles, especially as costly high capacity machinery similar to that in the car plants is used for component and cab manufacture. The process of integration is continuing with the decision of MAN and Bussing in 1969 to establish their own gearbox producing capacity to avoid the need of buying out from ZF. It would appear that to justify tooling up to produce engines, gearboxes, axles and so on required in 1971 an output of at least 12 000 a year. This allows production costs per unit to be reduced to a level where the prices charged are profitable and still competitive with those charged by pure assemblers buying components from outside specialists. The 1965 price list, for instance, for Atkinson and Magirus-Deutz for equivalent vehicles in their respective home markets showed that the U.K. vehicles' prices were very similar to those of the German firm. However, the integrated German producer produced over 12 000 vehicles in 1965 compared with 1000 by Atkinson. Since then, a decline in German demand for heavy vehicles due to a slow-down in economic growth between 1964 and 1967 and uncertainty concerning the German Government's transport policy*, had seen a fall in output by all the main makers of large vehicles: subsequently demand and output recovered again. (*Table 5.10*)

Table 5.10

OUTPUT OF COMMERCIAL VEHICLE PRODUCERS

Manufacturer	1965	1967	1969
Bussing	3 534	2 478	3 864
Daimler-Benz	58 867	53 468	91 492
Hanomag	28 395	23 489 ⎫	45 305
Henschel	4 110	2 534 ⎭	
Deutz	12 281	9 062	14 417
MAN	11 880	9 635	12 563

Between 1964 and 1967 some firms were more badly hit than others, Daimler-Benz and MAN improved their share of production but Deutz and Henschel suffered greatly. In terms of shares of the domestic German market Mercedes accounts for 45% of total CV registrations; in the sector for vehicles over six tons gross weight Mercedes is even more dominant having over 50% of the market. In second place is MAN with almost 20% of the market, having overtaken Deutz which had about 14% of the market.

The effects of this decline in total production had been extremely serious for the capital intensive German firms. Most seriously hit was Rheinstal hence the willingness to sell to Mercedes in 1969. The possibility of integrating Rheinstal's and Mercedes's output of major

* For instance, the so called 'Leber Plan' to virtually ban lorries carrying goods long distances; this was biased in favour of the railways.

components would allow significant economies especially to the smaller volume producer Henschel. The integration of Bussing and MAN would allow the same type of improvement with fixed costs being allocated over larger production. In addition, aggregate fixed costs should fall as the production of competing lines of components were phased out and the capital expenditures written off. (Further co-operation exists between MAN and Mercedes in the development of automotive gas turbine engines but development lags behind the U.K. and U.S.A.) Further integration of production occurred in the field of trailers. Unlike the U.K. or France, most trailers used by German hauliers are made by the CV builders. These include Mercedes, Bussing, MAN, Magirus-Deutz, while the only significant independents are the American dominated firms Freuhauf and Blumhardt-Trail-mobile, and the German owned firm Ackerman. Specialised trailers such as tankers and coal wagons are made by firms such as Struver and Krupp respectively. Most of the running units used by the CV firms are made internally but the independent firms buy from the major German axle company BPW or from the Eaton or Rubery Owen factories in the U.K.

In the EEC the German CV industry is dominant although it faces growing competition from Italy and Holland. MAN supplies all Saviem's engines above 140 b.h.p., and in turn MAN has increased its range by selling Renault vans through its own sales organisation. The German industry does not produce such a wide variety of commercial vehicles as the British one and no German firm could compete with the volume and therefore the prices of the British based mass producers of light to medium-heavy 'full size' commercial vehicles. Inside the EEC the U.K. firms would soon dominate this sector and would also more than hold their own in the lightest and heaviest fields. Even outside the EEC British mass producers can still influence the development of the German market. For instance, neither U.S. Ford nor GMC has yet used their British subsidiaries to any great extent as a means of improving their share of the German market, say through the assembly of U.K. designed and produced parts into complete vehicles in their German subsidiaries Opel and Ford Taunus. In 1967, however, General Motors established a separate company in Germany. This firm was to sell Bedford trucks and buses in Germany quite separate from Opel but possibly through the same dealers. This solution to GMC's German CV problems was decided upon after disagreement between Opel's ambitions and the plans of GMC's head office. In Ford's case various plants in the EEC assemble farm tractors from parts and components made in the U.K., this integration of

European activities could point the way towards German Ford assembling and marketing a complete range of British Ford vehicles. Such developments could have serious repercussions for the relatively high cost German (and Continental) CV makers and also for the U.K. CV industry. In the latter's case the output of the CV plants would increase in order to supply the German assembly plants. This would both reduce the real cost of production in the U.K. even further and increase U.K. exports.

One final point concerning the West German motor industry. We have suggested that although the car industry is extremely strong on the marketing, technical and production sides, the CV industry is less strong on the production side when compared to the British. As regards technical development and marketing the U.K. industry also appears to have an edge although on the sales side the Germans dominate the European market, safely protected by the common external tariff of the EEC. Further strength is conferred on the German industry by the size and expertise of the entire German machine tool industry. This manifests itself very clearly in the number of German firms which produce presses and tools required by the motor industry. Little of the equipment needed is bought abroad*, whereas U.K. manufacturers often have to buy abroad either because U.K. engineering firms are unable to supply the sophisticated equipment needed or because their delivery dates are too long.

ITALY

The final major vehicle producing country in the EEC is Italy. The Italian motor industry is unique among the major motor industries of the world in that its growth, prosperity and development depends largely on one firm, Fiat. Another unique feature is that the Italian market is the only major car market without a local American owned firm, but the significance of this has declined with the complete removal of tariff barriers within the EEC and the creation of a European market. We shall return to this point later.

THE STRUCTURE AND DEVELOPMENT OF THE ITALIAN MOTOR INDUSTRY

The Italian motor industry comprises of one giant producer, Fiat, which controls the medium-sized car firm Autobianchi and the

* Although some designs are made under U.S. patents.

commercial vehicle producer OM. Fiat also absorbed Ferrari, the small specialist producer of high performance cars, in 1969, and Lancia in 1970, for a nominal £1041. The rest of the industry is made up of the medium-sized firm, Alfa Romeo, and the general engineering group Innocenti, although the former bought the latter in 1971. Alfa Romeo is state owned and now, through its Innocenti subsidiary, assembles and partly manufactures BMC designs under licence. Innocenti was a large engineering and machine tool complex producing goods ranging from motor scooters to most of the giant body presses used by the Italian motor producers. The latter were made to U.S. designs, similar to those made by Vickers under licence in the U.K. Before being absorbed by Fiat, Lancia was an independent firm falling between mass and custom building. The emphasis on high quality and hand-finishing meant that Lancia did not control its costs as well as it might have done.

The slump in the Italian market in 1964 affected the producers of luxury cars in the over 1500 c.c. class most of all. This was not surprising as production of this type of vehicle had more than trebled between 1961 and 1963. Both Alfa Romeo and Lancia concentrated on this type of car, and with the burden of heavy investment in manufacturing and assembly facilities, a sharp fall in their market would increase unit costs and eliminate profits. As Lancia's direct and unit fixed-costs were already high, the extra burden of further cost increases hit the company very hard. The company's recovery after 1964 was slow and 1969 saw the company in a very vulnerable financial position with output at less than half the company's capacity of 100 000 units.

However, Fiat, Alfa Romeo and Innocenti had prospered during the boom in the Italian market which began in 1965 and which was still evident in 1971, and there did not appear to be any compelling reason for Innocenti's merger with Alfa Romeo. The remaining manufacturers such as Maserati, Ferrari, Lamborghini, Iso and Abarth produce high performance sports and touring cars. Maserati was purchased by Citroen in late 1968 and together with Fiat's absorption of first Ferrari and then Citroen has meant that both Ferrari and Maserati came under Fiat's control. Lamborghini is the prestige motor car division of an agricultural tractor making group, rather analogous to the position of Aston Martin in the U.K.

Other small firms such as Iso, Abarth or OSCA produce exotic high performance vehicles. Often production is highly integrated although a number of firms are mainly assemblers. The low capital investment of such firms, even the integrated ones which still largely hand-build major components such as engines or axles, allow them to withstand slumps in the market. At the same time, increased national income does not in itself allow these firms to increase production significantly as their labour intensive production methods preclude a rapid build-up of output volumes. Hence firms such as Ferrari and Maserati tend to have a steady output figure of 500 units a year allied to an order book of varying length. Occasionally a severe slump leads to such a large cancellation of orders that actual production schedules are revised downwards. In such an event the low fixed-costs of labour-intensive assembly and manufacture allow a firm a great deal of flexibility as regards profitable output levels.

The changing output of the Italian motor industry over the period 1946 to 1969 is shown in *Table 5.11*. The rapid growth in the annual

Table 5.11

ITALIAN VEHICLE PRODUCTION 1946–1969

Year	Cars	Commercial vehicles	Total
1946	10 989	17 994	28 983
1950	101 310	26 537	127 847
1960	595 907	48 710	644 617
1967	1 439 211	103 458	1 542 669
1969	1 477 366	118 585	1 595 951

total output has been during the 1960s. The industry developed from a medium-sized operation into a large one and by 1967, in terms of car production, it was almost comparable in size to the French and U.K. industries. By 1968 the industry provided employment, directly or indirectly, for 2·3 million people or 18% of total Italian employment in industry and services, and the Fiat group alone employed almost 160 000 people.

FIAT: AN INDUSTRY IN ITSELF

Of the individual manufacturers Fiat was clearly the largest. It was in effect the only large scale Italian producer, as all other firms were either medium scale or small scale (*Table 5.12*).

Fiat accounts for a massive proportion of the total output of the Italian motor industry at 87·5%. This situation is unique in that no other of the world's major car producing countries has such dominance

Table 5.12

ITALIAN VEHICLE PRODUCTION IN 1967

Manufacturer	Cars	Commercial vehicles
Fiat	1 233 892	78 323
Autobianchi	37 778	2 948
OM	—	17 947
Alfa Romeo	76 831	1 987
Lancia	43 172	1 464
Innocenti	46 026	—
Others	1 512	67
Total	1 439 211	102 736

by one firm. In terms of Fiat's share of the Italian market the situation is somewhat different, due to the existence of imports and because of Fiat's higher export ratio compared with the Italian medium-sized firms. In 1963, when the tariff reductions within the EEC began to have real effect, Fiat's share of the home market had fallen to 63% compared with a post-war norm of 90% before the creation of the EEC. By 1968 this share had climbed back to 75%, despite the lowering and final abolition of EEC tariff barriers and expensive attempts by all-comers to establish themselves in the Italian market. This relative recovery was due mainly to the huge expansion of capacity undertaken by Fiat and partly to Italian government help. For instance, in 1964, in an attempt to curb consumer spending, the Government introduced stiff import levies which were responsible for destroying a promising sales drive by U.K. Ford. Fiat's maintenance of its market share at between 70 and 75% means that as the Italian economy expands rapidly so does Fiat's sales and productive capacity. The Italian motor industry and motor market is like all other major motor industries in that output is concentrated into very few hands, and the Italian industry presents the most extreme example of this, with the largest firm approaching a position of monopoly.

The period 1946–1970 did not see any significant-volume car producer leave the industry and there was only one entry, that being Innocenti. However, both Lancia and Innocenti, together with a number of smaller firms, were absorbed by larger competitors.

The fact that Italian motor cars are taxed by the cubic capacity of their engines and real incomes in Italy are low by West European standards has meant that the bulk of production comprises of cars up to 1000 c.c. (*Table 5.12*).

Table 5.12

PERCENTAGE OF CAR PRODUCTION
BY ENGINE SIZE (1967)

Engine size	%
Up to 1000 c.c.	58
1000 c.c. to 1500 c.c.	33
Over 1500 c.c.	9

The comparatively low level of per capita real incomes allied to the fast growth rate of the economy indicates that the Italian car market should be the fastest growing in Europe during the 1970s. In 1967 the total car population was only $7\frac{1}{4}$ million compared with $10\frac{1}{2}$ million in France and the U.K. In terms of car densities the number of cars per 1000 people in Italy in 1967 was less than 140 compared with over 200 in France. The growth in demand should be for all types of cars, for small ones as new customers enter the market and for larger types due to the graduation of existing owners to larger and more expensive types. Such an event should help both the main Italian firms especially Fiat. Why should this be?

Foreign firms point to the size of Fiat's home market as the main cause of its success in the 1960s. A market which was growing quickly allowed Fiat to introduce new models, production techniques and equipment with the certainty that the investment involved would be justified by the sales made. The existence of a large home market also allowed the maintenance of high production levels which in turn allowed full utilisation of capacity and therefore low cost production. This allows low prices to be charged at home and abroad which should have further favourable effects on demand. The characteristics of the Italian market, as well as its size, proved valuable in making Fiat such a formidable organisation. Due to the economic factor of relatively low real incomes and the physical factor of many narrow roads—especially in towns—Italy is a small-car market. At the same time the Italian customer wanted high performance even from the smallest motor car. Consequently the bulk of Fiat's output consists of small, high performance cars—which was the type of vehicle which became so fashionable in the rest of Europe during the 1960s.

FIAT THINKS EUROPEAN

Until about 1960 Fiat put its foreign sales effort more on partly- or
wholly-owned firms outside Italy rather than on direct exports. This
policy gave Fiat a 10% stake in NSU in Germany, and Fiat's licencee
in Spain, Seat, in the late 1960s had 57% of the Spanish car market,
with a production level greater than Vauxhall's. This type of policy
allowed Fiat to engage in enormous deals in the U.S.S.R. to build
integrated car plants, and to a lesser extent with other East European
countries. However, the neglect of direct exporting left Fiat without a
good sales and service organisation in many important markets,
particularly in Europe. Since 1960, and more particularly since 1965,
this defect has been remedied and direct exports have soared. This
change coincided with a change in Fiat's organisational structure,
whereby younger executives were given a free hand in independent
jobs at ages younger than was Fiat's normal practice, and induced the
company to think in terms of gaining a very large proportion of all
EEC car sales. This contrasted with Fiat's earlier obsession with the
American car industry's financial and physical dominance and its
desire for a European cartel to prevent further U.S. penetration. The
instalment of the younger and outward looking Signor Giovanni
Agnelli as chairman of Fiat signalled the elimination of defensive
mindedness in favour of aggression.

As Fiat's sales horizons have widened so has the model range. Apart
from British Leyland, Fiat is the only European producer to produce
a range of cars spreading from small 500 c.c. saloons to luxury Ferrari-
engined cars of 2·5 litres. While firms, like VW trying to rid itself
of the 'beetle' image, introduce completely new models, Fiat keeps its
existing models up to date by gradual alterations and by exchanging
parts between different models. At the same time, one or two new
models are introduced and by the same process of interchange and
development give rise to many different variations.

This policy in regard to the development of new models cuts both
development costs and the gestation period. Most European companies
take three to four years to take a car from the drawing board into
production. Fiat do the job in about 2½ years by incorporating many
existing ideas and components. For instance, in 1964, with a slump on the
horizon, plans for a 1000 c.c. car were scrapped and an 'economy' model
of 850 c.c. was quickly developed in its place. Very few firms could
successfully change course in mid-stream as Fiat did in this instance.

Until the mid-1960s Fiat was essentially an Italian company in that its product planning, marketing and pricing policy was dictated by the conditions in the Italian market. Up to this time the company was too busy satisfying home demand to pay much attention to exports, for between 1950 and 1968 the Italian market had grown fifteenfold. It could be that despite the figures previously quoted concerning vehicle population, vehicle density and the fact that Italian average incomes are still way below the West European norm, the short-term prospects of a growing Italian market are not good. This is mainly because of the sharp dichotomy of Italy into the prosperous North and the under-developed South. Taking northern Italy alone the market would have similar real income levels and vehicle densities to the rest of Western Europe, therefore potential growth is lower than the all-Italy data would suggest. On the other hand, the southern market provides a long-term growth market, but it could be ten years before income levels increase sufficiently for people there to consider buying cars in any great numbers. So considering the lack of effective demand in the south, the Italian market may be approaching temporary saturation. In 1968, 75% of Fiat's domestic sales were replacement deals*, and the company expected its turnover to increase by 6% a year over the next four years compared with the 15% to 20% of the period 1958–1968. If growth in domestic sales does level off during the 1970s the company has endeavoured to sustain former growth patterns through increased exports. As an exporter Fiat is proving very success-ful, as shown in Chapter 11. The ever-widening range of vehicles, high volume production and long-lived models allow low-cost production and successful marketing. Although the company is not strike free, labour-relations are generally good and conducive to the maintenance of smooth production runs. During the late 1960s Fiat spent more on its foreign sales and service network than any other European motor company.

Financially and economically Fiat is an impressive organisation. Despite the fact that over 70% of Fiat's output consists of cars of under 1000 c.c. which are priced at between £300 and £460 in Italy (prices which include dealers margins of about 15% and a sales tax of about 12%) and on which Fiat's profit margins must be quite small, the sheer volume of output and the long life and amortisation period given to each model generates a sufficient cash flow to compensate for the low percentage margin. Huge investment projects are financed which still

---

* Earlier we mentioned that of every 10 cars sold in Italy only 2 replaced scrapped vehicles compared with 7 in the U.S.A. Here we are talking about replacement sales *per se* with no mention of scrapping; after all, most replaced vehicles in a market like Italy's will be snapped-up in the second-hand car market by low income customers.

leave large pre-tax profits. *Table 5.13* shows the comparable position for three different firms in 1967.

Table 5.13

FINANCIAL POSITION OF THREE MAJOR EUROPEAN PRODUCERS (£ MILLION)

Firm	Sales	Pre-tax profit and depreciation	% on sales	Pre-tax profit	% on sales
Fiat	£796	£80	10	£66	8·3
BMH	£467	£9·8	2·1	—£3·2	—0·7
Leyland	£305	£27	9	£18	5·9

Fiat's return on sales was even greater than that of a highly efficient producer such as Leyland which traditionally added a high profit margin to each unit. Fiat has, however, gradually moved away from the small 500 c.c. and 600 c.c. cars that were its staple product between 1954 and 1964. They still account for over 50% of turnover and abroad they are the cheapest and smallest cars available in most markets and they have no serious competitors, but because they did not show much profit the policy of the 1960s was to steadily introduce larger and larger cars. Between 1960 and 1967 this policy was very successful for cars up to 2000 c.c., at which point Fiat came up against competition from such firms as Citroen, Mercedes, BMW and Volvo and in the event the company did not do very well with its larger vehicles. Since 1967, however, the introduction of 2·3 litre coupes and 2·5 litre Ferrari engined coupes has allowed the firm to make some progress. Fiat's greatest success nevertheless is in the range between 500 c.c. and 1·6 litres, with prices ranging between £300 and £750 in Italy, while it hopes to use its Lancia subsidiary to compete with the other quality car makers of Europe.

THE OTHER ITALIAN PRODUCERS

Much space has been used to discuss Fiat because Fiat is in many ways *the* Italian motor industry. This contention is reinforced by an examination of the overall structure of the Italian motor industry and the Italian CV industry, although the firm producing the remaining 8% or so of Italian car output is significant in some ways. Alfa Romeo's current output is around 77 000 cars a year, and comprises three basic models in the 1300 to 2600 c.c. range. Traditionally Alfa Romeo and

Lancia competed for the market in high performance quality cars of between 1 and 3 litres, and this market was left to these two firms until the 1960s when Fiat began to strengthen its range of cars in the 1·5+ litre category. During the 1960s Fiat was not strong in the prestige saloon market but the link with Citroen and the absorption of Lancia gave the company a ready made range of 2 litre saloons. Any plans to market or even assemble Citroen vehicles on a large scale would pose a threat to Alfa Romeo which may have been one reason why Alfa wished to absorb Innocenti and thereby strengthen its vehicle range. Furthermore, by 1970 it was evident that the state-controlled Alfa Romeo company was attempting to turn itself into a large-scale producer of small-medium saloons as well as maintaining its traditional range of quality cars. This explains the establishment of a large integrated car plant at Pamigliano d'Arco near Naples in impoverished southern Italy. Completed in 1971, the plant has an annual capacity of 300 000 cars and at full capacity it employs 15 000. This will create another 7000 jobs in newly established ancillary activities in the area and will cause further increases in income.

Fiat condemned the move as creating over-capacity in the Italian industry but it marks the emergence of significant competition in the Fiat-dominated sector for cars of between 1 litre and 1·4 litres for the first time. Fiat criticised as over optimistic Alfa Romeo's market research which forecast that the number of cars in Italy would increase from 122 per 1000 in 1966 to 200 per 1000 in 1981. However, by 1967 the figure had already increased to around 140, so even if the growth rate falls considerably the Alfa Romeo estimate could easily be attained and indeed exceeded.

Traditionally Fiat has had a pessimistic outlook towards marketing conditions. The emergence of younger executives in the mid-1960s largely changed this but a residue remains, especially concerning short-term prospects in the Italian market. One suspects the main motivation behind Fiat's hostility was not so much fear of Alfa-Romeo creating excess capacity in the industry, but dislike of the prospect of having a reasonably large-scale domestic competitor for the first time. Fiat would then face competition on the two fronts of home and abroad for the first time.

The opportunities open to a vigorous firm armed with a competitive range of products in the small and medium car markets was exemplified by Innocenti. The rise from a position of obscurity in 1960 to an output greater than Lancia's in 1967 was achieved by producing three BMC models in the 800 to 1100 c.c. range. Most of the expensive components such as body pressings, engines and axles were imported from the U.K. for assembly in Italy, and despite the effects of tariff barriers inflating prices, Innocenti's output and share of the market increased steadily during the 1960s.

THE RANGE OF VEHICLES

The Italian industry produces a wide range of vehicles and not simply because of Fiat's contribution. Engine capacity for the mass produced vehicles is in the 500 to 2800 c.c. range, and in 1967 all but 5867 of the 1 439 211 cars built were in the under 2 litre category. This was partly due to the fact that Italy, like France, taxes a car by the cubic capacity of its engine—hence the very high taxation on cars over 2 litres*. Cars over 3 litres are produced by firms such as Ferrari, Maserati and Lamborghini for customers who are affluent enough to completely discount vehicle taxation. Alfa Romeo at present concentrates on traditional sports machines featuring engines of between 1300 c.c. and 2600 c.c. and in many cases special bodies by specialist producers. Fiat's Autobianchi subsidiary produce two basic models both with Fiat engines. Lancia produce high performance and large quality-built saloons of between 1100 and 2800 c.c. Innocenti produces family saloons of 850 and 1100 c.c.

Fiat alone covers all the vehicle ranges made by the other producers. In 1970 the daily output of about 5000 cars consisted of small family saloons between 500 and 850 c.c. medium-size vehicles of between 1100 and 1600 c.c., and larger vehicles of up to 2300 c.c. In addition, a range of sports coupes are manufactured, the largest incorporating a Ferrari designed engine. Retail prices in the Italian market range from the Fiat 500, 600 and 850 saloons at £300, £368 and £459 respectively, to £760 for a medium-size Fiat of 1500 c.c.; an Alfa Romeo or Lancia vehicle of 1·3 litres costs over £1300 which is equivalent to a Fiat saloon of over 2000 c.c. Specialised machines produced by Ferrari or Maserati cost between £4000 and £7000.

* For instance, in 1970 the tax on a Fiat 500 c.c. model was about £5, that on a 1000 c.c. model over £15, the tax on a 1500 c.c. car was almost £50, on a 2 litre over £50, and that on a 4 litre over £140! So the larger the car the disproportionately heavier the tax burden.

ORGANISATION: ITALY LACKS AN INDEPENDENT COMPONENTS
INDUSTRY

Turning now to the overall structure of the Italian motor industry
where the degree of vertical integration varies greatly between Fiat on
the one hand and the other major producers on the other. Amongst the
major European producers Fiat probably attains the highest degree of
self-sufficiency. This is due to the economic history of Italy and the
traditional dominance of Fiat in the engineering sector. The backward
nature of the Italian economy with its small industrial base during the
first half of the twentieth century meant that a motor producer had to
make the most of his own requirements as there were no outside
firms in a position to do so. This situation has in fact continued in
Fiat's case, for the firm is too large in relation to Italian industry
generally for any other producer to be in a position of being able to
satisfy Fiat's needs. So the tradition of self-sufficiency has been reinforced during the rapid post-war expansion of Fiat in particular and
the Italian motor industry in general. Hence Fiat, or the subsidiaries
and affiliates it has established over the years, makes most of its own
electrical parts, brakes, carburettors, diesel injections and injection
pumps, rubber products, paint and enamel. In addition, the firm has its
own steel making complex which ranges from blast furnaces and strip
mills through to foundries and forges; this allows Fiat to convert
ingots into various finished products. The company has the most
elaborate organisation for metal making and shaping of any motor
vehicle producer in the world. This applies not only to steel, but to
castings in iron and aluminium, and tubes, sheets and wires in a variety
of metals as well. Of the 158 000 people employed by the Fiat complex,
over 120 000 are employed in the complex of plants scattered in and
around Turin, which means that in excess of 50% of the city's population is dependent on Fiat in one way or another. It must also be
remembered that about 10% of turnover is derived from activities
unconnected with vehicle building such as aircraft manufacture, civil
engineering and construction, railway equipment and nuclear energy
equipment.

In some ways this self-sufficiency has had drawbacks in that Fiat
has been unwilling to take bold technical advances in processes outside
its own control. After 1966, however, with the advent of Fiat's younger
management, this was no longer the case. The new willingness to
accept recent advances was shown by the fact that although for years
Pirelli had sold radial-ply tyres to many Italian and other motor

makers, Fiat had remained aloof, but after 1966 radial-ply tyres were used. Again, Fiat had the designs to build transverse engined front wheel drive vehicles on a mass-production basis at the same time as BMC, but seemingly not the will power; however, 1969 saw the introduction of the Fiat 128 built to this design to compete with the Peugeot 204 within the EEC and the Innocenti 1100 in Italy. Any disadvantages such reticence had was of course overshadowed by Fiat's ability to control cost and quality at all stages of motor manufacture, from the metal-making and shaping processes to final assembly.

The presence of Fiat had placed smaller companies like Alfa Romeo and Lancia in a difficult position. They were too small to have their own components industry, either directly controlled or outside specialist. Any attempt to establish such organisations would have entailed huge investments and such high unit costs of production that to cover them prices would have been at such a level as to price the companies out of the market. The items they did make, such as engines, transmission units and bodies, imposed higher unit costs of production which Lancia and Alfa Romeo tried to hide through better quality. Other components they either had to buy from Fiat or as in most cases from Germany, France and the U.K. The abolition of EEC tariff barriers plus the Kennedy Round reduction in the common external tariff was a godsend to the smaller Italian makers in that they were able to buy items at a reasonable cost. This alone, however, was insufficient to save Lancia. Innocenti was the least integrated major Italian producer, being mainly an assembler of parts produced in the U.K., but as output increased more items were manufactured as and when it became economic to do so. The merger with Alfa Romeo could mean a sharp increase in the manufactured content. However, one of the few areas where outside firms are significant is in the production of wheels where three firms supply most of the industry.

One sector which is wholly in the hands of outside firms is tyre production where firms such as Pirelli and Goodyear are dominant. Another prosperous sector is that of the independent bodybuilder. Most of the Italian industry's body requirements are supplied by the car firms themselves, but models with small production runs have bodies produced by independent specialists. For instance, many Alfa Romeo and Lancia vehicles are bodied by firms such as Bertone, Ghia, Zagato, Vignale or Pininfarina. In the case of the specialist cars such as Ferrari, Maserati or Abarth the independent bodybuilder supplies the majority or even all of the car firms' needs. In total there are over forty specialist bodybuilders operating in Italy. These firms have a worldwide reputation and the Italian flair for imaginative thinking has given Italy the world leadership in body styling. Hence many foreign car firms produce cars with bodies either made or designed in Italy—Aston Martin, BMC, Triumph, VW and Peugeot, to name but a few, are firms which have done this.

COMMERCIAL VEHICLES

Again the dominant name is Fiat and its subsidiary OM. Other builders are Alfa Romeo, together with a very small number of vehicles made by the trailer maker OMT, the latter being fitted with AEC diesel engines. There are also Meridicinali 'Aerfer' and Viberti, two firms making buses of integral construction mainly incorporating Fiat mechanical components. Lancia's production was quickly phased out by Fiat.

Fiat was even more dominant on the commercial vehicle side than it was in the car market, producing over 96% of Italian vehicles and accounting for the same proportion of vehicles annually newly registered in Italy. This position had been maintained during the 1960s despite the reduction of the EEC tariff to zero. Fiat and OM dominate the medium-van and pick-up market and this position is repeated right up to the heaviest vehicles. Fiat and Autobianchi dominate the light-van sector. OM was purchased by Fiat before World War II, and as little integration took place, OM had operated as a vigorous competitor to Fiat in the CV market. Even as regards very important items such as engines, little standardisation occurred, with OM building diesels under licence from the Swiss Saurer concern and in return allowing the Swiss company to sell its vans in Switzerland. However, after 1966 a slow process of component standardisation occurred, as well as a degree of product standardisation, with OM specialising at the smaller end of the range. Despite this the two firms have a difference in outlook in both marketing and production. OM sells through eighty of its own specialised dealers quite independent of the Fiat sales network. Each dealer has a large area to cover in order to give him sufficient turnover and profits to make it worthwhile specialising on the sale of OM vehicles. OM is much less self-sufficient than is usual in the Fiat complex, for instance its engine research is done by Saurer in Switzerland. The company is not very interested in establishing its own sales network abroad, unlike Fiat's policy in the late 1960s, and any foreign sales are made through other companies, for instance, OM supplies vans to Unic, its French sister company, and vans are sold by Saurer in Switzerland. So in many ways the company leads an independent existence which is exemplified by the fact that OM is geographically separated from Fiat, being established in Brescia, some 200 kilometres from Turin.

The present state of the Italian market points to a prosperous future for Italian commercial vehicle production. Over 35% of all trucks in Italy are over 10 years old, and the market is still underdeveloped compared with other European markets. It was only in the late 1960s that many Italian tradesmen and merchants were able to afford a medium-weight van or pick-up of any sort, whereas others were for the first time in a position to buy medium-weight vans of between one ton and two tons carrying capacity. To take advantage of this growth in the market, OM expanded its productive capacity and simultaneously strengthened its range of medium-weight vans and light trucks.

Fiat also expanded its capacity and by doing so was installing fully developed transfer lines for the production of major CV components for the first time. In fact it may have been that Fiat remained committed to labour intensive and under-capitalised manufacturing and assembly techniques for rather too long. Until 1960 the volume of CV production did not justify the use of faster, more specialised, and expensive equipment; however, after 1960 the position had changed. Yet it was not until 1968 that production techniques were changed to more capital intensive methods which, although initially expensive, allowed the new higher production levels to be manufactured at lower unit cost. In terms of heavy vehicle production Fiat's unit costs in 1970 were probably still higher than the output leaders in Europe, Mercedes-Benz and Leyland. In the medium-weight sector Fiat was second only to Mercedes on the continent, but neither firm could compete with the output volumes and unit costs of production experienced by the British based mass producers.

In terms of exports most of Fiat's growth has been in sales to third markets, mainly in Asia and Africa. In Europe the company finds it hard to compete with Mercedes-Benz but nevertheless the Italian company is gradually expanding its EEC sales. Most sales are made in France where Fiat has both its Unic subsidiary and its own sales and service organisation. The French market was vulnerable to foreign penetration once the EEC tariff walls were first reduced and then eliminated, hence the successful sales drive made by German and Italian makers, and by Dutch and Swedish manufacturers. Fiat had the same flexible approach to exporting as Leyland, if it could not sell complete vehicles in a market because of local restrictions it would establish local assembly plants which were either wholly or partly owned. Again, Fiat has been satisfied in just selling expertise and content with a steady royalty income.

In terms of production the Italian industry has expanded rapidly as shown in *Table 5.14*, but in terms of total output the industry is much

Table 5.14

COMMERCIAL VEHICLE OUTPUT

Year	1946	1950	1960	1965	1966	1967	1969
Number	17 994	26 537	48 710	71 616	81 512	103 458	111 585

smaller than that in France, West Germany, or the U.K. This reflects the growth potential remaining in the Italian market and also the low level of Italian CV exports in the 1960s. Both these markets can be expected to expand and most of the expansion will be met by Fiat; consequently Fiat's growth potential on the CV side is extremely great. If we consider that Italian production by 1980 is likely to exceed 200 000 units, Fiat's output would be of the same order and therefore the company would be the largest CV producer in Europe. Over 100 000 units would comprise of light-vans, medium-vans and pick-ups, but close on 60 000 medium-weight trucks and 40 000 heavy vehicles could be produced. As a result Fiat and perhaps Mercedes-Benz would be in a position to challenge U.K. supremecy in the medium-weight sector, and Fiat would be a match for Mercedes and Leyland in the heavy-weight sector. It is possible that a larger part of the Italian market will fall into the hands of foreign producers, or even into the hands of Alfa Romeo, if they establish links with other firms to produce vehicles under licence. This would reduce Fiat's growth potential but even so the company should develop into one of Europe's dominant CV makers during the 1970s, and take up position alongside Leyland, Mercedes, Bedford, and U.K. Ford. Indeed Fiat guards its own base vigorously and cuts prices savagely if the need arises; in the CV market it is quite prepared to use short-run price reductions as a market weapon.

Alfa Romeo and Lancia made a few commercial vehicles, as shown in *Table 5.15*. Unlike in the U.K., there is virtually no sector filled by independent specialists. Alfa Romeo makes medium-weight vans and pick-ups for carrying loads up to two tons, plus a few large buses. The company has had links with the French Renault group and it is possible that light- to medium-weight trucks could be produced under licence. Before its absorption by Fiat, Lancia produced medium-weight vans and pick-ups, medium-weight trucks and large buses. So in neither case

Table 5.15

COMMERCIAL VEHICLE OUTPUT IN 1967 AND 1969

Firm	1967	1969
Fiat	78 123	91 953
OM	18 169	19 198
Autobianchi	2 948	2 982
Total	99 240	114 133
Lancia	1 464	1 710
Alfa Romeo	1 987	2 698
Others	67	44
Total	102 758	118 585

did these small producers manufacture a wide range of vehicles or in any number.

Turning briefly to the range of vehicles produced. Apart from the small number of vehicles produced by Alfa Romeo, the range of vehicles made by the Italian industry is dependent on the range of vehicles made by Fiat-OM. As in the case of cars it is Fiat and Leyland which produce the most varied range of commercial vehicles made by any producer in the European motor industry. Fiat and OM together make vehicles covering every size from 5 cwt. vans to 46 ton road trains. A wide variety of types are available in the medium-weight van and pick-up category, in the light, medium and heavy truck sectors, and a wide selection of bus chassis. Compared with the situation in the U.K. the Italian range of vehicles in the medium-weight sector is relatively weak and a greater choice of heavy vehicles are available in both the U.K. and West Germany. However, the range and quality of the Italian CV industry has been widened continuously and should allow Italy to compete strongly in the EEC and world markets.

As the industry is dominated by the self-sufficient Fiat group there is little scope for specialist outside suppliers. All the vehicle producers make their own engines and major components, although OM use a number of foreign designs. Alfa Romeo and Lancia purchased items such as diesel injector pumps from outside sources either from Bosch in Germany or Lucas in the U.K. If these two firms did not make an item themselves they had to purchase it from abroad or from Fiat. The market left for any outside supplier, after Fiat's self-sufficiency is taken into account, is not large enough to justify investment in production facilities or research. Profitable prices would be easily undercut by foreign producers or by Fiat★.

Apart from the production of tyres and wheels, the only significant sectors connected with the industry which are not part of the CV makers own activities are bodybuilding and trailer production. Trailer production is carried out by 15 firms, the dominant ones being OMT, Orlandi and Viberti. These firms are also concerned with container production but here the output leader is Fiat with an annual production of almost 20 000 units. Many vehicles are bodied not by the chassis builder but by independent specialists such as Viberti in the bus field or Talenti in the goods vehicle sector.

BENELUX

The three continental countries so far discussed covers all the domestic-ally owned motor production in the EEC apart from DAF† in Holland and Miesse in Belgium. So just a word about the Benelux motor industry.

BELGIUM

In 1969, over 767 000 vehicles were assembled or produced in Belgium. The vast majority were assembled from imported parts by Ford, GMC, Moskvitch, and the Leyland subsidiaries of Brossel Frere and Standard-Triumph. Only the small Miesse CV firm was a Belgian company and many of the major components used by this producer came from the U.K. In effect there was no Belgian-owned car industry and virtually no commercial vehicle industry.

THE NETHERLANDS

In the Netherlands the situation was slightly different. The Swedish CV firm Scania owns an assembly plant while the Verheul bodybuild-ing and CV company is a subsidiary of British Leyland, and in 1969 these and other assembly plants made just under 33 000 vehicles

---

★ When OMT tried to break into the truck market it purchased diesel engines from AEC in the U.K.

† Van Doorne's Automobielfabriek.

including over 26 000 cars. However, over 71 000 vehicles were manufactured by Dutch owned companies mainly by DAF, but also by Van Hool who used Fiat running units. DAF was by far the largest Dutch producer and its total output of just over 8000 commercial vehicles and 60 000 cars was roughly similar to that of Saab-Scania of Sweden who produced 12 000 commercial vehicles and 50 000 cars a year in the late 1960s.

DAF is a highly integrated firm although most of the major components are based on Leyland designs, albeit highly modified and developed. The company before 1939 only produced trailers, and between 1945 and 1950 the company's expansion was based on the growing trailer market. In 1950 the first commercial vehicles were made after the firm was given an order by the Dutch army. Initially, operations were largely based on the final assembly of Leyland components, but as output expanded more and more components and sub-assemblies were manufactured. Of the 6000 vehicles made in 1967, over 4000 were in the over 12 tons gross sector and the company held over 60% of the Dutch market for heavy vehicles in the late 1960s. On this solid CV producing base DAF first produced its own motor car in 1959.

The cars were a gamble on an idea: the use of automatic transmission in a small car by a unique type of transmission system designed by the DAF company. The original 600 c.c. vehicle made steady progress with annual sales around 18 000. In 1966 a redesigned vehicle with the engine enlarged to 800 c.c. was introduced, and this larger vehicle was able to tap a much wider market. In 1967 this larger vehicle sold 30 000 units compared with 20 000 for the original design which still remained in production. In 1968 a larger 1100 c.c. car was introduced and to avoid the heavy cost of time and money on design and research, a version of the French Renault 1100 c.c. engine was used. Total car making capacity was in 1971 in the region of 100 000 units a year. It would appear that firms producing between 50 000 and 100 000 vehicles a year can only survive by purchasing from outside those major components which cost vast sums to develop and to produce. Such firms can only survive by keeping internal production to a minimum and by buying-out over 70% of a car's value; in this way they are able to continue as firms mainly engaged on assembly. Saab of Sweden in the late 1960s bought their engine requirements from German Ford and British Leyland, Rover purchased a redundant GMC engine of advanced design and DAF purchased a unit developed by Renault. Although the optimum size of output on the assembly process is over 200 000 a year, that for engine production is over

1·25 million, so small firms make some savings by utilising the research expenditures made by giant firms. Add this to very long-lived production runs for all major body and mechanical components, and unit costs are controlled at a level not too much in excess of those experienced by the giant producers. DAF has succeeded in its gamble and in a period of 10 years it established itself as a car producer. The company in 1970 held fourth place in the Dutch market after Volkswagen, Fiat, and Opel, and sales within the EEC expanded as fast as the growth in the sales and service network would allow.

Ingenuity and drive partly explain the company's success but other crucial factors also played a part. The solid financial base provided by its CV operation was used to back a modest yet expensive entry into the car business. Another reason why cars and not CVs became DAF's main cause for expansion in 1967 was the injection of capital from three outside sources. These were the Dutch Government, Dutch State Mines, and the European Coal and Steel Community. The government provided a £12 million guarantee, the Mines took a 25% shareholding in DAF, and the ECSC lent £4 million. The reason for all this was the need to provide alternative employment for miners. When the Limburg Mine closed, DAF was prevailed upon to build a new car plant in the town for a new car model. All the men employed in the new plant were ex-miners. DAF's total employment amounted to 8500 people in 1970 based on the original Eindhoven plant and the new Limburg factory. Future plans to allow Eindhoven to revert to its original role as exclusively a CV production centre by transferring all car production to Limburg will allow DAF more CV capacity and will also allow the Limburg plant to move towards the optimum level for assembly operations. So the 1960s had seen the emergence of a new European producer of some importance; but what of the EEC motor industry as a whole?

THE EUROPEAN MOTOR INDUSTRY: A SUMMARY

Since 1968 there has been a dramatic acceleration in the pace of mergers, co-operation schemes and rationalisation in the European motor industry. This reflects the completion of the EEC's customs union which has had two effects*. Firstly, national producers have tended to co-operate more closely in order to strengthen their enterprises and therefore to be able to withstand the competition from other

* The creation of a customs union is merely a stage in the process of creating a European Economic Community.

European producers which followed from the elimination of tariffs and quotas. Secondly, as trading barriers were removed the prospect of creating a truly European industry faced with one large domestic market became a reality. This increased the attraction of creating a European-wide industry through international mergers or by foreign investment.

Following its creation in 1968 British Leyland has improved its European sales organisation and given priority to the expansion of productive capacity in Belgium within the EEC. The Fiat-Citroen plan for a full merger was thwarted by the French government but nevertheless Fiat initially gained a 20% stake in Citroen which can only be a prelude to a full merger. Daimler-Benz, having already absorbed Krupp's truck-marketing organisation, absorbed Henschel-Hanomag to maintain its position as the EEC's strongest truck builder. Peugeot's agreement with Renault began to bear fruit in 1969 with the production of a jointly owned engine plant near Lille. In the same year the independent German company NSU was absorbed by VW. Hence the number of separate car (and CV) companies in Europe tended to fall appreciably during 1968 and 1969.

From over 40 independent European car firms in 1960 the typical process of concentration is polarising around one national grouping in each country plus three American firms. This would mean seven firms at the most, one British, one French, one Italian and one German, plus GMC, Chrysler and Ford in Europe. This process is virtually complete in the U.K. and France, and was almost complete before it began in Italy, but there is still some way to go in Germany where three significant German-owned firms still remain. Within this movement there could be some international mergers. For instance, NSU was sought after by Fiat of Italy, Chrysler of America, Honda of Japan, and VW. In this VW won and the purchase was part of the process to establish one German giant car producer. However, in the case of Citroen no agreement could be found which suited either Citroen or the other French firms; as a result we then had the makings of a pan-European firm when Fiat was left as the only saviour of the ailing French concern.

THE EEC BECOMES THE DOMESTIC MARKET

Already by 1969 over 75% of the entire western European car market was in the hands of just seven producers. *Table 5.16* shows this situation, but ignores the production of cars for export to the rest of the world.

This would, for instance, put VW in top place as regards total production but because of the size of the firm's American market it is placed fourth in the penetration of the European market.

Table 5.16

MAJOR DOMESTIC CAR PRODUCERS

Fiat	18·9%
Ford	11·6%
GMC	11·1%
VW	10·6%
Leyland	8·5%
Renault	8·4%
Chrysler	6·5%
Others	24·4%

At present Fiat is the strongest, most aggressive and most successful European company. Its share of EEC sales have increased steadily over the past four years and currently stand at 25% compared with Renault's 12%. In every EEC market Fiat leads the list of importers, for instance, it is ahead of Opel in France, and in front of Renault in Germany. Fiat's marketing and prices were almost unequalled in the EEC during the later half of the 1960s. The company has been the largest investor in the development of a foreign sales network especially in Europe. This was all part of the company's plan to establish a pan-European enterprise. Although Fiat's present unassailable share of the Italian market may be challenged by Alfa Romeo, and although the sales of 500 and 600 c.c. Fiats in Italy make the company appear more dominant than it is in financial terms, the fact remains that Fiat is the major threat to all EEC domestic producers. This is because of its excellent marketing facilities and because of its profitable Italian base, which allows most overheads to be covered from domestic sales* and Fiat to sell at very competitive but profitable prices in the rest of Europe. The company can cater for every European market in terms of geography and in terms of income groups. Fiat produces more versions of each group of models than any other firm; the models range from the 500 c.c. 'basic motoring' model to the 2·8 litre Fiat 130 prestige saloon, in addition to which are the Lancia and Ferrari models. Fiat can therefore compete with Renault at one end of the scale and Mercedes-Benz and BMW at the other. Fiat and Leyland produce the largest range of cars in Europe. Another similarity is that both firms

* As we argue in Chapter 10 this is not a necessary condition to establish a successful export business.

are controlled by a single head rather than by committees. This gives both firms the drive, impetus and confidence to seek out new markets.

Although most Fiat and Leyland cars are in the family saloon category, both firms are in a position to challenge Mercedes' domination of the European market for heavy trucks and prestige cars. On the CV side, Mercedes-Benz's dominance has been consolidated by the technical superiority of its products compared with those of the French industry. In prestige cars, Mercedes-Benz retains its dominance, but here its position is being threatened. Until the 1960s only Citroen, with superb cars but poor marketing, was a real competitor, but now Mercedes faces a real domestic challenge for the first time in the shape of BMW as well as new prestige models from Fiat. Both these firms in the late 1960s introduced new cars in the 2 to 3 litre range which were aimed at the heart of Mercedes' marketing and product stronghold. As national income continued to grow at an annual rate in excess of $4\frac{1}{2}\%$ in the EEC, the market for prestige cars increased in size. A continuation of this together with traditional expertise in the production and marketing of quality cars should allow Mercedes to hold its current output growth of 8% a year. However, Citroen-Fiat and BMW will also benefit and via the cultivation of a more sporting image aimed at the younger executives and younger middle-class buyers, they could seriously threaten Mercedes' leadership. In its current expansionary mood Fiat could even contemplate some technical or financial link with BMW which would create the largest quality car complex in the world. Other firms likely to benefit from the general trading-up are Volvo and Leyland's Specialist Car Division. The former already has a large export market whereas the latter's problem is productive capacity rather than demand. Rover and Jaguar are faced with heavy excess demand despite the fact that their marketing organisation have yet to tap many potential markets, the EEC being one of them.

Renault, a state owned company, forms the nucleus of the French-owned car industry. A major step forward in this direction is the agreement with Peugeot to build a joint engine plant and to collaborate on research and the purchasing of materials and components. The companies' model lines overlap to a degree, but most Renault models are in the categories of 1200 c.c. and below, whereas Peugeot's range is mainly above this. The combined Renault-Peugeot range in 1971 concentrated on seven models, and consequently it did not cover the same range of markets as did Fiat's or Leyland's. Despite this, these two French producers manufacture a strong range of family cars noted for quality and technical excellence. This allied to a strong marketing effort had allowed Renault and Peugeot to expand rapidly, and their penetration of the EEC market in the 1960s was second only to Fiat. The individualistic design philosophy of Renault to produce functional vehicles which were typically French in conception, was nevertheless able to meet the requirements of the wider EEC market.

The other giant European car producer within the EEC is Volkswagen. The success of the company had been built up by one model, the VW 'Beetle'. Sales of this car were highly concentrated in Germany and the U.S.A., but in Europe the large sales were not as significant as popular mythology would suggest. Furthermore, in 1968 and 1969 sales of the Beetle turned downwards in the U.S.A., but recovered to a record 560 000 in 1970, and the model faced increased competition in Germany. During the 1960s the company attempted to break free from its single model philosophy, and now produces three distinct model ranges. In addition, the company has attempted to establish itself in the quality field with its Auto Union-Audi subsidiary, and further such models are provided by NSU. However, at a time when the rule of the Beetle may be waning in Europe, the new VW models and the original Audi range have not made a comparable impact. Despite the success of the 1969 Audi range, VW still remained very dependent on its basic Beetle, at a time when the market may in future fail to generate a growth in 'Beetle' sales. As a result a really successful wide-ranging German company capable of meeting Fiat on its own terms may have to await some linkage between VW on the one hand and Mercedes or BMW on the other. If such a German firm is to be an integrated car and CV producer then the only suitable partner for VW would be Mercedes.

The remaining companies which dominate the European motor industry are the American owned ones and Leyland. The latter has been engaged on a major sales expansion *vis à vis* the European market, part of which entailed direct investment in Belgium and other parts of Europe. The American companies have long thought in terms of developing a European market and this was one of the reasons why Detroit established firms in Europe in the first place. Also, the existence of European subsidiaries inside and outside the EEC led to the division of markets, the U.K. subsidiaries being concerned with the Commonwealth and EFTA, whereas the German and French subsidiaries concentrated mainly on the EEC and exports to the rest of the world. In both instances other markets were served but the main division was as stated. In view of this it was rather paradoxical that in 1970 the American firms were faced with the major task of trying to integrate their separate and quite independent European subsidiaries, a separation which had solidified over the years almost to the point of active animosity between British and German subsidiaries. After all, the relative success of one was seen as a threat to the continued existence of the other.

CAR DESIGNS CAN STILL REMAIN DISTINCTIVE

General Motors and Ford have had considerable success in catering for the demand for small-medium and medium-sized cars. However, both companies have had failures with their German and British ranges of large cars, both having miscalculated the market perhaps due to the influence of Detroit thinking and philosophy. Their cars have been too big and cumbersome, thereby suffering at the hands of the smaller executive saloons from, say, Rover or BMW. Their technical merit may also have been inferior to that of the likes of Mercedes-Benz or Jaguar, while the European customer able to afford a quality motor car did not want the most luxurious product of a firm mainly associated with the mass-production of popular family cars. Instead he tended to patronise the producer with a quality car image, mainly Mercedes, BMW, Citroen, Volvo, Jaguar, and Rover. In Germany especially, the range of large Opel cars had provided little competition for Mercedes or BMW. Any slight price advantage which the large American cars had was of little consequence in the European quality car market.

In the U.S.A. each firm has a quality car division which gives some distinction to the product; it is difficult to see how the same solution could be an economic proposition in Europe when it is considered that only 19 900 large Fords and 9200 large Vauxhalls were produced in the U.K. in 1968. It would appear that the American manufacturers will be unable to overcome firms like Rover or Mercedes in the luxury car field, or firms like British Leyland or Porsche in the sports car field. The main strength of the American-owned firms was in the field of medium-sized popular mass-produced family saloons. It is here that the American firms pose the greatest threat but here also the future growth of these firms could be less than that of the past. All three American firms in Europe produce the same kind of car and even in design and body styling they are very similar*. Hence it could be that unless they reverse this trend towards similarity, or even homogeneity, they will

---

* For instance the 1970 Ford Cortina was almost identical in body styling to the then current Vauxhall Victor.

be spending most of their time competing amongst themselves, while the more individualistic European producers tap the market for those customers wanting something different*. Human nature being what it is suggests that the European market as a whole will move increasingly in the latter direction. As incomes increase people will turn from basic motoring in almost identical tin boxes to basic motoring in the more individualistically styled tin boxes produced by essentially European firms. Hence the emergence of a single EEC market, clearly including the U.K., could find one American firm improving its position at the expense of its fellows, while the European producers as a whole found new markets and thereby improved their overall position *vis à vis* the American-owned firms.

The most vulnerable American firm is Chrysler, for all three of its European subsidiaries were financially unsound throughout the 1960s. Rootes in the U.K., Simca in France and Barreiros in Spain, all suffered declining market shares, heavy capital investment for re-equipment, and trading losses. All three firms were too small to find life easy in their home markets, so Chrysler's attempt to overcome this may result in one of the first truly European motor firms. The success of Chrysler's European venture could rest on the production of Anglo-French cars; engines and bodies could be made in one country only, with assembly occurring in both. This would allow something nearer optimum levels of production where the engine lines and body presses were concerned, as well as in the labour-intensive assembly shops where the optimum is much lower and where diversed assembly allows for better market coverage.

So the Americans must weld their separate companies together in order to rationalise production in different plants and to persuade managements to treat Europe as one market. Ford has started this task with a new management superstructure which could, however, lead to a longer chain of command and therefore production and marketing inflexibility. U.S. Ford established Ford of Europe in 1968 to undertake long-term planning for Europe as a whole, co-ordination of the national companies and the provision of services. In theory U.K. Ford and German Ford still run their own operations but in practice the new organisational structure tightly circumscribes their freedom of man-oeuvre. For instance, the U.K. firm was not now free to take decisions concerning marketing or the product range in total disregard of what

---

* As product differentiation becomes less the market becomes less imperfect and although 'brand' loyalty militates against the emergence of a perfect market price, differentials may become less. In short, the slope of the demand curve decreases.

G

Germany was doing, or of what the long-term planners at Ford of Europe recommend. At present there is no intention of forcing a common car on both operating complexes but this could only be a matter of time*. The possibilities of using joint components, of sharing production or design costs should offer significant economies and thereby lead inevitably to a joint production range. Similarly a common approach to marketing and to sales and service organisations should also evolve. Eventually the concept of two independent European subsidiaries will be as implausible as British Ford giving independence to each of its main production plants and allowing them to produce completely separate ranges which compete with each other. These initial moves by Ford must point the way to complete integration of European operations by all three American firms. This will come sooner or later as will the spread of the European giants across national frontiers.

Car imports in 1970 were already equal to 25% of total sales in France and to 22·5% in Germany and they rose sharply in the U.K. and Italy from 10% of domestic sales in 1969 to 15% in 1970. Hence Europe is already beginning to look like a unified market. Hence firms must judge when contemplating the production of a new car its likely impact in Europe as a whole and then plan its marketing and production strategy accordingly. The needs and wants of a German customer will soon become as significant to a French producer as the requirements of his French customers. How each firm will satisfy this need will vary from firm to firm, but there is no logical reason to suppose that all cars will begin to look alike or to look 'European' because different firms will come up with different answers all of which may be equally successful. At present there is no doubt that Fiat is in the van as regards changing its domestic horizons from Italy to Europe, with Renault in second place. The other European and American giants will also come increasingly to the same marketing conclusion, that each firm and market is essentially European rather than French, German or British.

THE LOCATION OF THE 'EUROPEAN' MOTOR INDUSTRY

The location of the European motor industry follows the diverse trend of the U.S. industry rather than the traditionally concentrated

* Indeed, in 1970 the new Cortina introduced in the U.K. was almost identical to similar Taunus models. The smaller Escort and Capri were made in both countries, and steps were afoot to produce a common range of engines.

U.K. industry. The British car producers protested vehemently against Government policy aimed at forcing them to expand away from the historic locations of the Midlands, Dagenham, and Luton. The French, however, have long since moved their expansion away from Paris, the largest traditional centre of the French motor industry. In Germany, Volkswagen deliberately decentralised and moved 200 miles away from Wolfsburg to find new labour supplies. The continental producer knew that expansion in a traditional centre would require the same degree of training for new labour as expansion in a 'green-field' site. After all, many German car workers were not soaked in the tradition of working with metal but were refugees from the farmlands of East Germany. Fiat in Turin derived most of their new workers from the underdeveloped peasant areas of South Italy. This realisation that expansion in a traditional centre meant the employment of 'green' labour meant that the firms knew that there was no real hardship caused by moving expansions to new localities.

In the U.K. the Midland car producer assumed that there was a perfectly elastic supply of labour with metal-working in their blood. They did not appreciate that this was not so and new green labour in Birmingham would need as much training as green labour elsewhere. This had two effects: a reluctance to move from traditional areas and a failure to pay enough attention to training, or to breaking the production processes down to their smallest components because of firms overestimating the dexterity of new labour in the traditional centres. This latter point has led to lost production, poor workmanship, and strikes caused by disillusioned operatives finding work more onerous than they were trained to cope with. The Continentals avoided both these pitfalls by a more thorough appraisal of the real advantages of remaining in traditional areas or moving elsewhere.

The EEC motor industry is widespread in a national and a European context. Its plants spread from La Rochelle in the West to West Berlin in the East, from Emden in the North to Naples in the South. As integration proceeds, the American structure will emerge with single plants being built for each major component which in turn will supply numerous body and car assembly plants dotted all over the EEC. Within the national frontiers this process is already at work. In Germany, the six main VW car factories are spread out from the Emden plant on the coast to the main Wolfsburg complex near the frontier with East Germany, plus a plant in West Berlin. Opel has plants scattered over 400 square miles of central West Germany. Ford is mainly concentrated on Cologne. Mercedes is situated in the South with plants in Stuttgart, Sindelfingen, Worth on Rhine,

Mannheim and Gaggenau. BMW is located in Bavaria. In short, each large German town has some sort of motor plant near it, the location is diffuse, with no high concentrations in one or two areas.

In France the motor industry is not so widespread as in Germany; however, there is no concentration of the industry into a few local and precise areas. Rather, the industry is concentrated into two very broad areas of France; the north from Rennes in Brittany to Lille near the Belgian frontier, taking in Paris and the towns between Paris and the coast, such as Flins and Rouen, and the mid-west from Strasburg to Dijon. Nearly all the northern plants are owned by either Renault or Citroen whereas the mid-west is the home of Peugeot and some of the Citroen factories. Simca's operations are extremely diffuse with the main complex situated at Poissy north-east of Paris with other factories in Dijon in central France and La Rochelle on the west coast.

The picture painted by France and Germany is one of motor plants scattered all over the northern area of the EEC. This is reinforced by the movement of German (and British) producers into Belgium where assembly plants have been established to take advantage of adequate labour supplies, and slightly lower labour costs. The Ford plants assemble vehicles from both German and British parts and although managed by Ford of Germany are a pointer towards the Ford of Europe concept.

The Italian motor industry is akin to the British one in that it is highly concentrated in just a few localities. This is a result of the historical separation of Italy into the relatively prosperous industrial north and the poverty ridden peasant south. Italian engineering has been highly localised around a few northern cities such as Turin, Milan and Brescia and this is where the motor industry grew up. The north provided favourable conditions for production and it was here that the vast bulk of the early Italian motor car market was situated. Turin is the capital of the Italian Motor Industry with Fiat, Lancia and Abarth plants as well as many famous bodybuilders and also a large number of component and accessory makers. Milan is the second largest centre with Alfa Romeo, Autobianchi, Innocenti and Iso, followed by Brescia which contains the OM commercial vehicle complex. A further concentration is in Emilia where most of the specialist car firms are located, such as Ferrari, Maserati and Lamborghini. This latter locality is sufficiently near the other main centres for easy contact to be maintained with various suppliers, but sufficiently far for the small specialists to keep their highly skilled operatives away from more remunerative employment in Turin or Milan. Recently the motor industry has begun spreading south with large integrated plants being established by Fiat and Alfa Romeo in Naples and Pamigliano d'Arco respectively.

6

THE OVERSEAS MOTOR INDUSTRIES: JAPAN AND THE NEW PRODUCING COUNTRIES

The main motor producing nations of Europe and North America have been discussed. All that remains to be done is to examine the only other major motor producing country, Japan, and some of the new motor producing countries such as Spain, Sweden and Russia.

JAPAN

The Japanese motor industry has risen from obscurity to a position second to that of the U.S.A. in only 20 years. The phenomenal rise in output is illustrated by the fact that in 1947 total vehicle output was only 11 320, but by 1967 it had soared to 3 146 486—which included 1 375 755 cars and 1 743 368 commercial vehicles. Of all the major car producing countries Japan was for a long time unique in that commercial vehicles outnumbered cars. After 1964, however, the growth in car output was far greater than that of commercial vehicles, and in 1968—for the first time—the annual car production exceeded that for trucks and buses.

Probably the most remarkable feature of the world motor industry in the 1960s was the huge expansion of Japan into a major vehicle producer. The growth during the 1960s was based on an explosive home demand allied to the selective penetration of overseas markets.

Currently, in 1971 Japanese producers had not made major inroads into the U.K. or into the rest of Western Europe, the large sales being achieved in the Far East, Australia and in the U.S.A. Intensive marketing has resulted in the rapid growth of Japanese penetration in the U.S. market for small and second cars*. The industry in 1971 was still heavily protected at home by very high tariff barriers; for instance, a British Leyland Mini selling for less than £600 in the U.K. cost around £900 in Japan, likewise a Volkswagen 1300 selling for £460 in West Germany cost over £970 in Japan; similar Japanese models cost around £620. However, the industry was under increasing international pressure to negotiate on the removal of such grotesque tariff levels as well as allowing the entry of foreign capital to participate in the Japanese motor industry.

We will briefly consider Japanese reluctance to liberalise their car market later, but either way there is considerable scope for the continued expansion of the Japanese market. The car density in 1971 was just under 40 cars per 1000 people, compared with a figure of around 140 in Italy. Given this as well as the rapid growth of the average Japanese income and the emergence of a more sophisticated credit-finance sector, the potential growth of the Japanese market during the 1970s and 1980s should be startling. Probably the comparative car density figures for different countries is not a unique guide to growth potential. It could be that road space and the car population per mile is a stronger limiting force to the growth of car ownership. Hence Western Europe may never equal the car densities in the wide open spaces of North America or Australia. This is of particular relevance to Japan where, until the mid-1960s the road network was pitiful. Subsequently a concerted and far reaching programme for the construction of urban and inter-urban motorway complexes was undertaken. At the same time, the average Japanese annual wage now exceeds the total retail price of a popular family saloon, i.e. of between 1000 and 1500 c.c. and costing between £600 and £700. This appears to be the threshold or take-off point for a really rapid increase in the domestic sales of mass-produced motor cars, being relevant at one time or another to all the major vehicle producing nations. This could also be a useful rule of thumb in predicting a sales explosion in cars.

---

* In 1970 (compared with 1969) Toyota increased its U.S. sales by 54%, to 196 400 units and Nissan by 71% to 104 100 units. BLMC's sales rose 2% to 69 400 and VW's by 3·3% to 560 000. This illustrates German apprehension concerning the Japanese sales drive in the U.S.A.

THE ORIGINS AND DEVELOPMENT OF THE JAPANESE MOTOR INDUSTRY

The basis of the Japanese motor industry was laid during the 1930s with government encouragement. Official help was forthcoming to establish capacity capable of producing large numbers of vehicles, especially for military use. After 1945 the industry was in partial ruins for a second time, having first been paralysed by the earthquake disaster of 1923. However, the need for road transport to help in the industrial development and reconstruction of Japan meant a large market for commercial vehicles. The development of this sector was further helped by the U.S.A.'s policy to use Japanese vehicles for military and foreign aid purposes in the Far East. Hence the early take-off of the Japanese industry was based on CV production, and as industrial growth proceeded so the need for such vehicles grew. At the same time, the general growth of incomes meant a growing car market. Nevertheless, until the early 1960s over 90% of car demand was basically non-private—cars were purchased mainly as taxis or official transport by Japanese firms and industrialists. Consequently most cars were over 1500 c.c. and £800, expensive to run and beyond the pockets of the vast majority of Japanese between 1945 and about 1962. Since 1965 the growth of incomes and credit facilities has led to a boom in private motoring and seen the emergence of the 'popular' and 'small-medium' car as the Japanese car industry's largest sellers.

The comparatively late development of the Japanese motor industry and the recognition that commercial success meant adequate capital as well as technical and marketing prowess has meant that the industry has bypassed the infancy stages experienced by the industry abroad. This meant that the existence of numerous small producers has never been a feature of the Japanese industry. From the creation of the industry in 1907 up to the present time there have been 52 separate enterprises* concerned with the production of motor vehicles. Between 1907 and 1916 the industry's output was very small. World War I induced some growth, but the significant developments occurred during the 1930s with the establishment of a war-orientated economy. Between 1936 and 1939 production of motor vehicles increased from 8800 to 41 300. Of the 1939 figure, car production was only equal to 2600.

Because of the mountainous character of Japan and its poor roads, pre-war Japan was dependent on shipping and railways for long-

* G. R. Doyle and G. N. Georgano, *The World's Automobiles 1862–1962*, Temple Press, London (1963).

distance traffic. It was only the needs of the 'war lords' which established a motor industry of any significance. By 1941 there were only 140 000 civilian motor vehicles in Japan, 64 000 of which were trucks; at the same time the Japanese army held 62 500 trucks*. Nevertheless, roughly 50% of the vehicles used in Japan were from foreign sources, illustrating the smallness of the industry in pre-war Japan.

Even in the 1930s the industry was highly concentrated with almost all the 41 300 vehicles made in 1939 being produced by just two firms. Nissan and Nissan Diesel, and Toyota together employed about 21 000 people and made most of their own component requirements. The remaining output was in the hands of Isuzu, Toyo Kogyo, Hino, Daihatsu and Fuji. The only firms in existence prior to the mid-1930s were Hino, which was established in 1917, and Nissan, which can trace its origins back to 1912. The Japanese vehicle producers escaped the worst of the effects of World War II and the two largest firms suffered no direct bomb damage at all. So as early as 1946 the industry was able to produce over 14 900 vehicles and the first post-war cars appeared in 1947 when 100 units were made. This set the picture for post-war Japanese output with the motor industry being heavily geared to CV production. It was not until 1954 that car output reached five figures and not until 1960 that six figures were achieved. However, by 1967 car output reached almost 1·4 million with CV output almost reaching 1·75 million, which meant that in terms of motor vehicles the Japanese industry was second in size only to that of the U.S.A.

DUOPOLY: THE TRADITIONAL STRUCTURE

The Japanese car industry has always been concentrated in terms of ownership and especially output. Before 1939 nearly all Japanese cars were made by two firms, Toyota and Nissan, the only other producers of any significance being Daihatsu and Toyo Kogyo. The commercial vehicle industry was also dominated by these firms although three other producers Isuzu, Hino and Fuji were of some significance. Every one of these firms, apart from Hino and Nissan, came into the motor industry during the 1930s, with Toyota and Toyo Kogyo producing their first cars in 1935, and Daihatsu in 1937. Isuzu entered the CV industry in 1937 to be followed by Fuji a year later. In 1969 the industry was showing signs of duopoly with Toyota and Nissan producing over

* *Motor Vehicles: A Report on the Industry*, Political and Economic Planning, London, p. 122 (1950).

75% of all Japanese cars, the rest being shared amongst five firms. This situation was not new. Its origins go back to the pre-war dominance of these two firms, and also to the post-war history of the industry.

In 1960, of the 10 firms making cars, many were comparative newcomers to the car side of the industry. Unique amongst the major vehicle producing nations, the Japanese industry was in 1970 less concentrated than it was pre-war, but the trend in the 1960s was towards the restoration of the extreme duopoly of the period 1935–1945. Seven of the firms only began producing cars in any numbers in the late 1950s and early 1960s. For instance, between 1958 and 1960 the CV producers, Toyo Kogyo, Mitsubishi, Fuji, Hino and Isuzu began car production, and in 1958 and 1962 respectively the two motor cycle makers Suzuki and Honda entered the car industry for the first time. Only Daihatsu, Nissan and Toyota were car producers of long standing. An eleventh independent firm was Aichi which concentrated on CV output, having attempted to enter the car industry during the early 1960s. This firm is now a Nissan subsidiary.

Many of the Japanese firms entered the car industry with the help of foreign producers' technical expertise. Isuzu and Hino built Rootes and Renault models respectively under licence before producing vehicles of their own design in the early 1960s. Nissan was quite heavily dependent on help from Austin during the late forties and early fifties. Toyota, however, spurned foreign contacts and continued to rely on its own reserves—technical, financial and marketing—on which to base its post-war recovery and development. So during the 1950s the Japanese car market was composed mainly of Nissan, Toyota, Daihatsu and Prince models, with other firms only entering at the end of the decade. All these new entrants found it difficult to build up large markets, the only real success being achieved by Toyo Kogyo. Hence the traditional extreme duopoly of the Japanese car industry is likely to reappear unless certain conditions are satisfied. We will return to this later.

The present distribution of Japanese vehicle output is shown in *Table 6.1*.

Toyota absorbed Hino in 1966 and Daihatsu in 1967; Nissan purchased the Prince Motor Company in 1965 and Fuji in 1969. At the time of writing some signs point to a possible link being forged between Toyota and Suzuki. Isuzu recognised its vulnerability as a small-scale producer faced with competition from larger firms. Consequently it tended to desperately seek out partners. In the mid-1960s the company became linked with Fuji, but when Isuzu attempted to bring Mitsubishi into the grouping, Fuji objected on the grounds that the two companies were highly competitive in the air-frames

Table 6.1

JAPANESE VEHICLE OUTPUT IN 1967 AND 1969

Firm	Cars 1967	Cars 1969	Commercial vehicles 1967	Commercial vehicles 1969
Toyota	476 807	964 088	355 323	507 123
Daihatsu	60 473	104 840	165 017	159 435
Hino	4 692	55	28 046	39 315
Suzuki	26 454	121 871	89 114	116 243
Nissan	352 045	697 691	385 074	469 222
Fuji	94 398	124 877	78 682	62 513
Aichi	—	—	42 568	22 041
Mitsubishi	105 950	127 812	211 428	209 446
Isuzu	38 716	36 429	94 084	118 774
Toyo Kogyo	129 051	201 132	259 272	227 094
Honda	87 169	232 704	62 120	131 583
Others	—	—	3	52
Total	1 375 755	2 611 499	1 770 731	2 062 841

industry. As a result Isuzu changed partners and linked with Mitsubishi. However, in 1969 Mitsubishi showed signs of forging links with Ford, and due to the Japanese firm's massive financial backing derived from the entire Mitsubishi engineering complex such an agreement would be one made among equals. On the other hand, Isuzu felt that its identity would be soon lost in such a grouping with its voice drowned by those of its two larger partners, hence the link between Isuzu and Mitsubishi was severed in 1969.

Consequently the Japanese car industry is now composed of only six independent producers, so already production is highly concentrated. The real picture is even more significant as the Toyota group, including Suzuki, and Nissan accounted for over 74% of all cars produced in 1967. If we add Toyo Kogyo's output, then the three largest firms account for over 83% of vehicles produced. At the same time these three firms held 81% of the domestic market in 1967 but by 1969 the figure had increased to 89%*.

Most of the increased penetration by the Big Three was due to the growth in Toyota's and Nissan's output, with Toyo Kogyo's market share being squeezed. At the same time, the market share left to

* *The Sunday Times*, Business News (9 March 1969).

Mitsubishi, Isuzu and Honda tended to fall as well. Honda, however, only entered the industry in 1962 and with aggressive price cutting, intensive marketing and superior products continually increased its market share. This meant that Toyo Kogyo, Mitsubishi and Isuzu found their continued existence as significant car producers being threatened. Consequent to these developments it appears that Japanese vehicle production is returning to the traditional duopoly of the pre-war period. As a result, the emergence of many new firms as car producers in their own right during the 1950s and early 1960s is likely to be replaced by the disappearance of a number of producers during the 1970s, either through mergers or through firms leaving the industry completely because of unprofitable output levels.

During the 1960s the boom in demand had allowed all Japanese car firms to earn a living. The development of the post-war car market in Japan has been different to the emergence of car markets elsewhere. Instead of their dual origin in the U.S.A. and U.K. as the toys of the rich and as the tin boxes for the use of the masses, in Japan as recently as 1960 fewer than 10% of the then total car output of under 100 000 was sold to private buyers. The rest went as taxis, government cars, or to private industry. Hence cars tended to be large status symbols of between $1\frac{1}{2}$ and 2 litres. From 1960 to 1966 demand expanded considerably, the real boom in output occurring between 1966 and 1968 with annual car output more than doubling from less than one million to two million units. The incomes of the 'petit bourgeois' and of skilled workers rose enough to allow them to buy cars within the 360 to 1500 c.c. class, the total output of which was just over 380 000 in 1965 but over 960 000 in 1968. All car firms were faced with rising demand and consequently they were able to sell all they produced.

For the smaller producers, however, this was only an apparent prosperity. As late as 1965 Nissan and Toyota accounted for under 45% of all Japanese car production, but the other firms all had a small slice of the available market and were mainly under-capitalised and debt-ridden. The smaller concerns needed new money merely to remain in business, let alone to expand productive capacity to maintain their share of the market. This was the situation facing firms in Europe and the U.S.A. some 30–40 years earlier. Only Nissan and Toyota were financially and commercially strong, and between 1965 and 1969 they took a number of vulnerable firms under their wing; they also had sufficient resources to be able to embark upon rapid investment schemes to turn themselves into international giants able to satisfy the burgeoning domestic Japanese demand. So paradoxically the real boom in demand between 1966 and 1968 saw the other producers losing ground, being unable to match the expansion programmes of Nissan or Toyota or to compete in price while at the same time making adequate profits. Between 1966 and 1968 the smaller Japanese firms made only marginal profits.

THE ROLE OF MITI AND THE LIBERALISATION OF TRADE

The period 1962–1970 has therefore been notable for two reasons. Firstly, the re-emergence of duopoly in the Japanese car industry, and secondly, the refusal of the remaining smaller firms to merge with each other in order to produce a viable grouping outside the Big Two. Isuzu's efforts have already been mentioned. The Japanese Ministry of International Trade and Industry (MITI) has been extremely concerned with the position of the smaller producers. In 1968 it drew up a plan which would require all other car makers either to merge with Toyota or Nissan or to merge with each other to concentrate on making specialised cars and commercial vehicles. Hence the Japanese Government has been anxious to see further mergers in the car industry, and the creation of two, or perhaps three, commercially strong and viable groups.

The main factor influencing MITI officials in their apparently strange posture of attempting to reduce competition, is their realisation that the protection of the Japanese industry from foreign competition cannot last indefinitely. If the industry remained as scattered and unco-ordinated as it was in 1971 the Japanese producers eventually would not be in a position to compete with American and European firms. The feared holocaust among smaller producers would give foreign firms the opportunity to fill the void in the market and to pick up a large number of retail outlets. It also appears that the Japanese Government feels that the continued prosperity of Nissan and Toyota can only be guaranteed if either: they share all the present domestic market between them and thereby reduce unit costs to a level where foreign firms can be met on equal terms, or if they were faced with a third large domestic grouping which was concerned with 'orderly' marketing rather than the cut-price and low profit margin policies of some of the smaller producers.

The problem of foreign competition is reduced to the dual question of foreign capital on the one hand and trade liberalisation on the other. Foreign capital would have three possible outlets in the Japanese motor industry: (1) participation in existing motor firms; (2) financing entry into the motor industry by other Japanese firms; (3) the establishment of foreign-owned subsidiaries. As the industry becomes more and more mature, with the largest firms approaching the optimum size for most of the stages of assembly and manufacture with marketing arrangements to match, the cost of new entry becomes prohibitive even for firms as powerful as Ford or GMC. Hence (1) becomes the only practical possibility. In theory, capital investment in the car industry becomes free in 1972; this could allow 50:50 arrangements between Japanese and other firms. However, it could be that certain regulations and conditions would be imposed on foreign investment which effectively close the door again to any form of foreign participation which could lead to the foreign parties gaining financial control. Japanese thought in 1971 highlighted two fears: (1) if the foreign partner was strong it would overwhelm its Japanese associate; (2) if they were relatively weak they would be of no use to Japanese firms. Presumably Nissan and Toyota would have no need of foreign capital but most of the other firms would be overwhelmed by large American or European firms. The one really strong 'outsider' is Mitsubishi Heavy Industries. The financial strength of this complex would allow it to stand up to the largest American firm which wanted to invest in its motor vehicle division. Hence the announced link between Mitsubishi and Chrysler to establish a jointly owned concern after 1972, with Chrysler taking 35% of Mitsubishi's equity in its vehicle subsidiary*.

In 1965 the importation of complete cars into Japan was partially freed in the sense that quota and foreign exchange restrictions were eased. Since the largest Japanese makers were then not big enough, and as the small makers were quite incapable of producing economic volumes before the early 1970s, trade liberalisation meant very little. The combination of a Japanese commodity tax (based on c.i.f. values) and a duty of 40% meant that the retail price of a foreign car was close to 100% greater than its home market price. This price disadvantage meant that quota restrictions were meaningless; in 1964, for example, only 13 500 foreign cars were sold—70% of the permitted quota. Hence the Japanese market would only be liberalised when tariffs were reduced to much lower levels.

Despite increasing foreign pressure to allow imports a larger share of the market and to allow the participation of foreign capital, this would only be heeded when the government-promoted scheme for further mergers was finally accepted by the smaller producers. Two major obstacles here have been the problems of what to do with the top

* After initial contacts with Ford, Mitsubishi eventually deemed Chrysler to be a more suitable partner.

executives of the weaker firm as they were unlikely to vote themselves out of a job, and which bank to drop if the merging firms had different banks as important shareholders. If a shareholding bank felt that the new group would take its business to a rival bank, it could often veto a proposed merger. However, it has been suggested* that as the motor industry is a post-war phenomenon and because it had grown so fast the link between a company and its bank was not as strong as in the older Japanese industries. Obviously some car firms are more strongly linked with their banks than others, but generally car firms appear more autonomous of their banks than is the general rule in Japanese industry.

The Japanese industry shows a high degree of concentration in ownership and output despite the fact that the industry is composed of a larger number of independent producers than is usual in a major motor industry. In many ways it was the existence of these quite weak smaller firms that gave the Japanese Government the excuse to delay the liberalisation of the Japanese motor market. The liberalisation that took place in 1965, when quotas were abolished, was accompanied by the removal of duty concessions on imported parts. This effectively killed the assembly of foreign vehicles in Japan. Consequently liberalisation meant in effect greater restrictions. As a major producer the Japanese should in 1971 now be in a position to genuinely liberalise trade, and to allow the participation of foreign capital in 1972. If this fails to occur then some form of tariff discrimination against Japanese vehicles could follow, although harming world trade in the short run this could be beneficial in the long run if it opens the way to genuine two-way traffic. Unfortunately a trade war is likely to harm Japan less than most, for due to the huge home market substantial exports may still only be a tiny proportion of total output. In 1969, of a total car production of over $2\frac{1}{2}$ million units total exports—although substantial at 560 000—were only about 20% of total output. In comparison the West European export ratios are around 50%. So in any generalised trade war the Japanese and American car firms would not be the main sufferers.

PATERNALISM AND VERTICAL INTEGRATION

The overall structure of the Japanese industry shows a very high degree of vertical integration. Either suppliers are owned by the car firms or they are dependent on their orders to get credit from the

* *The Sunday Times*, Business News (9 March 1969).

banks. There are a few very large independent suppliers which produce specialised components such as springs, wheels and electrical components. Such firms are the exception and most suppliers, although nominally independent, are effectively controlled by the vehicle producers. The use of many small firms impose a cost disadvantage on the vehicle producers, as their suppliers are not reaping all the available scale economies, although they do provide the production process with a certain degree of flexibility.

Superficially, the Japanese motor producer appears less integrated than the American or European, adding just over 30% to its value compared with about 50% elsewhere. The bought out parts, however, come from a subsidiary company or a smaller affiliate, dependent on the motor producer for all his orders and, indirectly, much of his finance. In other words, only with a motor producer's order in his pocket can a small producer obtain credit from a bank, the order is regarded as collateral.

In Japan there are fewer than 350 main producers of components and of these, the 21 with over 2000 employees supply one-third of the motor vehicle industry's requirements. Another 45 firms with between 1000 and 2000 employees account for another 30%. However, these 350 firms call upon thousands of small sub-contractors; the last industrial census listed 8000 with fewer than 10 employees and between 20 000 and 30 000 even smaller firms with less than 4 employees. This type of structure is typical of Japan. These small men give the main firms both flexibility—they can reduce the amount of sub-contracting in poor times—and cheaper labour. The loyalty of these small men is rewarded, with Toyota being especially paternalistic towards its smaller suppliers.

To overcome the problem of too many small firms the component suppliers are being encouraged to integrate themselves around Toyota or Nissan. This is proving easier than at the car manufacturing level because the smaller car producers tend to buy their supplies from the same pool of firms as the two largest vehicle producers. As a result, there is no question of a third group of integrated component makers being formed to serve the smaller car firms. Hence the process of forming two main component producing complexes being controlled either *de facto* or *de jure* by Nissan or Toyota proceeded quite quickly in the late 1960s. The Japanese car firms are therefore more akin to the American ones in structure than to the U.K. ones; it is unlikely that Japanese equivalents of Lucas, Automotive Products or Smiths, which supply almost all the industry, will become usual. Occasional instances may nevertheless arise, such as Borg Warner establishing a jointly owned subsidiary to supply almost all the Japanese needs for automatic transmission components.

MARKETING AND EXPORTS

The range of vehicles in Japan stretches from very light vehicles of less than 360 c.c., which are popular because of the various tax advantages they enjoy*, to 2½ litre saloons. Almost 100% of output consists of vehicles of less than 2000 c.c. because of the considerable tax disadvantage incurred by cars exceeding that size. To a certain extent the taxation system has distorted design, with the emergence of very small vehicles of less than 360 c.c. peculiar to Japanese conditions and very difficult to sell on the export market. At the other end of the scale there is only a very tiny market for large prestige cars because the costs of owning and running such vehicles are inflated by the tax system. Hence the few that are made are extremely expensive, due to the low production runs, and in order to control tooling costs large CV petrol engines are used which tend to have different characteristics to those normally required by the owners of large quality cars. It is likely that the Japanese large car of over 2 litres will, like the French, be killed by the tax system unless the system is changed.

Within the range 360 to 2000 c.c. the Japanese produce a wide variety of well finished cars of conventional design able to stand up to rugged conditions. Since the mid-1960s the biggest growth in output has been for cars between 900 and 1500 c.c., with the result that the range and quality of such vehicles has improved considerably over this period. It is only with the emergence of these models that Japanese cars have been accepted in world markets in any numbers. At the present time the bulk of world trade in motor cars is in this type of vehicle. Compared with the main Western European countries the Japanese car industry is still highly orientated to the domestic market; only 15% of vehicles produced were exported in 1968 compared with 62% for West Germany and well over 30% for Italy, France and the United Kingdom. Compared with 1958, when only 5% was exported, the Japanese export performance has improved and should continue to improve. Exports are discussed more fully in Chapter 10, but it is relevant to point out here that at the moment the industry has a narrow product and geographical export horizon. Nissan and Toyota account for almost 80% of all exports with another 10% accounted for

* Taxation is one-tenth of 'normal' rate on such vehicles. For vehicles over 2 litres it exceeds the 'normal' rate.

by Honda and Toyo Kogyo. Apart from the large commercial vehicles sold by Mitsubishi and Isuzu the remaining firms exported very little. The growth in exports has resulted from the reduced real cost of producing marketable vehicles largely because of the increased domestic demand for cars between 900 c.c. and 1500 c.c. The growth in this market is shown in *Table 6.2.*

Table 6.2

JAPANESE DOMESTIC CAR DEMAND IN 1965 AND 1968

Size of vehicle	1965 (1000s)	1968
Large and medium (1500 c.c.+)	100	140
Small (1200–1500 c.c.)	280	450
Popular (360–1200 c.c.)	102	510
Light (360–under)	104	440

Cars of between 1000 and 1500 c.c. account for 46% of all production compared with 37% in France, 33% in Italy and over 58% in the U.K. and West Germany. These are the vehicles that compete most vigorously in world markets and where relative prices and quality are important. In terms of quality, the Japanese car, having first suffered badly in comparison, is now equal to the very best European standards. In terms of price the Japanese car is equal to equivalent European types if not slightly cheaper. As a result the output volumes achieved by Toyota and Nissan for their best selling models should allow production at a unit cost broadly similar to European levels, and the Japanese car industry should be fully competitive in terms of both price and quality with its international rivals. This conclusion holds even when we consider the low profit margins earned by Toyota and Nissan which was basically due to the expenditure on the capital investment which was needed to expand production to meet the expanding domestic market. An expansion which is illustrated by the fact that in 1960 Japan made 105 000 cars but in 1970 the industry produced three million.

There is no evidence to suggest that Japan will be able to sweep away all competition as it did in the market for motor-cycles. For one reason the European car firms are in a far stronger marketing, commercial and financial situation *vis à vis* the Japanese firms than were the European motor-cycle producers. The Japanese home market for cars, even when fully developed, will not be equal to the EEC market and only broadly equivalent to the EFTA market for cars; in the case of motor-cycles the vast Japanese market allowed Japanese firms to operate at a scale which allowed unit costs far lower than those obtainable by European firms. Another reason was that Japanese motor-cycles were, generally speaking, technically superior to European types. In the case of motor vehicles the Europeans are at least the equals of Japan in this respect, although Honda produces cheap high performance vehicles with very advanced engines and Toyo Kogyo may be the first firm to really mass produce Wankel-type rotary engines. Europe must therefore keep abreast of all technical developments and by doing so should be able to meet Japan on equal terms. On the marketing side the highly sophisticated European and American firms can easily equal the efforts and performances of Japanese firms. It is to be expected that saturation coverage of particular markets would allow Japan to improve its position, but it needs to do this merely to equal the performance of the Europeans, so the problem of Japanese dominance does not arise. As always, efficiency will be the keynote needed by American and European firms to counteract the Japanese thrust and such efficiency is evident in many American and European firms. However, there is no natural law which means the inevitable domination of the world's motor markets by the Japanese.

The continued growth of Nissan and Toyota will produce two international giants able to meet the foreign producers on their own terms. This will mean a greater liberalisation of the Japanese market and hence a high degree of competition with foreign firms availing themselves of new marketing opportunities. Hence the Japanese motor industry will develop as one amongst equals, but the European fear of Japanese domination and the opposite fears felt by the Japanese should prove groundless. The world market will develop sufficiently to allow a number of American, European and Asian firms to reach optimum size and whose continued prosperity will depend on individual commercial and economic acumen in a competitive situation.

COMMERCIAL VEHICLES

Turning briefly to the Japanese commercial vehicle industry. The development of the Japanese motor industry as a major force stems from the production of trucks and buses. As we have seen, before World War II very few cars were produced but Japan had a CV industry designed and large enough for very considerable military needs. As a result all the main suppliers to the motor industry were geared to supply the needs of CV production. This in turn proved a hindrance to the post-war development of the car industry with the need to establish the capacity and expertise to supply components suitable for use in cars. It is only since the mid-1960s that an industry properly geared to supplying technically suitable low-cost components and materials to the car side has been really established on a basis similar to that prevailing in the CV industry. The output of the Japanese motor industry up to and including 1967 was the opposite of that in other major vehicle producing countries in that CV production was greater than car output. The year 1968 saw more cars made for the first time, although CV output in absolute terms is immense (*Table 6.3*).

Table 6.3

MAXIMUM COMMERCIAL VEHICLE OUTPUT

U.S.A.	1 751 805 (1965)
U.K.	464 736 (1964)
West Germany	259 474 (1964)
Japan	2 000 000 (1968)
U.S.S.R.	477 400 (1967)

From *Table 6.3* it can be seen that Japanese CV production is greater than that of the U.S.A. or indeed any other vehicle producing country. However, the product mix is important here when we are comparing the Japanese situation with that of abroad. In 1968 just over 580 000 units were mini-trucks with engines of less than 360 c.c. and about 50 000 of these were three wheeled vehicles. About a further million were light vehicles, medium-sized vans or car derivates. Although these considerations make it quite clear that the U.S.A. is still preeminent in the production of full-sized vehicles from between 4 tons gross to over 40 tons, Japan still produces more full-sized vehicles than the large European countries.

As the Japanese economy expands it is quite possible that total production will fall although the 'carrying capacity' made by the industry each year will continue to increase. It appears that the small van and truck market is saturated. As business gets larger their owners are replacing one all-purpose vehicle by one larger truck and an ordinary car. The scope for reducing numbers by using bigger units appears to be considerable.

In the case of mini-trucks designed to benefit from the Japanese tax concessions on such vehicles, it will be difficult to replace a declining home market with export sales. It has proved possible to export some of these vehicles in the past, especially to South East Asia and South Africa, but the overseas markets are rather limited. Also the decline in output of such vehicles cannot be immediately offset by increased car output. The production lines on which these vehicles are made, and in Nissan's case even the engines, are quite separate from car production. Hence some expensive re-equipping would be needed to allow these lines to produce cars on an economic basis.

Apart from the possible decline in small vehicles, the Japanese industry as a whole is in a very strong position. The small to large 'full size' trucks and buses are highly competitive in terms of quality, technical merit and price. Large markets have been established in the selected areas of South America, South Africa and Australia.

The greatest threat to European and especially U.K. producers is in the market for light- to medium-heavy trucks and large buses. There are virtually no heavy vehicles over 20 tons gross weight produced in Japan hence no Japanese producer is in a position to threaten firms such as Leyland or Mercedes here, except in the market for buses. But Japan is very strong in the production of vehicles of between 4 and 20 tons gross, the area where the British based mass-producers are pre-eminent. It appears that Japan is the only country that can compete on price in the rather price conscious market for mass produced trucks. A Japanese Hino truck of around $3\frac{1}{2}$ tons carrying capacity costs £1250 in Japan compared with £1200 for an equivalent Ford vehicle sold in the U.K. A Toyota 6 ton vehicle costs around £1600 compared with about £1500 for a similar Ford or Bedford complete with an ordinary truck body. So in terms of medium sized vehicles the U.K. producers can still hold their own, but it is likely that Japan will prove to be their main future competitor.

In terms of output, Toyota produces around 60 000 medium-weight vehicles, which puts the firm on a par with Bedford and Ford; hence the unit costs of production should be basically similar given the known efficiency of these three firms. The Japanese market for medium-heavy vehicles of between 12 and 20 tons gross is dominated by Hino, Mitsubishi and Isuzu, the latter two firms specialising on the heavier type of truck and bus. Another firm significant in this market is the Nissan Diesel subsidiary of the Nissan Motor Company.

The Japanese firms are proving very competitive on price, quality and marketing in the market for heavy vehicles. Only Mitsubishi and Isuzu are able to match the output volumes of Leyland, Mercedes and GMC's Truck and Coach Division, and it would appear that production costs are basically similar. However, Leyland does not use as much expensive capital equipment as the other producers, finding that output volumes of less than 50 000 a year requires very little in the shape of very expensive transfer machines or presses. Leyland's prices and costs therefore appear to be lower than those of other heavy vehicle producers who may be using much of their equipment at sub-optimum levels, in addition to buying more expensive equipment in the first place. Consequently Leyland is able to meet successfully the competition from the Japanese producers, even in markets where the Japanese have a transport cost advantage.

THE NEW PRODUCING COUNTRIES

These then are the main vehicle producing countries of the world and the ones which are the U.K.'s greatest competitors. Obviously, there are other nations where the motor industry is, or is likely to be, a major force.

SPAIN

The Spanish industry, although dependent on outside capital and foreign expertise, is likely to reach significant output levels by the mid-1970s, perhaps exceeding one million cars and 150 000 commercial vehicles. The main Spanish heavy-vehicle builder Pegaso is already exporting to South America and aims to establish assembly plants in overseas markets; Leyland owns about $7\frac{1}{2}\%$ of the capital in Pegaso as well as supplying technical expertise.

SWEDEN

Sweden, of course, has a strong domestic motor industry, with cars and trucks made by Volvo and Saab-Scania. Up until 1959 Sweden made more cars than Japan, but now the Asians make fifteen times as many. Total Swedish output is around 200 000 cars and 20 000 commercial vehicles a year, with Volvo producing 150 000 cars and 8000 commercial vehicles, compared with 50 000 cars and 12 000 commercial vehicles by Saab and Scania. The firms survive in an industry where annual output volumes of more than $1\frac{1}{2}$ million units are required to reap all the significant economies of scale. They do this by buying from the world source which offers the best value for money. Both firms import many of their components and materials; indeed, Saab now buys all its car engines from the U.K. and West Germany, and Volvo's foreign content is between 35% and 40% of total vehicle costs. In addition, the cost penalty of sub-optimum production is to a certain extent compensated by having a longer 'pay-off' period, with the same basic body being used for well over 10 years and engines being used for almost 20 years. Hence capital equipment is amortised over a longer period as are all other fixed charges such as design and development costs.

The influence of Volvo especially, in being willing to buy anywhere if the price and quality was right, has forced Swedish industry generally to look at its cost structures. Before Volvo became a significant force in the Swedish economy during the 1950s, high prices in the domestic market meant high costs of production rather than high quality. The significance of Volvo as a buyer has forced firms to introduce the most efficient methods in order to compete with foreign suppliers. As it is, about 35% of the cost of a Volvo is made up of imported parts, about 10% of the cost being accounted for by U.K. made items. The Swedish car and CV firms have established a strong export trade by concentrating on a few markets at a time to build up adequate sales and service networks to back up the sales of vehicles. The success of this policy can be judged by comparing exports in 1950 and 1969 (*Table 6.4*).

Table 6.4

SWEDISH MOTOR VEHICLE EXPORTS

Year	Commercial vehicles	Cars
1950	1 865	317
1967	15 375	123 020
1969	18 833	141 775

The overall export proportion was in excess of 64% of total production in 1967. A number of assembly plants have been built abroad, for example Volvo (Canada) assembles around 5000 vehicles a year and Scania commercial vehicles are assembled in Holland to serve the EEC.

THE U.S.S.R.

Behind the Iron Curtain both East Germany and Czechoslovakia have significant car and commercial vehicle capacity, while Austria has three domestic producers manufacturing cars and commercial vehicles. Switzerland supports two producers of quality commercial vehicles—Saurer-Berna and FBW—but total production is only around 1000 units a year. The main producing country outside those already discussed is the Soviet Union, where a considerable expansion of motor producing capacity was taking place in the early 1970s.

THE ECONOMICS OF RATIONING

Output of vehicles in the U.S.S.R. is as shown in *Table 6.5*. Even

Table 6.5

U.S.S.R. VEHICLE OUTPUT IN 1967 AND 1969

Vehicle	1967	1969
Cars	251 400	293 600
Commercial vehicles	477 400	550 700

when considering the relatively low income per head the output of cars bears no relationship to the potential effective demand. The output of cars in Spain for instance, where the income per head was basically similar to that in the U.S.S.R., amounted to 274 458 in 1967; the Russian population is roughly 10 times that of Spain. Further figures point to the lack of development of the Russian car industry and market (*Table 6.6*).

Table 6.6

CARS OWNED PER 1000 PEOPLE

Country	1958	1967	1969
Japan	2	75	115
U.S.S.R.	2	5	5
U.K.	90	192	200
U.S.A.	330	410	419

Despite a significant increase in national income over this period the consumer durable sector did not develop. The resources allocated to car output under the various Soviet economic plans did not lead to a significant increase in output and did nothing to satiate the pent-up demand for car ownership. In 1967 the total car population of the

U.S.S.R. was only $1\frac{1}{4}$ million units compared with $1\frac{1}{2}$ million in Brazil, $3\frac{3}{4}$ million in Japan and $10\frac{1}{2}$ million in the U.K. The emphasis placed on capital investment had meant the evolution of a large Russian CV industry with annual output levels being exceeded only by the U.S.A. and Japan. The total CV population in 1967 was $4\frac{1}{4}$ million units compared with 2 million in the U.K.

That effective demand was greatly in excess of supply at the beginning of the 1970s was shown by the fact that the real price of cars was greatly in excess of the official price and waiting lists were extremely long. The official price of a new $2\frac{1}{2}$ litre Volga saloon was 6000 roubles, but almost-new second-hand models exchanged for between 12 000 and 15 000 roubles on the Moscow market and 18 000 roubles in provincial cities. In 1969 18 000 roubles equalled 15 years' wages for a factory worker. Hence immediate motoring is beyond the pockets of the great mass of the Soviet population. Vast numbers are nevertheless prepared to buy vehicles at the official price, even though finding the money is still a struggle. The waiting list for a new Russian 'Peoples Car', which in 1969 was already two years behind schedule in being put on the market, was already closed; its length was 10 years! The situation is summarised in *Figure 6.1*.

Obviously the Soviet second-hand car market suggests that the official price and output of new cars is too low and therefore demand exceeds supply, as is shown by the waiting lists. The answer is to expand output from OX to OX^1 with the official price at P^x. It is quite possible that with an increased scale of output that long-run average and marginal cost will be lower and hence the supply curve will fall from left to right. As a result the new output will be greater, but produced at a lower unit cost which could mean a reduction in price.

RUSSIAN 'FIATS': FOR DOMESTIC OR FOREIGN CONSUMPTION

The signs are that the Soviet Union has recognised that car ownership is not necessarily a bourgeois, anti-socialist, anti-Soviet phenomenon, and has taken steps to increase car output. Hence the firm agreement with Fiat to help establish the Soviet motor industry on an efficient mass-production basis; other agreements could eventually be made with Renault and Leyland. The Italians are building a new integrated car plant at Togliatti on the Volga which will produce just one type of car based on the Fiat 124 saloon. The designed capacity of the works

Figure 6.1

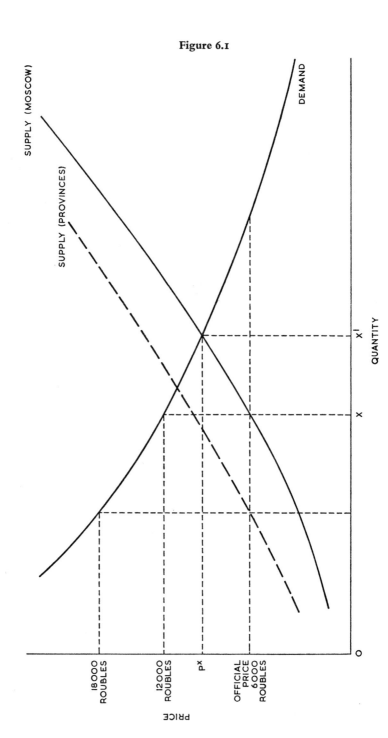

is 660 000 units a year, which will go far to realise the Russian plan to increase car output to a million units a year by the early 1970s. The total cost of the Volga plant was around £100 million, two-fifths of which was met by the Italians. Also Italy extended credits of over £15 million to meet the costs of purchasing equipment in third countries. The Russians are taking a leaf out of the Swedish book and are shopping around the world in search of the best equipment for particular tasks; the Japanese have supplied a plant to produce 13 million car engine filters a year which will supply the entire Russian vehicle industry; metal-cutting machine tools have been bought in the U.K.; various components are being purchased from Bulgaria and Hungary under the Comecon arrangements.

Everything else being equal, Western Europe should help to provide the U.S.S.R. with a highly efficient car industry fully able to meet a domestic demand at low real cost and price. However, the planned output of one million cars a year still seems inadequate to meet the Russian demand for cars, especially if the lower real cost of production is passed on in terms of lower official prices. Hence other European firms may be invited to help establish other car plants, while in Leyland's case they may be responsible for establishing an economically efficient bus plant. As a result the U.S.S.R. is unlikely to provide a major threat in world markets, although some cars will be sold abroad to obtain foreign exchange.

Under these circumstances the foreign price will bear no relationship to domestic price, for instance the Moskvitch 408 saloon costs the Russian buyer £1786 but is sold for 37% of this price in the U.K. and 33% in France. It is unlikely at the U.K. and French prices that this sale is still contributing to domestic fixed costs of production. This is because a car plant operating at around 80% of capacity finds that only about 15% of total costs are fixed costs; in other words, it is unlikely that all variable costs are covered and consequently an economist would say that Russian cars are 'dumped' on international markets in order to earn foreign exchange. This has had little effect on the world's market for cars as such supplies are limited by productive capacity and by bilateral agreements on the one hand, and by the lack of demand for solid but rather outdated Russian cars on the other. The emergence of Fiat-based cars at less than marginal cost on world markets would produce a greater demand but the two supply constraints would still exist, although underdeveloped countries anxious to purchase a supply of cheap cars could have some marginal effects on the traditional exporters. The 1970s will see the emergence of the U.S.S.R. as a major car producer, but it should be the 1980s which sees its emergence as a strong competitor in international markets, being too busy supplying the home demand in the interim*.

Assuming that Togliatti reaches its planned output of 660 000 vehicles a year, this is only scratching the surface of the Russian motorist's problems. In the first place he may still have a long wait for his car and secondly, when he receives it his problems begin again. Moscow with a population of $7\frac{1}{4}$ million has 19 repair centres and 105 petrol stations, and virtually no private garages to shield cars from the long Russian winter. Elsewhere in the U.S.S.R. the situation is worse. In other words, merely producing more cars highlights the lack of a motoring infrastructure. To alleviate this the planners would have to allocate considerable resources to aiding the private motorist. This would highlight two further problems: the inefficiency of the Russian system of the distribution and allocation of goods, such as spare parts for cars, and the fact that many car parts are not made in Russia at all but in the satellites. At the moment most Russian cars are owned by officials and private motoring has yet to appear. The new political climate caused by the discontent felt by a motorist watching his new, expensive, hard-won motor car, deteriorating or immobile because of the lack of adequate roads, garages, repair facilities, and so on may have very profound consequences.

COMMERCIAL VEHICLES

Due to the prominence given to investment in the Russian economic plans the U.S.S.R. has developed into a major producer of commercial vehicles; vehicles needed to transport the increased volume of merchandise produced by an economy with both a high growth rate and a growth rate geared to investment and away from consumption. The U.S.S.R. mass-produces lorries on a scale which is probably unequalled even in the U.S.A. or Japan; even in 1964 one factory was making 4000 units a week† or around 200 000 a year. By 1970 the planned output for the Russian CV industry was between 600 000 and 650 000 a year, the majority being vehicles of over 6 tons gross weight.

Despite the high volume of CV production, output has scarcely kept pace with home demand and the U.S.S.R. has had to import in

---

* At the time of writing it would appear that the domestic price of the Fiat based car will exceed 4500 roubles, or four years' average wages. Such a price may point to the intention to make considerable export sales at very low prices.

† *The Economist*, Supplement on Selling to the Motorist (24 October 1964).

considerable numbers from the Czech Skoda and Tatra concerns, as well as from Icarus in Hungary. In addition, it appears that the plant and equipment used in the Russian CV factories has been old and inefficient which has meant high volume high cost production. Attempts to overcome this have been made, but the reconstruction of the Likhachov motor works in Moscow which produces Zil trucks had in 1970 already taken seven years! Finally, many of the vehicles made have been of a poor quality with the added disadvantage of outdated design and technology. Many trucks still produced in 1970 were based on the designs of U.S. army Dodge and Chevrolet vehicles supplied to the U.S.S.R. during World War II. As a result of all this the Russian CV industry has not been able to make the best use of scarce resources and sales even to the underdeveloped world has not been great. It is possible, however, that this could change in the future and the Russian CV industry could become a force in the free market for such vehicles.

The present range of products plus the more rapid introduction of more efficient productive methods is putting the industry on a much surer footing. Allied to the sheer volume of medium and large CVs produced in the U.S.S.R. the real costs of producing modern CVs could be reduced below those prevailing elsewhere. If this occurs and the operation is backed by an effective marketing organisation, Russian CVs could become a real threat to the U.K. industry.

As in the case of car production the U.S.S.R.'s programme for the expansion of CV output depends on the reconstruction and modernisation of various enterprises. In 1970 the U.S.S.R. planned to produce between 600 000 and 650 000 vehicles. The reconstruction depended on the rapid installation of the most modern equipment. In effect this means introducing the most efficient equipment from different world sources. West Germany, for instance, is selling the U.S.S.R. machines for establishing automated lines for castings and mouldings*. The Japanese are supplying automated lines to produce truck doors as well as painting equipment and a plant capable of making 13 million engine filters a year. The U.K. is supplying expertise concerning all aspects of CV manufacture and assembly, as well as component and tool production. Particular emphasis is placed on British help to establish the capacity and technology to produce the diesel engines necessary. As the U.S.S.R. has mainly built petrol-engined trucks this has meant that Russian vehicles have not been easy to sell overseas. Hence Russian trucks sold in Belgium use Perkins engines; this helps sales as

* Daimler-Benz and Renault are building plants in the U.S.S.R. for the production of Russian commercial vehicles.

the large petrol engined CV is both technically and economically inefficient.

At the moment the U.S.S.R. imports over 2000 heavy diesel-engined vehicles from Hungary and Czechoslovakia plus almost 7000 trailers. On the export side, some 34 000 vehicles were exported in 1967. Well over 70% of these went to other Communist countries and the rest to countries such as the United Arab Republic as part of bilateral barter trade agreements. In a word the export of Russian commercial vehicles on the free market has been negligible, the sales that have occurred being part and parcel of bilateral arrangements. With the developments now taking place within the Russian motor industry the U.S.S.R. may develop as a long-term competitor in the open competition which is a feature of multi-lateral trading.

The organisation and structure of the Russian CV industry is non-competitive. Each plant of the Soviet motor industry concentrates on producing a very few basic models. Although this results in a multi-plicity of names, competition is non-existent and each range is com-plementary to that made in another plant. The five main Russian truck plants are the Moscow, Gorky, Byelorussian, Minsk and Krem-euchung motor works. The Likhachov motor works in Moscow, for instance, which produces the Zil six-ton truck, is part of a complex of plants. The main plant is served by other Zil plants in Moscow and elsewhere which provide vehicle parts. There are also close ties with other specialised plants which supply parts, units, and materials. The Gorky works produces the Gaz five-ton lorry and the Minsk works produces the Maz eight-ton lorry. All three plants are of much the same capacity and have similar production techniques and equipment. Each plant has a capacity of well over 150 000 units a year, making them the largest CV assembly and manufacturing plants in the world.

With the introduction of new equipment and products the unit cost of production in real terms should be extremely low. The Minsk factory also builds very heavy dumper lorries of between 25 and 65 tons gross weight on a mass-production basis! Again, if the product was good technically the Western CV producers could find their costs and prices undercut by a truly efficiently run Russian plant. Whereas the Zil, Gaz and Maz ranges cover the medium-weight market, the Kremenchung plant produces the heavy vehicles used on Russian highways. The Kraz six-wheel lorries cover the market for vehicles of between 16 and 22 ton gross, which is the lighter end of the heavy vehicle range. Other vehicles produced are for towing semi-trailers with the total weight involved being anything between 30 and 50 tons. Some of the Maz and Kraz vehicles use diesel engines. The Byelorussian plant produces super-heavy tip-up lorries for use in quarries and construction sites; these Belaz vehicles are made on a mass-production basis. So given Western levels of efficiency in production, marketing, and vehicle technology, the future Russian CV industry could produce all types of vehicle at very low long-run average cost levels which could undercut Western price levels. On the bus side minibuses are built in Riga, Kurgon, and Pavlavsk. Larger buses and trolley buses are made at Lvov and Likino. Again, very large production volumes are involved.

When one considers that 10 plants will be producing a total of around 650 000 vehicles in 1970 then one must conclude that the potential efficiency and strength of the industry is enormous. The early Five Year Plans, which laid the foundation of the motor industry, concentrated almost entirely on the production of commercial vehicles with a carrying capacity of between 2 and 5 tons. These light to medium vehicles were of poor quality technically. The post-war period had seen the emphasis placed on medium-weight and heavy-weight goods vehicles and buses*. Together with the U.S.A. and Japan, the U.S.S.R. is the only country which can rival the U.K. as a mass producer of medium-weight vehicles. In this field and in the field for heavy and super-heavy products the U.S.S.R. could emerge as one of the world's most efficient producers and provide strong competition to Western and Japanese firms. This is especially so following the planners new awareness concerning the need to improve the transport sector to aid growth.

In terms of car output, the Moscow works produces the low-powered Moskvitch, the Zaporozhye plant makes the Zaphorozhets mini-car, the Gorky plant makes the large-medium Volga and the large 'state-occasion' Chaikas based on the GMC Cadillac. In 1967 nearly all of the U.S.S.R.'s car output was of Volga and Moskvitch models; however, in the 1970s the largest single output will concern the Fiat based car from the Togliatti plant. The capacity of this latter plant is 660 000 units a year which should give extremely low production costs. So as in the case of commercial vehicles the 'Planned economy' can insist on the production of a few basic models. This should result in the optimum use of capacity in the existence of an homogeneous product, and in the imposition of a fixed price which approximates to a perfectly elastic demand curve. This would approximate to the economist's ideal of a 'perfectly competitive' market but without the competition. There would also be a welfare loss from the

---

* Even commercial vehicles were neglected in relation to the U.S.S.R.'s demand for transport services as was the entire transport sector. In the socialist economy distribution and service are the poor relations to production.

non-availability of choice, a choice which is given by imperfect competition.

OTHER PRODUCERS

Undoubtedly new world production centres will emerge. Nevertheless, the vast majority of the capacity and the capital will be controlled or dominated in one way or another by the world's existing major producers. The Latin American Free Trade Area is attempting some sort of integration for the highly fragmented motor industry within its boundaries*. The results to date have been disappointing, with 67 foreign firms producing over 200 basic models and 10 000 components in a market amounting to 650 000 vehicles in 1967. As countries insist on domestic assembly and, in time, domestic manufacture, rather than continuing to import complete vehicles, they impose 'domestic content' legislation. Firms failing to achieve these targets are faced by very steep tariffs on their imported parts. The establishment of a domestic industry on this basis leads to very high real costs of production. In the reference cited below it is stated that in Mexico a light CV with a domestic content of 'only' 63% costs 58% more than the imported equivalent, parts cost 119% more than imports. Brazil insists that vehicles made in the country should have a domestic content of 99% which imposes an 80% cost penalty on the same truck that is made in Mexico. Hence the proliferation of models plus the need to manufacture items locally means that significant scale economies are sacrificed. Firms are nowhere near short-term, let alone long-term, optimum production levels. Countries other than those mentioned use the same policies, and the emergence of nearly fully fledged domestic motor industries in Australia, Spain and South Africa is due to the same policy of economic nationalism.

The domestic assembly of vehicles from imported parts could be carried out with little cost disadvantage, if countries kept their 'import content' figure above 60%. The production facilities which allow the domestic content in total vehicle costs to exceed 40% are very costly, facilities which include those for making engines and transmissions and sheet metal bodies†. It is these items which on average account for 60% of a vehicle's costs and require huge investments in large-capacity high

---

* Jack Boranson, 'Integrated Automobiles for Latin America?', *Finance and Development*, Vol. 5, No. 4, International Monetary Fund (December 1968).
† British Leyland's Chilean assembly plant uses glass-fibre bodies, the cost of which at annual volumes of below 20 000 is much less than working in steel.

initial-cost body presses, automatic transfer machines, and other machine tools. The Australians impose a domestic content stipulation of over 95% for cars, the 5% of value left being imported virtually duty free. Firms failing to reach this proportion have to pay very high duties which more than compensate for the lower real cost of the imported parts compared with domestic manufacture. The firms in South Africa, Australia and Spain are either wholly foreign-owned subsidiaries or locally owned firms with exclusive contracts with foreign firms.

In all cases the domestic product costs more to produce than in the home country. The two factors of a smaller home market and the fragmentation of output between makes and models imposes a unit cost disadvantage. In South Africa 13 firms produced 26 different models in 1967; on average 4500 units per model were produced; in the U.K. the relevant three figures were 5, 35, and 60 000[*]. A large range of variations on a basic model can also add to costs, while the motor industry's suppliers have to produce a wide range of components and in small numbers. So in all cases a decrease in unit production costs requires both a growth in the market and a reduction in the range of models. However, in most countries the price premiums appear to be widening rather than narrowing, and many countries are finding that although it is relatively easy to establish a motor manufacturing industry the crucial consideration is the cost of doing so. This problem is now being recognised. Mexico for instance only allows the establishment of productive capacity if the potential output is large enough to give some economies of scale[†], and several firms have been excluded from the market on these grounds. Spain has a similar policy. Australia distinguishes between large and small companies when applying local-content targets. Even so the cost and price of cars produced by these 'newer' industries is greater than those prevailing in the home markets of the firms concerned, and the worst examples of high cost production tend to be found in Latin America. Even the huge investments required when the proportion of local content is pushed above 40% of total costs does not necessarily preclude in the short-run the existence of a large number of firms in the industry. In the long run the number of firms in the various industries could be reduced as price competition, allied to sub-optimum production, pushes firms out of the market. In Australia, for instance, Volkswagen

---

[*] I. C. Griffiths 'The South African Motor Industry', *Standard Bank Review*, Supplement (June 1968).

[†] Volkswagen is concentrating the production of certain components in its Mexican plant for use in overseas and German assembly plants.

has abandoned its local manufacturing facilities as the venture was proving unprofitable. The 'short-term', however, is in most cases proving very long and the present picture of fragmentation and many models leading to small production runs but at high cost is likely to continue. The likely exceptions are Spain and Australia where the process of concentration of output is gathering pace.

THE OVERSEAS MOTOR INDUSTRIES: SOME CONCLUSIONS

In the last two chapters the discussion has covered important and not so important vehicle producing nations. In terms of efficiency the low-cost American firms cannot be equalled, and the American consumer receives more car for his money and at lower real cost than any other car buyer. In Europe the technical and economic efficiencies of the car producers are broadly similar, although Volkswagen and Fiat probably have some cost advantage. However, although most of the major European car firms are at very similar positions on their long-run average cost curves, it would appear that the process of demand and cost-inflation in the U.K. has tended to push direct and fixed costs out of line. Mainly due to increased direct costs the short-run average cost curves in the British economy have perhaps tended to be above those experienced by European counterparts. Devaluation has tended to neutralise this but it will only be a 'once and for all' improvement if the U.K. car industry does not improve its labour productivity, partly by improving its labour relations and avoiding strikes, by reducing over manning, by using the most efficient capital equipment and by closing small inefficient plants. Once production costs are controlled further economies of scale could come from an improved marketing initiative. This must entail the final acceptance that the consumer is to be wooed, and is no longer to be regarded as someone who should be thankful for being given the privilege of owning a British car. Both the manufacturer and retailer have a role to play here if the U.K. motor industry is to successfully meet the challenge presented by the motor industries in these countries.

There are no intrinsic reasons why the British motor industry should not compete successfully with the motor industry in other countries. After all, even companies as strong as Volkswagen—the largest car firm in Europe—show some alarming weaknesses; despite numerous attempts to diversify the company is still essentially a one product firm, and of a total output of over $1\frac{1}{2}$ million units in 1969, over 1 million were 'Beetles', the other two car ranges and commercial vehicles accounting for the rest. The company's products are not as popular in Germany as they are abroad, indeed, more VWs were sold in the U.S.A. in 1969 than in West Germany, for while over 500 000 were sold in the U.S.A. less than this were sold at home. Indeed, lack of design ideas which would have enabled VW to push its share of the

Table 6.7

1969 OUTPUT TOTALS FOR MAJOR EUROPEAN PRODUCERS

Volkswagen	1 530 000
Fiat	1 210 000
Renault	910 000
British Leyland	850 000

home market above 32% was one reason why the company purchased NSU, a small company with an interesting range of current and projected models. Fiat began experiencing severe labour problems in the late 1960s, often the result of pressures by politically motivated unions in pursuit of wider political and social aims, such as improved housing. Nevertheless, some discontent has been caused by Fiat's paternalistic attitude to workers and other strikes are based on tactical reasons when collective contracts come up for renewal. Although such strikes are mainly official, and tend neither to be protracted nor persistent (unlike the endemic nature of strikes in the U.K.), nevertheless their incidence in the early 1970s was increasing. In the German car factories absenteeism has become a feature of the 1970s and employers have faced increasing difficulties over incentive schemes, changes in production methods, and the need to find workers overseas which often means expensive training. This is not to say that Continental firms have not in many ways shown themselves more aware of the needs of the market or to pay a greater deal of attention to labour relations than British ones. What it does suggest is that an efficiently run British motor industry could easily hold its own in world markets.

The events of the early 1970s clearly indicated that while the 1960s was a decade when profitability, growth and investment in the U.K. was poor[*], at a time when the main Continental producers presented a picture of dynamic and profitable growth, competitive pressures could easily change commercial fortunes. Successive currency revaluations by West Germany, labour unrest and higher wage demands in France and Italy, the staggering growth of Japanese vehicle production, the

[*] See Chapter 9.

attempt to instil long-needed efficiency improvements into British industry, all tended to challenge the trends of the 1960s. The financial results returned by the firms shown in *Table 6.8* in 1970 show that the Continental producer has no unique claim to efficiency and financial solvency.

Table 6.8

FINANCIAL PERFORMANCE OF THE MAJOR
EUROPEAN PRODUCERS IN 1970

Firm	Net profits (£ million)	Change on 1969 (%)
Volkswagen	23	−42·4
Audi NSU	−76·3*	—
Opel	30	−41·7
German Ford	30	−10·0
Daimler-Benz	20·7	−10·5
BMW	4·1	−25·1
Fiat	3·5	−86·0†
British Leyland	4·0	−85·5
British Ford	21·1	−45·0

* — £76·3 thousand, not million as shown in all other instances. Audi showed a profit of £1·5 million in 1969.
† Estimated figure.

In some instances these results were both cause and effect of executive and managerial strife at the highest level, as at VW in 1971, which only reinforces the point that Britain's motor industry, given the correct attitude to product development, marketing, labour relations, and investment in the most efficient techniques, can remain a significant commercial force. Although the British industry had fallen behind in terms of scale of operation during the 1960s, size in itself is not a sufficient condition for survival in competitive markets. The control of costs, the degree of competition, production, scales and future model

Table 6.9

TURNOVER OF THE MAJOR EUROPEAN
FIRMS IN 1970 (£ MILLION)

Volkswagen	1 797
Daimler-Benz	1 329
Renault	1 177
Fiat	1 141
British Leyland	1 020

policy, are all major problems which size may help to solve, but there is no guarantee that would occur. *Table 6.9* allied to the profit figures in *Table 6.8* clearly illustrates the thin edge between profit and loss experienced by even the giant European producers.

It would appear that at the time of writing the main British producer although overshadowed in gross turnover terms is not alone in facing economic and financial difficulties, and indeed there are signs that British Leyland could make up much of the lost ground in terms of profits and output during the 1970s, given the new marketing and product philosophy of the new management structure, points which receive elaboration elsewhere. The question is begged here as to whether Leyland Motors, by using its truck and quality car base, would have been better advised to concentrate on developing these facilities, instead of burdening itself with the task of reviving the ailing BMC combine. Daimler-Benz, by concentrating on such a policy, had done extremely well. However, the passage of time may prove the industrial logic of the Leyland-BMH merger.

7

THE DEMAND FOR MOTOR VEHICLES

In 1904 the total number of cars in use in the U.K. amounted to 8465; by 1968 the figure was 11 078 000. Clearly the market for cars has expanded enormously since the beginning of the century. In 1904 there was approximately one car for every 3890 members of the population; by 1969 the ratio was almost one car for every five persons. In the early years up to and including World War I the motor car and motoring was for the few. People who had sufficient purchasing power plus the desire to own motor cars were relatively few in numbers; in 1914 just over 130 000 cars existed in a country with a total population of around 37 million people. Before 1914 the number of people wanting cars, even if they could afford them, was small*. World War I changed all that.

War-time service trained more and more people in the use of cars and a fair number received a gratuity at the end of the war. These two factors meant that now nearly everyone appeared to want a car and a large number of people could afford to buy a medium priced vehicle, the demand for which was largely satisfied by Morris. In addition, the production of shells, mines, and munitions generally, had trained manufacturers to mass-produce. One element of the social revolution caused by the war was the realisation that the horse had

* Here is a fascinating quotation: 'This year will see a colossal weekly output of motor cars . . . the total . . . per week is not far short of 250 . . . To the casual observer it doubtless appears that soon this rate of supply must diminish, since all those who require motor cars will have been supplied', *Birmingham Post* (20 April 1907).

failed under modern demands but the motor vehicle had not. The 'socialites' and leaders of fashion saw that the car could help in their sporting activities rather than hinder them, for instance the development of the horse-box. All these factors brought more and more people into favourable contact with the motor car. Morris, realising that the car was for the masses and not for the few, was in a position to satisfy this growing market.

THE GROWTH OF CAR DEMAND

The original growth in demand for cars came from people who could afford to buy a motor car and who also had the inclination to buy one because of the value, satisfaction, utility or what you will which the product had for them. Before 1914 this meant the rich and that section of the rich who were regarded as procurers of vulgar trinkets. The really 'respectable' people still gave their favour to the horse. The typical price of the cars bought by such people were between £800 and £1000 or at 1970 prices £4800 to £6000. After the war Morris supplied cars at prices in the region of £340 or at 1970 prices at around £850. This initial growth in demand, which was based simply on the demand for a new product, may have lasted until 1956 when less than 9% of domestic car sales were for replacement purposes. It has been suggested that this stage was reached by the U.S.A. in 1921[*], but the slower early development of the British industry plus the pent-up demand caused by World War II meant that the initial forces of expansion in the demand for new cars remained active for longer in the U.K.[†]

Once this initial period was over then the growth in the demand for cars became less a function of the exploitation of a new product in an existing market but more dependent on other factors such as the growth of income and variations in the supply of credit. It is to the demand for vehicles in a fully developed market that we now want to turn.

[*] P. de Wolff, 'Demand for Passenger Cars in the United States', *Econometrica*, Vol. 6, pp. 113–129 (January 1938).

[†] As late as 1953 many second-hand car prices were *above* the list price when new. By 1954 things had eased and especially after 1956 when the large capital expansion of the industry between 1954 and 1958 began to bear fruit.

EMPIRICAL CAR-DEMAND FUNCTIONS

In a mature market M. J. Farrell stresses that the prime motivation is not the demand for new cars as such but a demand for car ownership[*]. Normally cars are sold before they wear out. Consequently a car owner can be flexible in deciding whether to replace his car or not. If he postpones or accelerates replacement then new car sales will vary but the demand for vehicle ownership will be constant.

In a mature market, a function explaining car purchases will include family disposable income, relative prices, the stock of cars, the number of households and the 'creation' of demand through the introduction of new models. Other factors could be the relative growth rates of rural and urban population, the availability of alternative means of transport, the trend of road and town planning and construction, traffic legislation, society's attitude to the car, and congestion. This last factor measured in terms of cars per mile may prevent British ownership levels ever reaching the American cars per head figure. To these items we must add the very important 'credit conditions' factor, but even then we are leaving out one very important variable. This is the aforementioned fact that car purchases can be postponed and people may use the same car for a number of years. Hence in a recession consumer demand for cars falls and the ratio of consumer durable demand in general to family disposable income will fall.

The non-proportionality of the consumption-function for durables was noted by Roos and Szeliski[†]. They attempted to cover this problem for assessing car demand by making car purchases a function of 'supernumerary' income. This was defined as the income left after paying for the basic necessities of life. The hypothesis was that supernumerary income fell even in a quite small recession. However, for post-war years this is not really borne out in either the U.S.A. or the U.K.; even in the most severe post-war recessions disposable income hardly fell at all, for the 'built-in stabilisers' in the economy, such as progressive taxes and unemployment pay, tend to maintain disposable incomes. Hence a valid hypothesis states that many consumers would reduce car purchases even if their own incomes are not reduced. In other words, a key variable explaining car demand could simply be expectations. We could be faced with a situation where, if people

[*] M. J. Farrell, 'The Demand for Motor Cars in the United States', *Journal of the Royal Statistical Society*, Series A (General), Pt. 2, Vol. 117, pp. 171–198 (1954).
[†] C. F. Roos and V. Szeliski, 'Factors Governing Changes in Domestic Automobile Demand' in *The Dynamics of Automobile Demand*, GMC, New York, pp. 21–95 (1939).

think times will be adverse, they would not purchase cars even though they are not directly affected. The Survey Research Centre of Michigan University built an exogenous attitudes index in order to measure attitudes. In practice it has been found that if the demand for cars is depicted as

$$C = f(Y),$$

i.e. consumption is a function of income alone, then the attitudes index takes on an important explanatory role. In consumption functions utilising more than one explanatory variable the 'subjective' attitude index can be successfully substituted by other more objective factors without harming the explanatory role of the function. F. G. Adams in one study[*] and I. Friend and Adams in another[†] found that generally speaking the length of the work week is a better explanatory variable representing general cyclical movements and their effects on car purchase.

During the 1950s it was thought in the U.S.A. that the cycles of good years and bad years for car purchases was due to tastes and the effects of style changes when new models were introduced. However, as the period 1960 to 1968 as a whole was a period of good years, model changes as an explanation of good year and bad year cycles has largely been discounted. There is little evidence suggesting that new car sales were higher when firms introduced new models than in years when only slight face lifting occurred[‡] Once a cyclical attitude variable of one sort or another is introduced the explanation of vehicle purchases can be made without the need to introduce a 'taste' variable.

Typical car demand functions look like this:

$$C_c = a + b\ Y - \left(\frac{Tr}{Pc}\right) - c\left(\frac{Pa}{Pc}\right) - dUu - eX_s \qquad \S$$
$$+ f\ Cr - g\ (a) - 1 \qquad R^2 = 0 \cdot 916$$

or

* F. G. Adams, 'Consumer Attitudes, Buying Plans, and Purchases of Durable Goods: A Principal Components, Time Series Approach', *Review Economics and Statistics*, Vol. 46, No. 4.
† I. Friend and F. G. Adams, 'The Predictive Ability of Consumer Attitudes, Stock Prices, and Non-Attitudinal Variables', *Journal of the American Statisticians Association*, Vol. 59, No. 4, pp. 987–1005.
‡ A better case can be made for the reverse hypothesis: that more new cars are introduced in good years than bad. The existence of prosperity improves the chances of a successful launching of a new model.
M. K. Evans, *Macroeconomic Activity Theory Forecasting and Control*, Harper and Row, New York, pp. 168–172 (1969).

$$C = a_o + a_1 Y + a_2 Y^2 + a_3 L_1 + a_4 L_2 + a_5 R + a_6 N_a$$
$$+ a_7 N_b + a_8 N_c \qquad \bigstar$$

or

$$D_t = f\left(Y_t \; P_t \; h_t \; S_{t-1} \; t\right) \qquad \dagger$$

In the first function the R^2 of 0·916 is the coefficient of determination, and is the ratio of the explained variation to total variation. Roughly speaking, over 91% of the variation in car demand is explained by the independent variables in the first equation. This formula says that the purchase of cars (C_c) is a function of: (1) personal disposable income (Y) minus transfer payments (Tr/Pc) which gives a figure for 'super-numerary' income; (2) the relative prices of cars (Pa/Pc); (3) the attitude variable given by the numbers unemployed (Uu); (4) by a dummy variable for supply shortages (eX_s); (5) by a dummy variable for credit conditions (Cr) and (6) by the stock of cars (a), that is, the value of the total number of cars in the economy. A plus sign says that, for instance, as 'supernumerary' income increases by 10 units it is associated with an increase of car demand of 1·346 units. A minus sign suggests that an increase in unemployment of 10 units is associated with a reduction in car demand of 4·3 units. The terms a to g are the parameters of the model.

In the second equation expenditure on cars is made a function of; disposable income (Y); the age brackets of the head of each spending unit $(a_1 - a_5)$; the numbers of adults, children and income earners in each spending unit $(N_a, N_b$ and $N_c)$; whether the family unit is in a rural area or an urban one $(L_1$ and $L_2)$; and R the race of the spending unit. No stock variable is included here but if the proportion of income spent on cars falls as income increases then it supports the hypothesis that the demand for cars decreases as the stock increases but increases as incomes increase. This is simply the capital stock adjustment principle $I_t = I_a + hY_{t-1} - jK_t$ where K is the capital stock in period t, and h and j are constants. If output, Y, increases while K is constant then investment increases. If K increases with Y constant I will fall as the desired stock of capital is quickly reached. In other words, the change in the consumption of cars is a function of changes in income.

The third formulation makes car demand (D) a function of per capita real income (Y), relative prices (P), hire-purchase (h) conditions and a time variable (t). S_{t-1} accounts for the lag in adjustment from the present stock level to the desired level. The data covered the years 1948–1956 compared with 1955–1957 for the Bennett analysis and 1948–1964 for the first demand function.

Other studies exist* but they largely cover the ground mentioned already. As we proceed we will bring in some of the results suggested by these theories covering the relationship between price and income changes on the one hand and variations in the demand for cars on the other.

THE DEMAND FOR CAR OWNERSHIP AND THE DEMAND FOR NEW CARS:
A DIFFERENCE

Before looking at the demand for new cars in a little more detail it should be stressed that often the demand for vehicle ownership makes itself felt in the market for second-hand cars. The market for second-hand cars is broadly equivalent in size to the market for new cars, although in the case of CVs this is not so. These conclusions are drawn from the record of hire-purchase contracts recorded by H.P. Information Ltd.† and the annual summary of new vehicle registrations‡. In the U.K. in 1967 for instance, 1 143 015 new car registrations were recorded and in the same year 1 158 581 new hire-purchase contracts for used cars were made. Clearly not all cars are sold on credit— roughly two new cars in seven are sold this way—and consequently the market in used cars exceeds that for new vehicles.

Many people become car owners for the first time by buying second-hand vehicles and the growth in car ownership is more a function of second-hand purchases than of buying new cars. In turn, second-hand cars are sold to become third-hand cars and so on. The desire for car

* R. H. Bandeen, 'Automobile Consumption 1940–1950; *Econometrica*, No. 25, pp. 239–248 (April 1957).
   H. S. Houthakker and J. Haldi, 'Household Investment in Automobiles: An inter-temporal cross-section analysis', in I. Friend and R. Jones (eds.), *Consumption and Saving*, University of Pennsylvania Press, Philadelphia (1959).
   G. C. Chow, *Demand for Automobiles in the U.S.A.*, North Holland Publishing Co., Amsterdam (1957).
   A. C. Harberger (ed.), *The Demand for Durable Goods*, University of Chicago Press, Chicago (1960).
   D. Suits, 'The Demand for New Automobiles in the U.S.A. 1929–1956', *Review of Economics and Statistics*, Vol. 40, pp. 273–280 (August 1958).
   L. J. Atkinson, 'Consumer Markets for Durable Goods', *Survey of Current Business*, pp. 19–24 (April 1952).
   † *Motor Industry Reporting*, SMMT, Vol. 1, No. 6 (December 1969).
   ‡ *Motor Industry of Great Britain*, SMMT, Table No. 23 (1968).

ownership for different income groups can be satisfied by entering the car market at different levels. The student can purchase a tenth-hand 'banger' for £25 whereas the company director purchases a £10 000 limousine. With increasing prosperity following from higher real incomes the owners of very old cars 'trade-up' to newer ones and the owners of slightly newer cars do the same with a number of people at the top of the scale entering the new car market for the first time. The greater the demand in the second-hand market the higher the prices; this in turn leads to better trading-in allowances for people selling cars to buy new ones, and in turn this activates the market for new cars. This readiness to replace one's car by a new one reinforces the demand for new cars following from higher incomes. So it must be realised that most new car buyers already own cars; hence their demand for new cars is a replacement demand. In other words, nearly *all* new registrations reflect a replacement demand but because of the second-hand car market there is still a net increase in society's stock of vehicles (*Table 7.1*).

Table 7.1

Year	New Registrations (1000s)	Change in Stock (1000s)	Net New Demand (%)
1960	820	570	69·5
1961	756	464	61·4
1962	800	592	74·0
1963	1 031	841	81·5
1964	1 216	889	73·1
1965	1 149	695	60·5
1966	1 091	616	56·4
1967	1 143	807	70·6
1968	1 145	524	45·5

We see that normally over 50% of all new car sales add to the car stock. Conversely, less than 50% are replacement sales in the sense of maintaining society's vehicle stock in terms of car numbers. It is likely, however, that nearly 100% of all new car sales replace existing cars, so almost all the increase in car ownership comes from people entering not the new car market but the second-hand car market. Consequently the basic demand is, as we have said before, not a demand for new vehicles but a demand for vehicle ownership and it is because of this that the stock of vehicles increases in a mature car market.

Farrell, Chow, Bennett and Evans measure the demand for car

ownership; Atkinson, Roos and von Szeliski, de Wolff and Suits look at the demand for new cars although Suits introduces elements allowing new car purchases to depend indirectly on ownership. The 1961 NIESR study of car demand in the U.K. looks at car ownership, but the 1967 NIESR model* together with O'Herlihy's estimate† looks at the current demand for new cars directly without introducing the concept of car stock or needing to estimate replacement rates.

The difference between the demand for car ownership and the demand for new vehicles has the following result. If the price elasticity of demand for car ownership is one then a 10% increase in price reduces ownership by 10%. If the car population or the ownership level is 12 million 'new car units' and depreciation is 25% a year then annual replacement demand is 3 million cars. With a price increase of 10% consumers will want to reduce their ownership level by 10% or by 1 200 000. This they can do by buying less than 3 million new cars. If the entire adjustment of ownership is made in one year only 1·8 million new cars will be purchased. This is a decline of 40% in new car purchases. So the elasticity of new car purchases with respect to price is − 4, which is four times the price elasticity of ownership.

Because new purchases of durable goods are normally smaller than the total stock, the effect of a change in an independent variable on the stock of durables is less than the effect on net changes in stock. In economics this magnified effect is part of the 'acceleration principle'. The degree of magnification depends on two factors: (1) the annual rate of depreciation and (2) the extent to which customers make the full adjustment to their required stock level in any one year. This second factor is very important for cars in particular and durables in general. In our example we had a four year life cycle plus full adjustment in one year. An increased rate of depreciation plus a longer adjustment process would have reduced the price elasticity of new car purchases. The studies concerned with ownership derive the changes in new car sales from changes in ownership. Those studies estimating new demand directly avoid introducing the concept of a car stock, the annual replacement rate and the adjustment period. In many ways these models are superior because estimates of car and commercial vehicle demand are of course very sensitive to the assumptions made concerning replacement and adjustment rates. On the other hand car ownership does utilise the basic demand motivation in a mature market.

* C. St. J. O'Herlihy *et al.*, 'Long Term Forecasts of Demand for Cars, Selected Consumer Durables, and Energy', *National Institute Economic Review*, No. 40 (May 1967).

† J. O'Herlihy 'Demand for Cars in Great Britain', *Applied Statistics*, No. 162 (1965).

Only O'Herlihy, Bennett and Farrell bring in the interdependence of new and second-hand markets and deal with the demand for cars of all ages.

THE INCOME ELASTICITY OF DEMAND

In analysing the factors governing the demand for cars all studies stress the importance of personal disposable income. Any change in income will produce a change in vehicle demand of the same sign. In all the econometric studies mentioned the long-run income elasticity of demand is to be found somewhere in the range from 1·1 to 4·2. Evans suggested that a 1% change in income would lead to a 1·1% change in consumption in the long-run, while the short-run result suggests a figure of 2·2%. At the other end of the scale, Suits puts forward an income elasticity of 4·2. Leaving aside the extreme values, the income elasticity of demand was generally found to be in the range 1·43 to 3·0. The U.K. figures are within the region of 2·4. Obviously any increase or decrease in domestic disposable income will have a profound effect on new car sales, and also on total production and employment given the size of the export ratio. In a mature car market personal disposable income is the most important independent variable. On some occasions a time-trend variable may appear to be equally significant, but this is normally a combination of other factors such as tastes, population increase, and relative prices, the influence of which has changed systematically over time at a constant rate. Consequently they can all be combined in a constant growth trend; the 1961 NIESR model reduces to $C_t = f(Y_t t)$, changes in the net stock of cars being a function of disposable real income and a time trend.

THE PRICE ELASTICITY OF DEMAND

However, most empirical demand functions attempt to isolate factors other than income and to gauge their influence on car demand. One important factor is the relative price of cars, that is, the ratio of car prices to consumer prices generally. A change in this ratio is equivalent to a change in real relative prices and the effects of this on car demand can give an estimate of the price elasticity of demand. In the various empirical studies the long run price elasticity varies from −0·6 to −1·5; Evans's short-run estimate is −5·1. It must be stressed that all these studies relate *total* car demand to different explanatory variables;

to relate the demand for the cars of a particular firm to such variables
would probably give different results. The price elasticity of BMC
cars if BMC cut its prices relative to those of its competitors would
probably give a larger elasticity of demand, perhaps as high as -4*.
In general, empirical studies indicate that around 80% ($R^2 = 0.8$) of the
variation in car demand is explained by income and relative prices.
The factors affecting demand which are still to be considered should
be seen in this light.

HIRE-PURCHASE AND ITS EFFECTS ON VEHICLE DEMAND

Given that annually about one-quarter of new cars are sold on hire-
purchase credit and over one million used cars, the general climate
of credit conditions could be an important factor in explaining car
demand. Since 1953, when records began, hire-purchase sales have
become more important. Concentrating on hire-purchase tends to
under-estimate the impact of credit sales but no comprehensive data is
available for cars bought on other forms of credit, say personal loans
from commercial banks. The hire-purchase position is given in
Table 7.2.

Table 7.2

HIRE-PURCHASE CONTRACTS

Contracts	1953	1964	1968
New cars (1000s)	26·5	329·3	296·6
Proportion of total (%)	9	27	26
New CVs (1000s)	13·5	67·8	65·4
Proportion of total (%)	13	28	26
Used Cars (1000s)*	167·6	1 065·2	1 160·8
Used CVs (1000s)	26·2	141·5	84·5

* Official estimates suggest that between 40% and 50% of total second-
hand car sales involved H.P. contracts.

Consequently an x% change in vehicles sold on hire-purchase will
have a $0.26x$% effect on total new car sales, and about a $0.4x$% effect
on all car sales.

A number of studies have looked at the influence of hire-purchase
credit on car demand. These include analysing the pattern of contracts
taken out—whether for one year, two years or longer—and the rate at

* See later an estimate of the elasticity of demand for Rootes cars in 1968–1969.
p. 275.

which these are completed*. Not surprisingly, most contracts are taken out for the maximum permitted period although this is more marked with new cars than with second-hand ones. As expected, as the maximum period is diminished by credit squeeze, then the proportion of maximum length contracts increases as the upper time periods are compressed. Most contracts run for their intended life-span, although some are terminated early.

The relationship between old contracts and fresh contracts has also been studied. The analysis did not support the idea that the completion of contracts at maturity influenced the degree of fresh hire-purchase business. Nevertheless, a relationship was found between the taking out of some fresh contracts and the early completion of existing ones; however, as it was difficult to predict early completion this relationship was of limited value in forecasting. That is, only about 25% of the variation in fresh contracts was associated with variation in early termination: Y (early completions) $= a + 0.25Y$ (change in fresh contracts). Therefore determining when hire-purchase contracts end is of little importance in forecasting changes in car ownership of old or new cars.

Other studies look at the effects of hire-purchase controls on private car sales† and find that the effect of an increase in severity of hire-purchase controls leads to a decrease in the rate of growth of new car sales on hire-purchase and vice versa‡.

The 1961 NIESR study introduced a variable measuring changes in hire-purchase conditions but found that the annual demand data was not sensitive enough to detect any significant relationship between changes in such conditions and changes in the stock of cars. However, Evans found from U.S. data that changes in credit controls were highly significant. In his basic model he used a dummy variable but found that the effect of changing credit conditions was better represented by changes in the monthly repayment burden. Although variations in interest rates would affect hire-purchase conditions, consumer demand was fairly interest-inelastic. The significant items were the percentage down payment and the maximum repayment period. Given the price of the product, it was variations in these items which greatly affected

* *Bank of England Quarterly Review*, Vol. 7, No. 3, pp. 268–275 (September 1967).

† P. Galambos, 'A Note on the Effect of Hire Purchase Control on the Sales of Private Motor Cars in the U.K. from February 1952 to December 1960', *Yorkshire Bulletin*, Vol. 14, No. 1, pp. 37–54 (May 1962).

‡ In the early 1960s only 6% of used cars and 4% of new cars were financed by credit other than H.P. (*Economic Trends*, C.S.O., 1965). However, by 1971 the growth in personal loans initially caused by tax incentives and then by avoiding H.P. restrictions, must have grown considerably.

the monthly repayment burden and hence the demand for cars. Evans produced a monthly 'payment term' of

$$P = \frac{Pc \, (1-D) \, (1+F)}{Ps \, . \, M}$$

where P is an index of the average monthly payment, Pc is a price index of cars, D the percentage down payment, F the finance charge rate, M the length of the contract and Ps a value of money index, so that $Ps \, . \, M$ are dollars measured in constant terms. Any change in hire-purchase control conditions would vary the monthly repayments.

One point to note is that as car demand is price elastic, any increase in car prices with credit controls constant must still increase monthly repayments and therefore reduce demand. Even if the repayment period was lengthened to offset the price increase so that P remains constant, unless it is argued that cash buyers have an elastic demand but credit buyers do not, then demand must still fall. This conclusion would follow from the inclusion of a separate car-price index Pa/Pc.

During periods of economic prosperity the growth in income would in itself increase demand. The importance of credit sales, however, means that with the easing of credit controls, demand increases by $0.75x(Y) + 0.25x$ where x is the total number of cars bought. As credit sales are about a quarter of total sales, any increased demand following from an increase in disposable income is only three-quarters of the total potential increase. If the other quarter of the market is to grow proportionately it requires an easing of credit restrictions.

In a recession increased controls reinforce the squeeze caused by the reduced growth of incomes. Following the boom in car output and registrations in 1964 the minimum deposit on cars was increased from 20% to 25% in June 1965. In July 1965 the repayment period was cut from 36 months to 30 months, in February 1966 to 27 months and, in July 1966 to 24 months, and the minimum deposit increased to 40%. This coincided with a slump in new registrations from 1 216 000 in 1964 to 1 091 000 in 1966, the net increase in car stock falling from 889 000 in 1964 to 616 000 in 1966. In 1967 hire purchase restrictions were eased considerably with the result that new registrations increased to 1 143 000, a net increase in stock of 807 000 or 70·6% of total new registrations. This was at a time when the economy was being squeezed by monetary and fiscal measures and real disposable incomes grew very little. In November 1967 hire-purchase controls were hardened again with a further tightening in November 1968. Although new registrations increased marginally in 1968 to 1 145 000 the stock of cars only increased by 524 000, 54·5% of new registrations being used to renew society's stock of vehicles.

Since 1952, when hire purchase restrictions were first introduced, variations in the rate of growth of the car stock have been closely connected with credit conditions*. Consequently the abolition of all official restrictions on hire-purchase (i.e. no officially specified down-payment on repayment period) in July 1971—for the first time since October 1958—was aimed at increasing the effective demand for cars. This marked the end of a period of restriction in the vehicle market which had lasted since June 1965—the longest squeeze faced by the British economy in general and by the vehicle market in particular.

It should be indicated that the above conclusion would not be held universally. A study by M. A. Ali suggests that changes in the minimum deposit rates and maximum repayment period would only effect the demand for cars to a limited extent†. However, the analysis is mainly concerned with the elasticity of the degree of responsiveness of car demand to changes in hire-purchase controls. As the elasticity co-efficient is significantly less than one it is concluded that changes in hire-purchase conditions would have little effect on total car demand. In reply to this it could be argued that here, as in the case of income elasticity, the important consideration is whether the coefficient is greater than zero, not as in the case of price elasticity whether it is greater than one. If elasticity is very low but greater than zero, then changes in hire-purchase conditions could still significantly affect the absolute volume of car sales, even if in percentage terms the change in demand is small relative to the change in hire-purchase controls. For instance, if total domestic car demand is one million units a year, restrictions are then eased by a factor of 20%, and car demand increases by 4%, then although the elasticity coefficient is only $-0·2$, car demand still increases by 40 000 units. This would be a considerable amount when it is remembered that car makers are able to sell extra cars without lowering their prices and at lower unit costs.

Other financial factors include the effects of tighter credit conditions generally, which reduces the borrowing facilities at the banks to finance vehicle purchases. It is also probably true to say that between 30% and 50% of yearly new car registrations are accounted for by business and commercial organisations. Furthermore, the need to protect a corporate image necessitates the use of newer cars. Con-

* A. Silberston, 'Hire Purchase Controls and the Demand for Cars', *Economic Journal*, pp. 32–53 and pp. 556–558, (March and September 1963).
    P. Galambos, *Yorkshire Bulletin* (May 1962).
    † M. A. Ali, 'Hire Purchase Controls and the Post-war Demand for Cars in the U.K.', *Journal of Economic Studies*, Vol. 1, No. 1 (1965).

sequently variations in investment allowances and depreciation provisions can greatly affect the real costs of cars and commercial vehicles to the individual business unit. In fact, despite the slow growth in incomes, tax allowances such as these have helped to maintain commercial demand for cars. In 1969 over 50% of all cars registered were for business purposes compared with 40% in 1967–1968. In short, business demand fell less than private demand during an intensified squeeze.

THE STOCK OF CARS

The other significant independent variable is the economy's stock of cars. In early consumer durable studies stocks were found to be insignificant as an explanatory variable, although this may have been because of unsatisfactory treatment of the stock measurement. To calculate stock either by counting units or straight line depreciation does not give a true stock value. Chow's study was a breakthrough in that he held that the market did not regard all cars as being equivalent. Chow measured the car-stock in terms of new-car equivalents, the 'weights' used being different relative prices of cars of different ages. Other studies use similar techniques often depreciating cars of different size classes at their own appropriate rate. For example, large cars depreciate quicker than small cars; a Ford Zodiac Six Mk IV depreciated 24% in the first year compared with 12% for a Cortina 1300*. If cars are divided between small, medium and large the three totals can be combined into a single figure measuring vehicle stock. This is done by counting small cars as one unit, medium cars as two, and large cars as three, or any other arbitrary scale. The net stock can then be measured in small new car equivalents. Chow found an annual rate of depreciation of 23% for the period 1920–1953. This rate had fluctuated little, reflecting the same market conditions over the entire period, i.e. those of a mature fully developed market.

Different markets show different rates of depreciation. As incomes increase and a market reaches maturity people change their cars more often thereby increasing the stock of used cars. As a result used car prices tend to fall. Hence the average rate of depreciation in the U.K. is about 15% compared with 23% in the U.S.A.†. Since the war the rate of depreciation of British cars has steadily increased, for instance, in 1955 a five year old Morris Minor was 80% of its new price, in

* *Motorists Guide* (February 1970).
† *The Economist*, p. 391 (24 October 1964).

1964 a five year old Morris 1000 was 45% of new price, and in 1970 a five year old was 44% of new. Depreciation rates in France and West Germany are higher than in the U.K. This is partly explained by the fact that the car ownership per head tends to be higher than in the U.K., in other words they are more mature markets. Other factors can explain a larger rate of depreciation however; (1) a rapid surge of new car sales as prosperity increased thereby limiting the market for second-hand cars; (2) distribution of income, for instance in Italy car buyers can afford either a new car or a very cheap one, there are very few people in between; (3) the sophistication and strength of the second-hand car market itself. Bearing this in mind, different depreciation rates may be applicable in different countries and at different times but when the market reaches maturity then depreciation becomes fairly constant.

In demand studies the demand for cars varies directly with changes in income but inversely with stock changes. Consequently a stock level which is high in relation to some calculated maximum required level will depress sales and vice versa for a low stock. Furthermore, in a period of prosperity replacement is accelerated which can bring together a high stock of cars and a low average age of vehicles. The rapid replacement increases net demand, and as the actual stock of cars approaches the required, then net demand falls off. This elementary 'trade cycle' model would reduce car demand quite irrespective of the level of prosperity. So before incomes fall car demand has already fallen. However once the downturn begins, the large stock of young cars means that replacement can be postponed for quite lengthy periods. The usual 'trade cycle' conclusion would predict that the higher the level of sales in the boom the worse the slump in new car sales is likely to be in the following recession. Another point is that in the short run an increase in income will first manifest itself in increased demand for consumer durables; as the stock increases to the new required level the long run increase in consumer durables will be less. In Evans the short-run income elasticity falls from 2·2 to the long-run level of 1·1.

MODEL CHANGES

It was once thought that in a saturated market one of the most important influences on new car sales was the stimulus given by the introduction of new models. Although one firm or one car may improve its market share there is little evidence to suggest that car sales were higher in years when new models appeared compared with years of only slight 'face-lifting'. Other factors such as a cyclical attitude variable, or hire-purchase conditions or changes in relative car prices were better explanations of any change in demand. Closely linked to this 'innovation theory' was the view that in an upswing consumer durables are bought first, then after the equilibrium stock is achieved consumers switch to more liquid assets. This theory was very popular in the U.S.A. during the 1950s. It was thought that the explanation of relatively poor car sales in 1956 and 1957 was that the economy's stock of cars had reached equilibrium at the expense of other assets in 1955, so in 1956 and 1957 people switched spending to restore their stock of other assets. This theory also explained the widespread view in the 1950s that car sales would not remain at high levels two years running. However, during the 1960s sales were constantly at a high level especially between 1960 and 1965. Clearly there were other reasons for the good year bad year pattern such as variations in H.P. controls, people's attitudes to future prosperity, relative car prices, and so on. The fall in car sales in 1956 in the U.K. has been cited as an example of postponed demand in anticipation of the new models introduced for 1957. However, 1957 sales did not significantly exceed those of 1956 and the 1956 performance can be explained by the fact that between 1951 and 1955 H.P. terms had eased considerably each year. Hire purchase monthly terms in 1956 were little different to those in 1955, and the rate of change of H.P. conditions was not maintained, which may have discouraged many buyers.

OTHER FACTORS AFFECTING CAR DEMAND

Other factors having a direct relationship with the level of car demand are: the number of separate households in the economy; the view that families with more than one adult spend more on cars; the lower the average scrapping age the higher is annual car demand. Inverse relationships have been detected in relation to the number of children per family and the higher the ratio of urban dwellers to rural families[*]. This final point can be explained by the lack of a public transport system in rural areas plus the need to travel longer distances to arrive at any planned destination. On these grounds urban dwellers have less need of a car than rural dwellers, although if a rudimentary rural

[*] W. B. Bennett, 'Consumption of Automobiles in the United States', *American Economic Review*, Vol. 57, No. 4.

transport service exists one would expect the consumer to make do. The annual cost of motoring in the U.K., given an average family car, is around £350, including hire-purchase payments and depreciation. At a cost of 3·5p a mile, assuming an annual mileage of 10 000, the mere inconvenience of rural living itself is unlikely to increase car demand. If a car is already owned then inconvenience will no doubt increase vehicle use. This is especially so when it is considered that the private motorist very rarely depreciates his car and more often than not only takes account of the petrol costs as an indicator of costs per mile. As the demand is for vehicle ownership rather than for a transport facility there may not be much wrong with the motorist's rule of thumb. He is paying for and receiving the utility derived from vehicle ownership and acting rationally by only taking into account the short-run marginal cost of motoring. Motorists may, however, as indicated below, underestimate both the short- and long-run marginal costs of car ownership.

Another factor affecting car demand is the socio-economic grouping of the population. In the U.K. it has been found that even with the same income, households belonging to different socio-economic groups are not equally likely to have a car★. Bennett comes to the same conclusion in that American Negro families spend less on cars than Caucasian families with similar incomes, locations, and family composition.

A mention must be made of seasonal variations in demand. Due to pent-up wartime demand, the fluctuations in export markets, and the economic control of the economy in general and of car sales in particular, the pre-war phenomenon of seasonal variations in demand in the U.K. did not reappear until 1959. Sales are generally highest in the spring in readiness for summer motoring and the lowest in December and January during the depths of winter and near the costly Christmas period. Before the war, firms introduced new cars at the October motor show in order to try to boost sales during the lean period. Now, however, they tacitly admit the ineffectiveness of such a policy by introducing vehicles as and when they are ready, but in the U.S.A. the traditional autumn close down in preparation for the new range of vehicles continues. Consequently the demand for cars falls off as 'obsolescence time' draws near. In the U.K. current sales are not adversely affected because the general public is unaware of the new models' 'launch time'.

★ R. Meron, 'Discriminant Analyses of Factors Affecting Car Ownership of Households'. A paper presented at a conference of the Royal Statistical Society held at the University of Sussex in March 1967.

Another factor affecting demand may be the variable costs of vehicle use. At the present time total running and maintenance costs for an average sized family saloon travelling 10 000 miles a year amount to about £150 a year. Adding insurance, excise duty and driving licence fees to this gives a figure near to £190. Depreciation and hire purchase charges also have to be included, bringing annual costs up to around £350. If private motorists fully costed their car ownership charges such a calculation could greatly affect annual demand both by reducing the number of owners, and by postponing replacement until the increased maintenance charges offset the reduced annual depreciation provisions. As it is, the majority of private motorists look little beyond petrol costs—hence car ownership appears to be far cheaper than it actually is.

Another point is that it is quite possible that increased monthly hire-purchase charges due to various factors affect demand less than an increase in the down-payment requirement. Although a larger down-payment reduces the monthly repayment, the difficulty in finding the extra finance needed initially frustrates a potential sale*. Between February 1955 and January 1961 the minimum deposit ratio was the prime variable, the repayment period being constant at 24 months. The easing of the deposit requirement was accompanied by increased sales, tightening of the deposit requirement by a reduction in sales. In April 1960 a reduction in the deposit ratio from $33\frac{1}{3}\%$ to 20% was accompanied by an increase in car sales from 657 000 in 1959 to 820 000 in 1960. An extension of the repayment period from 24 months to 36 months in January 1961 was not accompanied by an increase in sales until 1962. This largely *a priori* view concerning the relative effects of deposit ratios and monthly repayments is clearly a fruitful area for empirical testing. It could well be that increases in running costs have little effect on car ownership. For one thing, increases tend to be gradual and small, hence they are absorbed and accepted by the car-owner before he fully realises that such increases have in fact occurred. In addition, the motorist either (1) ignores most charges or (2) regards them as being a cost fully compensated by the utility derived from car ownership.

* This tends to be a 'once and for all effect'. Once the deposit ratio changes, potential customers have to save that much more or less. Once savings reach the new required levels, car demand can increase again.

THE DEMAND FOR BUSINESS CARS

It is likely that the factors affecting business-car demand may differ slightly from those affecting private-car demand. The former are more akin to commercial vehicles and are affected more by changes in investment and the general business climate than by changes in consumer income, purchase tax and variations in hire-purchase controls. Consequently it is important to know the proportion of private to business car demand before one can predict the effects of changes in hire-purchase controls or of national income on car demand.

Some estimates place business car demand at 40% of the total* in general, and at 35% in a boom, i.e. the change in private car demand is more volatile than business demand in that a proportionate change in income has a greater effect. A survey reported in *The Statist*† suggested that of 6 million cars in the country about $5\frac{1}{2}$ million or 81% were for private use. A further 17% of all private cars were subsidised by employers but this still left 71% of the car population as private cars. All company cars were under 5 years old but only 40% of private cars; indeed, 12% were over 15 years old. Clearly the need to maintain a smart image dictates rapid business-car replacement and the greater the proportion of business cars the higher would be the annual demand for cars. A further survey‡ analysed this problem, the sample covered suggesting that 53% of new cars were bought for business purposes and 18% of used cars. However, only 41% of new cars were accepted by the Inland Revenue as business purchases. Business cars were generally of larger engine capacity than purely private cars. For example, 54% of business purchases of new cars were over 1400 c.c. but 38% of private cars. Of the total number of business cars bought, about 25% were for the distributive trades and 20% for manufacturing industry. Furthermore, of cars bought on hire-purchase about 30% were new business cars but only 6% of used cars bought on hire-purchase were so described. For new cars not bought on hire-purchase some 45% were business cars and about 10% of used cars not bought on hire-purchase were for business purposes.

The business demand for cars, perhaps equivalent to 30–40% of annual sales should be more susceptible to changes in maintenance and running costs. In other words, business accounting should be fully aware of the total real costs of car ownership. But it appears that

* *The Economist*, p. 365 (22 October 1960).
† 'Economic Trends M.o.T. Survey Oct. 1961', *The Statist*, (5 July 1963).
‡ *Economic Trends*, C.S.O., No. 139, pp. xi–xviii (May 1965).

THE DEMAND FOR MOTOR VEHICLES

during periods when total costs increase by the greatest amount the proportion of business demand to total domestic demand also increases. Clearly the variable-cost factor is unimportant compared with the other determinants of car demand. Also the increase in cost would have to be extremely large to offset the increased costs derived from non-ownership, e.g. the time spent by the commercial traveller on a bus instead of using a car would lead to a colossal waste of resources. Replacement demand is another matter. The demand for a new vehicle could easily be postponed; however the business image comes in here. A new vehicle is seen as an advertisement for a thrusting dynamic firm; business prestige would be harmed by a fleet of older vehicles, especially as some competitors would be buying new equipment.

Another element in the business demand side is the 'rent a vehicle' scheme. Here the market is dominated by three firms Hertz, Avis, and Godfrey Davis which hire-out vehicles over variable lengths of time. In some instances firms hire cars over a period of years, hence avoiding large fixed outlays. In addition, a new car every year or so does not involve the hirer in recurrent fixed expenses. All the large hire firms have expanded from the car into the van and then into the medium and heavy commercial vehicles markets.

By and large one would expect business car and commercial vehicle demand to be mainly affected by the same factors as affect car demand in general. Variations in maintenance costs may be more important bearing in mind the closer control of total costs by the business sector. Their effect on the marginal efficiency of investment could also affect the total demand for vehicles at the margin. However, the road haulier and the hire car operators are the only business operators solely dependent on vehicle operation for a living. Most business cars and commercial vehicles are used for a 'distributive' function which is ancillary to the main operation of the enterprise. A bakery owning its own vans is not dependent on the profitable use of vehicles but rather on the profits from the sale of confectionary. Obviously overall margins are affected by distribution costs, but any increase is either passed on or absorbed and therefore written-down to sales promotion or to the convenience derived from owning ones own vehicles. So in many cases a firm could use its own transport when from a transport cost point of view it would be cheaper to use 'outside' transport facilities. Other 'benefits', however, may be adjudged to accrue which make vehicle ownership worthwhile. As these other benefits tend to follow from having a modern fleet, the demand for vehicles would be affected by factors other than maintenance and running costs. Even in the case of the professional haulier or taxi owner increased costs are unlikely to be specific to one firm, hence charges could be passed-on on an industry wide basis.

THE DEMAND FOR COMMERCIAL VEHICLES

Cars are often desired because of the utility conferred by car-ownership, but the demand for business cars, and especially commercial vehicles, is a derived demand. They are not wanted for themselves but because of the profitable use which can be made of them. The demand for an oil tanker is based on the demand for petrol. So although the relative prices may affect the type of vehicle bought it would not affect the total demand; the relative prices of the products carried is the appropriate price variable. Nearly every type of product is carried by commercial vehicles and hence a relative price variable is of little use. A change in the relative prices of 'everything' would leave total demand largely unaffected, as increased demand in one direction was offset by reduced demand elsewhere, except for changes following from variations in 'real balances', exports and so on. Consequently the price variable could often be omitted, unless particular weight could be attached to relative price changes in areas, such as the distribution of goods, the construction of buildings and the relative price of car derivative commercial vehicles. In this case relative price changes could have varying effects on demand because commercial vehicle use is 'skewed' to particular sectors. Another factor which could be discounted as a determinant of demand is the 'fashion' element which may have some slight effect on total car demand. Of course a new model is expected to be technically superior to the vehicle it replaces. This does not always prove to be the case (the BMC FJ range introduced at the 1966 CV show was a commercial disaster due to its unreliability) although the expectation is often one of product improvement. The demand function for commercial vehicles may therefore be something like this:

$$C_{cvt} = a + bY_{t-1} - K_{t-2} + dI_{t-1} - g\frac{P^\star}{Pg} - h\left(\frac{H}{T}\right) + R$$

where C_{cvt} is the demand for commercial vehicles at time t, $Y =$ income, $K =$ capital stock, $I =$ investment, $P^\star$ is the general price level, Pg the price of goods carried by commercial vehicles, $H =$ the number of professional road hauliers, $T =$ the total number of commercial vehicle users and $R =$ replacement demand.

Basically the demand for cars and commercial vehicles is affected by much the same factors and registrations tend to move together, although some differences occur and other variables may *a priori* be significant. CV demand is mostly dependent upon the growth in national income, for increased income means greater trade and the increased flow of goods. This demand for increased vehicle mileage can be partly satisfied by more efficient use of existing stock, but mainly it means increased investment in vehicles. Given a time lag to ascertain whether the increased demand is permanent and whether the existing fleet cannot be better utilised, increased demand in t depends on the change in income between period $t-1$ and $t-2$. Here the coefficient b is an approximation to the CV:Output ratio. Demand will also be affected by the level of income Y_{t-1}. The larger the capital stock in $t-2$ the smaller the increase in demand, i.e. the smaller the difference between the actual and the required capital stock.

Demand will also depend on investment generally: an increase in investment will indicate the need for increased primary and secondary activity. Hence the need to help in the actual process of investment and to carry the fruits of that investment. The increased incomes derived from the investment in $t-1$ will affect demand in t, i.e.

$$C_{cvt} = Y_{t-1} - Y_{t-2}$$

and

$$Y_{t-1} - Y_{t-2} = \Delta I_{t-1}$$

In other words, there is no time lag between investment and the change in income. Demand may be a function of the relative price level of goods accounting for the major part of the ton-miles 'produced' by vans and lorries plus the relative cost of bus travel. Little of the explanatory role of this variable is not already covered by fluctuations in income or the rate of growth of income. However, some role may be ascribed to relative prices, and its significance would increase the more was total ton and passenger-mileage 'skewed' to particular sectors.

Another variable could be the ratio of professional road hauliers to total CV users (H/T). Professional hauliers mainly buy vehicles from the specialist producers. Vehicles are built to give a working life of at least 10 years. In addition the length of journey is on average greater than for ancillary users*, hence the need for vehicles requiring long lives with the minimum of maintenance needs. The more hauliers there are as a proportion of total CV operators the smaller is the annual demand for new vehicles and vice versa. Consequently, although car

* Hence the haulier is more concerned with costs per mile, the short-haul user in costs per ton.

and CV demand may basically rest on income, CV demand may be better explained by changes in the level of income as well as by the absolute level of income. Another important factor would be the level of I especially if lagged by one time period.

The demand for cars is mainly explained by reference to income, stocks and relative prices, although some slight modification of this is needed to explain the demand for CVs. Probably factors in addition to the ones already discussed can have a role to play. In Japan the state of the roads and the need to prove ownership of a garage tended to restrict vehicle growth in the late 1950s and early 1960s. Vehicle density per mile can also be a factor (*Table 7.3*).

Table 7.3

VEHICLES PER MILE

Country	1968	1969
U.K.	59·2	61·2
Germany	48·3	51·6
Italy	45·1	49·9
France	26·0	27·0
U.S.A.	26·1	27·0
Japan	25·7	27·0

Source: *Basic Road Statistics 1970*, British Road Federation.

OWNERSHIP LEVELS: IS THERE ROOM FOR THE MOTOR CAR?

It may be that the U.K. will never attain American ownership levels on a population basis because of the compactness of the country and the high usage of the roads. The sheer misery of driving may turn people against private transport. At the moment it is the countries with the wide open spaces that have the largest car population per head of the population. So although vehicle use measured on a per capita basis is much less in the U.K. than the U.S.A. (just under one car in five compared with just over two in five in the U.S.A.) measured on a 'track' basis the U.K. market is more saturated than the U.S. In terms of vehicles per *square mile* the same conclusion holds. So whether car demand would grow sufficiently to give U.S. ownership levels in terms of the proportion of cars to the population will depend in the final analysis on whether the opportunity cost of car-ownership is offset by the benefits. If we value environment, then a social decision may be taken which would adversely affect the demand for cars at some future date. This takes us on to the final section in this chapter, the effect of the state and Government on vehicle usage and demand.

GOVERNMENT INFLUENCE ON USAGE AND DEMAND

TAXATION

In the U.K., motor taxation's incidence falls on the purchase price of cars* and on their running costs. The purchase price is inflated by purchase tax and running costs are affected by an annual licence, petrol duty and purchase tax on replacement items such as car tyres. Third-party insurance is compulsory by law, and generally speaking, increases with the performance of the motor car. This insurance, due to its compulsory nature, takes on the guise of a 'tax' on motoring. In the U.K. the tax burden of car ownership tends to be high relative to the case in say France, Germany or the U.S.A. This has been especially so during the period 1964–1970 when the withdrawal of purchasing power through high taxation was seen as a necessary part of a restrictive economic policy. As the elasticity of demand for car use† appears to be very low increased motoring costs are a good economic regulator. In addition, as the price elasticity of demand for car ownership appears to be over −1, any increase in car prices due to changes in purchase tax reduces total expenditure on consumer durables. So in various ways tax changes on the cost of motoring have immediate effects on aggregate economic activity.

Motor fuel taxation was first levied in 1909 at a rate of 3d. a gallon of petrol. The rate was 6d. in 1921 when it was repealed only to be reintroduced in 1928 at a rate of 4d. a gallon. Between 1928 and 1938 the rate climbed from 4d. to 9d. a gallon where it remained until 1950. The post-war period has seen a very large increase in the absolute rate of duty. From 1950 to 1969 the movement has been continuously upwards except for one reduction in 1957. Between 1950 and 1957 the rate climbed to 3s. 6d., falling to 2s. 6d. in the latter year. The next increase was in 1961 to 2s. 9d. where it remained until 1964. Since then the increases were fast and furious; duty was 3s. 3d. a gallon in 1964 and

---

* Purchase tax was levied on commercial vehicles in July 1950 for the first time; it was abolished in April 1959. The imposition of a value added tax would re-impose a sales tax on commercial vehicles.

† A. A. Walters, 'Subsidies for Transport?', *Lloyds Bank Review*, No. 83, p. 27 (January 1967).

it had reached 4s. 6d. a gallon by 1969. Between 1964 and 1969 the U.K. moved from one of Europe's low-price-of-petrol economies to one of the highest. In 1969 a gallon of premium petrol cost as little as 1s. 9d., the purchase price of 6s. 3d. being mainly duty.

Purchase tax is levied in the U.K. on the wholesale price of a motor car. Initially it was levied at a rate of $33\frac{1}{3}\%$ in 1940 and this state of affairs lasted until 1947, when a differential rate was introduced. Cars with a retail value of over £1280 were subject to tax at $66\frac{2}{3}\%$. In 1950 the differential was removed and all cars were taxed at $33\frac{1}{3}\%$. The subsequent picture is shown in *Table 7.4*.

Table 7.4

Year		Rate (%)
1951	All cars taxed at	$66\frac{2}{3}$
1953	,,	50
1955	,,	60
1959	,,	50
1961	,,	55
1962 (April)	,,	45
1962 (November)	,,	25
1966	,,	$27\frac{1}{2}$
1968 (March)	,,	$33\frac{1}{3}$
1968 (November)	,,	$36\frac{2}{3}$
1971 (July)	,,	30

Between 1951 and 1962 the trend was downwards, the tax rate reaching an historical low in the latter year. Between 1966 and 1968 the trend is upwards although even with purchase tax levied at $36\frac{2}{3}\%$ the rate is 'low' compared with the period 1951–1962. Between 1967–1968, total purchase tax on all goods raised £748·6 million, of which the car industry's direct share was £169·6 million, or 22·7% of the total. This does not include purchase tax on accessories or replacement parts. In 1966–1967 the car industry accounted for 21% of the total. In November 1962 when the U.K. purchase tax rate was equivalent to a sales tax rate of 21% the equivalent rates in Germany, Italy and France were 13%, 28% and 12%★. So even with purchase tax at an all time low the 'sales' tax burden was still high compared with some other countries. In 1970 with the U.K. rate at $36\frac{2}{3}\%$, the Tax on Value Added on cars in West Germany and France was 11% and $33\frac{1}{3}\%$ respectively†. In the Netherlands the total sales tax burden on cars is about 25%

★ *The Sunday Times* (11 November 1962).
† A purchase tax rate of $36\frac{2}{3}\%$ was equivalent to a value added tax of 30%

compared with 13% in Italy. In Sweden the VAT was increased from 11% to 16% in 1970. Hence the British car buyers face a higher tax burden on initial purchase than is usual in other European car producing nations, although the burden was eased slightly when the purchase tax rate was reduced to 30% in July 1971.

The annual excise tax on cars—once given the legendary title the 'Road Fund' Licence—is levied at a flat rate on all motor cars irrespective of size, engine capacity or performance. This was not always the case however. Between 1910 and 1947 the tax was levied at a rate of £1 per horse power, so cars with larger h.p. engines were subject to more tax. In 1947 this was replaced by a tax on the cubic capacity of the engine which in turn was replaced by a flat rate of £10 a car in 1948. Between 1948 and 1965 the rate had increased from £10 to £15 but between 1965, when it was increased to £17 10s. od., and 1968, the duty was increased to £25 a year. In practice, the latter increase in duty of £7 10s. may be an underestimate, because, faced with a lump sum outlay of £25, more people may have decided to purchase four-month licences at £9 3s. a time or £27 9s. od. a year.

The change-over from a differentiated to a fixed tax rate came as a result of repeated representations by the car industry to the Chancellor of the Exchequer. The h.p. tax influenced engine design by putting a premium on 'under-square' small cylinder bore and long piston stroke engines. It also reinforced the effects of petrol duty and insurance premiums in 'penalising' the users of larger-engined cars. Before 1939 the tax was on the basis of 15s. per h.p., so of itself it may have had very little effect on car demand, for instance, an Austin 'Seven' was taxed at £5 5s. od. whereas a Morris 'Twelve' cost £9 a year to tax, a difference of just over 1s. 5d. per week. It is certainly true that cars over 12 h.p. declined sharply in relative popularity between 1930 and 1938; but this would have been due more to the effect of relative prices. The prices of cars of 12 h.p. and below had declined greatly in the inter-war period thereby tapping a new market for car ownership. It was this, rather than the effect of 1s. 5d. or even 6s. od. a week extra h.p. tax, which led to the relative decline of large cars. However, it was true that the registration of cars over 12 h.p. fell from over 74 000 in 1930 to just over 60 000 by 1934, although in 1938 the figure had recovered to almost 62 000.

In other words, the h.p. tax may have had effects on car demand which were incommensurate with the absolute size of the tax. The whole question of taxation may have been magnified by its psychological impact on the mind of the motorist, so that tax avoidance may have become an obsession. In the early 1930s this obsession was reinforced

by advertising which hailed each new low h.p. car as a 'tax dodger'*.
Another possibility is that although the tax difference per week was
small as a lump sum difference it may have been important. It is
doubtful, however, if this was a significant consideration to more than
a few buyers; the fact that a 8 h.p. car would require a tax outlay of £6
compared with £9 for a 12 h.p. would be irrelevant compared with the
fact that the 8 h.p. car in the late 1930s cost little more than £100
compared with around £200 for a 12 h.p. model.

We must conclude that the h.p. tax did not bias demand in favour
of small and medium sized cars and against large cars. The main factor
here was the level of disposable incomes and the fact that unlike the
Americans the British motorist had little need of a large powerful
car to travel vast distances at high speeds and in comfort. A more
important factor may have been the inducement given by the tax
system to car firms to concentrate on small cars, but again the level of
incomes was surely a more important factor. So the production of
small cars which could not compete in markets where the demand was
for large-engined U.S. models cannot be fairly placed at the door of
the taxation system. After all Morris, Austin and Ford in particular
built large-engined cars mainly designed for the 'Empire' market.
Another contention, that the graduated tax system helped protect the
domestic market against large-engined American models, appears
plausible, but again the $33\frac{1}{3}$% import duty was obviously the overriding factor.

The cost of petrol, insurance premiums and the h.p. tax may have
had a slight influence on diverting demand to small-engined vehicles
which were economical to run, although any influence these factors had
was minute compared with the importance of income levels and the
relative prices of different sized cars, on demand. The tax system, the
petrol duty and insurance premiums also had little effect on the demand
for American cars compared with the influence of import duty,
income levels, and relative prices. In terms of design, the h.p. tax
may have influenced the designs of engines. The trend towards
'squarer' engines with large bores and short strokes began after 1947,
being discouraged by the h.p. tax. This type of engine is technically
superior to the 'under square' unit which had put small and medium
British cars at a disadvantage in terms of performance when compared
with their European rivals. The development of 'fast-running' engines
in the U.K. removed this disadvantage. The agitation to remove the
h.p. tax was on the grounds of its effects on design, effects which were

* *Motor Vehicles: A Report on the Industry*, Political and Economic Planning,
London (1950).

producing technically inferior engines. In turn, these technical efforts were based on the false assumption that the h.p. tax had a significant effect on demand.

After the introduction of the flat-rate tax in 1948 the popularity of the small and medium car was unaffected. In fact, the 1950s saw a rapid growth in small car production at the expense of medium sized cars. During the 1960s the production of small cars fell significantly whereas medium cars increased. This was due to 'trading-up' by customers as real disposable incomes increased relative to car prices.* Clearly the continued development of the small car market after the abolition of the h.p. tax and its subsequent decline in the 1960s illustrates that the relative market shares of different sizes of car had little to do with taxation, but everything to do with real income. If the graduated tax was based on a *more than proportionate* increase in taxation per h.p. then demand may be severely affected, it would appear that the disappearance of French cars over 2·2 litres or the absence of many Japanese or Italian cars over 2 litres is due to such a tax system.

Although at first sight one would estimate that the burden of purchase tax, petrol tax, excise tax and insurance premiums taken as a whole must affect total demand, in all probability only changes in purchase tax would significantly affect overall demand. Given that the elasticity of demand for cars is over one, any change in initial price will have a significant effect on car sales in the domestic market. Unless the private motorist estimates such things as the present value of the net utility yields it is unlikely that factors affecting running costs would materially affect car demand. In this case the net utility yield is the excess of annual utility over annual running costs so any increased taxation, on say petrol, reduces the net yield. Few motorists would make any such calculation. Even where business demand is concerned, the net cash yield from car ownership is perhaps a minor consideration when the other factors concerning business car demand are considered. Between 1938 and 1967 total 'recurring' taxes have increased from £87 million to £1093 million or from £28·73 per vehicle to £85·97 per vehicle. The addition of purchase tax made the total £1267 million in 1967†. This was still an incomplete picture because it excluded purchase tax on items such as spares and accessories. At the same time the growth in real incomes has led to an explosion in car ownership.

* At 1970 prices a 1939 Ford Prefect cost £740 compared with £672 for a 1970 Ford Escort. Both cars tended to serve the same sector of the market. Over the same period real incomes more than doubled.

† *Motor Industry of Great Britain*, SMMT, Table 123 (1968).

I

In the future, extra taxation to take account of social costs, e.g. the effects of congestion or despoiling the countryside, could be levied. However, any road pricing scheme would only affect car demand and car usage if the demand is elastic with respect to changes in running costs over the relevant ranges of the demand curve. What evidence there is points in the direction of inelastic demand. Really severe road pricing schemes plus a degree of prohibition of car use may eventually meet a real social need in protecting environment and making it worthwhile to restore and improve public transport. Such moves could severely affect future car demand especially if people really turn against their cars as despoilers of environment. There could come a time when although the consumer may want cars and therefore more roads, he may show that he wants to preserve 'green fields' even more. The car, by moving down the consumer's scale of preferences may suffer a decline in demand.

LEGISLATION

Legislation has had considerable impact on the demand for commercial vehicles and on their development. We have already noted the reimposition of petrol duty in 1928; however, diesel fuel was not taxed until 1933 and even then at a lower rate. Rates were not unified until 1935. This difference in duty may have provided impetus to the development of heavy oil engines; Crossley produced the first diesel engined bus in 1931 some two years after the appearance of the diesel lorry*. Compared with the petrol engine the diesel is a more complex and expensive unit but it gives greater thermal efficiency. This advantage is particularly marked in the case of heavy lorries travelling long distances or in the case of buses continually 'stopping and starting'.

As a result, the diesel engine opened up the market for long distance transport to the road haulage operator. That is although the development of cheap highly efficient petrol lorries after World War I, especially by Bedford and Ford between 1928 and 1931, had meant their substitution for horse drawn traffic over short distances, the low thermal efficiency of very large petrol engines meant that road transport was not fully geared to carrying large loads. Consequently this type of haulage was carried by either steam-powered road vehicles or by the railways. The development of the diesel engine meant that large loads could be carried long distances relatively quickly and

* D. Noble and G. McKenzie Jenner, *Vital to the Nation*, SMMT (1947).

cheaply by road vehicles for the first time. For instance, in the mid-1920s total running costs of a six to seven ton capacity steam lorry were 6d. to 7½d. a mile compared with 8½d. to 9d. for a petrol lorry. Furthermore, such loads were outside the scope of all but the most specialised and expensive petrol engined vehicles. By the mid-1930s the total running costs of a six to seven ton diesel lorry was 6½d. per mile at the lower duty level★. The steam lorry had a low payload to gross weight ratio and their use was complicated by many legislative measures. Taking the inherent and legislative disadvantage of steamer operations, perhaps it was only the imposition of the full heavy oil duty in 1935 which prevented the diesel engine sweeping away all steam and petrol driven competition. As it was, wartime measures virtually killed the steam wagon. It is certain that even without the duty-advantage, diesel engines would have been quickly introduced in large long-distance commercial vehicles; however, the duty-advantage may have speeded up the process. This increased the demand for heavy vehicles as the diesel engine opened up new transport markets to road haulage. In its early years diesel power was only used in large goods vehicles and buses. However, in 1938 Seddon with great foresight and faith produced the first light truck powered by a diesel engine. After the war this company opened up new markets in the five ton gross range for Perkins diesel engines, and so successful was Seddon that between 1945 and the mid-1950s all the mass producers offered Perkins-engined vehicles in their light-medium ranges. As the market expanded the mass producers gauged it worthwhile to tool-up for the production of their own diesel engine designs. Between 1952 and 1957 Ford, Standard-Triumph, Rootes, Austin and Bedford introduced their own medium powered diesel engines† for vehicles in the five ton to seven ton payload range.

Construction and Use regulations affect all motor vehicles, but especially commercial ones. When the regulations are amended so as to allow the use of larger lorries and buses on the roads, there is always an upsurge in the sale of the heaviest vehicles as customers wish to avail themselves of the larger permitted payloads. In the 1960s the surge in demand for heavy vehicles, and especially articulated units, was a direct result of the 1964 amendments to the Construction and Use regulations. This, however, only affects the incidence of demand and not the total demand for vehicles, except inasmuch that one very large vehicle may replace two smaller ones. In other words, the growth in national income has had a proportionately greater impact on

★ E. L. Cornwell, *Veteran and Vintage Commercial Vehicles*, Ian Allen (1963).
† Morris-Commercial had produced a Saurer-designed engine since 1948.

aggregate vehicle carrying capacity than on the growth in the stock measured in individual units. Hence the basic demand is for ton-mileage capacity rather than for actual units.

Precise legislation such as the Road and Rail Traffic Acts of 1930 and 1933, the Nationalisation of road haulage in 1947 and its partial de-nationalisation in 1952, the subsequent Transport Acts of 1962 and 1968, Plating and Testing requirements (1968), CV annual licence fees and speed limits, have all had some effect on CV demand.

The Acts of 1930 and 1933 which affected bus and truck operations respectively were quickly followed in 1934 by severe increases in the annual taxation of commercial vehicles, and the package of regulations was completed by a more strict enforcement of speed limits. The sailways, being traditional monopolists, tended to charge what the market would bear, with little account being taken of costs per unit per mile. This system was all well and good under conditions of monopoly, but in the 1920s a new situation arose. This period saw the rapid emergence and development of commercial vehicles. Ex-servicemen used their gratuities to establish road haulage enterprises after demobilisation, firstly with ex-war department vehicles and then with new ones. The improved products and production methods reduced both the first costs and running costs. The emergence of buses and lorries presented an alternative transport service to that provided by rail. As road charges were based on costs, the 'valuable' freight transferred to road, whereas cheap and bulky goods remained on the railways. In 1935 the cost of carrying coal from London to Birmingham was 10s. 5d. a ton, but drapery cost £2 15s. 2d. a ton. Charging what the market 'used to bear' meant that coal remained with rail but drapery transferred to road; the road cost was £1 2s. 6d. per ton for the same journey no matter what was carried*. In addition road transport did not have to provide regular services. If road operators chose to do so they were not protected from 'pirates'. The Acts of 1930 and 1933 were passed to limit entry and the conditions of operation within the road transport sector. These measures may well have reduced the short-term demand for trucks and buses but it is unlikely that long term demand was affected. If the Acts of 1930 and 1933 restored equilibrium via 'legislation' rather than through the operation of the free market, then the size of the road transport sector would have been unaffected in the long-run. This seems to have been so in the road haulage sector where prices were left free and entry if harder was far from impossible. It was only the 'A' licence which was at all hard to

* *Motor Vehicles: A Report on the Industry*, Political and Economic Planning, London, p. 72 (1950).

come by, the 'B' and 'C' licences being granted quite freely. On the bus side the restriction of entry and fare regulation was severe. The system of 'cross subsidisation' may have adversely affected the size of bus fleets in the long run by driving people to use cars. One suspects, however, that this possibility can be largely discounted as the growth in car demand, being dependent on income, would have occurred anyway.

The increased taxation of lorries in 1934 was designed to overcome the criticism that road transport received a subsidy through the public expenditure on roads. Taxation on goods vehicles has been based on unladen weight and for buses it has been based on seating capacity. Operators sought to maximise the payload capacity for any given unladen tonnage, and this tendency, although constrained by the Construction and Use regulations, does affect CV design. As a result of large increases in the post-war period, but especially between 1965 and 1968, the level of lorry taxation is now such that for each extra quarter-ton unladen weight over $3\frac{3}{4}$ tons tax increases by £13 10s. So whereas a car derivative commercial vehicle pays £25 a year in road tax, a 10 ton lorry pays £459*. The drafting of the 1968 Transport Bill came close to introducing a 'wear and tear' and an 'abnormal load' charge in order to cover the social costs imposed by large CVs, but after considering the effects of these provisions on transport charges, domestic prices, and exports, the proposals were dropped in favour of increased tax rates. In the highly competitive road transport industry not all increases in charges such as these can be passed on. The result has been a large number of bankruptcies and mergers within the road transport sector. Such developments, however, tend to leave the nation's overall vehicle fleet unaffected as efficient firms grow at the expense of the inefficient ones. Consequently overall demand is unaffected. Any general increase in rates may drive some existing traffic onto the railways but such has been the long term trend of traffic switching from rail to road that such an effect would be swamped.

The 1968 Transport Act abolished the A, B and C licence system introduced in 1933 and replaced it by a single Operators or O licence. For vehicles with an unladen weight below 30 cwts (or $3\frac{1}{2}$ tons gross) no licence was needed. For owners of vehicles over 16 tons gross (5 tons unladen) wanting to travel distances in excess of 100 miles as the crow flies it was proposed that they must have a 'Special Authorisation'. In 1970 the Conservative Government dispensed with this requirement, making this quantity licensing provision an addition to the normal 'O' or 'quality' licence. In many ways the 1968 Act made

* *Roadway*, Road Haulage Association, p. 50 (April 1968).

road transport a freer market. Apart from the need to show competence as a vehicle operator, no restriction would have existed on the operation of vehicles of 16 tons and under. For the lightest vehicles no licence was needed at all. It is possible that road hauliers, to avoid the need for Special Authorisation, would have replaced one 32 ton vehicle by two 16 ton vehicles. From society's point of view this would have been undesirable. Firstly, resources would have been used less efficiently as the percentage payload would have fallen from 83 to 73% of gross vehicle weight. Secondly, running costs excluding depreciation would have almost doubled. Thirdly, the use of more vehicles to carry the same ton-mileage would have added to congestion and to the wear and tear on the roads. As *Table 7.5* shows, capital and maintenance costs per vehicle are very much higher where heavy vehicles are concerned:

Table 7.5

PERCENTAGE OF TOTAL COSTS ALLOCATED
TO MAIN CLASSES OF VEHICLES

Class of vehicle	Capital costs	Maintenance costs
Cars and Taxis	41	41
Goods Vehicles		
Not over 3 tons	18	14
Over 3 tons	30	35
Buses and Coaches	9	7
Motor Cycles	2	3

Source: *Road Revenues and Costs*, Transport Holding Co., p. 50 (October 1964).

The Ministry of Transport also suggested that only 6% of all vehicles on the road—the heaviest ones—cause 26% of road wear. So a reduction in the use of heavy vehicles could have reduced total road expenditure and depreciation. Nevertheless, this must not be pushed too far, for the tax paid by the average goods vehicles over all roads was equivalent to 2·6d. per mile, a figure which varied from 1·9d. for the lightest to 4·3d. for vehicles of 5 tons unladen weight or over, whereas the cost per mile varied from 0·7d. to 2·6d. for the heaviest vehicles. For vehicles of an unladen weight of 8 tons or more the taxes paid per mile have been estimated at 5·2d. and road expenditures at 3d. to 3·5d. per mile. In other words if the heaviest vehicles are 'wasteful' of resources, they still cover their full costs and still prove to be the most efficient and profitable load-carrying vehicles. In addition, the use of smaller vehicles would still add to congestion and private costs. (Obviously, large vehicles impose social costs, but less social costs than imposed by the substitution of one large truck by two smaller ones. Furthermore, against the social costs of road transport must be added social benefits. If the former offsets both the latter and the private costs of transport, then an attempt to recoup this deficit may adversely affect the demand for commercial vehicles.)

Uncertainty caused by nationalisation, threats of nationalisation and so on may have had slight adverse effects on demand in the short-run. However no evidence exists to suggest that the effect is more than marginal. Indeed in 1964, 1965 and 1966 the domestic registration of commercial vehicles reached record levels despite the existence of a Labour Government sympathetic to the principle of state ownership. Also, over the entire period of the 1960s, road hauliers who found competition in the industry too severe tended to approach British Road Services (the state haulage concern) with a view to selling out. This process had started before 1960, that is long before the election of a Labour government in 1964. The nationalisation of bus companies had always been piecemeal, with private operators voluntarily selling out to the state. In 1948 Thames Tilling, in 1950 Red and White United Transport, and in 1968 the British Electric Traction Group, all sold their bus interests to the state. Other smaller concerns were also absorbed. In 1970 about 70% of all buses and coaches were either state or municipally owned, compared with 56% in 1950. Despite the fact that nationalisation was always a possibility, the demand for buses and coaches in the post-war period showed no sign of being influenced by this. The need to satisfy the demand for route-passenger-mileage was always the overriding consideration.

Legislation concerning speed limits could hardly be said to have affected domestic demand, but it has affected engine and vehicle design, sometimes with an adverse influence on costs. During the 1930s the speed limit for vehicles exceeding $2\frac{1}{2}$ tons unladen weight was 20 m.p.h. and lighter vehicles were limited to 30 m.p.h. During the war the shortage of lighter materials meant that vehicles were manu-factured with the use of heavy metals. Consequently the 'demarcation' weight was placed at 3 tons unladen*. It was not until 1957 that all vehicles were allowed to travel at 30 m.p.h. Due to the differential speed limit the normal horsepower per ton for heavy lorries was 5 to 6 compared with 10 for lighter types. As a result of the speed limit there

* This also affected design in that manufacturers attempted to produce large capacity vehicles of less than 3 tons unladen. This has meant that British com-mercial vehicles have tended to be lighter than foreign models and this could have a favourable influence on sales abroad.

was no demand for very powerful engines and the largest lorries used engines of only 120 h.p. In export markets where larger lorries and higher speeds were allowed such engines were unsuitable. Consequently the U.K. producers had to produce quite distinct 'running units' for home and abroad, and this tended to increase unit production costs. The British construction and use regulations tended to prevent the use of the size of vehicle allowed on foreign roads, so U.K. producers often had to supply two distinct ranges. The multiplicity of specifications which resulted may have affected costs which in turn may have affected foreign demand and therefore the total demand for commercial vehicles. However, the excellent export record of the industry suggests that any effect must have been slight. The increase in the speed limit to 40 m.p.h. in 1964, the 'Construction and Use' amendments, and the emergence of large-scale motorway travel increased the demand for larger and more powerful British CVs. As we have already seen, in some instances these new conditions found British producers slow in responding to the increased demand for large powerful vehicles.

The growth of the motorway networks has tended to emphasise the decline in the proportion of traffic carried by rail. The road haulier can almost match the speed of long distance rail hauls and consequently the haulier's market is growing. This adds to the demand for vehicles.

The 'Plating and Testing' regulations which commenced in 1968 are concerned with the legal gross weight and roadworthiness. These regulations could shorten depreciation cycles as maintenance costs could increase to meet these new requirements, thereby offsetting any reduction in annual depreciation charges which result from a longer life cycle. The upsurge in Ford's sales in 1967[*] may have been due to this as well as to their own efforts in marketing a new CV range. CV operators fearful that their vehicles would have been banned from use because of failure to match the new standards increased their demands for new vehicles. The traditional market leader Bedford was unable to cope with this extra demand, hence operators switched to Ford because of the latter's ability to quote earlier delivery. In gross terms, domestic demand for vehicles in 1967–1969 was about normal for the period 1964–1969, but the demand for vehicles over 3 tons unladen weight was above normal. Any increase in the rate of depreciation given the same vehicle stock must mean an increase in the demand for CVs.

Future legislation concerning a minimum brake-horsepower per ton ratio could result in the replacement of the existing vehicle stock by more powerful types. Such legislation is already in operation in West Germany. The legislation however, would only apply to newly

★ *The Sunday Times* (17 December 1967).

registered vehicles, so it is unlikely that total demand would be affected.

A final point here concerns the influence of outside agencies on design. From about 1912 until the early 1930s the War Department had largely controlled CV design through its subsidy schemes. Their need was for a solid, dependable, if rather slow vehicle, so these were the parameters of the specifications offered by firms such as AEC, Albion, Daimler, Leyland and Thornycroft. Consequently the vehicles produced by these independent companies were basically similar although different in detail. The subsidies paid to the operators of these vehicles reduced their operating costs, hence they were likely to patronise a firm producing vehicles qualifying for subsidy. In return for these subsidies operators would have been required to turn over their vehicles to the army in times of need.

From all this it is obvious that legislation of one sort or another has played a part in the development of commercial vehicles. However as in the case of cars the effect of all these factors has been of small import-ance when compared with such basic factors as changes in national income, investment and consumption. Some legislative factors may have affected the demand for certain types of car and CV, or may have influenced design in some way or other*. The effects on aggregate car or CV demand may have been much less significant, apart perhaps from the effect of the 1968 Plating and Testing regulations on CV replacement cycles, and the relative costs of road and rail transport. Other important factors affecting total demand are exogenous to the domestic situation, for instance, the level of exports depend largely on factors in foreign countries. Any domestic influence would come from the 'push' imposed by a declining home market or alternatively from the effect of reduced unit costs and CV prices resulting from a growing home market. These factors will be discussed in the chapter on exports.

CONCLUSIONS

The demand studies covered in this chapter are largely concerned with medium-term forecasts of from 1 to 10 years, although some of the analysis covers variables which are important in short-run models. The motor industry's own economists are mainly concerned with demand conditions up to one year hence, and here factors such as

---

* At the moment there is concern that the 70 m.p.h. maximum speed limit may affect engine design in a way that disqualifies U.K. products from foreign markets.

variations in purchase tax, hire-purchase conditions and credit generally, budgetary and monetary policy, changes in the pattern of used car prices and the level of used car stocks, are found to be the main explanatory variables. However, over the short-period, factors such as per capita income are less significant than they are in medium-term studies.

It has been found[*] that in short-term studies an 'attitude index' is the best explanation of movements in car demand. (Clearly 'seasonal variations' are important in short-run studies, but much effort is expanded in producing seasonally-adjusted sales forecasts.) A sample of the population is asked for its views as to the likely course of events in the economy in the immediate future. This gives an indication of people's attitudes, and it is found that car demand is highly correlated with people's short-term expectations concerning the likely occurrence of certain eventualities. The attitude index constructed explains 70% of the variation in car demand, whereas the results of a direct market survey (e.g. are you going to buy a car in the next 12 months?) only has an R^2 of 0·23 when related to car demand. Few attempts have been made to estimate the car stock, or car demand, over very long periods of time, mainly because the majority of demand models project future growth trends from past trends.

In the long-run such an approach may be invalidated by the appearance of market saturation, so to estimate car ownership in the more distant future involves projecting growth in the light of past trends *and* of expectations as to future market saturation. The approach of John Tanner of the Road Research Laboratory,[†] however, can be used to make a sophisticated extrapolation of the car stock at the end of the century by means of a logistic curve (or cumulated log normal function, or an S-shaped growth curve). This takes cognisance of the saturation problem by increasing the importance of the effect of this factor on the long-term trend of demand. The car stock approaches a limit of 0·45 cars per head. Such estimates are of great interest to road and town planners, but as present data gives no indication of market saturation they are of less immediate significance to vehicle producers who tend to take shorter horizons.

---

[*] See: R. J. Eggert and P. W. McCracken, 'Forecasting and the Automobile Market' in *How Business Economists Forecast* (W. F. Butler and R. A. Kavesh, eds.), Prentice-Hall.

[†] J. Tanner, 'Forecasts of Future Numbers of Vehicles in Great Britain', *Roads and Road Construction*, Vol. 40, No. 477 (1962).

APPENDIX

Estimating future demand is of more than academic interest as clearly this provides a 'service' to the motor industry in that it can plan future short- and medium-run production levels and long-run investment plans. Furthermore, Government is provided with an indication of how activity in general is likely to develop in the economy, and also the type and magnitude of official intervention needed to change motor vehicle demand both as a policy in itself and because of the effects of the motor industry on the economy at large. It was to be expected, therefore, that the Government and motor production and distribution sectors would be active in collecting data and in producing short-, medium- and long-term demand estimates and models. However, some comment on the Government's role in estimating future demand and production potential is called for.

The exact value of the National Economic Development Council or the economic assessments it made of the future is impossible to estimate at this juncture, except that it put the Treasury under official pressure to show the assumptions on which it manages demand in the economy or plans the growth of public expenditure. The National Plan* of 1965, although published under the auspices of the Department of Economic Affairs, had the NEDC closely associated in its preparation. The Plan was prepared by the Labour Government of 1964 in co-operation with both sides of industry in the private and nationalised sector. As a result of medium-term demand and supply projections, the overall Plan was designed to facilitate a 25% increase in real national output between 1964 and 1970; estimates of future demand and supply magnitudes in the motor industry were, of course, included. In the event, the Plan was sacrificed to the short-term need to correct the balance of payments and to protect sterling. This resulted in a policy of economic restriction. Nevertheless, in order that the Central 'planning' body, the NEDC, could more correctly guess both the implications and feasibility of a particular target growth-rate for particular industries, the Labour Government established Economic Development Committees (the Little Neddies) for individual sectors in the late 1960s. The Motor Industry EDC established in 1968† had a forerunner in the Treasury/ Motor Industry Joint Working Party of 1967 which was comprised of representatives of both sides of industry, the Government, and independent specialists, including academics. Various sub-committees are

* *The National Plan*, H.M.S.O., Cmnd 2764, London (1965).
† There is also a separate Motor Vehicle Distribution and Repair EDC.

formed periodically to look at specific topics, such as the effects of Regional Policy or Government economic policy on the industry. The EDC has become an excellent source of motor industry statistics and information, and at the same time it has made various short- and medium-term demand forecasts. Indeed, by 1971 the original 'planning' function of the NEDC–Little Neddy complex had largely disappeared, partly, but not entirely, due to the election of a Conservative administration in 1970. The Motor Industry EDC had become almost entirely an advisory and information service rather than a forum for discussing the feasibility and implications of a planned growth rate.

Statistical material, including periodic short- and medium-term (and occasionally long-term) forecasts referring to the motor industry, also come from a variety of Government Ministries such as the Department of Trade and Industry, the Ministry of Transport Industries, and so on. These estimates are made as a 'service' to industry or any other interested party, and also as a basis on which policies can be formulated and introduced. However, it would be wrong to imply that the motor industry is dependent on outside sources for vital information. The motor manufacturers, the motor traders, and organisations such as the Society of Motor Manufacturers and Traders, all make estimates of future short-, medium- and long-term demand prospects, some of which are based on quite sophisticated models which have been rigorously tested.

POSTSCRIPT

The 1971 Finance Act stated the intention to replace the British purchase tax system by a VAT. If the British VAT rate was equivalent to the German, i.e. 11% on most items, then the sales tax on cars will be substantially reduced: by spreading the tax load those items which incurred purchase tax will be reduced in price, whereas those formerly tax free items will increase in price. More important even than this 'once and for all' tax reduction for the long term development of the car industry, is the probability that for administrative reasons the Government would find it more difficult than where purchase tax was concerned to use VAT tax variation as a regulator or at least to single out particular industries for changes in their tax levelling.

However the 'kit car' industry could be adversely affected by the replacement of purchase tax by VAT. As VAT would be paid on parts and components the tax on an unassembled car and on a completed vehicle would be the same, apart from the cost saving stemming from a lower labour content where no assembly is undertaken. Formerly purchase tax was only levied on a completed car, hence the advantage of buying a kit car from the likes of Marcos or Lotus. Finally a purchase tax rate of $36\frac{2}{3}\%$ is equivalent to a VAT of 30%, hence if the proposed VAT on cars is around 11% then it becomes advantageous to postpone car purchases until VAT is introduced. As more and more consumers become aware of this fact the short-term effects on car demand and therefore on car producers could be severe. Hence to prevent disruption in the car industry the Government would be advised to gradually reduce purchase tax rates to the level of the expected VAT rate.

8

THE SUPPLY OF MOTOR
VEHICLES

In this chapter I want to deal with three main topics: the method of vehicle production, the short-run cost structure, and economies of large-scale production. These factors are crucial in that they determine the quality of the product and the efficiency with which it is manufactured. Allied to the conditions of demand these supply concepts determine the profitability of the motor industry and its constituent firms. Here we shall concentrate on the car side of the industry, although where appropriate commercial vehicle production will be introduced.

THE MANUFACTURING PROCESS

Motor vehicle production consists of the processing of raw materials in order to manufacture the components necessary for incorporation into the final product, and the final assembly of all these finished items to create a motor vehicle. Each car contains about 4000 separate items, and with duplication the total number grows to over 20 000. Up to the present time most items consist of metal—mainly steel, sheet steel, cast iron and aluminium. Certain car and commercial vehicle producers make great use of glass-fibre and plastics, but generally speaking metal reigns supreme. Furthermore, although plastics and aluminium are being increasingly used, the steel industry satisfies the vast majority of the motor industry's requirements. There are of course other important raw materials such as glass and rubber, all crucial to the orderly workings of the motor industry.

The manufacturing processes mainly cover the casting, forging, machining and pressing of metals. All this requires the use of much capital equipment especially at the machining and pressing stage where large numbers of machine tools and cathedral-type presses are used. As early as 1948* the motor industry used more machine tools than any other U.K. industry. In addition, when working at near capacity, as in 1964, the industry takes almost one-third of the sheet steel used in the U.K.

THE TECHNIQUE OF ASSEMBLY

The assembly of the complete vehicle occurs at different stages. Certain components are themselves assembled into complete units, for instance, electrical units such as alternators or mechanical units such as petrol pumps. Other items are built up as sub-assemblies; these include vehicle bodies and the major running units such as engines, axles and transmission units. In some ways the body assembly line is the key to final assembly in the modern motor car industry. The various body pressings such as doors, boot lids and roof units are assembled into a complete body. This complete body sub-assembly is transported to the final assembly line where other major sub-assemblies and other components are fitted into the body. The modern car is of unitary construction: that is, there is no separate chassis on which the body is placed. The body itself is now built-up and assembled in such a way as to serve as body and chassis. This was not the case pre-war, when complete bodies were added to a chassis, complete with sub-assemblies, at the final assembly stage.

Unitary construction has become the normal practice since the late 1940s in Europe, when the first post-war models appeared. In the U.S.A., the large size of the cars initially militated against the use of unitary construction, but the 1960s saw a universal swing towards this type of production. With unitary construction the body must be sufficiently stressed to take the place of a conventional chassis, and the larger the body the more difficult it is to do this. However, during the 1960s techniques were developed to allow the successful and efficient use of unitary construction in the U.S.A.

The use of unitary construction has had profound effects on the

* *Motor Vehicles: A Report on the Industry*, Political and Economic Planning, London, p. 21 (1950).

capital intensity of production and the life cycle of different models. In the car industry it is most successfully applied when the body is made up of different pressed-steel components. Turning sheets of steel into pressings requires heavy investment in huge automatic or mechanical presses together with expensive dies of the required kind. The expensive equipment plus the high annual output of such machines requires their maximum utilisation in order to spread the large fixed costs involved. The expense and long-life of such equipment also means that over-heads are spread over a large number of units for as many years as possible; this reduces the annual capital charges to be allocated to any one year's production. As a result, access to large financial reserves is needed by vehicle builders and model changes must be kept to a minimum in order to make the investment worthwhile at competitive product prices. Car producers therefore keep the same basic body shell for anything between five and twenty years or even longer (as in the case of the Morris Minor). Annual body changes cannot be afforded—even in the U.S.A. the basic body shell is retained for up to five years. The apparent use of annual fundamental body changes is due to the successful modification of a few body panels.

Previous to World War II, however, the annual model change was a feature of the motor industry. This was possible because the amount of capital involved in the manufacturing process was much less. In the U.K., although mass-production, flow-line production techniques, and a degree of mechanisation were features of the industry, the equipment and techniques used were not so sophisticated or costly as today. In addition, body making consisted of attaching steel sheets to a basic frame made either of wood or metal; the use of large pressed items was very much the exception until the mid-1930s. Bodybuilding was, as a result, a much less capital intensive process than it is now. The equipment used was also of the general purposes type and could be easily modified to do different tasks. This is in contrast to the special purpose equipment now used, which is expensive, but which produces a vast number of units at low unit costs by performing just one task. Pre-war the annual body change was an economic proposition as it did not involve the wholesale scrapping of presses and dies. The cheaper equipment used also meant that it was less expensive to 'stop the machinery' to change dies. Nowadays it is only economic to use large high speed special purpose presses if the high fixed cost is to be spread both over a large number of units and by continuous running of the equipment. This situation is shown in *Figure 8.1*.

Pre-war production totals justified a plant size SAC^1 (where SAC is short-run average cost); the expansion of the car market in the post-

Figure 8.1

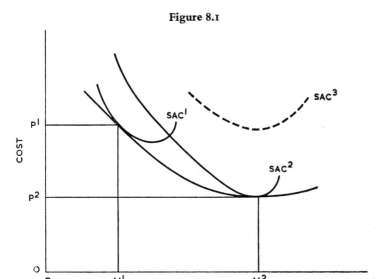

war period justifies plant size SAC^2 with a different technique of production. Output in the post-war period is M^2-M^1 greater than pre-war but cost and price is P^1-P^2 lower than pre-war. However, if output fell to OM^1 the more capital intensive post-war technique gives higher production costs than the pre-war plant size. In addition, if the position of SAC^1 is calculated on the basis of annual body changes, but SAC^2 on a five year body life and amortisation period, then attempts at annual body changes pushes SAC^2 upwards to SAC^3. In this case unit costs would be higher than pre-war at optimum output levels, and costs would be in excess of revenue. As a result it would be commercial folly to attempt annual body changes given the present high volume and potentially low cost production techniques.

In some instances complete cars do not roll off the assembly lines, rather components and sub-assemblies are sold so that a complete vehicle is purchased in unassembled form. Only specialist car producers do this for the internal market but all manufacturers export vehicles in a 'completely knocked down' (c.k.d.) form. In many instances where countries are attempting to establish domestic motor industries this is the only way imports are allowed in. Less shipping space and lower factory costs are involved, thereby reducing the vehicle's value and consequently the burden of *ad valorem* duties. In 1968, about 40% of all car exports and 12% of all commercial vehicle exports were c.k.d.

Other items produced or assembled at stages prior to final assembly may not be used on the final assembly lines. Instead they represent the manufacture of spare parts for domestic and foreign retailers, and for the producers' own stocks. Indeed, manufacturers still produce parts for obsolete and replaced models current as long ago as 1940*.

THE EMERGENCE OF AUTOMATION

As the demand for vehicles has increased, different production techniques have become appropriate. Indeed, with the growth in the output of a standardised item, production techniques can be altered in such a way as to reduce unit costs. First and foremost increased mechanisation becomes economically justifiable, as machines can be installed to do just one function for long periods of time. This has been done in two stages. During the inter-war period there was a gradual introduction of mechanised production techniques. Moving assembly lines became usual and machines were used to produce individual items on a continuous basis. Machinery was manually operated and parts were manually transferred from one machine to another. The post-war period has seen the second stage in mechanisation with the introduction of automation. Here there were two approaches. In the U.S.A., 'special purpose' machines were introduced capable of performing several operations at once, but they were often specific to one particular set of operations on a particular part of a vehicle. As a result the equipment was replaced when the vehicle model changed. Being specific to the parts concerned, the machinery had to be amortised over the life of these items; consequently it was only worthwhile introducing this equipment at very large output volumes.† Otherwise the fixed cost burden per unit would make production by such methods uncompetitive. The second approach was to add control devices to standard engineering machines to turn their operation into an automatic one. These machines were cheaper to install than special purpose units of the American type, and in addition they could be readily adapted to differing requirements so that product modifications did not require the wholesale scrapping of equipment. The lower output volumes prevailing in Europe made these machines more economic than the U.S. equipment; the fixed cost was lower and different sizes of component could come off the same line.

* *Motor Transport*, Supplement on British Leyland, p. 1 (14 November 1969).
† *Some Aspects of the Motor Vehicle Industry in the U.S.A.*, OEEC Report, pp. 17–18 (1952).

The European industry has never really introduced the type of inflexible high capacity machinery that equipped the U.S. car plants between 1945 and the late 1950s. During the 1950s the growth in demand for European cars made it worthwhile to move on from sole reliance on automated standard machines linked by mechanical handling devices to high speed automatic transfer machines. However, the Europeans came up with a different answer to this problem than did the Americans. The Europeans built automatic transfer lines based on adapting standard machines; this allowed the standardisation of machine heads and the equipment used to transfer pieces between work stations which facilitated the quantity production of this equipment. In addition, the basic standard machines can be used again when a model change occurs. Such adaptation is expensive but cheaper than scrapping the entire transfer machine. Whilst the French and British used standard limited purpose machines as a basis for producing transfer machines, the Germans linked standard general purpose machines to form automatic production lines with automatic handling. This however, appeared to be inferior to the British and French production methods, leaving scope for cost reduction in material handling and in the combination of machining operations*. By 1960 the Germans and the Americans followed the French and British predilection for adapting standard machines, substantially modifying them and coming-up with an automatic transfer line. As early as 1955 the Americans showed signs of moving away from their high cost inflexible lines towards the automation of single machines and automatic lines incorporating standard types of machine. By 1966 the considerable standardisation of tools and equipment by the Americans was evident†.

The European pioneer of automatic production methods was the Renault concern which adapted standard machines to create an automatic transfer machine. In this country they were quickly followed by Austin, although Ford and Vauxhall had already installed American type automatic transfer equipment. In 1950, Austin, with the help of James Archdale and Company, commenced building its own machine tools after the rest of the machine tool trade had turned the job down‡. Austin built machine heads and electronic devices while Archdale supplied bases and transfer mechanisms. The units produced could machine engine blocks and gearbox castings, transferring items through dozens of 'stations' without handling. Automation transformed the industry; in 1939 Austin's 19 000 workers produced 1700 vehicles

---

* 'Motors in the Boom', *The Economist*, p. 14 (22 October 1955).
† 'Cars: The Continental Divide', *The Economist*, p. 8 (9 July 1966).
‡ G. Turner, *The Car Makers*, Penguin, London, p. 36 (1964).

during a 52½ hour week; by 1960 their 23 000 employees turned out 6750 vehicles in a 42½ hour week. Automation increased production and reduced labour and other costs per unit. Austin gave the saving in direct labour costs as almost 85%, Renault pointed to large savings in maintenance costs when each special-purpose machine replaced ten standard machines.

Austin continues to build and design its own transfer machines adapting as much as possible standard machines as a base to build upon. They have also developed the 'link line' as an alternative approach to automation which on suitable components gives greater flexibility than the automatic transfer machine. The 'line' consists of 20 or 30 standard machines linked by mechanical handling devices. It costs less than a transfer machine and is easily adapted to differing requirements. So whilst greater volume justifies the use of the relatively flexible type 'European' transfer machine at some stages in the production process, such as making cylinder blocks, present volumes do not justify the universal use of transfer machines. Where greater flexibility is required the old idea of linking-up standard machines to form an automatic line is the best answer. AEC introduced a similar system in 1955 for the flow-line manufacture of diesel engines. The system increased output per man in the production of engine parts by between 300 and 600%.

THE ADVANTAGES OF MASS-PRODUCTION

Increased output volume not only facilitates mechanisation but also allows a basic change in the method of production. At very low output levels bespoke production methods may prevail, at higher output levels batch production will be used, to be superseded by flow production at even higher outputs. With the large scale production of a standardised product, equipment is laid out in sequence so that the product 'flows' from 'station' to 'station'. The high throughput justifies using a machine full-time on a particular task. With lower output levels the use of such special-purpose equipment would mean that it was idle for much of the time. This would increase the unit costs of production. Consequently at smaller output levels, a machine after doing one particular task would be quickly re-set to do another. In this case batch production would be used. In other words, a batch of parts are machined on one piece of equipment and then passed on to another for further processing. The first machine is then re-set to process some other item often in a different way. With flow-line production a flow of parts continually passes from one special purpose machine to another. With extremely large output volumes and mass production 'par excellence', individual special purpose machines are replaced by automatic transfer machine, a machine able to perform several functions at once as each transfer machine is in effect a mini flow-line.

If the output volume justifies it, flow production is preferable to batch production. In the experience of one CV manufacturer, it reduced the amount of work-handling and the level of stocks. In addition it allowed further mechanisation and some automation; this in turn reduced the direct labour content in each unit of output and allowed a reduction in the total work-force. The use of either individual general-purpose or special-purpose machines gave these advantages; however, the introduction of automatic transfer machines brought further benefits to this manufacturer. It had been found that the main production bottleneck had been the time spent on loading and unloading. Automation reduced this time significantly and costly machinery was used much closer to optimum capacity as the operating speed was allowed to increase. Flow-lines, and especially automated flow-lines, also make better use of work space as the amount of material stacking is reduced. The quicker production process also reduces the capital tied-up in work-in-progress in addition to reducing stocks generally. Less direct labour is needed especially when transfer machines are used. The greater degree of machine utilisation stemming from automated production processes and control systems allows significant short-run economies to be reaped as firms are able to operate closer to their technical optimum. Added to the economies of scale derived in the long-run, automated flow-lines give considerable reductions in average total unit costs of production (*Figure 8.2*).

SAC and LAC depict short-run and long-run average costs respectively. Given bespoke production, say Foden commercial vehicles or Aston-Martin cars, the scale of plant and the unit costs of production are given by SAC^1. An increased size of market allows the use of batch production methods, as in the heavy vehicle plants of the Leyland Motors Corporation or in the Jaguar car factories. This increases plant size to SAC^2 and gives considerable reductions in unit costs. The introduction of flow-lines in the mass-production car and vehicle plants utilising individual general and special-purpose machines gives plant size SAC^3 at cost and output AB, BO respectively. A further enlargement of the car market means that automatic transfer machines and control systems can economically replace individual standard machines and reduce costs to $A^1 B^1$. Consequently between plant size SAC^1 and SAC^3 there are long-run scale economies to be reaped,

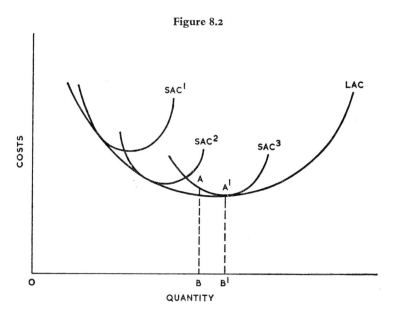

Figure 8.2

whereas along SAC^3 from A to A^1 the law of variable proportions allows a cost reduction of $AB–A^1B^1$.

THE SHORT-RUN COST STRUCTURE

Turning now to the typical short-run cost structure of a British mass-producing car firm. No two firms have exactly the same cost structure but a general picture does emerge. In discussing the cost structure of a British built car one must first make reference to the output level in relation to the capacity on which it is based. Any figure arrived at is based on a producers' budgeted costs based on an assessed utilisation of capacity[*]. It would appear that normal capacity is regarded as being 80% of maximum capacity; working at this level is on average the optimum annual utilisation of capacity possible due to normal demand fluctuation[†]. Hence we may assume that scheduled output on which the cost structure is based is equivalent to around 80% of capacity.

At this level of output a noteworthy feature is that the 'bought-out' content in total vehicle costs is very high. For example, 30% of a

[*] *The Effect of Government Economic Policy on the Motor Industry*, National Economic Development Office, London, p. 26 (1968).
[†] *The Economist* (5 January and 17 August 1963).

Leyland truck and 40% of a BMC truck in value terms is made outside British Leyland, for a BMC car it is 70% and for a Jaguar 60%. Over the period 1960 to 1967, taking the U.K. car industry as a whole, material costs have never accounted for less than 62% of budgeted costs*. Material costs include all raw materials plus semi-finished and finished components entering into the finished product. In a fully integrated highly automated car plant direct labour charges account for about 8% of total costs†. Other variable costs incurred from both production and commercial activities account for about 14% of total costs. At the same time, fixed overheads during the period 1967–1968 were around 16% of total works costs‡. These fixed costs cover development expenses, the manufacture of special tools such as body-dies and other fixed factory and commercial expenses such as depreciation charges on the one hand and advertising and general sales promotion on the other. From this we have a generalised cost structure for a firm working at 80% of capacity as shown in *Table 8.1*.

Table 8.1

A TYPICAL CAR'S COST STRUCTURE IN 1968

Variable and Fixed Costs	%
Bought-out components	
Other materials	62
Direct Labour	8
Other Variable Costs	14
Total Variable Costs	84
Development and tooling and other fixed expenses	16
Total Fixed Costs	16

Given this data plus some information concerning the output volumes of different motor firms and their total fixed costs, it is possible to work out an approximate picture of a motor firm's short-run average cost curve. In other words we are dealing with the position when some factors of production are fixed in supply; for instance, the plant size cannot be varied, but output can be increased by adding factors which are variable in the short-run to the fixed factor. More

* *The Effect of Government Economic Policy on the Motor Industry*, NEDO, London, p. 26 (1968).
† *Some Aspects of the Motor Vehicle Industry in the U.S.A.*, OEEC Report, p. 76 (1952).
‡ *The Effect of Government Economic Policy on the Motor Industry*, NEDO, London, p. 26 (1968).

labour can be employed for example. If we look at the position during the first years of the 1960s, a number of car firms had a gross operating investment of around £60 million. If we take this as an indication of total fixed costs and assume plausibly that our largest producers had a scheduled output capacity of around 600 000 vehicles a year then we derive some notion of the nature of the average cost curve facing the individual firm. In this analysis we will assume that variable costs per unit of output are constant. From these figures the rough estimate of fixed costs per unit of output can be fixed at £100. From *Table 8.1* fixed costs at this level of output were 16% of total unit costs, hence total unit costs are £625. So at 80% of maximum capacity estimated total costs are £625, fixed costs being £100 and variable costs £525. Using a cost index, it is possible to estimate the percentage change in costs as output deviates from the scheduled level (*Table 8.2*).

Table 8.2

OUTPUT AS A PERCENTAGE OF MAXIMUM
CAPACITY AND SCHEDULED OUTPUT

Percentage of maximum capacity	Percentage of scheduled output	Index of costs
20	25	148
40	50	116
60	75	106·5
80★	100	100
100	125	96·8

★Scheduled output.

What this indicates is that a percentage change in output of say 25% of scheduled output means that costs vary between 6·5% and 3·2% of the planned cost level on which its marketing and pricing strategy is based. However, given the level of unit variable costs, variations in output by as much as 25% from the planned optimum level have only a slight effect on total unit costs, whereas a variation in variable costs would be much more serious for at optimum output levels variable costs are much more important than fixed costs. Obviously at very low production levels the heavy fixed costs impose a tremendous burden, but the fixed costs per unit over a wide range of output levels either side of the scheduled optimum are relatively slight★.

★ This section relies heavily on A. Silberston and G. Maxcy's *The Motor Industry*, Allen and Unwin, London, p. 65 (1959).

The popular view that heavy fixed costs in the motor industry must always have a large effect on the total unit costs of production can therefore be shown to be wrong. Tooling costs in the motor industry, for example, are less significant than one may think, despite high initial expenditures. The extra tooling costs involved in producing a mechanically advanced car like the BMC Mini or 1100 was perhaps of the order of £2½ to £3 million. Even this only adds £5 to £6 to the cost of each car over a model run of 500 000. In this case, some existing parts, such as engines and gearboxes were utilised*. A totally new model like the Ford Escort cost £15 million in new tooling and production facilities. The model run was expected to be around 1½ million units, so fixed costs were £10 per car. (As body dies may need replacing before this total is achieved, the fixed cost per car may be somewhat higher than this.) This shows that despite extremely large fixed expenses, the fixed costs per unit in the region of projected output levels is quite small. Again, if 'General Motors amortises a given die which costs $40 million over 4 million units in 2 years, the unit cost is $10'†.

Of course a commercial failure is extremely expensive; the failure surrounding the Edsel cost the Ford Motor Company $250 million‡, which gives some idea of the total fixed costs incurred in producing a motor car. If, however, this model had achieved its 'scheduled life time output' of some 4 million units, then total unit fixed costs would have been around $62·50. Under conditions such as these the car producer's main task is to control direct costs. 'Where he is using many parts that are not made for any other maker, he may well find that his production costs are higher than those of makers of conventional cars. BMC found this a problem with the Mini§.' Similarly, increased material and labour costs generally are just as dangerous to the level of the short-run average cost curve. So although a decline in output will have little effect on unit costs except when the fall is very large, increased variable costs have a profound effect on total unit costs and on a firm's pricing policy‖.

* 'Cars: Does Innovation Pay?', *The Economist* (15 December 1962).
† J. A. Menge, 'Style Change Costs as a Market Weapon', *Quarterly Journal of Economics*, Vol. LXXVI, No. 4 (November 1962).
‡ J. D. Scheel, *Cars of the World*, Methuen, London, p. 182 (1962).
§ 'Cars: Does Innovation Pay?', *The Economist* (15 December 1962).
‖ In 1969–1970 car prices increased five times in fifteen months due to the effects of inflation on direct costs.

Although short-period output changes will normally have negligible effects on costs, the small increase in fixed costs per unit of output coming from variations in output of up to 25% from the projected optimum can still greatly affect profits. So in this respect the attention paid to heavy fixed costs is justified. For instance, between 1955 and 1958 Vauxhall doubled its capacity from 130 000 vehicles a year to 260 000 vehicles. There was a movement from one short-run cost curve to another. The old plant size had been used to capacity with the result that profits per vehicles were of the order £45 to £50 and net margins on sales between 8¾% and 10¼%. In 1958 with the new plant size in operation output was about 67% of maximum capacity, profits per vehicle were £4 10s., or less than a 1% margin on sales. Although we have two different cost curves here we can still indicate that output at near maximum capacity gives profits per unit of around £50; at around 67% of capacity they had fallen to £4 10s. From our approximate cost index we deduce that the change in average fixed costs arising from variations in output would not greatly affect costs per unit of output over this output range. However, profits per unit of output are greatly affected by this small increase in fixed costs per unit of output: a 5% increase in total unit costs equivalent to say 5% of £625 or just over £31 would cut a 10% profit margin by 50%. This together with any fall in output would reduce aggregate profits by over 50%. To this extent movements in profits and output bear a direct relationship. Increases in variable costs at given output levels, all the same, are likely to affect profits even more given the large proportion of costs made up by variable costs at scheduled output. When profit margins are tight to begin with then any reduction in output will place severe pressure on margins. For instance, between 1961 and 1962 BMC earned between £6 10s. and £5 10s. per unit; in 1968–1969 Rootes earned £2 8s. per vehicle with output at under 60% of maximum capacity. In the case of Rootes, unit costs at this output level were perhaps some 7% above those prevailing at scheduled volume. Any further reduction in output would almost certainly have led to losses: a 0·5% increase in the costs of a car costing £600 to produce would result in losses. Of course any slight percentage increase in variable costs would be even worse.

Quite clearly Rootes' break-even point between total costs per unit and total revenue per unit was reached at just under 60% of maximum capacity. This leads us in to our final point here.

With a given cost curve and with output within 25% of scheduled volume any increase in demand will have little effect on short-run average costs per unit. Similarly, if a firm wishes to increase its output by reducing price, it is quite likely that total costs will increase more than total revenue. That is even though demand is elastic and a price cut increases total revenue, the increase in total costs is likely to be even greater as variable costs form a large proportion of total unit costs; hence profits are reduced or losses increased. As a result there is a tendency for short-run prices to remain constant*.

We can show the possible results as follows. The point to note is that at any point where total revenue equals total costs excluding profits, the smaller is the proportion of fixed costs to total costs at the going 'break-even' output, the more difficult it is to break even following a

Figure 8.3

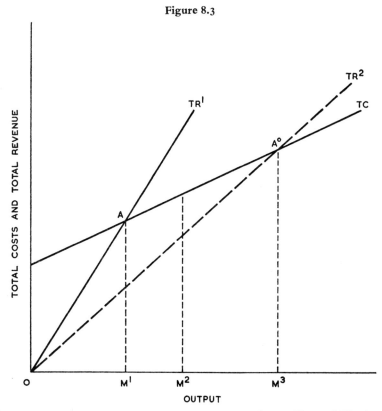

* See A. Silberston and G. Maxcy, *The Motor Industry*, Allen and Unwin, London, ch. 5, (1959); also, *The Dynamics of Automobile Demand*, GMC, New York (1939).

fall in price. So if the demand for a firm's cars are elastic a price reduction increases total revenue, but if at the original output level variable costs per unit predominate then any increase in output increases total costs considerably. For instance, if variable costs per unit are constant and if the average cost per unit is £10 when 100 units are produced, then an increase in output of 10% increases total costs by 10% if fixed costs are zero; if variable costs per unit are zero then total costs remain constant. In short the smaller the proportion of fixed costs to total unit costs at the going volume the larger the proportionate increase in total costs when output expands. So if fixed costs are 16% of total unit costs then a 10% increase in output increases total costs by about 8·4% or £84. If the 10% increase in output followed from a 1% fall in price then the elasticity of demand is 10, and total revenue increases by about 9%. Hence profits are increased. However, if the 10% increase in demand only follows from a 2% fall in price, then total revenue increases by about 8% and profits fall. So where fixed costs are a small proportion of total unit costs only a very large magnitude attached to the price elasticity of demand will increase profits given a price reduction. Two points emerge; under many conditions the price elasticity of demand will not be sufficiently large to restore a new break even point and even if it was the increase in output required would be impossible given the capacity of the plant involved.

Given a price reduction the total revenue curve falls from TR^1 to TR^2 at OM^3; A^0M^3 is greater than AM^1 at output OM^1, therefore demand is elastic. However, as capacity is OM^2 the break-even output OM^3 cannot be achieved (*Figure 8·3*).

At present (1971) the fixed cost element in total unit costs is around 16%, compared with 9·9% in 1967* in the U.K. motor industry. Hence any increase in output will increase total costs quite considerably and in a 0·84:1 ratio with output. Assuming constant variable costs per unit of output and a further decline in the proportion of fixed costs per unit as output expands, an increase in output of 10% from the present output level may increase total costs by around $8\frac{1}{2}\%$. Under these circumstances the elasticity of demand must be around 6·6 if profits, as distinct from revenue, are to increase.

---

* *The Effect of Government Economic Policy on the Motor Industry*, NEDO, London, p. 26.

THE ELASTICITY OF DEMAND AND PRICING POLICY

Empirical studies* place the price elasticity of demand for cars at between 0·6 and 1·5, most results being in the range 1·2 to 1·5. So where the average total cost curve flattens out and the fixed cost element per unit is small then price cuts will not increase profits. That is the increase in revenue is insufficient to offset both the price reduction and the increase in total costs following from an increase in demand and output. If, for instance, total revenue increases by only 0·2% when the price elasticity of demand is 1·2, then only if a large part of total unit costs are fixed costs will profits increase, and then only if output increases over a narrow range for fixed costs per unit fall rapidly here.

These empirical studies refer to car demand as a whole. As the elasticity of demand facing the individual firm is normally greater than that facing the entire industry, would an individual U.K. car firm be likely to increase short-run profits given a price cut? Some indication follows from the position of the Rootes Group in 1968 and 1969. Between November 1968 and July 1969 the company reduced the prices of most of its cars by an average of 5%. In 1968 Rootes sold 189 000 cars and 194 000 in 1969; at the same time total car registrations on the domestic market fell from 1 117 000 to 980 000, a fall of just over 12·2%. Applying this to the Rootes output its 1969 total should have been 166 000, but the actual total was almost 17% above this. Working on this crude basis the price elasticity of demand works out at 3·4. As the company was working at around 60% of capacity in 1969, without the price cut it may have been working at just 50% of maximum capacity. From our notional cost index we can see that average unit costs fall by just under 5% over these output ranges. At the same time average revenue falls by 5% so the Rootes Group would suffer a slight decrease in profits, indeed during the year 1969–1970 compared with 1968–1969 the company's losses increased.

Hence in the short run there is an incentive to keep prices constant. Any decrease in price with output 25% either side of schedule is likely to reduce rather than increase profits. Similarly given any decrease in demand, caused by exogenous factors such as income changes or hire-purchase restrictions which reduce output, this will hardly increase unit costs at all over a large range of outputs. The fall in costs will therefore almost be commensurate with the fall in revenue, so given a reasonable profit margin to start with there will be little

* See Chapter 7, p. 228.

need to increase prices. An exogenous increase in variable costs is another matter for it is such changes which provoke nearly all short-run price variations. If variable costs were constant over time then prices would have little need to alter.

It must be made clear that it is not suggested that firms should increase their fixed cost element per unit just because this means that with increased output the increase in total costs would be that much less and the probability of increased short run profits following a price cut would be that much greater. The analysis shows that when total revenue (TR) equals total cost (TC), the smaller the proportion of fixed costs the less likelihood that a price reduction will be successful in restoring a break-even situation or a previous level of profits. However, the smaller the level of fixed costs the smaller is the break-even output level given a particular price and rate of profit (*Figure 8.4*).

Figure 8.4

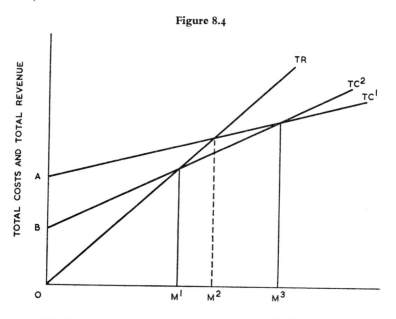

With the same TR curve two firms have different production methods and cost structures. Firm A with TC^1 has a higher capital: labour ratio than B. With low fixed costs BO break-even output is OM^1, with fixed costs at AO it is OM^2. However, as output continues to increase the firm with the higher investment, by needing less variable factors, finds its average costs per unit of output falling faster than does firm A. Beyond output OM^3 the highly capitalised firm has lower unit and total costs than the 'labour-intensive' firm. So the smaller the fixed cost element the smaller the break-even point (with zero fixed costs the break-even output is zero), but as output increases such a firm's costs increase faster than a highly capitalised one. From pieces of information percolating from vehicle producers, actual break-even points in the period 1968–1970 can be tabulated (*Table 8.2*).

Table 8.2

OUTPUT AS A PERCENTAGE OF
CAPACITY WHERE $TC = TR$

Firm	%
VW ('Beetle' output)	14*
Br. Leyland (Bathgate)	80†
Br. Leyland (Albion)	40†
BMC Cars (approx.)	70
Rootes	60
Ford	70
Overall Cars	64
Heavy CV Makers	25

* *Motor*, (p. 13. 27 December 1969,)
† *The Sunday Times*, (p. 29. 4 May 1969,)

The very low Volkswagen figure is due to the full amortisation of many fixed cost items over the period 1939 to the present. Items such as design and development costs, expenditure on special tools and presses have been largely paid off. The heavy CV producers have little capital equipment although design teams are large, at the same time gross profit margins of over 10% per vehicle produce unit profits of anything between £290 and £510 depending on the firms involved. Albion's capital equipment largely involves the ingenious use of low cost and/or home made equipment*. The car plants are much of a muchness although Rootes' low break-even point is noteworthy.

The break-even point depends not only on fixed costs but also on the profit margin per vehicle; the lower the margin the higher the break-even point (*Figure 8.5*).

TR^1 includes a higher profit margin than TR^2; with a given TC curve TR^1 gives a lower 'break-even' output. The heavy CV makers have low fixed costs and high profit margins; but BMC was heavily capitalised with inefficient and badly used equipment† and only low

* *Automobile Engineer* (January 1964).
† *Motor Transport*, Supplement on British Leyland, pp. v–vi (14 November 1969).

Figure 8.5

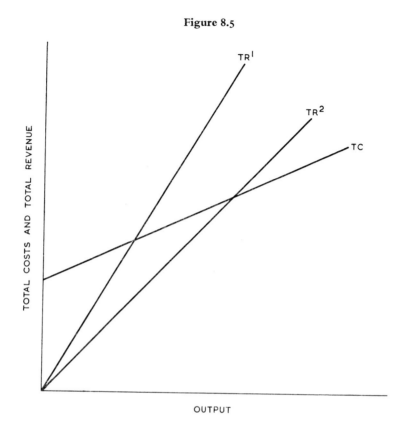

profit margins were added to full cost because of strong competition from Ford and Bedford. This situation is shown diagrammatically in *Figure 8.6*. *TR²* and *TC²* are the Bathgate conditions if *TR¹* and *TC²* are the conditions facing such efficient assemblers as ERF, Seddon and Atkinson; Foden is more highly capitalised but profits per unit are very high.

In conclusion then, once a firm is at a break-even point the smaller the fixed cost proportion and profit margins per unit the greater the likelihood of reduced prices leading to reduced profits. In some instances the increased output required to offset a price reduction and to restore break-even conditions may be greater than plant capacity. In other instances the elasticity of demand would not be large enough to restore a break-even position. However, the smaller the fixed cost element and the larger the profit margin, the smaller the break-even output; the greater the profits the greater can be the minus deviation from scheduled output before losses appear.

At present the car industry as a whole is highly capitalised and striving to reduce its absolute variable costs (by standardising components and reducing the labour force) in order to reduce the slope of the TC curve. Hence its overall break-even point is a quite commendable 64% of maximum capacity. However, the Big Three U.S. firms have break-even points around 50% and Volkswagen has a very low figure of around 20%. Given broadly similar production methods the U.K. problem seems to be inefficiency, both in the use and type of equipment, but more importantly in too high a level of variable costs. In addition some margins may have been placed at too low a level *ad valorem* especially on small cheap cars, e.g. BMC's earnings of £5 10s. a car during much of the 1960s was mainly due to the pricing of Mini cars. Fixed costs should not be a problem at all if firms produce in the region of their 'scheduled-output' volumes. In

Figure 8.6

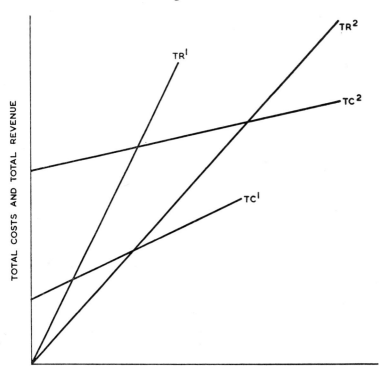

the U.K. it is direct material, component* and labour costs† which have been internationally out of line.

In the short-run it has been indicated that without changes in variable or direct costs prices would have no incentive to vary. In the long-run however, the firm can shift onto a lower short-run cost curve by moving along its long-run average cost curve. This it can do by either changing the product to meet the price appropriate to current demand and competitive conditions, or by increasing output to reap economies of large-scale production.

ECONOMIES OF LARGE-SCALE PRODUCTION

The problem here is to decide whether there is some technical optimum value of production beyond and below which long-run average costs per unit tend to increase.

If a technical optimum exists it is obvious that it changes over time as technological change occurs. In some instances technological change can reduce the magnitude of the optimum output but in most cases it does the opposite. Another point is that in an industry where there are distinct processes and operations the technical optimum occurs at different levels of output depending on the process involved.

Broadly speaking the car industry contains four main processes: assembly, foundry work, forging and machining and pressing. Where the optimum is different for different stages in the productive process then the overall optimum for the plant-complex is the lowest common denominator of each optima. So if assembly optima is assumed to be 180 000 units a year, engine machining 1 000 000 a year and 'boot' pressings 2 160 000 a year, then the overall technical optimum for the firm requires 12 assembly plants, two engine plants and one pressings plant, the lowest common multiple being 2 160 000.

The duplication of either plant or equipment does not affect unit average cost at all. A car firm producing 360 000 units has the same unit assembly costs as that producing 2 160 000 units; however, it is not able to justify the use of the most efficient engine or body equipment available at such an output level. Techniques which are cheaper for the small firm may give higher unit costs than those incurred by the capacity use of more expensive but higher output equipment which the larger firm finds it profitable to use. To utilise such equipment the small firm would have to leave it idle for much of the time,

* *The Economist*, p. 1126 (15 December 1962).
† *The Sunday Times* (6 November 1966).

with the result that unit costs would be too high. If the large firm producing 2 160 000 units is competing with one making 4 320 000 units then it is at no cost disadvantage; the absolute normal profit and net cash flow would nevertheless give the second firm a financial advantage.

The existence of increasing returns to scale is often explained by the fact that larger output allows greater specialisation of process and division of labour. The laws of probability are involved to explain why stocks need not increase as rapidly as sales to maintain an optimal sales to stock ratio; this is related to the greater stability and predictability of large numbers. Other instances result from physical relationships, for instance the materials needed to enlarge a storage area are related to the square of the surface dimension, whereas capacity increases by the cube of the surface dimension. This is then applied by engineers as the '0·6 Rule'*, a rule of thumb relating the increased cost of equipment generally to the increase in output. What does not explain varying returns to scale is the use of different inputs with different optimal capacities. Just because each assembly plant produces 180 000 units compared with 1 080 000 units for each engine plant does not necessarily mean that the decrease in total unit costs beyond 180 000 units is a sign of economies of scale. Here, all we are saying is that there are discrepancies between actual and optimal input sizes because certain inputs are not available in certain sizes. This problem is the indivisibility of input units or, a related problem, the lack of perfect adaptability. If the operation is able to expand proportionately and by large enough increments to overcome these problems then constant returns to scale may prevail. So when we said economies of scale exist in the car plant-complex we meant that an engine plant turning out 1 080 000 units was different and more efficient than one capable of producing 180 000 engines. However, to overcome the indivisibility and adaptability problem posed by a machine with an optimum output of 1 080 000 units requires six assembly plants, otherwise the engine plant is out of balance with the assembly plants and unit costs increase. If given the correct balance, unit costs remain constant then the *minimum* optimum has been exceeded and further increases in output means the duplication of existing techniques.

---

* The increase in cost is given by the increase in capacity raised to the 0·6 power.

ASSEMBLY

In trying to gauge the motor industry's optimum output level we must analyse what is the optimum in each of the four major processes involved. First of all we shall look at vehicle assembly.

The modern assembly line with its mass of overhead conveyers and sub-assembly lines feeding the main assembly line is, surprisingly though it may seem, a small-scale activity in the context of the scale of operation in the car firm as a whole. In the U.S.A. the Big Three producers have almost 50 assembly plants between them, giving an average plant capacity of about 200 000 units per year. In the U.K. there are nine major mass-production assembly lines*. Taking the estimated output of these plants in 1964, which is the peak production year to date, the average annual output per plant is just under 200 000 units. At the time of writing (1971) this optimum may have doubled again. Both the U.S. and U.K. figures are based on two-shift working schedules. Between the early post-war period and the late 1950s it would appear that the optimum assembly output had doubled from 100 000† units to 200 000. Probably the main reason for this is greater mechanisation; although assembly is still relatively labour-intensive, the developments in such spheres as automatic welding techniques have increased capital intensity and thereby enlarged the optimum output level. In addition, the emergence of new electrophosphoric paint plants with a capacity of 42 units an hour gives an annual output, on a two-shift, eight hour day for 48 weeks basis, of around 200 000 units. At one time the assembly of 200 000 units would have meant the duplication of much equipment, including the number of assembly lines in each assembly plant. However, although some duplication exists one long assembly line as at the Rootes plant at Ryton-on-Dunsmore will produce 180 000 units a year. Obviously the larger British companies are large enough to reap all the economies of scale at the assembly stage. With high demand conditions the total production of each firm would be well in excess of the assembly optimum.

Economies of scale in assembly are important then up to 200 000 units a year. The switch from 'bespoke' to batch and then to mechanical flow-lines brings significant cost reductions. Small commercial vehicle specialists have benefited by switching from bespoke production at

* These are the major Ford, Vauxhall, Rootes, BMC and Triumph plants. They do not include Jaguar, Rover or the Abingdon sports-car plants.
† A. Silberston and G. Maxcy, *The Motor Industry*, Allen and Unwin, London, ch. 6, p. 77 (1959).

one station to single multi-station flow-lines. As output increases firms find it worthwhile to introduce more mechanisation such as moving assembly lines; the culmination of this process is found in the vast assembly-halls of the mass-producing car firms. In these plants, general purpose machinery is used to assemble many different models on a single assembly line at any one time. The correct components are brought to the assembly line by the use of computer control which selects the correct items for loading on to the conveyers which feed the main assembly tracks. The same principle can be used on mass produced car lines and on heavy vehicle lines. Variety and changes of model impose none of the extra costs at the assembly stage that they do when machining and pressing is involved. The use of electronic controls keeps disruption to almost zero.

The various sub-assembly lines are basically similar to the final assembly line and have similar optima. The most important line is the body line; here the welded sub-assemblies, such as roofs and sides, are put together in the main assembly jigs by automatic or hand welding. After painting, the body enters the final trim shop from where it moves on to the final assembly line. The equipment used in body assembly is largely non-specialised apart from the jig and some welding equipment. Because it is uneconomic to transport complete bodies most European and American final assembly plants have body assembly plants attached. Only in the U.K. have complete bodies been transported in any numbers, due to the survival of Pressed Steel for so long as an independent body maker. After BMC purchased Pressed Steel in 1965 this tended to change, and now only body panels are transported to the main body assembly plants. The Linwood plant presses body parts for the Rootes group, some of which are transported to the Coventry plant and other bodies are assembled in Linwood for the main car assembly plant next door. The existence of many body assembly plants suggests an optimum similar to final vehicle assembly; even if further economies are available, they are insufficient to offset the differences in cost between transporting individual pressings and complete bodies.

Consequently flow-line assembly appears to give optimum output levels at around 200 000 units a year. The process is relatively labour intensive, the product complex, and the equipment for the most part is of the general purpose kind; hence a somewhat limited optimum size prevails. Further developments in the field of automatic control with high speed computers controlling final assembly plus the development of less labour intensive assembly methods could lead to further economies and therefore larger optimum output levels. The need to achieve optimum assembly levels is stressed by the fact that, in one form or another, assembly costs account for over 20% of the budgeted total unit costs of a car.

THE FOUNDRY

Casting is done partly in foundries owned by the car firms and partly by independent suppliers. In all, there are over 50 outside foundries meeting the iron castings needs of the motor industry; this appears to suggest that economies of scale are not easily attainable in this branch of the industry*. Between 1950 and 1965 iron foundries making car parts increased production from 335 000 tons to 939 000 tons. Increased production though, did not lead to equivalent increases in the size of foundry. Of the 1100 foundries existing in 1965, only 59 produced over 10 000 tons of castings a year, roughly 200 tons a week, the amount produced by big foundries like Darcast in one morning. At the other extreme, over 350 foundries produced less than 200 tons a year†. Castings production is very labour intensive and most equipment is of the general purpose variety; this equipment is used in conjunction with a wide variety of shapes and sizes of castings, so specific items need not be produced in very large numbers to fully use the capital involved.

The survival of a large number of different foundries of different sizes, even in supplying the motor industry, probably means that economies of scale are unimportant beyond relatively small volumes. This is borne out by the 'survival principle' for determining optimum size‡; if particular plant or firm sizes survive over time while other sizes disappear the size of firm which survives is the optimum size. Within the different firms there are basic differences in attitude and production methods between different sizes of companies. The small firms produce castings with little or no mechanised plant, labour-using methods being prevalent. In the biggest foundries, such as the Birmid and Qualcast plants, machinery is used for most processes and transfers between processes. Between these extremes are foundries with varying stages of mechanisation.

Small firms survive because of the amount of capital needed to

* M. E. Beesley and G. W. Troup, 'The Machine Tool Industry', *The Structure of British Industry* (N.I.E.S.R.: C.U.P., Vol. 1, p. 379, 1965), point to the survival of independent firms with only 24 foundries owned by the motor industry.

† 'Cars and Their Components', *The Economist*, p. 22 (23 October 1965).

‡ G. S. Stigler, 'The Economies of Scale', *Journal of Law and Economics*, Vol. 1 October 1958).

modernise a foundry, certainly in excess of £1 million, plus the realisation that 'under-capitalised' small firms are still able to compete on price. The cost-conscious car industry, which is by far the foundries' biggest single customer, has been unwilling to transfer allegiances to big firms for small producers can still compete effectively. The buying policy of car firms used to militate against large capital investment; car firms called for tenders from a large number of foundries on an annual basis. The annual scramble meant that firms could not guarantee work for more than a year at a time and hence were reluctant to base expansion on car industry orders. Car firms now guarantee to buy from only two or three foundries for all their requirements of any particular component and foundries are assured of a particular production level over long periods. Allied to this is the changing demand patterns of the motor firms towards more expensive and advanced types of castings. In 1964, 12% of the cast-iron used by the car firms was of this nature, and over 50% of the requirements were supplied by two foundries owned by one firm*. The concentration of demand on fewer suppliers may change the position in favour of larger, highly mechanised output. This in turn may increase the optimum size where foundry average production costs are at a minimum.

However, the wide variety and nature of the castings used by the motor industry suggests different optima for each. For instance, even motor firms with their own foundries have to 'buy-out' a wide variety of castings. While it is quite easy to operate a foundry making the less complicated castings such as cylinder blocks, it is more expensive to establish capacity able to make the wide range of high quality castings now wanted. No foundry group produces a complete range of castings needed by a car firm. A completely different type of foundry and process is needed to produce small, light castings compared with those producing heavier and cruder items such as cylinder blocks. Consequently there is a place for the specialist foundry which has developed sophisticated techniques for the mass-production of specific components; these firms are much smaller than the organisations producing heavy castings, but even here the position is fluid, only the largest groups having a sufficient net cash flow to provide capital for research and development into the new alloys likely to be used by the car firms in the future†.

So at present the optimum size of foundry is quite small, but the

* 'Cars and Their Components', *The Economist*, p. 32 (23 October 1965).
   'It is also now evident that the merger movement is beginning to affect the Steel Foundry Companies,' *Daily Telegraph* (7 February 1970).
   † This section draws heavily on 'Cars and Their Components', *The Economist*, p. 32 (23 October 1965).

increased use of machinery plus the need to work with new sophisticated metals may increase the optimum, especially if more specific
equipment is used. At present it would appear though that greater
mechanisation means largely the increased use of general purpose
equipment. Therefore the optimum is quite small, as shown by the
continued existence of many small and medium-sized firms. Consequently although their cost levels may justify their continued
existence, the capital needed for both increased mechanisation and
research into new metals could eventually mean the disappearance of
small firms for financial reasons.

FORGING AND MACHINING

It would appear that as regards assembly and foundry work the car
firm producing 200 000 units a year is at no cost disadvantage. But
when it comes to the machines making up the production lines for
parts, and manufacture by large presses with their attendant tools and
dies, the situation alters greatly. It is here that the most efficient
techniques require the use of astronomically expensive equipment
which is tied to the manufacture of just one basic type of component or
vehicle model. Consequently to reduce unit costs below that prevailing with the 'next-best' technique needs very high annual volumes to
justify the use of such expensive equipment.

The production of engines, gearboxes, transmissions, radiators,
carburettors and so on is capital intensive. Economies are derived from
the production of great numbers, hence manufacture is concentrated in
a few specialised plants. These parts are small in relation to their
value and it is therefore an economic proposition to transport them
over long distances. This is also true for many 'bought-out' parts;
by supplying the industry rather than the firm, Lucas can produce on a
large-scale and gain significant economies. In addition, the longer the
production run over time, the greater the amortisation period and the
lower the fixed-cost per unit. These factors tend to shift the long-
run average cost curve of the car firm downwards.

At the end of the 1950s the optimum output of engines on a two-
shift five day week basis was between 360 000 and 440 000 a year in
the American Motors Plant*. However, the industry's optimum was
above this: as early as 1953 it was reported that an hourly production
rate of 144 units existed at Ford's Cleveland Plant†. This suggested an

* *Administered Prices: Automobiles*, Senate Committee Report (November 1958).
† *Some Aspects of the Motor Vehicle Industry in the U.S.A.*, OEEC Report,
pp. 17 and 310 (1952).

optimum output level, using the most efficient equipment, of nearly 700 000 units a year. In 1970 the figure for optimum output was reported by one manufacturer as being around 1 million units a year. The same type of equipment is installed in the U.S.A., Europe and Japan. In the U.K., Japan and Western Europe, one, two or three basic engines will power a number of different models, whereas the Americans may use about a dozen types. So at present the optimum output of engine blocks is around 1 million a year, and similar equipment is used in the U.K. and the U.S.A. The optimum output level for equipment making items such as gearboxes and transmissions is probably similar to this, although British firms tend to use cheaper and more flexible equipment with an optimum capacity of around 250 000–300 000 units a year.

American producers making over two million cars a year have to duplicate equipment used for the production of major components; in fact most producers find it worthwhile to build two or three separate engine plants. Most of the equipment used for assembly or casting is multi-purpose, but in machining it is mainly special purpose. Although the less rigid transfer machines can allow some modifications, say to the cylinder block, only one basic engine can be made. BMC's A-series engine was first introduced in 1951, but with antecedents going back to 1939, and powers all Mini and 1100/1300 vehicles. Together with engines made for stock, export and replacement, total annual output of A-series engines could exceed 850 000. The basic Ford unit powering the Escort, Cortina and Capri models is produced in numbers in excess of 700 000. With output levels per engine type within about 80% of optimum, the largest U.K. firms can find it economic to use the technically most efficient equipment available. The high initial capital cost is spread over a large volume; and with a 'write-off' period of 10 to 15 years* the high volumes now prevailing also allow full amortisation over a realistic time period at a competitive rate. Even the car firms in the U.S.A. tend to maintain the same basic engine for 10 to 15 years, being unable to afford the huge outlays involved in tooling-up for completely new units much more often than this†. During the 1960s the same basic U.S. engine had a life of over 10 years, slight modifications to body design occurred annually and completely new body-shells were introduced every three to five years.

Although optimum engine capacity together with other major components is around 1 million units a year, even higher figures

* 'Does Innovation Pay?', The Economist, pp. 1135–1136 and p. 223 (15 December 1962 and 12 January 1956).
† 'Cars: The Continental Divide', The Economist, p. 8 (9 July 1966).

exist for the production of individual forgings. In 1969 GKN introduced a fully automated forging plant able to produce circular forgings
nearly 10 times faster than by conventional press forging methods.
This one machine was in a position to confer real economies to the car
industry if firms sped the process towards using common components.
The one machine was run by two or three workers and produced
4200 forgings per hour, or on a three-shift basis working at 75% of
optimum capacity, about 12 million forgings a year*. Even if five
such forgings were used per car the largest firm only produces around
320 000 units of its largest selling car with total output of around
$1\frac{1}{4}$ million vehicles at capacity working. Hence to reap the full benefits
of such equipment the entire car industry must use the same forgings.

SHEET METAL PRESSES

The same situation exists in that the techniques and equipment needed
to manufacture vehicle bodies requires very large outputs to give
efficient use. The huge presses can use different dies but such is the
expensive nature of these cathedral-type pieces of equipment that to
stop their operation in order to change dies is a very expensive operation. The continuous use of such equipment to do one task by utilising
costly dies to turn out maximum volumes in the minimum of time
reduces unit costs per pressing to the minimum. Each one of the large
number of dies used per car model is specific to that particular model.
If there is any change whatsoever in the size or shape of a particular
body panel then a new or reworked die is needed. To do this is expensive. The costs of each expensive die can be measured in millions of
pounds, and these costs multiply, as more and more sheet metal
parts alter the more extensive the style changes. One British producer
reported that it costs between £4 and £6 million to tool-up for a new
body. Another manufacture claimed that it cost at least £10 million to
tool-up for a completely new body, while a simple face lift effecting
only a few front pressings cost £1 million. The magnitude of the
resources used is illustrated by the fact that by using the same size of
door in both two and four door versions of the Morris Marina, BLMC
saved over £300 000 in tooling costs.
    However, dies wear out at different rates, faster if they have to draw
out the steel deeply as in the case of roof panels, more slowly if the
pressing is shallow, such as body side-panels or boot lids. Some dies
appear to wear out after 250 000 units have been produced, others may

* *The Daily Telegraph* (20 June 1968).

last for 4 million units. This explains why, in contrast to popular mythology, the Americans do not alter complete bodies every year. Instead, a minority of body parts are altered yearly, mainly those produced by dies which wear out yearly. The complete body change generally comes every three to five years when even the most durable dies are well worn. In contrast the machinery for making mechanical parts lasts almost indefinitely, hence American engines have a life of 10 to 15 years. It is the skilful changing of a few body panels plus the interchange of other body parts that gives the impression of frequent model changes.

This explains the life-time capacity of body tools but it does not indicate the optimum output per year. The optimum capacity is dependent on the operative speed of each press. Properly maintained, each press has a long life compared to the special dies used. In addition, every large volume producer has similar presses in their stamping plants. Some have more than others but no cost reduction is involved because there may be duplication of existing equipment. It would appear that the optimum capacity for most presses is 2 million per year* although in 1952 the figure for maximum optimum output was around 4000 pressings a day or almost $1\frac{1}{2}$ million a year. As in many areas of car production, the increased use of automation has tended to increase the optimum production level; before 1939 the 'stamping' optimum was around 250 000 units a year†. In addition the use of all-metal bodies and then the development of unitary construction contributed to this process.

THE OPTIMUM SIZE OF THE MOTOR CAR PRODUCER

The overall optimum of the integrated car firms appears to be around 2 million units a year. The assembly-optimum is around 200 000 units a year and in all probability the foundry-optimum is not much greater than this. The machining-optimum is around 1 million units a year, and the overall optimum is governed by the pressing-optimum of around 2 million units a year. As regards the optimum production level of bought-out components it is likely to be high for electrical components and some forgings. Only in the case of circular forgings, however, is it likely to be over 2 million units a year; beyond that

---

* J. A. Menge, 'Style Change Costs as a Market Weapon', *Quarterly Journal of Economics*, Vol. LXXVI, No. 4 (November 1962).

† A. Silberston and G. Maxcy, *The Motor Industry*, Allen and Unwin, London, p. 83 (1959).

duplication of equipment is needed. Of course, if components such as bodies and mechanical items were bought-out, then the optimum capacity of the firm would be quite small at around 200 000 units a year. If the industry standardised on engines, gearboxes and basic body panels then in theory external economies of scale equivalent to the present internal economies would be reaped. It is the development of completely integrated firms that has pushed the firm optimum up to around 2 million units, rather than technological developments as such.

It is possible that technological developments in the future could reduce the optimum size. For instance, if steam or electric traction becomes economically feasible for car propulsion it is likely that these basically simpler units, compared with the internal-combustion engines, could give lower unit production costs even though the optimum output of the equipment used was lower. Another development could be the use of plastics for the production of complete bodies on a mass-production basis. Already it is suggested that the mass-production of plastic bodies by using metal dies and large presses is more economic up to annual volumes of 170 000 than the production of metal bodies*. Beyond that point however the techniques used in steel-body making gives lower costs. Further developments could result in the production of plastic bodies at optimum levels below 500 000 units a year, but nevertheless at lower unit cost than steel bodies. This would greatly alter the optimum size of the car firm. This of course is pure supposition, and at the moment the present overall optimum appears to be around 2 million units a year. A reversal of the integration process is unlikely, and from the point of view of customer choice and product variety would probably lead to a loss in economic welfare.

Given the above overall optimum only GMC, Ford and Chrysler in the U.S.A. achieve the required output. In Europe only Fiat and Volkswagen approach the figures quoted with their world car output totals of around $1\frac{1}{2}$ million units. The real problem is only found in the stamping department. All the European giants meet the requirements for assembly and castings optima. Because of the wide utilisation of one basic engine a number of these European firms produce mechanical units at or near optimum levels, and the American firms and their main European rivals use basically the same equipment at near optimum levels. Where body-pressings are concerned the American firms gain cost advantages in two ways: (1) the continuous use of body presses, without the requirement to stop production to change dies and (2) the

* *Motor Transport*, p. 70 (8 November 1963).

spreading of tooling costs over more units, so that amortisation costs per unit are lower.

Concerning the first point, only a yearly production rate for each pressing of around 2 million could allow the maximum utilisation of each body press. Even though European producers use common body panels for many models there is a limit to this process. The highest European body production levels is achieved by Volkswagen in the production of around $1\frac{1}{4}$ million 'Beetles' per year. Other producers use the same body presses to produce more than one item or, utilise them full time on one component but at less than optimum rate. Consequently the American firms have a cost advantage here.

As regards the second point, the European firms can offset the American advantage to some extent by not changing the basic body style so often. During the 1960s the car firms in the U.S.A. changed the basic body style every three to five years*. In the U.K., for instance, the basic Mini and 1100/1300 body shells in 1970 had remained unchanged for over 10 years and 7 years respectively; the 105E type Ford Anglia lasted 10 years; the Volkswagen in 1971 had lasted over 25 years, and so on. The total tooling costs for a car like the Ford Escort exceeded £15 million, hence initial costs must be spread over sufficient volumes to minimise unit tooling costs. In Europe this means a long-lived product cycle. In the U.S.A. the annual volume of a basic model can often approach 1 million units, and given the wide interchange of body-pressings the production of individual parts can exceed this. Ally this to a life-cycle of three to five years and total production can be between 3 and 5 million units. In the U.K. the largest annual volumes tend to be around 300 000 units; for example, the Ford Cortina and BMC 1100/1300. So U.S. production is around $3\frac{1}{3}$ times as great on an annual basis. Over a 10 year life-cycle total 1100/1300 output may approach three million, although a slow build-up would give a figure of $2\frac{1}{2}$ million. Between 1959 and 1968, $1\frac{1}{4}$ million 105E Ford Anglias were made, tooling costs were amortised in the first four years. However, the U.K.'s disadvantage in terms of total volume can be reduced to between 2:1 and nothing. In the case of Volkswagen, the annual 'Beetle' output of around $1\frac{1}{4}$ million with a lifetime output of over 10 million units means that in this one case a European firm can equal or even surpass the extent to which the Americans can spread tooling costs. So the longer 'style-periods' can improve the European cost position *vis à vis* the U.S. firm. Economies derived from the continuous operation of press equipment are lost and can

---

* 'GM . . . are entering the third year of the present "A-body" cycle,' *Motor*, p. 28 (20 September 1969).

only be achieved if annual output approaches the optimum. This is shown diagramatically in *Figure 8.7.*

Figure 8.7

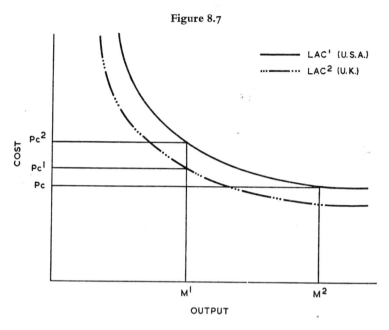

The U.S. firm's long-run average cost curve is LAC^1 with the British at LAC^2. The U.K. curve is lower due to a smaller fixed provision *per year,* that is amortisation is spread over a longer period. U.S. costs and prices at optimum output OM^2 are OPc. If the U.K. firm used the same amortisation period as the American but with output OM^1 its costs would be OPc^2; with LAC^2, however, output is sub-optimum but costs are OPc^1. That is above OPc but below OPc^2. In fact, the U.K. firm's costs at output OM would not be as depicted by LAC^2, because at output OM some equipment would wear-out quicker and amortisation would be between the levels shown by LAC^1 and LAC^2.

THE LONG-RUN COST CURVE

Given the information already discussed we can produce a rough picture of the economies of scale won by the firm and the industry. That is, the lower costs per unit which result from larger production and which is derived from financial, marketing, managerial and risk-bearing factors as well as from technical economies. *A priori* one would expect the greatest cost saving to occur from zero output up to 200 000 units a year, for up to this point economies are available from all four main categories of production. Beyond 1 million a year the cost saving would be less as only the pressings department is contributing to cost reduction, all other areas of production are duplicating their existing equipment*.

The Society of Manufacturers and Traders estimated a cost saving of 15–20% when, given flow-line techniques, output increased from 50 000 to 100 000 units a year†. Up to 50 000 units a year the same source implies that batch production would be more efficient than continuous-flow production. *The Economist*‡ produced a very rough estimate of the proportionate cost savings at higher output rates. An increase in output from 125 000 to 175 000 units per year reduced costs by 5% to 6% and an increase in output from 300 000 to 1 200 000 per year reduced costs by 17%. In other words, the 'cost-elasticities'

Figure 8.8

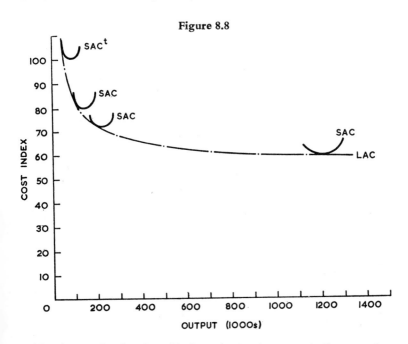

* In other words, a function of the form $Y = A = 1/x$ assymtotically approaches a limit as x (i.e. output) increases. Also, as x increases Y's rate of decrease falls.

† *Report on Proceedings*, National Advisory Council for the Motor Manufacturing Industry, p. 3 (1947).

‡ 'Volume and Costs', Motoring Supplement, *The Economist*, pp. 7–11 (23 October 1954).

over the three ranges mentioned are: 0·15 to 0·2, 0·12 to 0·10 and 0·06. As output increases the cost saving per unit falls.

The resulting long-run average cost curve LAC is approximate to that shown in *Figure 8.8*. Also shown in the figure are the possible short-run average cost curves. For example, SAC^t is the batch production short-period cost curve, the other SAC curves refer to different plant sizes each one more efficient than the next smallest at optimum capacity. Evidently as the firm's output grows unit production costs fall, as the industry as a whole grows each firm can reap external economies. A large industry, for instance, will develop industry-wide research organisations which produce benefits for each firm. The most important external economies, however, are derived from the expansion of outside suppliers, an expansion caused by the growth of the motor industry itself.

As in the case of the car firms themselves, the actual cost saving involved will depend on the shape of the supplier's cost curves, their initial size of operation, and of course the percentage of total output accounted for by the growing industry's demand. As regards the final point, suppliers vary concerning their dependence on the car industry; in general, the more basic the item the less dependent is the firm on the car industry. For instance, 25% of all castings and about 20% of steel production ends up in the car industry in one form or another, however about 60% of Lucas's output of manufactured components and 80% of Automotive Products's output ends up in the motor industry. Hence a given increase in the size of the motor industry is going to have a proportionately greater effect on Lucas than on the British Steel Corporation.

Where firms are already at optimum production levels then no cost saving arises from expansion. Many component producers, however, still talk in terms of a need for greater standardisation on the part of the car firms in the field of components. Early in 1949 the 'Big Six' formed their own Standardisation Committee following the Ministry of Supply's invitation to the National Advisory Council for the Motor Industry in 1946, to address itself to the concentration of production on a few basic models and components. Following upon this Joseph Lucas reduced prices to manufacturers by 4% to take account of cost savings following from standardisation*. It would appear that Lucas and other component makers feel that standardisa-

* *Report on the Supply of Electrical Equipment for Mechanically Propelled Land Vehicles*, Monopolies Commission, H.M.S.O., p. 47, para. 133.

The pre-war range of 48 different dynamos, 38 starter motors, 68 distributors and 133 headlamps were reduced to 3, 5, 3 and 2 respectively (*The Sunday Times*, 15 March 1970).

tion could continue with further cost savings, consequently the optimum production level is still to be reached. Lucas's *break-even* point for alternator production is 1½ million, the optimum is clearly greater. Following the development of their new forgings process Garringtons said that the new techniques could give the car industry real economies if firms agreed to use common components. Here cost saving comes from technological progress rather than increased output by the car industry; nevertheless, greater output would allow the increased production of standardised products and hence further cost reductions. Although further cost savings are possible the high degree of vertical disintegration and standardisation in the motor industry suggests that further economies external to the car firms are limited.

EXTERNAL ECONOMIES

Externalities can create diseconomies as well as economies. For instance the expansion of an entire industry can push up the labour costs of each producer either because less efficient labour is used or because the increased demand for labour pushes up wages. An expansion of the car industry based on a car of novel design often requires components of a novel design. As this output is marginal to existing production it requires components produced in smaller numbers than where conventional parts are concerned. A further externality can be the Government's Development Area policy in channelling expansion away from traditional areas. Short-run problems exist while labour becomes used to the new industry, both in terms of labour-relations and operative techniques*. Other long-term excess costs stem from increased transport costs, but any dispersal of plants whether to development areas or not would have caused this. In fact, little evidence exists proving that regional policy was disadvantageous to firms deciding to expand in development areas†.

Consequently we can say that the expansion of the motor industry can create externalities which can either increase or decrease the long-run direct costs of the car firm. Lower direct costs stem from greater spreading of fixed costs by suppliers. Long-run direct costs can increase

---

* *Regional Policy and the Motor Industry*, Economic Development Committee for Motor Manufacturing, p. 3 (March 1969).

† Investment Grants plus the regional employment premium have reduced private capital and labour costs. In 1970 the R.E.P. was £78 per year per man which in itself could greatly increase apparent profits, i.e. over 100 000 workers are employed in these areas by the car industry.

if the labour supply to the industry is less than perfectly elastic and if we do not assume homogeneous factors of production. Another point is that industries external to the car industry also have externalities and these may offset or reinforce the internal economies arising from expansion.

Optimum production levels are discussed in terms of zero technological change. However, it is quite probable that over time the greatest influence on growth and efficiency is technological change plus innovations in general. Vast sums spent on research, development and product improvement can both reduce production costs and produce a technically better product. Occasionally a technique is developed which means a lower initial capital outlay, but more often capital costs increase. This, in addition to the vast expenditure needed for research and development, means that it is the firms with the largest cash flow which will succeed. Even if the total average costs of production incurred in producing one million units a year are largely similar to those incurred in producing four million units, the larger cash flow makes the second firm financially stronger. It is the financially strong firm which can afford to innovate and to spend most on research; hence it is the large firm which is likely to produce the new product which the market wants and at the 'right' price. The large firm's 'lead-time' from original research to the final marketing of the product should be less than the small firm's. Vast sums can be spent to perfect the product and the productive process in the shortest possible period. A small firm must move slowly because it cannot afford to make a mistake; the large firm can explore several avenues at once and then arrive at a final solution rather more quickly. Technological progress and innovation by motor firm and supplier alike governs the long-run competitive success of firm and industry.

TECHNIQUES OF PRODUCTION IN THE COMMERCIAL VEHICLE INDUSTRY

No British commercial vehicle producer manufactures on the same mass-production basis as car producers. In the specialist vehicle field, to keep unit costs at a minimum, given the size of output and the size of the market, firms must operate as vehicle assemblers. If any manufacturing is done then again, given the scale of output, general purpose machinery is required for the most efficient use of resources. Engines, gearboxes and transmissions made by the specialist producers utilise batch produced parts which are built up by hand along a simple flow-line. The flow-lines use the minimum of mechanical equipment. These labour intensive methods of manufacture and assembly are probably the most efficient up to about 5000 units a year. Beyond that level, mechanical assembly lines plus the use of flow-line methods to manufacture a minority of items such as engine casings become worthwhile. On operations like these, flexible automatic transfer machines built-up from standard units can be utilised efficiently.

When operating as independent entities, firms such as Leyland Motors and ACV skilfully used simple mechanical methods to produce their own major components. Manufacture was partly on a batch-basis and partly continuous flow-line, the latter often occurring when the manufacturer himself developed ingenious methods to link up relatively inexpensive equipment. Leyland's Albion Motors plant produced gearboxes and other transmission equipment at a maximum rate of 400 a week*, which meant an optimum output for the techniques used of around 20 000 a year. The Leyland factories utilised many material handling devices of simple but efficient designs. Some units such as gearboxes were built on a continuous basis but batch production methods were used to make items such as relay boxes at a rate of 50 a week, or hub casings at a rate of 25 a week. The variety of components made, their size, shape and weight, presented problems in the mechanical handling of heavy parts. In general, special purpose machines are out of the question because of the relatively low production rates, so standard machine tools were adapted. No firm would be justified in tooling-up with special equipment to make engines, gearboxes, axles, etc., at output levels less than 20 000 a year. This helps to explain why mass-producing firms long kept out of the sector for vehicles over 16 tons gross. Subsequent expansion of that market has occurred but the large firms do not have the reputation for quality or durability that would make their products wholly acceptable to customers in the heavy-weight class above 16 tons gross.

As regards the mass-production of lorries for annual volumes over 20 000, an ingenious use of simple machinery would be preferable, but in fact producers tended to use more items of a special-purpose nature. Now that production levels of over 50 000 trucks a year are usual for some firms, tooling-up with more specialised machinery appears justified. BMC, Rootes, Ford and Bedford operate integrated CV plant-complexes. Chassis are assembled on moving trucks, although these do in some ways differ from the car lines. Where custom building is attempted, as at Rootes, the line stops for 17 minutes at each of the 11 stations. This allows quite complicated

* *Automobile Engineer* (January 1964).

assembly operations to be completed without quality being sacrificed. The chassis at Rootes is then transferred to a second 13-station continuously moving line. Items such as axles are assembled on their own lines as are vehicle cabs*; the latter being welded from bought-out pressings. Bedford, Ford and BMC produce more standardised vehicles, hence the assembly lines move continuously but much more slowly than those building cars or car-derivative vehicles. This is because of the more complicated assembly process, often needing the utilisation of very heavy components. The very complicated vehicles are first partly assembled off the tracks and introduced at a stage in assembly where they can be dealt with in the time allowed. Some 'stations' have more operatives than others depending on the complexity of the job.

High speed transfer machines built-up from standard machines are used to produce engine blocks but as output is around 120 000 units a year, in the case of Ford and Bedford, production is sub-optimum. Components such as axles are manufactured on lines of multi-purpose machines, often equipment that has been phased out by the car plants. Some components are still batch produced as this is the cheapest method given the volume involved.

Given the type of product the optimum output per assembly line is around 70 000 units a year, a figure regularly approached by Ford and Bedford. As regards mechanical items and cab pressings output is sub-optimal, hence the use of 'inferior' techniques at their optimum levels or near optimum levels.

The CV industry reaps significant external economies from vertical disintegration. This is especially so in the case of major mechanical items such as 'bought-out' engines, axles and gearboxes, as well as cab-pressings. Perkins produces engines at a rate in excess of 600 000 units a year or near the technical optimum, this volume is in excess of the total commercial vehicle output of the U.K. industry. Motor Panels supplies cab-pressings to a large number of firms, none of which could afford to tool-up for steel cab production on its own. The industry buys most of its chassis frames from Rubery Owen. These external economies shift the CV industry's long-run average cost-curve downwards (*Figure 8.9*).

SAC^1 and SAC^2 are the notional short-run curves for 'assemblers' and 'Leyland-type' firms respectively. SAC^3 and SAC^4 show the position for mass-producers. Given substantial external economies the long-run average cost curve falls from LAC^1 to LAC^2.

---

* *Motor Transport*, p. 10 (7 March 1969).

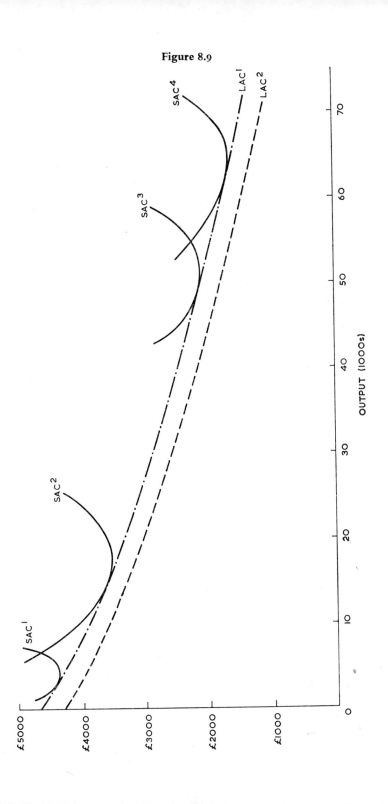

Figure 8.9

A SUMMARY

This chapter has covered various aspects of production. The costs involved are phenomenal; Rootes spent £25 million on building its Linwood plant in order to make one type of car; the same company spent about £35 million on tooling up and investing in press shops and assembly facilities for the Hillman Avenger introduced in 1970. Although a typical car's assembly time in the most efficient plants has been cut from 74 to 50 and then to $25\frac{1}{2}$ man-hours, or $2\frac{1}{2}$ clock-hours once the basic components have been gathered together, each model has taken from $3\frac{1}{2}$ to 5 years to develop from the 'broad specification' stage to the 'final announcement' of the production model. Firms like Rolls-Royce take over nine years to develop a new model! The equipment that produces items like engines at a rate of one every 40 seconds or so, has halved the labour required in the machine shops, but at an immense outlay; something of the order of £1 million for a cylinder block machine transfer line and £5 million for rear axle and gearbox automated machines*.

In the short-run, price reductions are unlikely to increase profits; in the long-run price reductions can come from economies of scale and consequently the producer has greater flexibility concerning his pricing policy in the long run. As well as the production technique the nature of the product can be fitted to a price, and variation in the product can also give price flexibility in the long run. So a new model's price can be controlled in the long-run by using the most efficient engineering practices, vast investment in the latest manufacturing techniques, and in the specifications of the model. The Rootes 'Avenger' project, for example, began five years before the vehicle was launched on the market. From the start of the project the emphasis was on low cost design; for instance, the use of larger body pressings reduced the number of spot welds from the usual 4500 to 6000 down to 2500. Similarly, the vehicle was technically straightforward in terms of overall design and in the minimum of complexity for individual components such as engine, springs and transmission components. Consequently the method of manufacture and assembly on the one hand and the nature of the product on the other can be modified so as to reduce the direct or variable costs of production. Simplified manufacture and assembly can also increase throughput thereby reducing unit fixed costs by increasing the optimum output of existing techniques.

* *The Times* (17 February 1970).

Vehicle production for a mass market involves a colossal investment, but at large output levels unit costs are low. In the previous chapter we considered those factors which determined the growth of demand and which by implication governed the level of output. In the next chapter we analyse the ways and means by which the output of one firm changes in relation to that of its competitors.

9

COMPETITION IN THE MOTOR INDUSTRY

The most obvious manifestation of changes in the competitive strength of different firms are changes either in their share of total production or of the home market or both. During the inter-war period the most notable occurrence was the competition between Ford on the one hand and Morris and Austin on the other and the variations in the market shares held. The 1920s forced the motor industry to rationalise and streamline itself under the dual impact of the slump and fierce competition. As demand increased a small popular market appeared for which firms had to be able to make standardised light cars on a large scale at prices which constantly kept them ahead of the competition.

COMPETITION IN THE PERIOD 1918–1939

A PERIOD OF STRESS

In the inter-war period, the artificial boom following the end of World War I broke in October 1920. This was followed by a heavy and serious slump which, although severest in its earlier years (1921 and 1922) lasted until the mid-1930s*. This had profound effects on the vehicle manufacturers. In 1918 Austin planned to concentrate

---

* Severe deflation was caused by the 'Return to the Gold Standard' policy. In 1929 the situation was aggravated by the Wall Street Crash and the restrictive policies accompanying the collapse of the Gold Standard.

almost exclusively on producing a 20 h.p. model; consequently the firm was totally unprepared for the switch in demand to the lightest cars which came as a result of the slump in aggregate income. In fact, an official receiver of debts had to be appointed. This period almost saw the disappearance of Leyland Motors; in 1920 the company was unable to pay a dividend and in the height of the slump in 1922 and 1923 Leyland £1 shares sold for 2s. 3d. At the end of 1922 a loss of almost £1 million was made which took several years to pay off before dividend payments could be resumed in 1929. Morris Motors took quick and drastic action in the face of a collapsing market. Production at the works was geared to making 60 units a week and commitments to suppliers was at a corresponding level. When demand fell from 276 to 74 units a month between September 1920 and January 1921 the position became serious. Morris's answer was to cut prices twice in one year, in February and October 1921. Despite this profits per car increased from £36 to £50 a car between the financial years 1919–1920 and 1920–1921. This occurred because of a shift to a new short-run cost curve; as output increased costs fell along the short-run average cost curve, but in addition the new body shop at Cowley achieved costs far below those at the Coventry plant which had used traditional craft methods. In addition outside suppliers assured of a larger market were able to pass on economies external to Morris which gave lower direct costs. Morris price cuts were on average of the order of 35% whereas output between 1920 and 1921 increased by over 50%; in other words, the price elasticity of demand was around −1·4. Given a short-run average cost curve and an elasticity of demand of −1·4, for the price reduction to increase profits the fixed cost element in total costs must exceed 70% of total costs. However, even at output levels equivalent to 25% of capacity, variable costs may exceed 66% of total costs. So it was unlikely that short-run profits increased. However, in the long run the movement to a lower average cost curve plus lower direct costs would improve the firm's position. Morris, unlike Austin, concentrated on the 12 h.p. motor car which was more suited to the demand conditions of the 1920s.

Austin had to develop a new market and this it did with the Austin Seven of 1922. Introduced at £225 by 1929 it sold for £130. This was the period of the box-shaped saloon made as cheaply as possible with the minimum of styling. By 1929 Morris, Austin and Singer held 75% of the car market, the first two holding 60% between them. Morris and Austin owed much to the longevity of their major models, the 12 h.p. Morris Cowley and the 7 h.p. Austin. The period 1927–1929 was one of mini boom after seven years of slump, and over the period Morris and Austin rose to a position of pre-eminence.

In the closing months of 1929 a world-wide slump hit all markets. As a whole, the U.K. market was relatively less affected than, say, the French or American markets, due to the slow development of the industry in the 1920s. This slow development of new industries in the 1920s, rather than the decline of old ones, was the major reason for the depressed U.K. economy during the period. In 1929, however, this proved an advantage, as U.K. output had less far to fall. Although the U.K. car industry as a whole was relatively unaffected the position of different firms was much more severely hit.

Morris's output of 63 000 in 1929 fell to 43 000 in 1931 with the company's market share falling from 51% to 38·5% in 1931 and 27·2% in 1933 where it more or less remained until 1939. As Austin faced the 1920 slump committed to a large horse power car, so Morris in 1929 was stranded with the 12 h.p. Cowley as his main weapon. The Morris Minor introduced in 1929 at £125 was not yet established in the market when the slump came. The Minor's price fell to £100 in 1931 but this did not stem the fall in the company's market position. Between 1928 and 1933 improved designs, differential taxation, and lower prices opened up mass markets to cars of and under 10 h.p., and whereas in 1928 only 25% of car sales were of models of 10 h.p. and under, by 1933 the figure was 60%. Consequently Austin with its 'Seven' already established in the market was not as seriously affected as Morris. Even so its market share fell from 37·3% in 1929 to 28·8% in 1933. The main gainers at the expense of the two market leaders were the American owned firms Ford and Vauxhall, especially the former. In 1931 the Ford 8 h.p. appeared which increased the firm's market share from 5·7% in 1929 to 18·9% in 1933. At the same time GMC's ambition to turn Vauxhall from a producer of specialist cars into a mass producer got under way. Both the Rootes Group and Standard with 9 h.p. models increased their share of total sales. Faced with this competition, Morris's fortunes did not revive until 1934 with the appearance of the Morris Eight. The new model was backed by a capital expenditure of £300 000 including the installation of a moving assembly line.

After 1933 the U.K. economy slowly recovered and the period 1934–1939 was one of steady economic advance. This was both anticipated and reflected in the production of the car industry which after two years of falling production in 1930 and 1931 recovered in 1932*. In 1933 total car production at almost 228 000 well exceeded

* For a superb account of the U.K. motor industry in the 1930s see *Cars of the 1930s* by Michael Sedgwick (Batsford, London 1970).

the previous peak of 171 000 achieved in 1929. Between 1933 and 1937 production increased continually to reach a pre-war peak in 1937 of over 379 000 units. In short, the inter-war period was one of continued expansion of the car market apart from short-lived setbacks in 1920 and 1930. No labour or material constraints to expansion were evident and improved techniques were introduced continually, both to the product and to the method of production. Output increased from 71 000 units in 1923 to over 379 000 in 1937, and although output was still comparatively small some economies of scale were possible. In fact, despite some sub-optimum working in certain areas and the increased variety of models, car prices fell continually during the inter-war period. The SMMT index of car prices using 1924 as the base date fell from 100 to 49 in 1938. Obviously the increased variety of cars or the possibility of sub-optimality did not adversely affect the price-cost relationship of the larger firms. The main reason for this was that not so much money was spent on tools, and cars were much simpler in design. So although Morris produced about 18 basic models between 1924 and 1935 this did not have the same effect on costs as it would have under present-day conditions. For one thing, bodies were made of sheet steel, wooden frames and fabric, so no expensive presses and fewer dies were used. In addition the same basic engine served in a number of different models. As a result the variety of models produced in the 1930s was not as harmful to costs as once thought, given the production methods and the type of product. Some cost penalty was however, inevitable, especially with the emergence of all steel bodies in the mid-1930s and unitary construction in the late 1930s.

METHODS OF COMPETITION

Competition in the market during the 1930s was made up of price and quality competition on the one hand and the yearly introduction of new models on the other. In the late 1930s, Ford and Morris dropped yearly models in favour of 'Series' models, with each 'series' to last a number of years. Even so, *The Economist* noted in 1933 that the number of models produced by the 'Top Ten' firms had increased from 46 in 1929 to 64 in 1934. As 'variety' competition became more important in the 1930s the motor industry became accustomed to laying-off workers during the late summer while new models were prepared for the autumn Motor Show. This, together with the seasonal variation in demand, led to considerable variations in monthly production and prosperity in the motor industry.

Price competition was a feature of the inter-war car market. However, most price changes were a function of changed input prices or of the introduction of new models. Price changes in existing models, as with the Ford Eight in October 1935, were few and far between. Competition was mainly confined to style, service and quality. Ford's price cut as a defensive measure against the new Morris Eight introduced in 1934 was accompanied by a fall in unit profits in 1936. As we saw in an earlier chapter, given the likely elasticity of demand, the capacity of existing plant and the proportion of variable to fixed costs, only very rarely can a cut in price be expected to increase short-run profits. Only with movement to a new lower short-run average cost curve, made possible by the expansion of the market, can a price reduction be likely to produce long-run profit increases.

Because of these considerations price competition, as a short-run trading weapon, was little used in the 1930s. In the 1920s, as a result of Morris's price cutting, such competition was more prevalent. Even then the 'market leader' reduced prices when new models were introduced and when changes in technique and input prices favourably affected costs. Long-run price competition associated with the introduction of new models was a significant feature of the car industry in the 1930s. This meant that new models in any class had to be priced at levels competitive with existing models. Obviously the greater the volume the lower the unit cost and price. A new model could only be profitable if it successfully appealed to the public's taste and consequently allowed its producer to operate at production levels similar to that of its competitors. So with a given price, commercial success depended on market penetration. The keenness of such price and quality competition led to a rationalising of the car industry as over 30% of the firms existing in 1930 had disappeared by 1939. Firms such as Talbot, Swift and Riley disappeared as separate entities, whereas firms such as Rover, Triumph, Jowett and Singer were forced out of the popular car market into the higher priced 'specialist' categories.

THE DISAPPEARANCE OF DUOPOLY

As regards the 'Big Six' firms, we have already mentioned the changes in market shares that occurred in the early 1930s. So profound was the change that whereas in 1929 the position was almost one of duopoly, by 1939 the two major producers had become six (*Table 9.1*).

A number of reasons accounted for this change in competitive strength, which were the forerunners of similar pressures on Nuffield

Table 9.1

PERCENTAGE OF TOTAL PRODUCTION

Year	Vauxhall	Standard	Rootes	Ford	Nuffield	Austin
1929	1·1	4·9	—	5·7	51·0	37·3
1939	10·4	12·8	10·9	14·7	26·9	24·3

Source: A. Silberston and G. Maxcy, *The Motor Industry*, Allen and Unwin, London p. 107 (1959).

and Austin in the post-war period. Management problems, especially at Morris, were partly to blame and only after the appointment of a new top management team did Austin and especially Morris recover their competitive edge. The shift in demand to small cars during the early part of the 1930s found Rootes, Vauxhall, Standard and Ford in a better position to meet this demand than Morris*. Even Austin lost sales to the new but established models made by its small competitors. A third factor was the emergence of the American controlled firms, Ford and Vauxhall, as a major force. The early 1930s was the period which saw the Detroit management determined to break into the British market to a considerable degree. In 1931 the new ultra-efficient integrated plant at Dagenham was opened by Ford and allied to this was the access to American research, development and technology. The Ford Eight appeared in 1931 as an American built and developed prototype to be followed by the Ford Ten in 1935. Both models owed more to quality than to price alone for their competitive success. Ford produced the best car it could at the conventional class-price rather than use the cost advantages conferred by its new plant and American contacts to undercut its rivals. Consequently the smallest Morris and Austin cars looked dated and flimsy against the new Ford Eight. At the other end of the mass market, Ford and Vauxhall produced new 20 h.p. plus models to compete with the largest British made cars. The Vauxhall Cadet (1931) was the first new model since the GMC purchase in 1926 and was the first non-luxury class Vauxhall. This was the company's first move into the price and quality area of the mass producers of motor cars, albeit right at the top of the mass market. Rootes and Standard avoided the main brunt of the American push by concentrating on the 9 to 10 h.p. field. In fact they were the only large firms in this growing market until the appearance of the successful Ford Ten in 1935. During this time interval Standard and Rootes about doubled their share of total production.

* See: M. Sedgwick, *Cars of the 1930s*, Batsford, London, pp. 267–290 (1970).

The final reason for the decline in the relative positions of Austin and Morris may have been their policy of rapid model changes and the production of a wide range of models. Although not to be over-emphasised given the production methods prevalent at the time, rapid replacement and wide variety must have reduced both the length and size of production runs. Consequently amortisation provisions ate into revenues so that profits were low and in some instances initial costs of models were not fully recovered*. This policy was the initial reaction to the new competition posed by Ford, Rootes, Standard and Vauxhall. In an attempt to offset the basic weakness of Austin's and Morris's range of vehicles in the face of the newer 8, 9 and 10 h.p. models from Ford, Hillman, and Standard, the two companies introduced a continual stream of models in an effort to tap the customer's purse. However, it was only with the appearance of the new Morris Eight in 1934 that Morris's position recovered, and this car was to prove to be the most successful produced by the British motor industry in the pre-war period†. Between 1933 and 1935 the production of cars was reorganised; assembly was mechanised and the machine shops overhauled. These new production methods allowed a great expansion of output at lower real cost and at the same time the car range was completely redesigned to suit the new production methods. Between 1933 and 1935 Morris's market share increased but thereafter fell almost continually to 1939.

It is probably fair to say that after the basic shift in market shares in the early 1930s the rest of the decade saw only slight variations as different companies were occasionally more successful than others in tapping the continually growing market for cars. Even so, the multiplicity of models gradually became more serious from a cost point of view. After the mid-1930s pressed steel bodies began to appear with an accompanying increase in expenditure on body presses, dies and tools. Even the number of basic engines began to multiply. The increased investment on specific equipment plus the low output runs explain the oft quoted difference between the cost of producing Ford V8 cars in the U.K. and in the U.S.A. during the 1930s‡. The relative output levels in Dagenham and Detroit were 3677 and 500 000, consequently despite the heavy transport costs the American made vehicle could be sold in Europe at a price 30% lower than the price of the British model in

* Andrews and Brunner, *The Life of Lord Nuffield*, Blackwell, Oxford, p. 194 (1955).
† Total production between 1935 and 1938 was 250 000 units, compared with 225 000 Ford Eights made between 1932 and 1939.
‡ *Motor Vehicles: A Report on the Industry*, Political and Economic Planning, London, p. 29 (1950).

third markets. This explains the pattern of U.K. car sales abroad in the pre-war period as we shall see later.

So during the inter-war period long-run price, quality, and style competition, was much more important than short-run price competition in explaining changing market shares. The U.K. industry competed and grew in a protected home market and what exports there were went to markets where the U.K. industry received 'Imperial Preference'. Even though competition and growing output led to a significant fall in car production costs and prices the industry was still too small to compete with Detroit.

COMPETITION AND MARKET SHARES SINCE 1945

THE POST-WAR EXCESS DEMAND FOR CARS

After World War II, supply was the only constraint on production. During the 1930s the emphasis was on long-run price competition and the introduction of new models in order to boost demand. After 1945 the world-wide shortage of cars presented the producers with a sellers' market; the main problem was supply and not demand. Changes in market shares would be a function of the success or otherwise of different firms in boosting output and in acquiring extra steel allocations. Material and labour shortages kept post-war output levels below that of the 1937 peak until 1949. In addition to the difficulties affecting aggregate supply, the home market between 1945–1955 was deliberately starved of cars. In order to earn sufficient hard currency to pay for imports, British Governments added to the motor car's role as a purveyor of luxury and pleasure the means whereby the economy could be rebuilt. During this period over 75% of annual production sometimes went abroad and over 90% for certain models.

As the public demand for car ownership was severely controlled, second-hand car prices exceeded the new car list price. Manufacturers attempted to frustrate profiteering by having customers sign documents preventing them reselling their cars for a specified period but this did not appear to have much effect. As late as 1953 the second-hand prices of a number of mass-produced cars were in excess of the new car price*. By 1954 increased productive capacity began to significantly affect total production and second-hand prices eased; however, it was not until the end of the 1950s that the boom in second-hand cars collapsed.

* *The Economist* (9 October 1954).

With the return of near equilibrium conditions in the car industry in 1956 it was evident that competition in the car market was taking on forms similar to the pre-war situation. Short period price competition when prices of existing models were altered independently of input cost conditions were rare. This was equally true of the period of excess demand between 1945 and 1955 when excess 'profits' were only earned by people re-selling newly bought cars, the manufacturers' prices altering in response to cost changes or the introduction of new models. The post-war phenomenon of demand, cost, structural and bottleneck inflation has led to frequent upward price revisions*. In all cases such cost increases have led to upward price revision by all producers within a short time of each other. All firms make such revisions in the light of expected price adjustments by their competitors. As such changes in input prices normally hit all firms to about the same degree each individual firm feels pretty confident that its competitors must soon revise prices in the same direction. Consequently oligopolistic features of collusion or price leadership have not been the causes of general price increases in the post-war period.

SHORT-RUN PRICE COMPETITION IN THE 1960S

The major instances of short-run price competition have been caused by the Rootes Group trying to improve a declining market share and by Ford passing on new economies of scale. In 1964 Ford reduced the price of the Anglia by £30†. This was a result of tooling costs being fully amortised after four years production and the savings available in moving from the small Doncaster plant where output was 300 cars a day to the new Liverpool factory which then had a daily capacity of 600 units. Reductions in costs were available from both sources independently of the state of demand, hence profits were unaffected by the price reduction accompanied by a movement to a lower short-run average cost situation. In August 1961 Rootes cut the basic price of the Minx by £41, the reason given as an attempt to boost sales in the face of increased costs caused by working at 50% of capacity. Although demand increased, the profits of 1960–1961 turned into losses in

* The problem became particularly acute in the period 1969–1970 when car prices were increased five times in fifteen months. Reduced output put pressure on profits and any increase in direct costs could only be met by increased prices in the short-run.
† *The Economist*, p. 154 (9 February 1964).

1961–1962*. Only with the large increase in car output in 1962 and 1963 did Rootes return to profitable operation. In October 1968 the price of the Hillman Imp was cut by just over £10 and in July 1969 most of the other cars in the range were reduced in price. These price reductions while boosting the company's market share failed to prevent profits falling by over 18%. As production was at about 56% of capacity increased demand would have very favourable effects on profits. These though are exceptional cases with short-run price competition being very rare.

MODEL-PRICE COMPETITION: A FEATURE OF THE INDUSTRY

Long-run model-price competition† has been extremely marked since the mid-1950s. In 1970 four basic cars accounted for 41% of car sales in the U.K. The British Leyland 1100/1300, Ford Escort and Vauxhall Viva are all light-medium cars, the Ford Cortina being a medium sized car. The 1970 Hillman Avenger was a new contender for the light-medium market and was priced near but below the four-door version of its established competitors. At £585 in its basic four-door form the Hillman was £32 cheaper than the Ford Escort, £20 cheaper than the Viva and BLMC 1100 and £40 cheaper than the BLMC 1300. Consequently Rootes had to take the price of competing models into account and attempt to produce a comparable vehicle at similar cost. In effect an attempt was made to simplify and cheapen manufacture and assembly thereby allowing a degree of price undercutting. When manufacturers' profits per car, in terms of a mark-up over costs at standard output, can still amount to less than £40 on a cheaper model, such price cutting as achieved by Rootes can only be done with severe price and cost controls, otherwise profits will suffer. The other manufacturers were dubious, and perhaps surprised, concerning the efficacy and validity of Rootes' pricing policy. However, retaliation in terms of short-run price competition did not occur even when the other firms felt that Rootes was 'spoiling the market'. Instead vigorous advertising campaigns to 'sing the praises' of competing models were undertaken.

* The Company suffered a thirteen-week shut-down in 1961 caused by a strike at its British Light Steel Pressings factory in North London.
† This simply says that the cross-elasticity of demand for cars is high. If a new model in a particular class of the mass-market is priced too high, then sales would be lost to lower priced models in the same class produced by competitors. The term 'model-price' was coined by Silberston and Maxcy in their excellent text, *The Motor Industry* (Allen and Unwin, London 1959).

Such competition for the mass-market has continued unabated since 1945 and the results of this in terms of market shares is shown in *Table 9.2.*

Table 9.2

PROPORTION OF TOTAL CAR PRODUCTION (%)

Year	BMC	Standard	Ford	Rootes	Vauxhall	Others*
1946	43·4†	11·5	14·4	10·7	9·0	11·0
1950	39·4†	11·1	19·2	13·5	9·0	7·8
1955	38·9	9·8	27·0	11·4	8·5	4·4
1960	39·5	11·2	26·8	10·0	9·1	3·4
1961	38·3	6·5	32·8	10·5	8·5	3·4
1962	38·0	6·4	29·7	10·8	11·7	3·4
1963	38·4	6·6	31·4	10·6	10·3	2·7
1964	38·5	6·5	28·0	11·7	12·6	2·7
1965	38·2	6·5	29·5	10·6	12·8	2·4
1966	(39·0)‡37·6	7·6	29·0	10·7	10·7	(3·87)4·2
1967	(36·1)34·7	7·9	28·4	11·7	12·7	(4·1)4·6
1968	(45·1)§33·6	7·6	30·5	10·4	13·5	(3·9)4·4
1969	(49·5)37·7	7·5	29·4	10·5	11·0	(4·3)4·7
1970	(48·1)35·8	—	27·3	13·3‖	10·8	(—)0·5

* Including Jaguar and Rover (figures in brackets refer to Rover and Jaguar). † Figures for Austin and Nuffield. ‡ BMH. § British Leyland. ‖ Now Chrysler (U.K.)

THE ADVANCE OF THE FORD MOTOR COMPANY

In general terms, the main features of the post-war position has been the relative improvement by Ford at the expense of nearly all other groupings, but especially BMC and 'others', and the decline of the independent producer. The latter category declined from a position where over 1 car in 10 produced in 1946 came from an 'independent' producer, whereas by 1968 only 0·39% of total production came from independent firms. The largest decline came between 1946 and 1960; in the earlier part of the period, firms like Jowett were left behind in the production race because their small orders with outside purchasers put them at the end of the queue for materials and components. Greater integration by the big groups cut off body supplies to the independent firms. The main problem however, was on the demand side, not the supply side. Independent firms producing in relatively small numbers could not profitably match the prices of the large firms in the mass market as their costs were higher. Consequently, the only specialists to survive were those producing 'something different'—either high performance sports-type cars or luxury saloons. Even here the differential purchase tax hit the producers of expensive large cars more than others, and even under a single tax rate the tax burden on more expensive cars was higher. So despite a high post-war demand for cars the independent firms faced many troubles and by 1960 only two significant firms remained outside the large groupings. During the 1960s those firms were absorbed by larger groups, leaving only Reliant as an independent producer with an annual output in excess of 20 000 cars, the majority of which were three-wheelers.

Little of the decline in the specialist share of the market in the 1960s was due to the appearance of competing Ford models, although this may have happened in the 1950s when firms like Jowett, Singer and Lea Francis competed in the popular market. Ford increased its market share by simply giving the market what it wanted in terms of product and in terms of value for money. In addition, the pre-war Dagenham plant was probably the most efficient in the U.K., and its full potential was used between 1945 and 1956, enabling Ford to win the race to produce as many cars as possible. The company's initial success was not due to frequent model changes or to a wide range of models in the period 1945–1956. Indeed for many years Ford only produced two basic models and it was only during the 1960s that the number of basic models was increased to finally number five by 1970. In terms of price competition, Ford abstained from short-run price competition except in the case of the Ford Popular in 1953 and the prior mentioned reduction in the Anglia's price. In terms of long-run price competition Ford was not particularly aggressive during the period 1945 to 1956, tending to build cars to the existing conventional price in each class. After 1960 Ford maintained its progress by widening its model range and using new model price competition to match the market thrusts of BMC, its main rival. The BMC Mini was countered by the Anglia 105E in 1960, the Morris 1100 introduced in August 1962 was matched by the Cortina 1200 in the following month. Whereas the BMC models were revolutionary the Ford cars were conventional packages which gave the customer a great deal of motor car for his money. Although the Anglia was almost £100 more than the Mini the Cortina was £10 less than the 1100. Ford was also fully geared-up to maximum production with a product largely devoid of teething troubles. In contrast, BMC insisted on announcing cars before any large numbers were ready for sale, and numerous teething troubles gradually manifested themselves in the production models. As a result Ford built up customer goodwill and a large market while BMC tried to catch up on its waiting list.

During the late 1960s the new Escort took over the Cortina's original market, the new Cortinas 'trading up' to a slightly different market*. The declining small car market was abandoned and left to the BMC Mini and the Hillman Imp. At the same time BMC did not really have a suitable car in the £850 to £925 category dominated by the 1966 series Cortina. So although BMC had a larger variety of cars than Ford during the 1950s and 1960s it was the latter firm which in the 1960s had more to offer the customer in the 1250–1500 c.c. market. In the early 1960s cars below 1000 c.c. accounted for $33\frac{1}{3}\%$ of the new car market, 'light' cars in the 1100 c.c. to 1500 c.c. accounting for $13\cdot5\%$ of total registrations. BMC's 1100 and Ford's Cortina were benefiting from the gradual change in customer preference for light cars which by the mid-1960s had grown to 22% of all registrations. By 1969 this market accounted for 37% of all sales, compared with 14% for small cars. Of BMC's two main models one was in the declining small car sector, whereas Ford had traded-up to have two successful vehicles in the light car market. In addition, in the over 1500 c.c. class Ford had taken sales from Rootes, BMC and Vauxhall with its Corsair range and to a lesser extent with its relatively unsuccessful big cars such as the Zephyr-Zodiac range. Another new market was tapped in 1969 with the sporting-type Capri, introduced at a time when BMC was bidding to increase its share of the market with the Maxi. However by the end of 1971 the Capri had been much the more successful model although both cars were in separate uncompeting sectors.

In 1970 almost 41% of all domestic car registrations were made up of just four models, the BMC 1100/1300, Vauxhall Viva, Ford Escort and Cortina. The remaining 30 or so basic mass-produced models plus various specialist cars competed for the remaining 59%. Ford's luck, or scientific appraisal, had allowed the company to be more consistently successful in judging the market's present and changing needs than any other firm. This was especially so during the early 1950s and again during the mid and late 1960s.

Throughout the post-war period Ford's unitary growth was only countered by merger by the main British firm. First Nuffield-Austin, then BMC-Jaguar and finally BMH-Leyland. In 1946 the constituent firms of British Leyland accounted for over 60% of total car produc-

* The 1970 range of Cortinas were generally priced in excess of £1000 compared with around £850 in the case of BMC 1100–1300 models. The original Cortina was marketed in the same price range as the BMC models.

tion in the U.K., in 1968 the figure was 44%, Ford on the other hand had increased from 14·4% to 30·4% over the same period. In other words, the two largest firms still accounted for over 74% of total production, the Rootes Group and Vauxhall accounting for 10·5% and 13·1% of total production compared with 10·7% and 9·0% in 1946.

THE LONG PRODUCTION-RUN VERSUS SHORT-RUN PRICE COMPETITION

Although the post-war period has been similar to pre-war in that short-run price competition is rare and that competition takes the form of the long-run model, quality and style competition, it is dissimilar in that a smaller variety of basic models exist and fewer model changes occur. Fewer models exist partly because fewer independent firms remain but mainly because each firm produces a smaller range*. In 1938 *The Economist* listed 40 different engines and an even larger number of chassis and body types produced by the Big Six. In 1970 some 18 completely different car engines and about 30 different body shells existed; but over 60% of output covered just three basic engine types and five body shells. The annual model change was disappearing in the late 1930s and the model 'series' has become universal in the post-war period. BMC tends to maintain models longer than the American controlled firms; the Mini and 1100/ 1300 were already a decade old in 1971, and the Minor was over 23 years old when discontinued in 1971, and so on. During the 1960s Vauxhall changed their basic body shells every three years, Ford tended to work to a four year cycle except for the 10 year old Anglia. With greater use of specific capital equipment and different manu-facturing processes annual basic body changes have been uneconomic. Even annual face-lifts where a minority of body dies are altered became extremely rare during the 1960s. Some manufacturers took the view that the long production runs of identical cars helped sales as the customer was unafraid of his car being outdated quickly by superficial facelifts. Whether this is a valid argument is difficult to judge, although Rootes the main 'face-lifter', did experience a declining market share in the 1960s.

In short, the great interchangeability of body pressings between models and the emergence of 'badge engineering' meant that the number of models listed by producers bore no relationship to the

* Compared with the Continental industry, a greater variety of models and more frequent model changes are usual.

number of basic models. In 1970 Vauxhall listed 40 different models but in fact only three different body shells and three basically different engines were made. Changes in basic body shells occur only rarely although some firms have different life cycles to others, changes in engines are even rarer. The large companies now aim at a model run of at least one million body units for their 'front line' popular models which allows the maximum spreading of special tooling and equipment costs even if sub-optimum working cannot be avoided completely. Under the conditions prevailing in the late 1960s this implied a life cycle of at least five years. This compared with the U.S.A., where a new body shell is introduced after three to five years, and the Continent of Europe where the non-American firms retain the same model for at least 10 years, and often for over 15 years and occasionally for over 20 years. In fact the smaller number of models and less frequent basic model changes could mean lower production costs for many Continental cars *vis à vis* their U.K. rivals. Ford and Vauxhall especially work on the basis that both the maintenance of existing sales and long term increase in sales requires a basic-model change every four years or so. As their products are technically straightforward compared with the more complex and expensive BMC models, more rapid model changes do not appear to impose a cost penalty. However, compared with conventional or advanced Continental popular cars, the U.K. product does appear to be more costly to produce when home market prices are compared.

Although short-run price competition is absent, the motor car market is nevertheless a highly competitive one. There is no question of monopoly and, despite the small number of significant domestic producers, little evidence of oligopolistic practices. Competition between domestic producers and between home and foreign car makers is intense. So although the car market is not 'perfectly' competitive it is nevertheless highly competitive.

The closest approach to monopoly is found in the heavy CV market where British Leyland typically accounts for 70% of the market for vehicles of 16 tons gross. Even here severe competition is faced from the small specialists and from Swedish imports at one end of the scale and Rootes, Bedford and Ford at the other. In terms of bus production the constituent firms of British Leyland have over 75% of the market and almost 100% of the market for stage-carriage buses. The jointly owned Leyland-National organisation* may in future offer the only domestic source of heavy duty buses. However, the threat of monopoly has persuaded new firms to enter the bus market.

* 50% of the equity is owned by BLMC and the British Government.

Firms such as Seddon and Metro-Scania received many orders from operators fearful of a BLMC monopoly, and faced with delivery delays.

COMPETITION IN THE COMPONENTS INDUSTRY

THE VARYING DEGREES OF COMPETITION

Turning now to the more particular manifestations of competition in the market for motor cars. In the field of components the vast army of outside suppliers gives the impression that the components industry is highly competitive, but because many firms concentrate and specialise on particular items the competition is somewhat limited. Some firms almost have a monopoly of particular items or groups of products, such as Lucas in the dynamo market or Smiths in the market for car heaters. In fact, the entire electrical components sector is comprised of near-monopolists or duopolists in its various sub-sectors. Again, only Rubery Owen and GKN-Sankey compete in the heavy pressings market in producing heavy side members for commercial vehicles. Even where a number of firms produce a product, competition is limited by each firm concentrating on different often non-competing forms of the product. For instance, in 1969 an agreement between Dunlop and GKN-Sankey left Dunlop as the U.K.'s biggest producer of car wheels, leaving the commercial vehicle business exclusively to GKN. The only alternative source of supply after this agreement was Rubery Owen, and as evidence points to the motor industry being unwilling to tie itself to one producer of wheels Rubery Owen stands to gain.

Competition is often limited by the buying policies of different car firms. BMC traditionally liked to deal with one supplier whereas Ford tried to maintain at least two sources of supply. In some cases the component maker is a subsidiary of the car maker and the parent tends to favour this source of supply; BMC tended to use SU car-burettors, but not exclusively, leaving Lockheed and Solex-Zenith to compete over the remainder of the market. Vauxhall only purchases items from its AC-Delco associate if prices are competitive with those of outside suppliers. In the event Vauxhall buys almost exclusively from AC-Delco, tending to buy-out only those items which AC does not manufacture. Lucas attempted to retain its market share by reducing the price of many items produced by AC-Delco; this had the effect of postponing Vauxhall's buying switch to AC-Delco for a little while.

in short, the existence of alternative sources of supply, especially if one is owned by the vehicle builder, leads to keen competition between component and material producers.

Competition tends to be limited by various licensing and patent agreements. Patents can make competition much more difficult but such problems can be circumvented by the appearance of a new design. However the problem is then one of finding an alternative design which is as good as the existing product. Often this has proved difficult and the lack of expertise on the part of new producers enables the existing firm to retain its dominance. The Ricardo company has no productive capacity of its own—it simply researches into the intricacies of the diesel engine. This has allowed it to become the world's foremost authority on diesel engine design, and Ricardo patents cover many aspects of diesel engine manufacture. The company sells its knowledge to engine builders and consequently the constant stream of new Ricardo ideas allows new engines to be built by many different companies. Here patents are no hindrance to competition; the main constraint would be expertise, which in the case of diesel engines is circumvented by using the independent expert. The rapid obsolescence of existing technology and the relative ease of finding new answers to old problems relegates patent rights to a very minor position in its effect on competition*.

THE MONOPOLIES COMMISSION

The activities of the Monopolies Commission and the Restrictive Practices Court showed that cartels have been quite active in the field of component production although absent where vehicle production was concerned. Many trade associations, such as the Society of Motor Manufacturers and Traders or the Motor Industry Research Association, have been based on collecting information and passing on research of one sort or another and are therefore non-restrictive. However, Monopolies Commission investigations into the tyre industry in 1955 and the supply of electrical equipment in 1963 showed that regulations concerning price agreements and conditions of sale did exist. Although it was mainly the retail and wholesale outlets which were affected, the countervailing purchasing power of the vehicle producers meant that keen competition existed between suppliers to supply original equip-

---

* Attempts were made in the motor car's early history to monopolise production by registering all-embracing patents. Such attempts were defeated in the various litigations that followed.

COMPETITION IN THE MOTOR INDUSTRY

ment to the vehicle builder. The fact that the large producers paid identical prices for tyres was not taken as a sign of a price agreement between tyre producers, but more of the bargaining power of the vehicle producers and the price leadership of Dunlop*. Although 'price leadership' suggests oligopoly the existence of identical selling prices for similar quantities is also a sign of a perfectly competitive market in equilibrium. The growth of Michelin, Goodyear and Firestone in the U.K. market has clearly increased competition since the mid-1960s. In 1963† the Monopolies Commission found that in the field of electrical goods that the main item against the public interest was the price differentiation between initial equipment and replacement sales. One or two firms (Champion and Lucas) had pricing policies which in some cases led to 'excess' profits and it was held that the abolition of resale price maintenance would have a favourable effect on competition and prices. The British Starter Battery Association's practice of exchanging information on prices and terms was also criticised. Most of these points, however, referred to the replacement market. As regards sales to the motor firms, the need was for optimal, and therefore in this case large firms, to produce items at minimum cost for the motor industry. In the initial equipment field the existence of near monopolists was not accompanied by the exercise of monopoly power as regards price and output policies.

In a sense original equipment prices may be partly determined by the nature of the replacement market. The two Monopolies Commission reports mentioned suggested that between two-thirds and one-half of all sales are made in the replacement market. Hence a firm will fight to improve its share of the very substantial original equipment market in order to build-up its share of the replacement market. This is working on the principle that owners will be influenced by the fact that a particular make of component if accepted by the car maker should be the best one for him to use. So original equipment sales may be something of a loss-leader to build up a larger replacement market where prices are higher. At the same time the countervailing power of large purchasers who had knowledge of market prices and production costs would in itself suggest that the original equipment market would be more 'perfectly competitive' than the replacement market where the supplier is dealing with thousands of small-scale purchases.

If price competition has often been absent in the retail market,

* Report on the Supply and Export of Pneumatic Tyres, Monopolies and Restrictive Practices Commission, H.M.S.O. (1955).
† Report on the Supply of Electrical Equipment for Mechanically Propelled Land Vehicles, Monopolies Commission, H.M.S.O. (1963).

even after the gradual abolition of resale price maintenance, since the mid-1960s other forms of competition have existed on the retail side. Different guarantee periods or larger dealer discounts can all be used to increase the size of a firm's market. However, where original sales are concerned the existence of oligopolistic market leaders and powerful buyers with a shrewd knowledge of their suppliers' costs can result in stable but low costs. All car producers tend to 'shop around' periodically to check that their existing suppliers' charges are still competitive; in most cases here it would appear they are, for buying-switches are the exception rather than the rule.

RELATIONSHIPS BETWEEN THE SUPPLIER AND THE VEHICLE BUILDERS

Considerations other than price do provoke vehicle firms to seek-out alternative supply sources. Fears of supply disruption caused by strikes in an exclusive suppliers' factory, or complaints concerning the quality of a product, can provoke firms to buy from more than one source. Leyland Motors, concerned that Lucas' electrical equipment was basically designed for cars, commenced producing American Butec components under licence. Standard-Triumph bought batteries from Chloride due to the rash of labour troubles at the Lucas factory in 1962. Other firms buy from more than one source fearing that when the vehicle firm works to capacity one producer over a long period of time would be unable to supply sufficient components to keep pace with the car firm's demands.

In the case of an absolute monopolist, the vehicle builder cannot threaten to take his custom elsewhere in order to keep the supplier's costs down. However, the firm could commence producing the part itself, and in some areas this is a very real sanction against excess profits or inefficiency on the part of suppliers. In other cases where specialised expertise and vast amounts of capital are needed for optimum production this may be a hollow threat. The fact is that absolute monopolies are rare. In the field of electrical components certain sectors are dominated by one firm but in all cases, except in the manufacture of dynamos, alternative sources of supply do exist. A further protection against the exercise of monopoly power would be the threat to purchase abroad. During 1969 Sir Donald Stokes implied that BMC's old 'Buy British' policy was no longer sacrosanct. Another possibility was, until 1971, the reference of a firm to the Prices and Incomes Board if it was suspected of unjustified price rises. In 1965 a component supplier attempted to increase the price at which it sold components to

Leyland Motors by 67%. Leyland's Sir Donald Stokes reported this to
the Prices and Incomes Board with the result that the supplier decided
upon a 5% increase instead*. In other words, firms usually have an
inducement to control both costs and prices and thereby manufacture
as efficiently as possible.

In general the atmosphere and relationship between suppliers and
vehicle producers is a good one. Any dissatisfaction results in suggestions
as to how to correct matters rather than in an immediate switching of
business. Trust is established over a long period of time when car
firms and supplier keep each other informed concerning new products
and expected changes in the rate of production. This position was
summed-up by Mr. Leslie Hewson of BMC: 'We can be tough when
we have to be but never beyond what is fair and reasonable. To over-
shoot these limits would be to deprive our suppliers of the profits they
deserve and which it is in our interests that they should make. Two-
way confidence and goodwill are the keys to the success of our purchasing operations†.'

It is possible that even if suppliers earned rather more than 'normal
profit' on their capital their prices would still be lower than those
experienced by the vehicle builder if he attempted to produce the
item for himself. For instance, 'know-how' and expertise are not
acquired overnight so a very long period of expensive mistakes could
follow. The supplier can save the vehicle builder from having to
invest in productive capacity, capacity which often has an optimum
greater than one firm's output. Therefore buying-out confers economies
that would otherwise be lost.

On the other side of the coin, dependence on outside suppliers makes
the car firm susceptible to disruption when delays in production in the
suppliers' factories occur. Hence the car industry's vulnerability to
strike action and labour unrest. The non-delivery of a component—
and all components are vital—due to a strike in a plant employing say
less than 300 people, can over varying lengths of time throw hundreds
of thousands of motor industry employees out of a job. For instance,
BMC only has a few hours' supply of Lucas components in its own
stock-rooms at any one time, hence a strike at Lucas can quickly
affect BMC. This is in contrast to a heavy vehicle factory where annual
demands are so small that component producers will often only accept
orders if they can batch produce items equivalent to many months
production of lorries.

From what we have said it is obvious that vertical integration is not

* *Motor Transport* (6 August 1965).
† *Autocar* (10 August 1967).

an unmixed blessing. Control of one's suppliers may avoid dependence on a monopolist and may overcome supply problems due to un-coordinated investment plans by vehicle builder and supplier. Labour relations may also improve so that a strike in a components factory will not throw a vast industrial organisation into chaos, although many such key plants owned by vehicle builders have been sources of unrest and strikes in these plants have been very disruptive. On the other hand, suppliers specialising on complex items should have lower production costs and derive advantages from years of 'know how'. At the same time from the vehicle producers point of view a downturn in demand means that it is the suppliers capital and labour which is under-utilised and not his own. No car firm would wish to take such a policy to such lengths that the suppliers' existence was threatened. Nevertheless, the fluctuating nature of the vehicle industry has induced firms to diversify production so as to meet demand from outside the motor industry; for instance, nearly half of Lucas' turnover is accounted for by supplying non-automotive demands such as the aircraft industry.

In short, suppliers—whether monopolists or competing firms—do not earn excess profits through their relationship with the vehicle builders. The Monopolies Commission on electrical goods made it clear that near-monopolists like Lucas and Smiths did not exploit their strong position *vis à vis* the vehicle firms in order to earn above 'normal' profits. Suppliers are in fact eager to pass on price reduction made possible by long production runs, and consequently many suppliers are in the forefront of the campaign for firms to standardise on components so that economies of scale can be reaped and passed on. It is unlikely that vehicle builders themselves could supply the same range of components at the same cost and price as their outside suppliers. The desire of Lucas, GKN, Smiths and other firms to supply a stand-ardised product in order to increase their own efficiency and reduce their prices suggests that even the strongest firms are not interested in harmful monopolistic or oligopolistic practices.

HOW THE CAR FIRMS COMPETE

The variations in market shares and the desire of firms to retain their market shares is indicative of the highly competitive nature of the car industry in particular and the motor industry in general. But an industry comprised of four large firms, each with substantial financial resources, is unlikely to be characterised by short-run 'cut throat competition' aimed at increasing long-run profits. The chances are that the 'long run' would be a long time coming and that even then the price cutting firm would be matched step for step by its equally strong competitors. In addition, due to reasons discussed in Chapter 8*, short-run price changes can only be rarely expected to have favourable effects on profits. Consequently short-run price competition is absent in the industry and short-run relative-price stability is the rule. In the long-run model, price competition occurs which amounts to very real competition. The *frequency* of model changes can also have profound effects on the profits of different firms.

In a rapidly growing market, short-run price competition may be a sound policy if the elasticity of demand is very high and the reduction of unit costs considerable, as when a firm starts from a base-output well below optimum. As the market reaches maturity those conditions no longer exist, then the best policy for monitoring or increasing sales and net revenues may be to introduce new and better models every so often. In the U.S.A. a model life of three to five years will be acceptable whereas in Europe a change of models over a period of less than 10 years can severely hit production costs of one sort or another. As production increased and methods of construction improved, unit costs were reduced. As model-price competition became prevalent from the 1930s onwards, this allowed the production of better cars at the same price, rather than continuing with existing designs at a lower price. As income increased customers were prepared to pay for a 'better' product rather than insist on a lower priced new model. In other words, the gradual improvement of old models was dropped in favour of better appointed new models. Apart from the quality of the bodywork the present day car appears to be infinitely better in all respects compared with the pre-war model designed to serve roughly the same market category†. The two-door pre-war Ford 8 h.p. saloon was priced at £100 between October 1935 and July 1937; the basic 1968 Ford Escort cost £515 before tax. Given that the purchasing power of a £ in 1937 was 20s. but 5s. 6d. in 1968, plus the fact that the 1968 car was technically superior and more comfortable, a car owner was receiving as much car, if not more, for his money in 1968 than he was in 1937. Comparing the Ford 8 h.p. as the cheapest car made with the cheapest car made in 1968 the £438 BMC Mini this conclusion is considerably strengthened. As tastes changed and customers desired 'something better' the demands of the

* Page 274.
† See *Autocar*, pp. 45–47, 23 January 1969, for a comparison of the 1932 Ford Eight and the 1968 Ford Escort.

low-cost motorist were still satisfied, mainly by the second-hand car market.

THE COST OF MODEL CHANGES

While the car market is not perfectly competitive, in most instances the industry appears to give the public what it wants. Hence the costs to the consumer implicit in the changed specifications of cars over the post-war period have been matched by benefits which have been willingly paid for. The cost to the consumer of such changes is the expenditure that would have been saved if, for instance, 1946 type cars had continued to be built but with the developing technology rather than see new models introduced. Although we could assume that this excess cost was willingly borne by the consumer, the argument is sometimes presented that resources spent on car model changes could be put to better use in the public sector*. Consequently some American economists thought it interesting to ascertain the order of magnitude of the resources used†. The extra costs to society came from: the costs of special retooling for new models; the direct costs of producing larger, heavier and more powerful cars; the costs of automatic transmissions, power brakes and advertising; the secondary costs paid out by car owners in the form of increased expenditures on fuel caused by the 'horsepower race' in the 1950s. They found that direct costs of model changes increased by between $380 and $470, or about 17% of the actual list price. Retooling costs attributable to model changes grew from $19·6 millions in 1950 to $6782 millions in 1961; per car this worked out at $2·9 in 1950 and $98·9 in 1961. Additional petrol charges in 1960 were $7109·5 millions, or about $44 extra spent on petrol per owner per 10 000 miles than if 1959–1960 cars had had 1949 specifications. If the presumption is still one of purchases being worth the money paid, the total extra cost per owner of $700 in the late 1950s plus $40 per petrol may appear to put a very high value on model changes. All figures are in terms of dollars of constant value.

If consumers had been faced with the choice of 1949 cars built with 1960 technology or 1960 cars built with 1960 technology they may have still chosen the latter, thinking it worthwhile to pay the costs

---

* J. K. Galbraith, *The Affluent Society*, Houghton Mifflin Co., Boston, p. 352 (1958).

† Fisher, Kaysen and Griliches, 'The Costs of Automobile Model Changes since 1949', *Journal of Political Economy*, Vol. LXX, pp. 433–451 (October 1962).

involved. However, when we realise that vehicles still produced in 1971 such as the Willys Jeep and the VW Beetle are basically products of the 1930s or that the Citroen DS series was introduced in 1955 and that many other European cars have model lives of over 10 years, it would appear that consumers often prefer that a long-lived model be brought up to date. So although the American customer willingly paid for model changes, if he had been brought face to face with the costs involved and the alternatives available, he may have chosen against such changes.

From the European experience it would appear that the consumer is willing to pay for model improvements but equally he is willing to pay for a long-lived model built under changing technology. Thus some customers want model changes and are satisfied by the cars produced by Simca or Vauxhall, while others want the same basic model *à la* Volkswagen or BLMC Mini*. The U.S. customer was not given the choice. Whether in fact the costs of model changes which were willingly paid were worth incurring in relation to their opportunity cost could in practice be answered in terms of a value judgement rather than by positive economic statements.

Model-price competition, in replacing old models by 'better' ones and by producing a wide range of vehicles, has been the type of competition which appeared to meet most closely the requirements of the car market. Producers tend to provide a range of vehicles in order to spread their risks and not become dependent on one model or one sector of the market. If consumers 'trade-up' producers also want to retain their custom, and they do this by offering a range of vehicles which cover the market. If a market sector declines then some firms may move out of it to leave it to just a few firms, for instance, when the 'Anglia' was replaced Ford left the small car market to British Leyland and Rootes. However, all firms wish to be represented in the fastest growing sectors—hence the emergence of the 1100 c.c. Vauxhall Viva in 1963 and the 1300 c.c. Hillman Avenger in 1970. On the retail side dealers wish to provide a range of choice in order to cover the widest possible market; therefore to maintain his dealer network intact a producer has to manufacture as wide a range of models as possible. So despite the fact that over 40% of all car sales in 1970 was in the 1100 c.c. to 1500 c.c. market, the vast majority of model types in terms of numbers were outside this sector.

---

* Only if the original product is advanced enough will long life-cycles be preferred. The 1932 Ford 8 h.p. was not an advanced motor car, whereas the Citroen 2CV, Citroen DS19 or BMC Mini had so much to commend them that they were not dated by newer models.

COMPETITION AND THE RANGE OF VEHICLES

The range of vehicles produced varies from country to country and from time to time. In France and Japan, the car taxation system, the average level of incomes and the state of the road system largely precludes the manufacture of cars of over 2000 c.c. In the U.K. a wide range of sizes exists from the BMC Mini to the Rolls-Royce V8. In the U.S.A. during the 1950s the range of cars narrowed so that all were physically large and powerful. The interchange of body panels between GMC's low-price Chevrolet and high price Cadillac range meant that although the latter tended to be larger than the Chevrolet the difference was relatively slight. In 1956 a 'basic' Chevrolet cost just around $2000 compared with between $4000 and $5000 for a Cadillac. This difference of 250% contrasts with a difference in vehicle length and engine capacity of less than 10%. In the U.K. in 1970 the price difference between an Escort and Executive at opposite ends of the Ford range was 140% but the difference in engine size was 173%. This situation had been usual in the U.K. motor industry since 1945, and contrasts with the American policy in the 1950s of trying to dress-up fundamentally similar cars in different clothing, then stressing the differences rather than the similarities, and producing a range of prices per manufacturer rather greater than the spread existing in the British motor industry.

During the 1960s the situation altered in the U.S.A. Firstly the increased market share gained by small foreign cars, and secondly the high cost of credit and rapid inflation during the late 1960s turned customers away from large American cars. The 'compact car' introduced in 1959 had a short-run influence on imports but the rapid growth of prosperity during the mid-1960s increased the demand for 'traditional' car sizes. However, the slow-down in economic growth in the late 1960s increased the demand for sub-compact imported cars at a time when total demand was falling. As a result the American firms had seen a large market of almost 750 000 units develop for small cars. To tap this shift in consumer demand all the American firms by 1971 were producing Cortina-size vehicles, some with engines still large by European standards, of around 3000 c.c. but others with $1\frac{1}{2}$ to 2 litre units. So changed market conditions had necessitated a widening of the range of American vehicles. This process had begun in the early 1960s, reversed itself in the middle of the decade, but reappeared in a very marked way with the introduction of the sub-compact Ford Maverick in 1968, but especially with the appearance of

Cortina-size cars such as the American Motor's 'Gremlin', and Ford's Pinto in 1970.

In the U.K. luxury cars are made by the specialist firms using relatively labour intensive production methods. In the U.S.A., due to high labour costs luxury cars are basically mass-produced models with many added features. Consequently although the price variation between British mass-produced cars is less than the American, the price variation between a Mini and a Jaguar is over 300% and the variation between a Mini and a Rolls-Royce is over 1000%! In the U.K. there is a greater variety of radically different cars in terms of size, performance and quality than exists in the U.S.A. However, the similarity between the Vauxhall Viva, Ford Escort, and Hillman Avenger, or between the Ford Cortina and the Hillman Minx, shows that forces exist in the British market which lead to a great similarity between different makes of car competing in the more important sectors of the market. This trend will be reinforced by British Leyland's resolve to produce cars of a conventional type to compete with the American inspired products. This would still leave the unconventional Austin range and the Specialist Car Division to provide variety; in addition substantial variations exist between the different models produced by any one manufacturer.

The individuality of British Leyland points to why the Continental firms, although each producing a smaller range of models than their British competitors, have traditionally produced a greater variety of types when one firm is compared with another. French, Italian, and German firms have always been ready to produce unconventional but long-lived models. In France for instance, only the American-owned Simca firm has concentrated on conventional models, although even here some unconventional models have appeared. Citroen has only produced five basic models since 1934, three of which remained in production in 1971. Although each model's lifetime was extremely long, often over 20 years, the difference between each type was profound. The same can be said of Renault, and Fiat in Italy. Peugeot tended traditionally to concentrate on one model but by 1971 it produced three distinct types of car. In Germany, Opel and Ford tended to produce conventional vehicles, Volkswagen distinctive and individualistic designs, BMW sports models, Mercedes-Benz quality cars and NSU very small rear-engined vehicles.

In Germany, the variety within each firm's range of cars was marked, but not nearly as marked as the variation between manufacturers. Revolutionary developments such as the mass-production of all steel bodies*, the development of vehicles of integral construction, rear engined vehicles and front-wheel drive cars, were mainly the result of individuality on the part of Continental producers. Because such vehicles were often so revolutionary and ahead of their time partly explains the very long life-cycles of many Continental cars. In the past when Continental markets were smaller than the British, their post-war production nevertheless utilised all the usual mass-production techniques. So the only way to operate profitably was to amortise models over a long period of time and to be protected from 'new' cars by very high tariff walls. In addition, the less mature Continental market often allowed short-run price reductions as costs per unit fell significantly with increased demand and output. Hence the long life of low price cars such as the Citroen 2CV, Fiat 600 and Fiat 500 was aimed at producing a low cost car for low income categories. This post-war tradition of long production runs has perhaps conditioned customers to the existence of the same models over a long period and consequently they do not expect nor see the reason for model changes every five years. Also it could be that the Continental customer regards his car as less of a status symbol and more of a method of transport than his British counterpart.

CROSS–ELASTICITY OF DEMAND: PRICING POLICY

Although short-run price competition is absent, mainly because of the relatively low price-elasticity of demand and the relative insensitivity of costs to output increases, the keenness of model-price competition and the similarity of prices charged by different firms in each class suggests that the cross-elasticity of demand is quite high. Although some customer loyalty can be counted upon, if the price difference between, for instance, a Viva and an Escort became pronounced, then customers would switch suppliers. If prices were above 'normal' for some time a producer would only be able to retain his market if he could persuade the market that the price difference is covered by superior quality or design. For instance, during the 1960s the Austin 1300 tended to be the market leader in the light car market although it was between 5% and 10% more expensive than its rivals. The BLMC

* It was the American Budd Corporation which pioneered and perfected the manufacture of all-steel car bodies. European firms availed themselves of Budd patents to develop their body building techniques. The American company, together with Alfred Morris, were largely instrumental in establishing the Pressed Steel Company.

1300 however, was a technically advanced car compared with its conventional rivals.

In some instances a car could be priced at levels equivalent to or just above its rivals, but if its production costs were considerably higher then profits would be lower. In the market for mass-produced cars, long-run model-price competition leads to similar prices in various sectors of the market but to different profitability. For instance, in 1956 Ford made £45 per vehicle, BMC £35 a vehicle, Standard £30 a vehicle and Rootes made a loss. Vauxhall made a profit of £80 a vehicle largely because at that time it was mainly dependent on CV output. In 1969 BLMC made £38 a vehicle compared with £16, £71 and £28 for Rootes, Ford and Vauxhall respectively. The market leaders in the car market, BLMC and Ford, were more able to set their prices solely in relation to their own costs than were Rootes or Vauxhall, who had to bear in mind not only their own costs but also the prices charged by their rivals as well. So if Rootes' unit production costs were higher than Ford's, but Rootes set its price largely on the basis of Ford's prices, then obviously it would make a lower profit per unit of output. If this conclusion was modified to say that Rootes only partly took Ford's prices into account, then Rootes could decide that it could charge a little above Ford's prices without harming its own market.

In the field of mass-produced commercial vehicles, such as the intensity of competition that the two market leaders Ford and Bedford price in relation to their own costs and in relation to each other's prices. Guy Motors in attempting to compete during the 1950s in a field which was being taken over by the mass-producers tended to price almost entirely in relation to the prices charged by its competitors and in this instance such a policy led to liquidation. So either a low cost firm could price at its rival's level when they were earning an 'adequate' return on capital and the low cost firm thereby earn an above average return, or the low cost firm could charge on the basis of its own costs and its high cost rivals could earn a lower return on their capital. Elements of both may be usual in the U.K. motor industry. The result is that the low cost firm could normally internally finance a great deal of its investment, but if a very severe depression hit the industry it could either reduce prices relatively to its competitors or hold prices steady while the competing firms increased theirs. As firms tend to increase their prices in unison this could indicate that the low cost firms are pricing more in relation to their own costs and therefore regard their resulting return on capital as no more than adequate.

The effects of competition on the long-run profits of firms could therefore be severe. However, not only long-run model-price competition is involved but also the economics of style changes. We have already seen earlier how style changes can affect society's use of resources, but also how the pace of style changes can affect the competitive strength of different firms.

THE ECONOMICS OF STYLE CHANGES

Competition can be severely curtailed because style changes have significant effects on total unit costs of production. In short, rapid style changes could bankrupt small car firms at no cost to the large firm. This follows because special tools and dies are designed specifically for particular models with a particular style of body and engine. Any die is used to produce a particular pressing so any change in the style needs a new or reworked die. Now firm A may have a body press which uses a die to stamp out rear boot lids at the rate of 1 million units per press per year. If the special die has a life of 2 million units the die is worn out in two years. Firm B having a smaller annual output only turns out 100 000 boot lids a year, so that the same press has its die periodically changed to produce boot lids, roof panels, bonnet panels and so on. At this rate firm B's die is amortised in 20 years compared with 2 years for firm A. Firm A is then able to use either the same type of die or to change the type of die and therefore change the style of the part pressed out. The cost of either course is the same, therefore the cost to A of the style change is zero. If B feels it has to follow suit and changes the style of its car, it must either scrap or rework a die which is only one-tenth amortised. Either way the cost is immense as the cost of expensive dies runs into millions of pounds. For example, the unit cost of the same £2 million die to A is £1 to B it is £20. If firm B is competing in the same market as A then its prices must be similar to A's. As a result its profits may be much lower or even negative. So if firms A and B take part in style competition, with B following A's leadership, then the way is opened towards B's bankruptcy. However, B may react to A's style change by introducing new equipment to produce a new car with special characteristics and advanced specifications. In other words, B may have found a new market where technical merit, quality, and economy were preferred to style changes. As an example, while GMC introduced three-yearly style changes, VW remained unchanged for 20 years. Some customers require style changes other do not; if the small firm attempted to match the product life-cycle of a larger competitor then bankruptcy would eventually occur. Instead, the smaller firm finds an alternative market weapon to style changes such as advanced technology. Therefore firm B may be on point X on short-run average cost curve SAC_1 instead of point Y on SAC_2. Firm A is at Z on SAC_2^* (*Figure 9.1*).

Figure 9.1

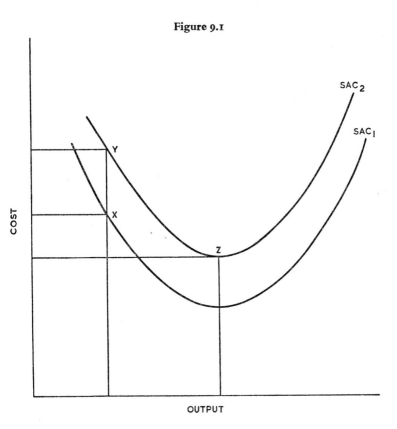

The replacement of price competition by style-competition still leaves the large firm in an advantageous position. If the smaller firm adopted a different strategy then it improved its chances of survival. In short, the smaller firm should not attempt to fight the larger on its own grounds but instead cultivate a new competitive weapon of its own. Having found such an alternative the smaller firm should not respond to an attempt by the larger firm, when entering the smaller

---

* SAC_1 is lower than SAC_2 as less capital is used per year, that is, the amortisation period is longer.

firm's 'new' market, to introduce sales strategies which are beneficial to the large firm. Turning now to other market strategies.

SALES PROMOTION

In an imperfectly competitive market sales promotion is an important part of the competitive war raged between producers. Prior to about 1956 when the seller's market was in operation and the main problem was one of production, attempts to maintain and expand a market through sales-promotion activities was not needed. Any advertising was aimed at preserving the goodwill of a market waiting patiently for new car deliveries. In effect prior to 1956 little advertising was carried out which attempted to stress the difference between products rather it was mainly confined to the information role. Since the mid fifties demand conditions became more important and the role of sales promotion in its many guises increased. In effect the tighter the squeeze on aggregate demand the greater was the amount of sales promotion used to try to maintain a firm's total sales and therefore to increase its market share in a declining market. In the period 1956–1966 advertising took the form of specifying the general superiority of one firm's products compared with another's. In the late 1960s a form of advertising almost unique in the U.K. appeared where one car firm would list the advantages of its own products not in general terms but in direct relation to the cars of its closest competitors. Firms tended to express the superiority of their product over that of A, B and C and show how and why it was better. This advertising which 'knocked the opposition' appears to have been a direct function of the most severe demand squeeze the industry had known, lasting from 1965 until the mid-summer of 1971. Whether such advertising* would remain usual under conditions of expanding demand remains to be seen, especially in the severe form existing in 1969–1971.

Advertising is one of the most widely used weapons of short-run competition. When Hillman introduced its Avenger in 1970, Ford immediately replied with advertising stressing the advantages, price and otherwise, of certain Ford Escort models. British Leyland stressed the longevity, advanced technology, and continuing market leadership of its 1100 and 1300 models. So retaliation to a new model was rarely manifested by price changes but almost always by an advertising campaign stressing the advantages of existing cars over newcomers, such inferences being either implicit or explicit.

* A type of advertising which is quite usual in the U.S.A.

Other forms of sales promotion such as increasing the number of model options, the length and conditions of product guarantees, and so on, are often countered by the other firms in the industry. If the move is regarded as a 'defensive' manoeuvre by a firm which is losing its market share, the other firms may not retaliate. If the move is interpreted as an 'aggressive' one on the part of a firm wishing to increase its market share then retaliation follows.

In the U.K. most advertising expenditure on motor vehicles appears in various sectors of the press and only rarely on commercial television. The written word is regarded as a more suitable medium in that people wish to spend time studying specifications and price and time is something they do not have with 'instantaneous' TV advertising. Even during the initial launching of a vehicle the manufacturer tends to mainly use press advertising backed-up by a TV campaign. Retailers and dealers in particular areas may, however, use TV and cinema advertising quite independently of the vehicle manufacturer. In short, a TV campaign may be useful in drawing attention to a product but press advertising is more likely to persuade a customer to purchase, as it gives him time to digest and absorb the characteristics and attributes of new and existing models.

THE COMPETITIVE ROLE OF THE RETAIL NETWORK

THE RETAIL OUTLETS

An important aspect of competition in the vehicle and especially the car industry is the size and quality of a manufacturer's chain of retail outlets. Initial sales and continued maintenance of the vehicle stock requires a chain of dealers with the expertise, equipment, and personnel, to carry out these functions properly. The image created by a particular manufacturer depends to a large extent on the quality of service and satisfaction that retailers give the owners of a particular make of car.

The geographical coverage of the dealer network is of some importance, as the potential customer may be attracted or deterred by the distance he lives or works from an official dealer of a particular manufacturer. If the customer wants a particular make of car sufficiently strongly this problem is of little consequence, but it may have some effect, especially where the purchase of foreign cars is concerned. Consequently firms try to match each other in dealer representation and obviously the number of sales per outlet varies with the size of the manufacturer. However, the largest manufacturer, BMC, has often been over-endowed with dealers and it does not match the number of sales per outlet of its somewhat smaller rivals. This had the effect of giving BMC too many under-capitalised small dealers unable to provide customers with the service that other manufacturers' dealer chains were offering. One of BMC's main problems therefore appeared to be the size and quality of its retail side especially when compared with that of Ford.

There is probably some optimum size for dealer representation. A firm with too few dealers may lose sales as customers prefer to be rather closer to a sales and service outlet. Too many dealers may mean too many small firms unable to generate sufficient sales to finance the establishment of first-class service facilities. Hence dealer representation must be measured not in terms of numbers alone but in terms of the volume and value of sales per retail outlet. In addition the sales and service outlets can vary in size. A number of small retail showrooms in the vicinity of a large distributor which has the financial strength and cash flow to employ the best in terms of equipment and personnel need not be detrimental to the quality of the retail network. Hence the number of sales outlets can quite safely be greater than the number of sales and service points.

The large number of retail outlets now existing is mainly a result of the strong competition which prevailed between manufacturers in the 1930s and, to a lesser degree, it is the result of the effects of the 1956 Restrictive Practices Act. The profits earned on new car sales was sufficient inducement to firms for them to clamour for the sales franchises of different manufacturers. The manufacturers in turn had to give firms sales franchises in order to induce them to risk sinking capital in establishing facilities and to hold sufficient stocks of parts and spares.

In the inter-war period the competition between manufacturers led to a large growth in the number of independent retail outlets. Competition increased as the percentage growth in retailers tended to exceed the growth in aggregate sales. Although little list-price competition occurred, price cutting did occur indirectly via the payment of discounts, despite the existence of the British Motor Traders Association's (BMTA) 'Book' of recommended prices or the wide use of the Glass Guide Service Ltd.'s *Guide to Used Car Values*★. Nevertheless, price competition was reduced to some extent by these publications as were the losses made on used car sales. However, in effect Resale Price Maintenance, which the BMTA had been established to insure,

★ See below, p. 336.

was not operative in the inter-war period. This was especially so before 1935*, when net prices were invariably affected by variations in trade-in values and dealers' discounts.

Between 1945 and 1953 the effective operation of resale price maintenance was faced with the opposite problem of excess demand. The BMTA introduced a scheme to discourage dealers from selling at above list price, and to discourage customers reselling their vehicles, almost immediately after receiving delivery, on the second-hand car market. The Association forbid its members to purchase or sell any second-hand car at prices above the current new car list-price; the retail buyer was forbidden by a covenant to resell within a year of purchase without the consent of the BMTA. In practice dealers and retail buyers easily circumvented these restrictions. After the end of this scheme in 1953 the Association continued to protect the manufacturers' list price for cars and accessories but the control of 'trade-ins' was not reintroduced after the war.

ATTEMPTS TO RESTRICT COMPETITION

The Restrictive Practices Act of 1956 made multilateral resale price maintenance illegal. One of the bi-products of this was that the motor manufacturer could not force dealers to be members of the BMTA by agreeing to supply only Association members with cars, and the BMTA could not issue a 'stop list' of firms failing to abide by the Association's rules on resale prices as such rules were deemed illegal. But the 1956 act made explicit what had only been conventionally accepted previously; the imposition of individual resale price maintenance by single firms. In the motor trade this was used to prevent inflated prices being paid for 'traded-in' cars or a discount being given for a cash sale where no 'trade-in' was involved. In the latter case the new car sale would have meant a reduced profit margin, but in the first case it meant that substantial capital would have been tied-up in second-hand cars until such time as they were sold, often at a loss.

In 1934 discontent among dealers had reached such a pitch that manufacturers realised co-operation between themselves and the dealers was needed. This led to moves which reduced the degree of competition. The British Motor Traders Association, founded in 1920 to maintain the wholesale and retail list prices established by manufacturers, took on a role of administering and enforcing the price policies formulated jointly by manufacturers and retailers. In 1934

* See below, p. 336.

manufacturers made it obligatory for their retailers to belong to the association and in 1935 the BMTA sought to eliminate 'excess competition' by publishing the National Used Car Price Book*. A dealer exceeding the maximum trade-in allowed or who passed-on larger discounts for new cars than he received from the manufacturer, was liable to a fine or, more seriously, to be suspended from the Association. The latter meant in effect expulsion from the new car trade because of the manufacturers' requirement that all dealers had to be members of the BMTA. A dealer not in membership would receive no new cars from the manufacturer. This scheme was only partially successful as the Association could not really control second-hand car prices without controlling the supply of new cars and the rate of scrapping of old ones. Uncontrolled variations in the stock of old cars affected the 'trade-ins' offered by dealers. However, after 1956 the BMTA remained only to help individual manufacturers enforce price maintenance, but in effect the 1956 legislation made no difference to the degree of retail price competition that was allowed. Collective control by the BMTA was merely replaced by individual control by vehicle manufacturers. The 1956 Act and the disappearance of the sellers market in the mid-50s (which culminated in the collapse of the boom in second-hand car prices in 1959) thus had some effect on the relationship between manufacturer and dealer.

A test case by BMC in 1957 showed that liability to registration under the 1956 Act was avoided if individual resale price maintenance replaced the old multilateral arrangements. The motor industry dropped its 'exclusive dealing' commitments, so any dealer wanting to stock different firms' products could now do so. In practice, larger margins were still offered to exclusive dealers and franchises were given to such firms in preference to others. Secondly, any firm satisfying the liberal minimum requirements could be put on the motor industry's list of dealers and so sell new vehicles. The dealer did not have to join the BMTA or abide by its rules. Finally, the motor industry introduced a new scheme which, because it was an enforceable formal agreement between manufacturer and dealer, was subject to registration with the Registrar of the Restrictive Practices Court. The industry fully expected the Court to agree that the scheme introduced in 1959 was in the public interest, but in December 1960 it was found unacceptable by the Court. The scheme contained a clause which was an integral part of the mechanism by which the motor industry enforced price maintenance. This was a clause by which the signatories

* *Motor Vehicles: A Report on the Industry*, p. 44, Political and Economic Planning, London (1950).

to a deal maintained prices for each other: manufacturers prescribed the prices and trade-discounts for products and insured that these were adhered to by dealers. However, the regulation of discounts and minimum standards for dealers by the vehicle producer was deemed against the public interest. This part of the agreement was aimed at controlling the selling conditions of a non-franchised dealer who had no contract with the vehicle producer. That is, following the 1956 Act dealers were allowed to sell any make of car they wished and there was no *contractual* way a manufacturer could enforce RPM on sales of his cars by a dealer with whom he had no franchise agreement. The attempt to regulate discounts and impose minimum standards was an attempt to get around this problem and to control franchise dealers more closely. Although the 'collusion' between dealer and manufacturer to maintain each others prices was thrown out, the use of individual RPM was not registrable under the Act and was in no way affected by the 1960 decision. Firms, however, were allowed to give what discounts they liked. In addition, the control of fleet-users discount by manufacturers was disallowed, leading to greater competition for the custom of fleet-users of vehicles and cars.

In some ways the abolition of collective enforcement in 1956 did introduce a free market in car prices, notwithstanding the 1959 scheme or individual RPM. In 1960 the downturn in the sale of Vauxhall cars allied to increased competition and reduced prices in the second-hand car market saw Vauxhall make no attempt to prevent its dealers from cutting prices. Before 1956 collective enforcement would have made such a move impossible and even after 1956 individual RPM could have precluded such activity. However, for the first time since 1945 a car firm stood aside from a situation where dealers were in effect setting their own price. This reduction in Vauxhall's prices was not a normal instance of short-run price competition because the manufacturer did not cut its factory prices, much to the annoyance of dealers.

The existence of RPM only reduced the area of competition between firms, not the degree. Dealers continued to give varying trade-in values, a fact recognised by the generous profit margins RPM allowed dealers. In another direction, dealers had been helped by manufacturers training their mechanics; this saved money for the dealer and insured a supply of competent operatives to protect the manufacturers good name. Also dealers paid out of their gross margins the full cost of a pre-delivery check, the first service of a new car, and paid something towards the cost of work done under makers' guarantees. The abolition of RPM in 1964 (Resale Prices Act), by the amendment to the

1956 Act, increased the dealer's competitive freedom. In most cases the manufacturers 'recommended price' was initially taken as the fixed list price, but the very severe squeeze between 1966–1971 tended to bring some flexibility into the system. As a result both sides of a bargain-allowance on the old car and the price of the new one became subject to bargaining, whereas technically only one side was previously subject to bargaining. In practice effective price reductions have always been possible if only on one side of the bargain. Higher trade-in values, free offers such as one year's excise tax, free petrol, servicing, and so on, all reduced total outlay. The 1966–1971 squeeze saw the greatest post-war use of such inducements because with the over expansion of the dealer network many firms in the contracting market were fighting for survival. Many weaker firms were pushed-out of business in the first real 'shake-out' the retail car trade had faced. Previously car firms had helped dealers by giving them special discounts on new cars for them to maintain their margins while engaging in effective price cuts. However, the severe squeeze which faced the car firms and the need for some rationalisation of retail chains saw little use made of such a policy by car producers during the late 1960s.

On the retail side the 1960s saw a strong trend towards amalgamation; Kennings, Henlys, Bristol Street Motors, and a number of other concerns, all grew into multi-million pound concerns with quotations on the Stock Exchange. Some distributors were encouraged by car firms to expand on the Continent in order to facilitate the growth of car exports, while others concentrated on domestic growth. Each manufacturer had a vested interest in seeing its best retailers grow in pace with those of its competitors. Hence the 1970s should see increased competition on the retail side but with franchises being much more difficult to come by than in the past. Consequently the great competition between car producers is being matched by greater competition by financially powerful retail outlets. Although the number of outlets per firm in any particular area may fall, the increased competition between firms should maintain the same high degree of competition between distributors and dealers. A further factor here is the increased penetration of foreign cars into the U.K. market and the competition which they provide for British firms and their retail outlets.

THE EMERGENCE OF A MORE COMPETITIVE ENVIRONMENT

Following the activities of the Restrictive Practices Court and the abolition of resale price maintenance, car dealers faced a more com-

petitive environment. Even so, the firms with sufficient turnover
were able to earn very good incomes. The margins for retail dealers
are $17\frac{1}{2}$% and distributors receive 4% for cars supplied to dealers.
Some differences occur between firms, for instance, BMC and Vauxhall allow an extra 1% to any dealer selling their cars exclusively,
Ford gives $18\frac{1}{2}$% to all dealers and Rootes give 5% to its distributors*.
Rising commission for hire-purchase deals effectively adds 2% to
dealers' margins when cars are purchased this way. As a result dealers,
on average had tended before the squeeze in the late 1960s to earn from
20% to 30% on capital. Of course some firms did very much worse
and some did much better. Quality of management rather than size
may be the main factor here as public companies earn from $7\frac{1}{2}$% to
25% on capital. When competition became fierce the larger garage
had an advantage. It was able to offer generous part-exchange allowances because they operated large second-hand businesses. Firms need a
stock of about 20 cars for a good balance and quick turnover was
needed for profits. The small dealer often resells his cars to other
dealers, receiving 8% less than if he had sold it retail†. The ending of
resale price maintenance may have increased competition somewhat
and trimmed gross margins, but even under the severest of squeezes
(1966–1970) no cut-throat competition was evident. The natural
competitiveness in this sector, however, inevitably meant that firms
were leaving and entering the industry. In fact, the squeeze in the late
1960s highlighted the need to rationalise the retail sector.

In 1970 there were some 12 500 retail outlets in the U.K. (*Table 9.3*).

Table 9.3

BMC	4 900
Other BLMC	2 100
Total BLMC	7 000
Rootes	2 200
Ford	2 000
Vauxhall	1 000
Others	300
Total	12 500

With 400 distributors and 4500 dealers the BMC network was too
large. It had 40% of the country's retail outlets but only just over

* Margins on accessories are even higher; distributors receive about 25% to
30% on batteries, 20% to 30% on lamps, and 30% to 45% on sparking plugs.
† Information from *The Economist*, pp. 65–66 (7 April 1962).

30% of domestic car sales. Ford sold almost as many cars but through just 16% of the country's dealers. Despite the creation of BMC as long ago as 1952, by 1970 no rationalisation of the Nuffield and Austin networks had occurred. This had meant considerable geographical over-lapping by dealers with the result that 3000 of them only handled 17% of BMC's business. Distributors were given considerable freedom to appoint dealers so that BMC had little direct control of sales, unlike Ford which worked through main dealers and dealers and retained control of all dealer appointments and the territorial division of the market. BMC found it impossible to make a proper assessment of sales potential area by area or to establish viable sales targets to be met per outlet. Having too many small dealers BMC had gained a large share of the rural market but had a weak hold on the big towns: although the rural per capita car population was higher, the absolute urban population was of course proportionately much greater. Small dealers were unable to exploit modern methods of marketing or cost reduction and in the larger towns were very vulnerable to aggressive competition from the selected and highly trained Ford and Vauxhall dealers. To strengthen its weakened grip on the market BLMC had to rationalise the old BMC sales and service network. In order to reach a sales intensity equivalent to that of Ford or Vauxhall the BLMC network of 7000 dealers should have been reduced by 50%. A selected number needed to be turned into main dealers in order to combine the function of distributing to small dealers with that of large-scale retailing, with BLMC controlling the entire network. Of Ford's 2000 outlets about 400 were main dealers and in Vauxhall's case 300 outlets were main dealers.

All the main producers have established separate CV distribution networks. Traditionally, the ordinary car dealers also sold commercial vehicles, but as the CV business grew and became more specialised the demand for full-time truck specialists also grew. After 1965, 165 of the 450 Ford main and retail dealers handling commercial vehicles were appointed truck specialists. These firms had largely withdrawn from the car side of retailing in return for the local monopoly of Ford truck sales. Bedford used a similar policy and BMC belatedly tried to do the same. Like BMC, the Rootes Group's retail network was too large with too many weak retailers. A long overdue rationalisation of the various networks making up the Rootes chain was commenced in 1969. The aim was to reduce the 1800 car and 400 CV dealers existing in 1969 to 1230 car dealers and 250 CV specialists. Of the car chain roughly one-quarter would be main dealers. Rootes, having originally developed from a retail car business in the inter-war period, had always owned a considerable proportion of its own network; the other manufacturers tended to operate through independently owned chains. Nevertheless, to succeed in the very competitive car market Rootes had to strengthen its retail network through rationalisation, thereby putting itself in a position to successfully market its range of products.

COMPETITION IN THE COMMERCIAL VEHICLE MARKET

THE BRITISH INDUSTRY AND TARIFF PROTECTION

During the inter-war period the American-owned firms Ford and Bedford tended to dominate the mass-produced truck and light bus market. The main British competitor was Nuffield which had entered the CV market with car-derivative vans in 1913. However, the CV market in the 1920s developed quickly around the one-ton truck, the market for which was dominated by imports, especially the U.S. Ford one-tonner. Nuffield seeing this growing market and the need for a British competitor produced their first 'real' CV in 1924. Light vans had been produced along with cars but the production of larger vehicles needed special facilities. As a result the Adderly Park plant was purchased and it concentrated on the production of trucks. In common with all mass-producers, the range of trucks was nearly always fitted with the same petrol engines as used in larger cars. The establishment of facilities by the mass-producers to produce special running units is a post-war phenomenon necessitated by the growth in size and complexity of mass-produced commercial vehicles. Within 16 months of Nuffield's entry into the one-tonner market the venture was earning profits. Between 1924 and 1931 the Nuffield CV range consisted of one-ton trucks, light vans and taxis. Similarly Ford and GMC concentrated their production in these fields, only moving up the weight scale in the 1930s.

Nuffield's successful entry into the CV industry in competition with the established market leaders Ford and GMC was partly due to the merit of the product and the growth of the market but mainly, one suspects, to the imposition of McKenna duties at $33\frac{1}{3}\%$ on CVs and vehicle parts for the first time in 1926. As a result, imported Ford and GMC vehicles and parts became much more expensive, and allowed Nuffield to compete on price with products produced at much higher rates of output in the American factories. In 1925 GMC purchased

Vauxhall cars but continued to assemble Chevrolet and GMC vehicles from imported parts until 1931. In 1932 the GMC assembly plant at Hendon was closed and CV production was transferred to Luton. The first Bedford trucks (i.e. British designed and built GMC commercial vehicles) of $1\frac{1}{2}$ to 2 tons appeared in 1931. Even with the tariff disadvantage on imported parts, GMC assembled over 54 000 vehicles between 1925 and 1931, so without its tariff protection Nuffield would have found the competition even stronger, perhaps too strong. Ford commercial vehicles between 1911 and 1928 were either imported or assembled from imported parts. The number of manufacturing operations undertaken in the U.K. however, gradually increased until the $1\frac{1}{2}$ ton truck chassis introduced in 1928 was clearly an all-British vehicle. Between 1911 and 1927 the Manchester plant produced 100 000 CVs but between 1928 and 1931 the output of $1\frac{1}{2}$ ton trucks alone totalled over 35 000. When the Dagenham plant opened in 1931 the model range was extended to include two-ton models and total truck output reached about 12 000 units in 1932. Consequently Ford was in a better position than GMC to bypass the detrimental effects of the 1926 tariff on vehicles and parts. The British 'content' of Ford vehicles was already at a high level, reaching 100% in 1928. Even so, Nuffield was placed in a slightly advantageous position between 1925 and 1928 and this allied to the excellence of the product and the efficient method of production allowed the successful entry of an all-British manufacturer.

Apart from the production of car derivative CVs Austin's only entry into the CV market was the production of a two/three ton lorry between 1913 and 1922. The company re-entered the truck field in 1939 with a three ton lorry powered by a new advanced type petrol engine which in 1971 was still the basis for the large petrol engines used in BMC trucks. The Rootes Group having purchased the established CV producers Commer Cars and Karrier at the end of the 1920s had a range of vehicles between eight cwt. and four tons in 1929, growing to five tons in the mid-1930s. The remaining giant American producer was Chrysler which assembled Dodge vehicles in the U.K. between 1923 and 1928. Although the $1\frac{1}{2}$ ton truck introduced in 1928 was largely a British project many American components were still used, and it was not until 1938 that the first entirely British vehicle appeared. This was a five-ton truck.

THE DOMINANCE OF BEDFORD AND FORD

As regards the mass-producers, the 1920s saw the emergence of British-built vehicles and the decline of imports, but the market leaders tended to be American owned firms such as Ford and GMC. In the 1930s the emergence of new productive capacity in the U.K. owned by Ford, Bedford, and Dodge, meant that these firms competed vigorously with each other and together with Nuffield dominated the market. In the 1930s the dominant firms from the 1920s tended to produce a wider range of vehicles. Between 1920 and 1931 the most popular vehicles were in the one ton to two ton category. In 1933 Rootes led the way up the weight scale in an attempt to find a new market niche away from direct competition with the larger firms. The company produced a three-ton truck to be emulated by Ford in 1935 which launched a new range of vehicles based on the V8 engine which had been introduced in 1933. In the pre-war period three-ton trucks were the largest vehicles Ford produced and the same basic range lasted until 1955 by which time it had reached the five ton payload category. In the 1930s Nuffield produced the widest vehicle range of any British-based producer. The company made vehicles from 10 cwt. vans to 7-ton trucks as well as single and double decker buses. The main market in the 1930s was in the up to three ton class, and between 1935 and 1939 the Bedford three ton vehicle was the most popular of the period. Summarising, in the 1920s and 1930s the market for light trucks was dominated by Ford, GMC, and Nuffield, with the first two fighting vigorously for leadership in the light truck field and Nuffield the market leader in the car-derivative sector.

THE SPECIALIST PRODUCERS AND THE DEVELOPMENT OF DIESEL-ENGINED VEHICLES

In the inter-war period the specialist market for commercial vehicles was dominated by Dennis, Albion, Dodge, Guy, Leyland, and AEC. In the 1920s these firms concentrated on the two to four ton market, which was outside the scope of the mass-producers. In the 1930s, when the maximum permitted weight for road vehicles was increased greatly from the $8\frac{1}{2}$ tons laden prevailing in the 1920s to the 20 tons gross permitted in 1934, the scope for long and short distance road haulage increased greatly. Firms demanded larger lorries and buses to

M

make maximum commercial use of the new opportunities opened up to road vehicle operators *vis à vis* their railway competitors. As a result Guy, Dennis, Albion and Dodge concentrated on the new market appearing for medium-weight vehicles in the four to six ton class, while firms such as AEC, Leyland, and new-comers such as Atkinson and Foden, began to concentrate on larger trucks and buses from six tons up to the maximum sizes allowed.

As we have mentioned before, the development of the diesel engine greatly facilitated the use of large lorries as for the first time the internal combustion engined lorry was more economic than the road steamer in the over six ton category. Other developments such as the pneumatic tyre and stronger wheels meant that the solid steel wheeled steamer was not the only efficient way to transport heavy loads long distances. Heavy-duty bus production in the 1930s was a highly competitive market led by Leyland, AEC, Daimler and Albion, although other significant firms existed such as Bristol, Crossley, Guy, Maudsley and Tilling Stevens. Bedford already dominated the market for light-weight buses.

In the 1930s the standardised nature of mass-produced commercial vehicles meant that model-price competition was a definite possibility. in the heavy vehicle and medium-weight sector the prevalence of one-off production, or the addition of a customer's particular requirement to a standardised chassis, meant a multiplicity of 'models'. Consequently model-price competition was not really possible in the accepted sense as each unit produced was often a different 'model' and sufficiently different to competing models so as to be priced differently. The prices of the medium weight products, of say Guy and Dennis, tended to be roughly similar but the price variation was still greater than was usual in the case of the mass producers. Constant variations in model types meant differentials in the prices charged by different firms. The three market leaders in the mass production field tended to price their products in relation to each other with firms like Rootes and Dodge accepting their market leadership. Price competition was almost always of the model-price variety.

In the 1930s and 1940s mass-produced vehicles were extremely simple in design and rather limited in versatility. The range of products was also extremely narrow, being limited to a few main types with little variation being offered. In the 1950s the range began to widen, a process which continued throughout the 1960s, until by 1971 each mass producer supplied a choice of vehicles ranging from car derivative vans to heavy duty trucks which competed with the products of the CV specialists. In the late 1940s and early 1950s when only petrol engined vehicles were made, the main mechanical units were common with those used in the manufacturers' motor cars. However, the Seddon company had in 1938 produced the first light truck to be marketed with a diesel engine. In the 1930s many firms utilised the expertise of specialist diesel engine makers such as Gardner to produce diesel-powered heavy vehicles; others such as Dennis, AEC, Leyland and Albion made their own. By 1939 the diesel engine was supreme in the heavy vehicles' field but development was much slower in the case of lighter vehicles. The development of compact and relatively cheap Perkins engines, however, made diesel power suitable for lorries of as little as five tons carrying capacity. Seddon's existence was due to this belief on the part of Perkins that diesel power was ideal in the medium-weight sector, and just before the war and then during the late 1940s and early 1950s Seddon established a market for light-weight diesel engined lorries★.

The development of small diesels in the U.K. owes a great deal to the Perkins company which from the late 1930s had believed that diesel power would be used for all classes of vehicle down to and including light delivery vans. As the demand for lighter diesel lorries expanded the mass producers began offering diesel powered lorries for sale, initially buying engines from Perkins. Although Austin, Bedford, Commer, Dodge, and Ford, bought from Perkins, Morris-Commercial introduced a five ton lorry in 1948 fitted with a Saurer designed engine of their own manufacture. This brought home quite forcibly to the other mass producers that a market existed for light-weight diesel vehicles. However, no company apart from Nuffield was prepared to risk finance in tooling-up to make their own engines, and hence they turned to Perkins. The mass-producers are indebted to Perkins for having faith in their product and patience to await the demand which they knew would come.

As the market for light diesel vehicles increased in the early 1950s it became economic for mass-producers to produce their own engines. Consequently between 1952 and 1957 all the mass producers developed and produced their own diesels. Ford's original designs first appeared in 1952 and Bedford's in 1957, and in 1966 and 1968 respectively both firms replaced their original designs with brand new units. In all cases diesel engines were made on specially adapted multi-purpose machines although special purpose transfer machines were used for some items. During the late 1940s and early 1950s the demand

★ It is interesting to note that by 1971 Seddon was quite clearly the largest of the specialist producers. This position was reinforced by its absorption of Atkinson in 1971, the combined output being close to 5000 units.

for diesel vehicles increased, and in addition a new demand appeared in the market for vehicles of between two and six tons carrying capacity. Competition for this new market became intense and each firm quickly supplied diesel engined vehicles, eventually with units of their own manufacture. Although diesels were more expensive than comparable petrol engines due to the heavier castings needed for the engine block and the costly components used, the greater thermal efficiency and longevity of such engines made them attractive to operators. As the output of smaller diesels increased the unit cost of production tended to fall; in addition, the development of new large petrol engines for commercial vehicles utilised techniques where a common engine block was used for petrol and diesel units. All this reduced the cost of diesels and increased their attractiveness. By 1953, for powering vehicles of over four tons unladen weight the diesel was supreme, but between three and four tons the petrol engine was still leading and substantially so below three tons (*Table 9.4*).

Table 9.4

DIESEL ENGINED VEHICLES AS PERCENTAGE OF TOTAL

| | Percentage of Total | | |
Unladen Weight	1947	1953	1967
Up to 1 ton	—	—	0·75
1 to 3 tons	4·2	22·0	30·0
3 to 4 tons	8·0	46·0	93·5
4 tons plus	52·0	85·0	98·7

At the same time as diesel-engined lorries were becoming more prevalent, diesel-engined agricultural tractors were becoming more popular. In 1947 less than 5% of new tractors were diesel powered whereas in 1953 almost 47% were so powered. So in 1947 less than 5000 diesel engines were used for automotive products compared with almost 15 000 in 1953. The total growth in the demand for smaller diesels in the 1950s justified the manufacture of diesel engines by the mass producers. By 1967 over 30% of all new CV registrations were diesel powered, or over 77 000 in all*. Add to this the export of another 200 000 units and the position becomes clear. All the large CV companies can produce their own diesel engines quite efficiently and smaller companies can 'buy out' from diesel engine specialists.

* In 1971 over 800 000 diesel engines of various types and for various applications were produced in the U.K. This clearly established the British diesel engine industry as the world's largest.

Competition between diesel makers is strong because each engine has its own merits and adherents. As a result specialist CV makers are called upon to supply vehicles with different makes of engine, and occasionally a mass producer will give a choice as well.

Very few large petrol engined cars are now made and, because the characteristics of a large CV petrol engine makes it unsuitable for meeting the engine specifications of a large car, petrol engines used in trucks are now quite different to those used in cars. Only in the one to three tons category does the petrol-engined truck reign supreme and even here the use of diesels is increasing.

THE MASS–PRODUCERS MOVE UP THE WEIGHT-SCALE

After 1945 the mass-producers were generally limited to producing trucks of three tons carrying capacity and less. In the late 1940s they all moved into the five ton weight category, and in the mid and late 1950s they moved into the seven ton category. By the early 1960s the mass producers moved into the 8 to 16 ton category, and in the late 1960s the mass producers began making vehicles of between 16 and 28 tons gross vehicle weight. The firm tending to lead the way up the weight scale was Rootes. Being the smallest of the mass-producers it found it difficult to compete by means of model-price competition and still produce a vehicle of the price and quality of its rivals without sacrificing profits. Hence it tended to seek new market niches away from the markets of its main competitors and thereby charge prices giving commensurate returns on capital. This model-*weight* competition has been the main feature of the mass produced CV market since 1945, and as one firm moves up the weight scale the others tend to follow eventually. In the 1950s firms may have lagged as much as three years behind the 'model-weight leader', but in the 1960s Ford and Bedford followed each other very closely when either of them followed Rootes. However, because of design problems BMC fell further behind during the late 1960s.

Firms tended to move up the weight scale not only because their competitors did so, but fundamentally because customers were 'trading-up'. If a mass-producer was not to lose custom to its competitors or to specialist producers it had to provide a range of larger vehicles to meet customers new requirements. Model-price competition, weight-scale competition, and specification competition have all been usual in the post-war mass-market. The mass-producers have been very successful in maintaining and expanding their market in the light- and medium-weight sector. In the heavy-weight sector they have not been so successful, for although their products were cheaper than the specialists, operators continued to demand quality and longevity which they were unsure of obtaining from the likes of Ford and Bedford.

The model-weight competition had a profound effect on the medium-weight vehicle specialist producers. Many small firms in the mid-1950s only produced vehicles in the two to seven ton payload range. Albion noted the market trend early, and seeing that the mass-producers were moving into the five ton sector in the late 1940s, sold out as a going concern to Leyland in 1951 after making record profits. Other producers were not so successful; Guy Motors failed to move with the times and remained in competition with the mass-producers and Thornycroft, Dennis, and Seddon tended to do the same. The profits of all these firms declined in the late 1950s, and in some cases disappeared altogether. Guy went bankrupt and Thornycroft sold its vehicle building subsidiary to ACV after making substantial losses. Attempts to compete on price with the lower cost mass-producers put all the medium-weight specialist producers in jeopardy. At the same time the specialist firms competing in the heavy vehicle market went from strength to strength as operators continued to trade up into the heaviest classes and as the demand for heavy vehicles increased with the growth in national income. Changes in legislation and improvements in the road system all helped to turn the market in the direction of Leyland, AEC and the independent firms.

COMPETITION IS BASED ON THE RANGE OF SPECIFICATIONS

Competition was very rarely on the basis of short-run price competition, the most notable example being the reduction in the price of Guy heavy vehicles in 1964. Jaguar cars did this in order to bring their prices more in line with Leyland's in an attempt to build-up output sufficiently to reduce unit costs. It was admitted that the new price structure was based on an output volume not yet achieved. In this case the subsequent increase in output was sufficiently large for the increase in revenue to more than offset the increase in costs, with the result that losses were turned into profits. In 1966, however, a new range of models was introduced which was priced in competition with Leyland. Throughout the CV market the product has become more sophisticated and the specifications wider. All the mass-producers manufacture a vast range of models, although a large number of common components are used. The great variety of specifications and models means that all price changes reflect *model*-price changes. Even if a model is reduced in price the reason is not short-run price competition but a reduction in the number of specifications or 'extras'. In the case of the mass producers it is possible to distinguish a basic model, whereas in the case of Foden or Atkinson each vehicle is different. In the CV market sales are made on the basis of individual contracts and in many cases therefore no list price can be given. A customer will shop around weighing up price, quality, and delivery dates from different manufacturers. As a result firms compete on price plus quality and specifications. The lighter or smaller the vehicle the more important does model-price competition become, the heavier the vehicle the more important does quality and individual specifications become in relation to price. Within the heavy vehicle sector different customers require different combinations of price and quality. One heavy vehicle specialist suggested that it was able to charge up to £500 above the equivalent Leyland model before sales began to tail-off. So some customers are prepared to pay more, and evidently judge what they buy to be good value for money. A sufficient number of people think in these terms for the heavy vehicle specialists to gradually increase their output, turnover and profitability. Firms such as Dennis who tended to operate further down the weight scale and which had no reputation for producing really heavy vehicles found the position difficult. The lack of concerted and clear policy objectives has often put some firms at a competitive disadvantage.

THE RETAIL NETWORK

The mass-produced vehicles and the more standardised ranges of some of the specialist producers are sold through the trade. Other manufacturers tend to rely on direct selling, especially in the case of very heavy trucks and in the case of buses. The growth of specialist dealer chains shows how important is the retail side in a competitive market. To meet growing competition from the mass-producers Leyland established a much larger and much more powerful dealer network to sell its lighter and more standardised vehicles. The distributors and dealers are backed-up by Leyland's own chain of depots. A lack of a suitable dealer network or depot chain has adversely affected some firms, notably Dennis which was very weak on the sales and service side and desperately attempted to remedy the position over the period 1969–1971.

Typically, almost 25% of all new-car sales but less than 20% of new CV sales were done via hire-purchase contracts. Leaving aside vans and concentrating on trucks and buses only, about 16% were via H.P. contracts. Consequently variations in H.P. restrictions were likely to have a relatively small effect on total demand. Another feature was that whereas more *used* cars, vans, and buses were sold via H.P. than were new ones, in the case of trucks the opposite was true. This was probably due to the rather small market in used trucks plus the fact that depreciation was so severe that cash purchases were often within the reach of the purchaser. With more severe conditions being imposed on vehicle operators, on the safety and maintenance side, the second-hand market is likely to be further restricted.

COMPETITION IN THE COMPONENTS INDUSTRY

Although detail modifications are being continually made and model-price and model-specification competition was almost a continuous process, many items on the CV side had as long a life-cycle as items on the car side. Major components such as engines remained in production for very long periods of time. For instance, the large petrol engines used in BMC three to five ton trucks was originally introduced in 1939 and the Ford V8 engine introduced in 1933 was only replaced in 1953. In terms of diesel engines Ford's original design lasted from 1952 to 1966, in the case of all the other mass-producers their diesel engines introduced in the mid-1950s were still in production in 1971. A number of the original designs introduced by Perkins in 1937 were still manu-factured in an improved form in 1971. In the case of the heavy vehicle specialists, ACV had by 1971 produced three distinct ranges of engines since 1932, although some factors have been common to all. Leyland had survived on two basic ranges since 1933. In all cases occasional additions are made to existing ranges, such as the ACV V8 in 1968 which was in addition to the main range introduced in 1964. Gear-boxes and other major components had equally long lives. Only the mass-producers make their own pressed-steel cabs, the specialists tend to buy-out or to produce fibreglass or wooden framed sheet metal units. In most instances a basic cab design is retained for over 10 years. In this way the sub-optimum use of expensive equipment, producing components, running units, and pressings, was not made worse by too brief an amortisation period which would either have deflated profits or increased costs, or both. In practice the U.K. manu-facturers tended to make skilful use of equipment which was not

necessarily as technically efficient as that used in the car plants, but
which was more economically efficient for the scale of output achieved.
In some instances diesel engines were not produced either on automated
transfer machines or on mechanically linked special purpose machines,
but were assembled by hand along simple moving flow-lines. This
method of production tends to be more labour intensive but avoids the
wasteful idleness of expensive capital equipment. The net result was a
more efficient method of production for the scale of output involved.

FORD AND BEDFORD: THE FIGHT FOR MARKET LEADERSHIP

The commercial vehicle industry generally is extremely competitive
with firms continually attempting to introduce models superior to
those of their competitors. Competition is mainly based on specifications, reliability, and of course price, the latter being more important
the lighter the vehicle. In the car-derivative and medium-weight van
and pick-up sector the absolute price variation model for model is
about £50 for car derivatives and £150 for 12 cwt. vans. In the market
for mass-produced trucks between 6 and 13 tons gross the price spread
between different manufacturers for similar models is around £150.
In the case of vehicles of 16 tons the spread of prices charged by firms
in the market is £200 for the mass producers and £550 for other firms.
In the 20 ton range the specialist vehicles are priced at about £500
above the mass producers*.
   The 1960s saw an intensification of competition mainly as a result of
an aggressive sales push by Ford directed at supplanting Bedford
as the main truck producer and at supplanting BMC as the main
producer of medium-weight vans. In 1964 Ford established a 'Special
Vehicles Division' in order to add further variations to the wide range
of vehicles offered, which together with the appointment of a director
of commercial vehicle sales represented the first really serious attempt
to place the company's CV activities on a par with its car business. In
addition the radical and crucial reorganisation of the truck and bus
sales and service network completed the groundwork for a serious
attack on the CV market. In 1965 the company introduced a new
range of trucks which in terms of quality, specifications, and styling,
put it on a par with Bedford and BMC for the first time. This replaced
the somewhat inferior Thames Trader range which dated from 1957.
In 1966 the Ford Transit range of medium-weight vans was introduced
into a market where BMC and Ford competed for market leadership.

   * From the manufacturers' price lists.

At a time when Ford was strengthening its supply position, the demand for medium trucks received a boost from government legislation which introduced 'plating and testing' in 1968*. Many older vehicles would have needed much expense lavished on them in order to satisfy the new requirements, consequently operators replaced them with new ones. As a result Ford was in a strong position to meet this upsurge in demand.

In 1967 Ford gained the market leadership for vehicles of over two tons payload by accounting for 25% of U.K. sales compared with between 23% and 24% for the traditional market leader Bedford. In effect, the £12 million invested in the D-series of trucks, which ranged from light 2 ton trucks up to 28 ton gross vehicles and which was deliberately planned with market leadership in view, had succeeded in its aim within two years. At the same time a new range of BMC trucks, introduced into the market for medium vehicles of five tons payload and over, proved a commercial failure due to delays in production and shortcomings in design which led to unreliability. In short, Ford's expanded market share occurred at a time of similar expansion by Leyland and consolidation by Rootes and Bedford, therefore Ford's advance was mainly at the expense of BMC (*Table 9.5*).

Table 9.5

MARKET SHARE FOR VEHICLES OF OVER TWO TONS PAYLOAD (%)

Firm	1965–1966	1966–1967
Ford	15	25
Bedford	25	23
BMC	19	11
Leyland	12	16
Rootes-Dodge	17	16
Others plus imports	12	19

Source: *The Sunday Times*, 21 January 1968, p. 33, and 17 December 1967, p. 36.

In 1966 when BMC's share of the truck market was taking a downward plunge the company was still dominant in the lighter sectors. It held almost 50% of the car derivative market, over 30% of the medium-weight van market, and 20% of the one to two ton truck sector. However, in 1965 Ford introduced its Transit range of medium-weight

* 'Plating' refers to regulations concerning a vehicle's gross weight and 'testing' to a new Ministry of Transport scheme to ascertain a vehicle's roadworthiness.

vans to cover payloads of from just over half a ton to almost two tons. This range in terms of choice and specifications appeared to be just what the market wanted, with the result that BMC's share of the market was greatly reduced (*Table 9.6*).

Table 9.6

MARKET SHARES IN THE MEDIUM-WEIGHT VAN MARKET (%)

Firm	1965	1968	1969	1970
Ford	19	32	38	44
BMC	34	24	n.a.	21
Bedford	23	20	18	16
Rootes	10	6	7	9
Others plus imports	14	18	n.a.	10

Source: *Motor Transport*, 24 October 1969 (Ford Motor Co., advertisement) and SMMT.

As a result of these market changes Ford had supplanted the traditional market leaders in the medium van market, and in the truck market for vehicles over two tons payload. Only in the car derivative market was Ford held at bay by the market leader*. In terms of total CV production Ford had overhauled the largest producer BMC in both 1966 and 1968, BMC only being so significant by dint of its production of about 50 000 car derivative vehicles annually.

Table 9.7

TOTAL COMMERCIAL VEHICLE OUTPUT 1960–1970 (1000's)

Firm	1960	1961	1962	1963	1964	1965	1966	1967	1968	1970
BMC	140	185	165	140	155	140	109	107	105	107
Ford	100	80	85	83	92	85	113	93	108	141
Bedford	105	95	75	84	107	112	102	89	97	102
Dodge-				10	13					
Rootes	40	27	29	27	29	30	40	29	27	32
Leyland	30	25	25	23	25	28	25	23	24	26
Rover	35	35	35	28	28	45	35	31	36	40
Others	10	10	10	5	6	12	9	8	11	10

* It is interesting to note that the introduction of a VAT will necessarily increase the price of commercial vehicles, vehicles which are at present exempt from purchase tax. Some 20% of car derivative van sales are sold to people who use them for private rather than commercial uses in order to avoid paying the purchase tax on the car 'equivalent'. With the imposition of VAT this inventive is very much reduced, although as the cost of the car is greater than the van some incentive will remain.

It is quite probable that without the dislocation to production caused by the replacement of the Anglia van by the Escort model in 1967 Ford would have retained overall leadership in that year. Despite the importance of export sales it is quite evident that the growth in Ford's CV output since 1965 is a function of its successful performance on the domestic market at the expense of its competitors. In certain sub-sections of the market other firms appear as market leaders, for instance, in the market for vehicles of between $1\frac{1}{2}$ and 4 tons payload BMC has a fine range of products holding over 55% of the market. In addition, in the market for vehicles of over 5 tons payload, Leyland holds $33\frac{1}{3}$% of the business. Even here the market share varies in different sub-sectors (*Table 9.8*).

Table 9.8

LEYLAND'S SHARE (%)

10 tons to 14 tons gross	11
12 ,, ,, 14 ,, ,,	30
14 ,, ,, 16 ,, ,,	36
16 ,, ,, 20 ,, ,,	90
20 tons plus	67

Table 9.9

PERCENTAGE SHARE OF COMMERCIAL VEHICLE PRODUCTION

Year	BMC	Ford	Bedford	Rootes	Rover	Standard	Leyland	ACV	Others
1938	30·7	20·0	24·6	5·5	—	—	4·1	2·1	13·0
1947	27·9	22·9	20·3	7·9	—	—	2·2	2·9	16·0
1954	31·8	15·4	20·8	8·9	9·4	2·3	11·4		
1957	33·7	18·7	20·4	7·6	8·7	2·3	8·7		
1960	28·4	21·8	22·9	5·6	6·6	3·8	11·6		
1961	40·2	19·6	20·7	6·5	7·4	1·1	3·3		1·3
1962	40·0	20·7	17·6	7·0	7·7	1·1	4·2		1·4
1963	35·2	20·6	21·1	7·4	6·4	0·6	4·7		3·7
1964	35·5	19·7	23·0	6·5	6·0	0·5‡	4·2		3·8
1965	30·7	18·7	24·6	6·6	9·9	(—)†	6·2		2·8
1966	25·0	25·9	23·2	9·3‡	8·1		5·8		2·6
1967	27·8	24·3	23·2	7·6	8·1		6·2		2·6
1968	25·7	26·4	23·8	6·6	9·0		5·8		2·0
1969	23·6★	27·0	24·2	6·6	8·5†		39·2†		1·9
1970	(37·8)†	30·9	22·3	7·0	(—)†		(—)†	(—)	2·0

Sources: *L'Argus*, *SMMT*, *PEP*. ★ Estimated figure. † British Leyland (including Austin-Morris, Rover, Leyland Truck and Bus Division–Guy, Leyland, BMC, etc.). ‡ Including Dodge in 1966 and subsequently.

Because of rounding totals do not necessarily add up to 100.

In the 10 to 14 ton sector Leyland faces strong competition from the mass-producers, although in the 12 to 14 ton sector the mass-producers are not quite so dominant. In the 14 to 16 ton sector Leyland competes strongly with the mass-producers, and with other specialists such as Seddon and Dennis. In the heavy vehicle sector Leyland is clearly the market leader, but faces more competition in the very heavy vehicle market than in the one for rather lighter types. In other words, firms such as ERF and Atkinson plus imported vehicles from Sweden are able to maintain a third of the total market in the face of Leyland's competition.

COMPETITION IN THE COMMERCIAL VEHICLE MARKET: CONCLUSIONS

In conclusion, competition in the CV market and industry is intense. Price is a factor especially in the lighter end of the market but variety, quality and specifications are also very important. This is shown by the fact that the Ford Transit models tend to be about £70 more expensive than equivalent BMC types, however this did not prevent Ford from appropriating BMC's market. The superior specifications and range of the new series of vehicles being sufficient to more than offset price differentials. BMC retaliated not by short-run price changes but by the introduction of new models, hence model-price or model-specification competition is the usual competitive weapon in the domestic CV markets. In the mass-produced truck market specifications are as important as price in the market place. Ford's new model-D truck range was more expensive than the range it replaced and as expensive as competing models. Nevertheless model-price competition when it meant producing a better quality product succeeded where model-price competition in terms of producing a cheaper product did not. In the heavy vehicle sector no list prices are produced, except by the mass-producers. Here model-specification competition is taken to the infinite degree. The variation in specifications is endless so a customer can only compare prices when he has tendered a number of manufacturers. The vehicle is built to a particular specification and then costed rather than attempting to produce to a particular price which is regarded as a normal one. In short price competition of any sort becomes subsidiary to model-specification competition. Customers deem that they are receiving value for money, even if a 28 ton Swedish vehicle or one built by the small specialists costs up to £500 more than a Leyland or £1800 more than a mass-produced vehicle.

The small-scale specialists are protected both by the 'service' they give their customers and by the size and nature of their market. Even where the mass-producers manufacture 28 ton trucks it would not be economic for them to produce in the same way as their smaller rivals. Therefore they cannot match their close attention to detail and quality during assembly and manufacture which is made possible by the labour intensive methods used by the specialists; this allows the small producers to survive by supplying their small but adequate market with the type of vehicle required.

In earlier chapters we have seen that the CV component suppliers compete very strongly with each other, therefore we need not dwell on this point here. However, we can mention a few points. The attempted market sharing between Dunlop and GKN, in car and CV wheels respectively, has been frustrated by Rubery Owen's vigorous competition in both markets. The attempt by the Cummins Engine Company to take-over the market for high-powered diesel engines provoked such a vigorous response from Perkins, Rolls-Royce, Leyland and Gardner that the American company's U.K. operation had to be reduced in size, subsequently a large number of redundancies in the British administrative side occurred. In other words model-specification competition proved to be very vigorous. In the field of diesel engine fuel pumps Simms competed for many years with Lucas-CAV, both firms indulging in bouts of 'component-improvement' competition. In the end Simms found itself paring margins to virtually zero in order to try to compete with Lucas. Although the Simms product may have been technically better it was more complex and therefore more expensive to produce. CAV made an item more suitable for mass production which allied to its larger output meant lower unit costs. As a result Simms sold out to CAV-Lucas, but both sides continued as separate entities and produced competing products within the Lucas empire. Vigorous competition exists in the body-building and trailer sector, all leading to the maximum choice for the customer at keen prices.

On both the car and CV side the 1960s has been a follow-up to the 1930s in that the firm gaining most from competition has been Ford. In terms of total output and shares of the home market, Ford has advanced mainly at the expense of BMC. As in 1952 and again in 1966 and 1968, BMC had to merge to maintain its market against competition. In 1964 BMC had 38% of all car production compared with 33·6% in 1967; Ford however advanced from 28·1% to 30·5% over the same period. Similarly BMC's share of total CV production fell from 35·5% to 25·7% with Ford moving from 19·7% to 26·4%.

The analysis so far has been in terms of domestic competition but, as we shall see in a later chapter, firms are more ready to cut prices in foreign markets than they are at home. Indeed, many export sales may be made at little more than marginal costs with overheads being mainly covered by home sales. Furthermore, as pointed out earlier, as 16% of average total costs at planned output levels are fixed then 84% are variable costs. Consequently prices must not be set below 84% of average total costs if a particular sale is to be worthwhile on a short-term basis. If home prices are equal to average total costs, including profits, as measured at planned output levels, and if ex-works export prices are more than 16% below home ex-works prices, then export sales will reduce short-run profits or increase short-run losses as the case may be. Ideally if only short-run marginal costs are covered then in the long-run the export market should be abandoned unless the government wishes to subsidise exports in order to earn foreign exchange. If short-run marginal costs are left uncovered then export sales should be dropped immediately, unless sales are made as 'loss leaders' now in order to earn profits later.

10

THE FINANCIAL POSITION

In this chapter a brief look is taken at the trend of profits in the motor industry, the level of investment, the place of the motor industry in the economy and the level of productivity. Firstly, then, an analysis of the trend in pre-tax net profits between 1959 and 1968.

THE PROFITABILITY OF THE BRITISH MOTOR INDUSTRY

VARIATIONS IN PROFITABILITY

It is quite evident from *Table 10.1* that severe fluctuations have occurred in the profitability of the motor industry both in terms of net pre-tax profits and in terms of profits per vehicle.

In absolute terms the profits of the four main car producers have fluctuated considerably, with pre-tax profits over the decade 1960–1969 failing to repeat the performance of 1960. Actually, trading profits in 1968 reached a new peak of £112·9 million, but because of record interest payments the net pre-tax profits earned were below those earned in 1964 or 1960. In terms of profits per vehicle the fluctuations have been even greater than that of pre-tax profits. An interesting feature was that whereas overall profits in 1968 were 11% below the 1960 peak, profits per vehicle were 25% below the 1960 performance. Also, up to 1962 profits per vehicle did not always move in the same direction as capacity utilisation, whereas from 1963 the two have invariably moved together. What this points to is this.

358

Table 10.1

Year	Index of Profits	Index of Profits per vehicle	Index	*Capacity(%)
1959	100·0	100	100	69
1960	117·6	100	134	93
1961	59·6	62	95	65
1962	43·6	40	107	74
1963	90·9	70	120	83
1964	110·9	73	127	88
1965	95·6	68	113	78
1966	58·3	44	99	68
1967	13·6	10	93	64
1968	106·7	75	126	87
1969	97·0	79	n.a.	n.a.
1970	14·0	9	n.a.	n.a.

* Output ÷ Capacity × 100.

Between 1960 and 1962 variable costs often increased sufficiently to offset the effects of falling fixed costs per unit on profits per vehicle. In addition, the growth in output between 1959 and 1960 was due to increased production of small cheap cars of below 1000 c.c. but there occurred a decline in the output of larger cars. This meant that *ad valorem* profit margins produced a smaller absolute profit. Between 1961 and 1962, however, small cars declined in output whereas larger cars increased significantly; hence the main cause of falling profits here was the increase in variable costs plus a decline in output of larger, more expensive commercial vehicles. In the period following 1962 profits per vehicle were highly correlated with changes in capacity utilisation. A 27% fall in capacity utilisation between 1964 and 1967 led to a fall in profits of almost 90%. This is a result one would expect from our previous analysis; although a 24 point fall in capacity utilisation only increases unit costs by around 6%, if profit margins were only 12% then profits would fall by over 50%. In the period 1964 to 1967, the increase in variable costs added to increased fixed costs per unit increased more than the increase in car prices and reduced profits to very low levels. In fact, net income after tax for the Big Four in 1967 was minus £2·9 million! The losses of BMC and Rootes offset the profits of Ford, Vauxhall, Leyland and the other smaller firms such as Rover and Jaguar.

Although the overall movement in profits between 1959 and 1969 had been erratic with the overall trend having a negative sign, the position of the CV specialists had been rather different (*Table 10.2*).

Table 10.2

INDEX OF PROFITS AND RETAIL PRICES

Year	Index of Profits	Index of Retail Prices* (1959=100)
1959	100	100
1960	140	101
1961	166	104
1962	182	107
1963	152	110
1964	202	114
1965	176	120
1966	256	124
1967	285	127
1968	371	134
1969	302	141
1970	400	150

* Compiled from Company Reports of Seddon, Dennis, Atkinson, Foden, ERF and the Transport Holding Company.

In no year during the decade did net pre-tax profits fail to exceed those earned in the base year. After 1964, when the car firms tended to do badly, the small CV specialist producers tended to do very well. Over the period as a whole the overall trend of profits has been strongly upwards. The figures for Leyland Motors and ACV are included in the car series, therefore the overall upward trend in Leyland profits between 1959 (£5·3 million) and 1967 (£18 million) would make the performance of the vehicle specialists even more impressive. After 1964 the growth in national income was on average around 2½% a year but the demand for large vehicles had grown by over 15% a year over the same period. The demand for other types of CV fell by 15% over the entire period 1964–1968. Consequently heavy CV makers continued to work to capacity, their main problem being one of sufficient supply rather than demand. Trading-up by operators and short-term factors such as the effects of 'plating and testing' legislation on replacement cycles meant full order books for the heavy CV producers in the 1960s. Any fluctuation in profits was due to increased variable costs rather than to excess capacity.

THE POSITION OF THE INDIVIDUAL FIRM

The overall picture concerning profits does tend to hide the individual picture. Some firms have been much more profitable than others. On the car side Ford, Vauxhall and Standard-Triumph (after the take-over by Leyland in 1961), have been the most profitable firms. Rootes had the worst record, making losses in 1962, 1963, 1965, 1966, 1967, and 1970, and only producing marginal profits in its good years. BMC's position fluctuated widely with a loss of over £3 million being earned in 1967 (*Table 10.3*).

Table 10.3

PRE-TAX PROFITS (£ MILLION)

Year	Rootes	BMC	BLMC	Leyland	Ford	Vauxhall
1957	0·8	11·2		6·1	18·4	0·6
1958	3·4	21·0		6·4	24·7	1·1
1959	3·9	15·7		5·3	32·2	13·5
1960	4·4	26·9		9·2	33·7	14·1
1961	2·9	10·1		6·9	22·2	14·5
1962	−0·89	4·2		5·5	17·0	16·0
1963	−0·25	15·4		10·98	35·0	16·3
1964	1·8	21·8		18·2	24·0	17·9
1965	−0·2	23·3		20·45	8·9	17·7
1966	−3·1	21·8		16·43	7·4	13·7
1967	−10·5	−3·28*		18·0	25·4	12·0
1968	3·9		37·95		43·0	12·2
1969	0·61		40·0		38·1	1·6
1970	−10·0		4·0		20·0†	−5·16

* British Motor Holdings.   † Approximate figure.

The most consistent and impressive financial picture in the U.K. motor industry in the period shown is that presented by the Ford Motor Company. Its profitability during the troubled times of the middle and late 1960s meant that on average it tended to be more successful in overcoming difficult market conditions than its competitors.

Leyland's reversal in 1961 and 1962 was due to losses of over £1·5 million a year sustained by its newly acquired Standard-Triumph subsidiary, but its overall growth during the decade was very impressive. Indeed, the recovery in British Leyland's profits in 1968 and 1969 was due largely to the Leyland and Jaguar components in the group. However, in 1970 the Austin-Morris division sustained very heavy losses of almost £16 million and even Standard-Triumph slipped into the red. The final positive balance was due to the highly profitable Leyland heavy CV sector and to Jaguar and Rover cars.

The commercial precariousness of the Rootes Group is evident from the time-series shown in the table. The profits made in 1960 of £4·4 million were a company record; this fact only exemplifies the very poor profits typically made by the company. Following various problems, culminating in a disastrous strike in 1961, the company's fortunes took a turn for the worse, and only absorption by Chrysler prevented liquidation. The American company's burden was illustrated by the cumulative losses made after 1965.

Recovering from a costly expansion in 1956–1958, Vauxhall's position reflected its dependence on commercial vehicles and medium-sized cars, all of which carried high mark-ups. The introduction of the first model Viva in September 1963 marked a change in company strategy through an attempt to enter the fastest growing sector of the car industry. Competition from the larger groups was severe and mark-ups were lower, as a result any divergence from standard output tended to have a disproportionate effect on profits. During the 1970 financial year the company made a pre-tax loss of £5·16 million, the highest in the company's history and only its third loss and its first pre-tax loss.

Thus the smaller groups have shown an erratic profits picture, as indeed has the largest British company, BMC; only Ford displayed a propensity to earn a net cash flow sufficiently large to ensure the company's survival. Clearly without BMC, Leyland would have continued to do well, in the same way as Daimler-Benz, by concentrating on quality products. It may have been better for a firm with a larger management structure, such as GKN, to have taken on the BMC problem. After all, most mergers seem to be undertaken not for the economies of scale they make possible but as a 'management consultancy' exercise, where the 'stronger' firm feels it can make better use of the 'weaker' firm's resources, which is more a question of short-run optimality than an attempt to reduce long-run costs. Vauxhall made a post-tax loss in 1969 and 1970 and a pre-tax loss in 1957. The latter caused by compressing a five-year expansion plan into three years the former due to a combination of the credit squeeze, increased variable costs, and labour unrest. On the CV side only Dennis Brothers and Bristol made any losses, the former due to under-utilisation of a large relatively capital intensive plant, and the latter due to restrictions placed on output by the 1962 Transport Act and the consequent need to make up for delayed investment when this restriction was removed late in 1964.

Table 10.4

PROFITS PER UNIT ($£$s)

Manufacturer	1954	1956	1961	1968	1970
Vauxhall	100	80	20	35	−33
Ford	65	45	53	59	47
BMC	50	35	6 10s. ⎫	38	−22
Standard	30	30	−21 ⎭		
Rootes	23	—	7	17	−46

Care must be taken in comparing one firm with another and one particular firm over a period of time. For instance, up until 1956 Vauxhall typically produced as many commercial vehicles as cars per year; also, until 1964 the company only produced medium sized cars. As a result the value of each unit was much higher on average than those produced by other car firms and hence unit profits tended to be high. BMC tended to be the small-car market leader and the proportion of its total output consisting of such vehicles was higher than that for other producers. In the early 1960s this percentage reached record proportions, hence the very low unit profits. Standard and Rootes, although engaging in model price competition still had to price in competition with larger firms, this tended to squeeze margins and made the firms extremely vulnerable to any factor which reduced output. Strikes, supply bottlenecks, and credit squeezes, which reduced output and increased unit costs by as little as 1–2% were enough to wipe out gross margins of $1\frac{1}{2}\%$ and produce losses. The fundamental improvement in BMC and Standard-Triumph margins was due to a linkage with Leyland Motors. Between 1961 and 1968 Leyland turned Standard-Triumph into a mass-producer of quality cars and ceased the attempt to compete with BMC, Ford, or Vauxhall, on price. This allowed an improvement in gross profits and profits per unit. Due to the production of large CVs it is impossible to deduce from Leyland's profit figures what car unit-profits were in 1961–1968, but an intelligent guess would put the figure at around $£25$–$£30$. BMC's improved profits were partly due to the influence of Leyland's quality cars and lorries but also the effect of Leyland's management improving the quality, output and sales of BMC's own CVs and cars. The change in the product of individual firms, for instance, the increase in Vauxhall's car:CV ratio, the reduction in Ford's small car: total output ratio, and so on, all tend to complicate the picture of profits per unit. Different firms also have different vehicle assembly to 'other activities' ratios, with the number of individual components, spares, and 'other products' varying from firm to firm and from time to time. All these factors affect the profits per 'vehicle' figure even if the number of vehicles produced remains constant.

FINANCIAL INDICATORS

THE 1960S: A PERIOD OF POOR RETURNS ON INVESTMENT

The variation in profits has been matched by the fluctuations in the return on capital measured on both a pre- and post-tax basis (*Table 10.5*).

Table 10.5

RATES OF RETURN ON CAPITAL (%)

Year	Pre-tax	Post-tax Motor Manufacturers	All Manufacturers
1959	—	12·4	—
1960	24·4	12·5	7·6
1961	12·6	7·7	6·4
1962	7·6	4·5	5·7
1963	13·8	8·0	6·1
1964	15·0	8·6	6·9
1965	12·8	9·9	7·7
1966	7·8	5·1	4·8
1967	1·8	−0·4	—
1968	12·6	10·4	—

These results are subject to the usual problems associated in measuring capital, for instance, do different firms value capital in different ways at different times, e.g. is the valuation on a replacement or historical basis?

The post-war return reached a peak in 1960 with a rate of return which was almost repeated in 1968, but by and large the 1960s was a difficult period for the motor industry. This was in sharp contrast to the period 1946–1960, when the return on capital was generally very good, although even in the 1960s the returns earned by the motor industry still tended to exceed those earned by manufacturing industry as a whole. The 1960s therefore reflected a more competitive situation which contrasted with the rapid growth of the 1950s. Consequently firms did not respond to increased costs by increasing prices quite so

readily. However, the period from July 1969 to December 1970 was
one when all the mass manufacturers each increased prices five times!
This was a result of an all-round increase in variable costs which
threatened to obliterate total profits.

DETAILED FINANCIAL EFFECTS

What has been the effects of fluctuations in profits and in returns on
capital? Here it is instructive to look at the relationship between the
cash flow on the one hand and gross fixed investment on the other*.
The cash flow means depreciation plus net income after tax plus payments to minority interests. From these statistics the following picture
emerges (*Table 10.6*).

Table 10.6

CASH FLOW AND INVESTMENT (£ MILLION)

	1959	1960	1961	1962	1963	1964	1965	1966	1967	1968
Net earnings	45·2	52·7	28·5	22·3	46·3	53·6	57·2	30·9	−2·0	54·5
+ Depreciation	30·6	31·9	32·6	42·0	47·3	53·8	61·4	66·2	69·8	77·0
Cash flow	75·8	84·6	61·1	64·3	93·6	107·4	118·6	97·1	67·8	131·5
Gross fixed invest-ment	—	60·1	88·2	87·5	86·5	89·0	97·2	97·5	86·9	47·4

The relationship between net earnings in year t and investment in
t is not particularly close, but the change in net earnings in t compared
with $t-1$ and the change in investment in $t+1$ compared with t is
highly correlated with the signs being invariably similar. On the other
hand, the opposite is often true where the relationship between
depreciation provision and gross fixed investment is concerned. This
is only to be expected where the fall in net earnings is partly offset by
increased depreciation provision. Over the entire period however,
depreciation has increased continuously, and since the mid-1960s it has
become the major part of the cash flow, whereas net earnings have
fluctuated widely, even becoming negative in 1967. Clearly then, given
a one year time-lag, gross investment is a close function of the level of
net earnings and the major factor explaining fluctuation in the cash
flow has been fluctuations in net earnings. Only in 1962 was the fall in
net earnings offset by increased depreciation allowances and even then
it was the sign of the change in net earnings between 1961 and 1962

* NEDO Data Book, *Motor Industry Statistics 1959–1968*.

and not that of the cash flow which explained the change in the level of investment in 1963 compared with 1962. The lower level of profits or net earnings tend to affect the level of internally generated funds, for lower profits adversely affect not only the means to expand but also the will, so changes in profits do appear to be a very important factor in maintaining gross investment.

Changes in the level of net earnings, however, do not produce commensurate changes in gross investment in the following year. So although changes in net earnings explain the sign of changes in gross investment it does not explain the magnitude of this change. Can changes in the total amount of internally generated funds explain this fluctuation, that is, retained earnings plus depreciation? From the data in *Table 10.7* it would appear not.

Table 10.7

INTERNAL FINANCING AND EARNINGS DISTRIBUTION ($£$ MILLION)

	1959	1960	1961	1962	1963	1964	1965	1966	1967	1968
Net Income	45·0	52·4	28·3	22·0	45·9	52·5	55·8	30·1	(2·9)	53·2
Preference Dividend	0·9	1·0	0·9	0·9	0·9	1·0	1·0	1·6	1·3	1·1
Ordinary Dividend	16·6	17·7	15·1	16·0	18·1	20·8	22·9	31·4	21·6	28·9
Retained Earnings	27·5	33·7	12·3	5·1	26·9	30·7	31·9	(2·9)	(25·5)	23·2
Depreciation	30·6	31·9	32·6	42·0	47·3	53·8	61·4	66·2	69·8	47·4
Total	58·1	65·6	44·9	47·1	74·2	84·5	93·3	63·3	44·3	70·6
Gross Investment (fixed)	—	60·1	88·2	87·5	86·5	89·0	97·2	97·5	86·9	47·4
Net Investment (fixed)	—	28·2	55·6	47·5	39·2	35·2	35·8	31·3	17·1	– 29·6

Fluctuations in internally generated funds do not produce commensurate fluctuations in the level of net or gross fixed investment in the following year. When internally generated funds increase then the opportunity is taken to reduce the dependence on outside sources of funds, when internal funds fall then increased recourse is made to outside sources. The one exception appears to be 1968 which followed the traumatic shock caused by the overall losses made in 1967. Any fluctuation in net income is mainly felt by reduced retentions, in other words dividends are maintained in the face of fluctuating profits. This was especially noticeable during the slump in earnings in 1966 and 1967 when dividends were maintained in an attempt to shore up the market value of the motor firms' issued capital. This was especially so in the case of BMC but also Vauxhall and Rootes. When net earnings increase, distributions are maintained as there is little need to artificially shore-up the market value of equity capital. There is therefore no sign of a deliberate policy of high distributions.

Generally speaking, retained earnings plus depreciation are the major source of funds. In contrast to the period 1946–1962, depreciation is a much more important source of funds than retained earnings, reflecting the larger capital stock of the industry in the 1960s and the pressure on profits caused by increased competition and the credit squeeze. As mentioned before, changes in output affect average unit costs very little, but this small change in unit costs is enough to produce considerable variation in profits. Apart from the early years of the 1960s, fluctuation in profits appear to be caused by under-capacity working with the attendant increase in fixed costs, plus intensified competition which has limited the extent to which prices have been increased in the face of increased variable and fixed costs. For instance, between 1959 and 1969 the index of retail prices increased by 30% but car prices before tax only increased by some 15–20% for similar models.

Although internally generated funds are the most important items, other sources of short and long-term capital have been more significant in the 1960s than previously, especially where fixed assets are concerned (*Table 10.8*).

Table 10.8

CHANGES IN ASSET STRUCTURE AND FINANCING ($£$ MILLION)

	1960	1961	1962	1963	1964	1965	1966	1967	1968
Assets Employed	706·1	734·0	733·3	869·5	986·1	1 069·5	1 162·2	1 153·0	1 240·5
Equity	376·6	388·9	398·0	427·8	469·9	516·3	526·5	494·4	502·6
Minority interest	5·3	5·4	7·3	8·2	6·7	9·8	10·8	11·5	9·0
Future taxes	39·1	21·8	19·3	30·2	37·9	25·6	24·3	19·3	32·8
Long-term loans	34·4	47·3	63·5	73·2	71·5	79·3	75·0	105·2	127·6
Bank loans, etc.	3·0	19·5	26·7	17·3	37·2	47·9	126·7	129·7	49·0
Other liabilities	247·8	251·1	258·6	312·9	363·0	390·8	398·9	393·0	519·5
Financing									
Fixed Assets	235·4	291·0	338·5	377·7	412·9	448·7	480·0	497·1	467·5
Trade Investments	6·4	8·3	8·7	10·5	14·4	11·9	13·6	16·4	18·7
Current Assets	464·3	434·8	426·1	481·3	558·7	608·9	668·7	639·3	754·3

Clearly changes in equity capital and bank loans have been important in financing changes in total assets. From almost zero in 1959 Bank loans had become an extremely significant item by the late 1960s mainly in financing liquid assets, but the continued high level of bank credit in 1967 suggests that much of the fixed investment occurring in that year was so financed. Similarly in 1961 and 1962 items such as changes in shareholders equity and long-term loans were obviously linked to changes in the stock of fixed assets. By and large the industry has depended on internally generated funds for its gross fixed investment and a fall in these items has led to a recourse to alternative sources of finance in the year involved*, and a fall in gross investment in the year following the fall in retained earnings. This is largely true of the level of net investment as well.

THE COURSE OF CAPITAL INVESTMENT AND PRODUCTIVITY

THE MAIN PHASES OF CAPITAL AND PRODUCTIVE EXPANSION

Since 1945 the expansion of the motor industry has been continual, with net investment being undertaken in most years. However, three separate investment booms are detectable. The first and smallest of the three occurred between 1950 and 1953. Firms were attempting to meet the pent-up demand caused by the war and make up for the acute shortage of machine tools which existed in the late 1940s. Expansion occurred in the traditional locations of the motor industry although the utilisation of ex-Government 'shadow factories' meant some expansion in 'new' areas such as South Wales. Between 1954 and 1958 a much more significant expansion took place again in the traditional areas. BMC expanded and re-equipped Longbridge, Vauxhall did the same at Luton and Dunstable, as did Ford at Dagenham. Simultaneously the heavy CV makers engaged on their first post-war expansion between 1955 and 1958. Vauxhall's expansion between 1955 and 1957 was an attempt to make up for lost time because previous investment plans had been too small to allow the company to remain a significant force in the car industry. The accelerated expansion programme of £34 million was financed largely by long-term loans (£20 million) plus a £3 million loan from GMC and a pre-tax loss of over £2·3 million; a relatively small proportion coming from internally generated funds. Ford's expansion was entirely self-financed, but BMC, Rootes and Standard made substantial recourse to outside sources. This expansion increased the motor industry's productive capacity from around

* A substantial fall in profits and hence the cash flow makes it difficult to float new equity or stocks on favourable terms.

1 300 000 cars and commercial vehicles, to about 1 900 000 vehicles a
year.

The third major wave of expansion occurred between 1960 and
1965 which brought total productive capacity up to about 2 400 000
vehicles a year. This expansion largely took place in new locations
as the motor firms were largely influenced by governmental direction
and financial inducements. In 1960 Ford moved its CV production to a
new plant near Slough, BMC moved truck production to Scotland,
Ford and Vauxhall brought their Merseyside plants into full operation
between 1963 and 1965, and between 1960–1963 Rover built a new
plant at Cardiff. In 1960 and between 1963–1965 expansion was mainly
internally financed but in 1961 and 1962 long-term loans increased
significantly and between 1959–1965 a large increase occurred in the
value of shareholders equity.

Since 1965 expansion has been strictly limited due mainly to the
stagnation in home demand and in total output. Such was the fall in
profits in 1967 and 1968, however, that a large proportion of investment had to be financed by long-term loans.

PRODUCTIVITY AND INVESTMENT: THEIR INTERDEPENDENCE

Turning now to productivity in the motor industry. Between 1961
and 1968 productivity increased by 23% with output per man reaching
a peak in 1968, whereas vehicle output reached a peak in 1966. The
reduction in the labour force after 1966 was partly due to a recession
in demand but also due to a reduction in the 'normal' labour force
employed by British producers. The largest 'shake-out' occurred at
BMC where the aim was to produce the same peak output as before
but with 12 000 fewer men*. On an inter-firm basis, in 1965–1966
BMC produced 8·5 cars per man per year compared with 9·7 at Ford,
10·6 at Vauxhall and 16 at Volkswagen†. Of course, the larger the
output the more capital intensive and more mechanised the productive
process, and the more economies of scale which are reaped the greater
is the productivity of labour.

In the U.K. the increase in output between 1961 and 1964 increased
productivity by 16%. The fall in output in 1965–1966 and the marginal
recovery in 1967 meant that productivity fell back to a level 12%
greater than it was in 1961. The upward surge in output between 1967

* *The Sunday Times* (6 November 1966).
† By 1968 it was suggested that each Ford worker made 11·7 vehicles compared with 5·6 by BMC workers, *The Sunday Times* (21 December 1969).

Figure 10.1

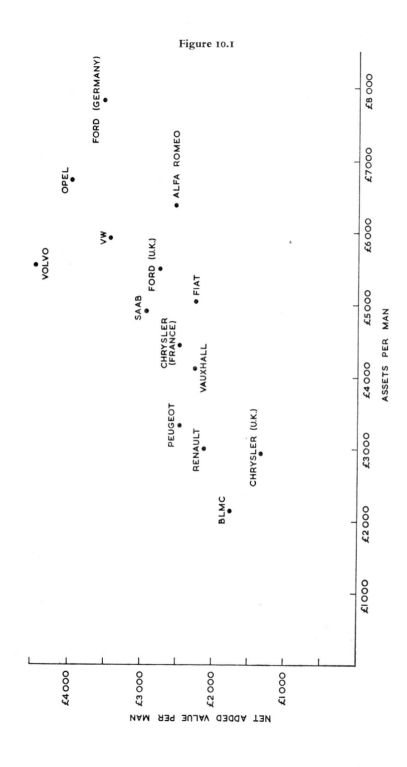

and 1968 increased productivity by 11%. This reflected both the labour 'shake-out' which had occurred between 1965 and 1967 and the greater utilisation of capacity in 1968. The relationship between output and productivity is illustrated by the fact that, whereas a U.K. mass-producer will produce 10 cars a year per man, a small specialist maker such as Aston Martin or Jensen may have a figure of 0·75 cars per man per year. In other words, not only the full utilisation of existing capacity but also the use of a different type of production method will increase labour productivity. Consequently the capital intensity of production is important in explaining different degrees of labour productivity. The U.S.A. reaches the highest levels of capital intensity. In 1968 the number of vehicles made per worker in the U.S.A. exceeded 18 and this was roughly 80% better than the U.K. average. However, compared with the situation in 1950 when the ratio was 10·7 cars per man per year in the U.S.A. to 3·3 in the U.K.* the situation had improved relatively. This reflects the larger relative increase in output, mechanisation, and capital intensity, in the non-American motor industries.

A comparison of British and European levels of productivity also shows the British industry in a rather poor light. Two tests of a company's efficiency are the capital assets per man and the value added per man per firm, and of course the two are highly correlated. Clearly the more capital intensive a company the higher the output:labour ratio; in other words the more machinery per worker the more can be produced (*Figure 10.1*)†.

The equation to be derived from the data in *Figure 10.1* is given as

$$Y = 1042 + 0·34X$$

where Y is the net value added and X the assets per man. The R^2 was 0·50 and the T statistic was 3·4. Using the logs of the data the R^2 was 0·60 and the T statistic was 4·2. This simply illustrates the close relationship between the two variables.

Of the five least capitalised firms in 1969 three were British, while of the five most capitalised three were German. The most efficient British firm was Ford (U.K.) and in 1969 the fixed assets per employee in the British industry were as shown in *Table 10.9*.

In international terms, the value added per employee of Ford (U.K.),

---

* J. T. Dunlop and V. P. Diatchenko (eds.), *International Comparison of Productivity*, McGraw-Hill, New York, ch. 15, p. 194 (1964).

† The assets per man referred to in *Figure 10.1* include all capital assets, e.g. fixed assets, stocks, work in progress, cash, etc.

Table 10.9

FIXED ASSETS PER EMPLOYEE ($£$)

Ford	2 709
Vauxhall	2 057
Chrysler	1 840
BLMC	964

the best British firm, compared unfavourably with its German rivals (*Table 10.10*).

Table 10.10

VALUE ADDED PER EMPLOYEE ($£$)

Ford (U.K.)	2 764
Volkswagen	3 355
Opel	4 878
Ford (Germany)	4 500

Clearly capital investment is a key factor affecting productivity but other factors are involved as well.

Clearly the volume of output is not the only factor which affects productivity, for in 1968 BMC produced over 714 000 vehicles compared with Ford's 661 000, yet Ford's productivity in that year was over twice that of BMC. In 1965–1966 BMC made over 700 000 vehicles compared with under 275 000 by Vauxhall; nevertheless, the latter company had a higher labour productivity. The high figure at VW may give a clue to part of the reason. Apart from over-manning and sub-optimum working, BMC produced a greater variety of vehicles than Vauxhall, Ford or VW. Concentrating on a few models should increase productivity per head. In 1965 VW made around 1 300 000 vehicles compared with 800 000 by BMC yet VW's productivity was twice BMC's. Continental mass-producers such as VW, Renault and Citroen produce a smaller range of vehicles than their U.K. rivals and change models less often. Consequently productivity may be higher because output patterns are less complex and less disrupted by different models emerging from the press shops and assembly lines. As model changes are infrequent, the firms' 'learning curves' tend to reduce the cost of each operation over time.

THE PLACE OF THE MOTOR INDUSTRY IN THE U.K. ECONOMY

Now to a brief survey of the place of the motor industry in both financial and economic terms in the economy as a whole. On average the industry accounts for about 16% of all manufactured exports in value terms and this was £617 million in 1960, £896 million in 1968 and over £950 million in 1969. Of this last figure, £322 million was generated by BLMC. The 1963 Census of Production (at the time of writing the last which is available) shows that the motor industry accounted for $7\frac{1}{2}$% of manufactured production, 5·1% of all industrial production, and nearly 6% of all manufacturing employment. On the expenditure side, in 1963 the industry accounted for 12·3% of all new building work, 7·9% of all plant and machinery installed and 9·0% of total net capital expenditure. It has been estimated★ that in terms of all direct and indirect inputs to industry the motor industry accounted for 5·1% of industrial production in terms of direct requirements in 1963, and 5·5% in indirect needs. So overall the motor industry accounted for over 10·5% of industrial production. The addition of capital items such as plant and machinery brings the current and capital direct and indirect requirements of the industry up to 12% of total industrial production. The same source attributes 32% of the growth in industrial production to the motor industry; in other words, fluctuations in the activity of the motor industry can have a profound effect on economic activity generally. If the value of the motor industry's output fell by 6% then total economic activity would fall by almost 2%.

The importance of the motor industry in the entire economy makes it an attractive weapon of economic policy. The extent to which economic policy can affect the motor industry can have a considerable effect on total activity. Clearly the impact of policy can have considerable impact on the physical and financial performance of the motor industry. The industry is under a dual influence as far as policy is concerned: particular and specific measures such as taxation, legislation and hire-purchase controls, and general measures which affect economic growth, output and expenditure in the economy as a whole. It has been suggested† that a 2% growth in national income affects

★ A. G. Armstrong, 'The Motor Industry and the British Economy', *District Bank Review*, pp. 19–40 (September 1967).

† A. Silberston, 'Hire Purchase and the Demand for Cars', *Economic Journal*, (March and September 1963).

new car sales by as much as would a fall in the minimum hire-purchase deposit from 33% to 20%. Consequently general economic measures are as important as specific measures in their impact on car demand. In terms of commercial vehicles the impact of general economic policy is much more important as so few non car-derivative vehicles are bought on hire-purchase or credit. Although the practice of leasing rather than buying vehicles is expanding, here again credit restrictions are not used. Consequently the impact of fluctuation in the demand for exports, which is independent of specific measures aimed at the car industry, plus the fact that business cars and commercial vehicles are more dependent on general economic conditions, means that much of the fluctuation in the demand for vehicles is unavoidable given that we need 'stop-go'. The high income elasticity of demand for motor vehicles, whether it is personal disposable income or national income is enough to cause wide fluctuation in vehicle demand quite independently of any specific measures.

Consequently the financial position of the motor industry will always be susceptible to changes in the general economic climate. In turn, variations in the activities of the motor industry will affect national income generally. Any reduction in car demand will have an immediate effect on domestic activity and if the fall in demand is caused by a fall in exports any adverse movement in the balance of payments will have a recessionary bias. This will have further effects on the economy and therefore on the motor industry and so on until the 'multiplier' has worked itself out.

11

EXPORTS

The British motor industry's position as an export leader is purely a post-war phenomenon. At the end of World War II the British Government, faced with a massive reconstruction programme, was presented with the problem of earning sufficient foreign exchange to finance crucial imports. At one time it was thought that 'traditional' exporters such as cotton would lead the export drive but a quick study of these industries showed that they were in no position commercially or technically to do this. Then it was realised that the world needed motor vehicles, and so the industry was placed at the forefront of the export drive. For the first time the industry became export orientated.

EXPORTS: A POST-WAR PHENOMENON

The British motor industry at home had been protected from foreign competition to a greater extent, and for a longer time, than nearly all the rest of British industry. It developed behind a wall of protection. As regards exports in 1938, only £18·6 million worth of U.K. motor vehicles were sold abroad. Of this a very large proportion went to empire and Commonwealth countries where the U.K. benefited from preferential tariffs. Despite Imperial Preference, the competition from large American cars, built in volumes and at costs with which the British industry could not compete, was intense, especially as U.K. producers often had to produce large Empire models especially for overseas markets*. American cars were generally more suited to meeting the needs of these markets than were any British cars†.

The British industry's general failure to compete with foreign—mainly American—producers was shown by the small export percentage which existed, even after the introduction of Imperial Preference in 1929. In 1938, 44 000 cars were exported, 75% of them to where the U.K. received a tariff advantage of one-third. Similarly over 85% of the total production of 341 000 cars was sold domestically‡, in a market protected by the $33\frac{1}{3}\%$ ad valorem tax on imported cars, commercial vehicles and vehicle parts. In other words, 97% of all cars produced in the U.K. were sold in protected markets! Even so, the value of exports at £14·9 million was about twice as much as for textile machinery, the other principal engineering export. Motor vehicle exports nevertheless represented only 3% of total U.K. export sales§.

The rapid expansion of exports after World War II is in marked contrast to the position after 1918. The 1913 figure was not matched until 1924, when 14 000 vehicles were exported, whereas the best inter-war figure was exceeded as early as 1946. Between 1929 and 1933 exports declined, recovering to 90% of the 1929 figure in 1933. Between 1933 and 1937 exports increased continuously, falling back from over 99 000 vehicles in 1937 to almost 84 000 in 1938. As we have seen before, the great depression of 1929 did not have such a profound effect on the British motor industry as on the American due to the very slow development of the industry in the 1920s. By 1933 total production exceeded the 1929 level. At the same time the U.K. increased its share of the world export market between 1929 and 1933 from about 7% to 22%‖. This relative advance was short term but the 1930s did see a considerable increase in absolute exports. The growth between 1929 and 1933 was mainly at the expense of the U.S.A. whose vehicle exports fell from 537 000 in 1929 to 65 000 by 1932. By 1937, American exports had recovered to 395 000 which was still well below the peak achieved in 1929. The depression in the U.K. saw the imposition of a general tariff on imported goods in October 1931 which marked the end of 'free trade'. The establishment of a general tariff wall allowed the U.K. to develop more fully a policy of

* The Morris 15·9 h.p. 'Empire Car' a powerful, roomy car designed to travel over rough ground was such a model.
† Michael Sedgwick, Cars of the 1930s, Batsford, London, p. 250 (1970).
‡ The Motor Industry of Great Britain 1968 (SMMT Yearbook).
§ The Motor Industry of Great Britain 1938 (SMMT Yearbook).
‖ Motor Vehicles: A Report on the Industry, Political and Economic Planning, London, p. 78 (1950).

Imperial Preference compared with when only a narrow range of duties was used. In 1919 Imperial Preference of one-sixth of full duty was imposed on certain goods, widened in 1921, and culminated in the Import Duties Act of 1932. In 1932 the U.K. received tariff concessions from the Dominions and under the Ottawa agreements a full-blooded policy of Imperial Preference was instituted. This allowed British cars to compete more successfully with American models in markets such as Australia and New Zealand. In addition, from 1931 when the U.K. left the Gold Standard and 1933, when the dollar was devalued, U.K. exports benefited from the level of the sterling–dollar exchange*. This was true not only in U.K.–U.S. trade but also in the Sterling Area where the U.K. experienced an exchange rate advantage over the dollar. Also the fall in output to less than 50% of capacity in the U.S.A. increased production costs, probably by as much as 20%. Finally, the slump caused a decline in purchasing power in many car importing countries, and the general increase in tariffs and internal duties tended to favour smaller cars of lower initial value and lower running costs.

Before 1939 U.K. vehicle exports therefore flourished mainly within protected markets. In terms of value and physical units the bulk of shipments went to the Imperial Preference market†. As regards the European market, Eire was the most important, followed by Sweden and Denmark, two countries which granted preferential rates to British vehicles under commercial treaties made after 1932. Even given such tariff advantages, the U.K. only dominated the Eire and New Zealand markets. India and Australia, two of the U.K.'s main customers in the late 1930s, both bought largely from the U.S.A., as did Denmark and Sweden. In 1937 the largest world importer of cars was South Africa which did not grant preference to U.K. vehicles; as a result, the U.S.A. sold four-and-a-half times as many vehicles there as in the U.K. In Europe, Germany was the most important car supplier, the U.K.'s efforts being matched by those of the French.

In the inter-war period a smaller proportion of vehicle exports went to the Empire than in the case of cars. In value terms, 81% of car exports in 1929 and 1937 went to the Empire compared with 73% of commercial vehicles. This was largely explained by the fact that New Zealand, which took nearly one-quarter by value of the U.K.'s car exports, took only 7% by value of her commercial vehicles.

Domestic protection for the British car industry began in 1915

* Between 1925 and 1931 the dollar-pound rate was over $4·84 to the £. Between 1932 and 1939 it *tended* to be below this.
† 81% in 1937 in value terms.

when the McKenna duty of $33\frac{1}{3}\%$ *ad valorem* was imposed on cars and components. Originally this was not a protectionist device but an attempt to improve the balance of payments and save cargo space during World War I. Apart from an interval in 1924–1925, the duty was retained after 1918 as a protectionist device. In 1926 the duty was levied on commercial vehicles and vehicle parts for the first time. In 1931 the McKenna duty was abolished and consolidated into the general tariff structure still at $33\frac{1}{3}\%$. Now, however, the rate could be varied more easily if so required; but it was not until 1956 that the first rate reduction to 30% occurred, followed by another in 1962. In 1962 the rate on cars, buses and parts was $27\frac{3}{5}\%$ with a lower rate of 24% on commercial vehicles. In 1963 the former rate was reduced to $25\frac{1}{5}\%$, and by 1968 the rate was down to 22%. The Dillon Round of Tariff reductions between 1961 and 1968 was followed by the 'Kennedy Round'. Between 1968 and 1972 the general tariff on cars and parts was to be reduced to 11% but commercial vehicles would remain at 22%—not because of the U.K.'s policy, but as a result of the EEC's need to protect its CV makers from U.K. competition. The Commonwealth rate gave a preference of one-third, and since 1968 the EFTA rate was zero. As a result of this we can conclude that between 1918 and 1956 the British motor industry was a highly protected 'infant' industry. Between 1956 and 1968 it reached a position of greater maturity, and by 1972 its tariff protection would be more appropriate to that of a fully matured and efficient industry.

DIFFICULTIES, DOMINANCE AND DECLINE

THE WHEREWITHAL OF NATIONAL RECOVERY

The immediate post-war period was characterised by a policy of exports at all costs, in order to earn as much foreign exchange as possible. At the end of the war the British motor makers were faced with a huge world-wide demand for vehicles in a situation where few vehicles were to be found. The European producers had been more badly hit by the demands and ravages of war than the British; in Germany especially, many factories were in ruins or 'lost' in the Russian zone.

In the U.S.A. the post-war domestic boom in demand tended to absorb most of the vehicles produced, while the world-wide dollar shortage meant that most countries (the U.K. included) had no dollars to spare to buy cars. American cars were also too large for the European roads of the 1940s and their demands on the restricted supply of petrol, which was partly rationed in the U.K. until 1953, was too great. As a result at no time during the 1940s did U.S. car exports, despite the world-wide excess demand, reach the levels achieved in the middle and late 1920s. In contrast, U.S. CV exports reached record levels in 1947 and 1948; countries were prepared to free dollars to purchase essential capital items such as trucks which were needed for reconstruction, development, and the facilitating of trade generally.

The void left by the American car makers in a world where the demand for cars was unprecedented could only be filled by the U.K. in the short-run; producers feverishly tooled-up in order to try to meet this demand, in a situation where the only problems were on the supply side. The situation in the U.K. at the end of 1945 was one of general dislocation and shortage, and the motor car was seen not only as a thing of luxury and pleasure but the means by which the economy could be rebuilt. The car firms were no longer at the beck and call of fashion or economic recession, but were seen by policy makers as the wherewithal to economic recovery.

The all-out drive to produce cars for world markets meant that production was primary and quality secondary. During the period 1946–1956 the poor reputation gained by the British car industry, especially in Europe, as producers of second-rate and unreliable vehicles proved long-lived. Only in the late 1960s was the industry able to start erasing this reputation from the minds of overseas dealers and customers. The production rush also meant that labour relations became secondary. Attempts by firms to ignore labour's increasing power, crushing it when possible and giving in when this proved impossible, was not the way for firms to establish good labour relations. This meant problems in later years with domestic and foreign sales being thrown into chaos by the frequent production shortages caused by strikes. Finally, the Government's pressure on the car industry to export as much as they could meant that the volume of exports became the sole criterion by which to judge a firm's performance. As a result, no time or finance could be diverted from production to the establishment of first-class sales and service networks abroad in order to back-up and consolidate the volume of sales made.

Hence criticisms levelled at the motor industry concerning its failure to retain customers' good-will because of the inadequacies and poor quality of their sales and service side in overseas markets was not altogether fair. The industry was doing what the Government wanted between 1946 and 1956, that is, maximising short-run sales in order to earn foreign exchange. This was what the Government wanted, and consequently it pressurised the industry to export at all costs. If the industry became over extended or was unable to establish a sales network of sufficient quality the Government was as much to blame for this short-coming as was the car producer.

GOVERNMENT INDUCEMENTS TO EXPORT

Government pressure on the car industry to export was exercised through the establishment of annual export quotas per firm, which if not achieved would lead to a reduction in the steel quota allocated to the firm involved. In many ways this was unsatisfactory. It assumed that all exports were 'good' and home sales 'bad'. On economic grounds, however, a greater volume of cars and commercial vehicles directed to the home market may have increased domestic growth and generated even more exports. This was tacitly recognised as far as commercial vehicles were concerned, for despite being warned of the dire consequences concerning their steel quotas or by the introduction of direct government direction of sales if they did not export more*, their export quota policy was regarded as a failure†. Firms failing to meet quotas were not penalised as Governments were more afraid of being labelled 'unfair' or as being cast as the prime cause of a firm's labour force being thrown out of work.

Hence the reduction of steel quotas was never in practice used to force firms to export. Nevertheless, the threat appeared real to the firms at the time, especially to the car producers. This was because sheet steel was in shorter supply than any other type and car producers used proportionately more sheet steel than truck and bus producers in terms of the value of final product accounted for by sheet steel. As this was so the steel quota and the threatened supply restriction was more real in the case of car producers than in the case of truck and bus producers. Another point was that initial allocations were based on past, that is pre-war, export performances. As a result, if a particular firm was in an improved position as regards production techniques and marketing in 1945 as compared with 1939 this was ignored. Consequently some firms received larger allocations in 1945 than their commercial strength at the time justified, whereas others were under-endowed.

In the event, *actual* steel deliveries to firms bore little relation to

* *The Economist*, p. 157 (1949).
† C.A.R. Crosland, *Britain's Economic Problem*, Jonathan Cape, London, p. 38 (1953).

allocations, mainly because the competing demands for steel led to an overall economy-wide shortage. Because of raw material, power and labour supply difficulties, output of cars in the late 1940s never exceeded 65% of capacity and was often well below 50%. The shortage of sheet steel, which was particularly acute, tended to favour CV production at the expense of cars. Even so, the U.K. motor industry was much better off, both relatively and absolutely, than its Continental rivals. In 1947 the British industry was allocated 13% of available steel supplies as compared with $5\frac{1}{2}$% of a smaller steel output allocated to the French motor industry★. After 1952 matters began to improve; the steel shortage which had held production in check began to ease, bringing with it a change in Government policy, and fixed quotas for deliveries to the home market were replaced by a percentage of production quota. In 1953 this was abandoned, leaving the industry to find its own export level. The improved situation was further exemplified by the reduction in purchase tax from $66\frac{2}{3}$% to 50% in April 1953. Furthermore, in 1954 new productive capacity started to come into use.

Apart from problems caused by steel shortages and steel quotas, most firms after the war experienced problems in obtaining adequate supplies of machine tools. In 1947 delays ranged from twelve to eighteen months for basic machines, and two to three years for special purpose units. Traditionally the latter had been imported from the U.S.A., but the difficulties experienced in obtaining import licences caused problems. The production of special purpose machines in the U.S. in large numbers meant that U.K. firms could purchase them at relatively low prices. Many items, in order to circumvent the import licence problem, were produced in the U.K. for the first time† in the 1940s, although at an obvious cost disadvantage. Where machines were not built in the U.K., the only practical alternative was for a car firm to 'hand build' a piece of equipment even if this sometimes lacked the latest improvements. In view of the recognised contribution which the car industry could make to the balance of payments and to the reserves, it was obviously short-sighted to restrict the supply of crucial American-made machine tools or to limit too severely the industry's investment in machinery generally. Some equipment was available from Government surplus stock and nearly 15 000 machines had been acquired during the war, 83% of which was suitable for post-war use.

★ *Modern Transport* (22 May 1948).
† Often under U.S. licences, for example, all the huge body presses in the U.K. are made by Vickers under U.S. licences.

Despite many difficulties, some of which were to leave a long lived legacy of ill-will, the British motor industry in the immediate post-war period became export orientated. This was quite unlike the situation in the pre-war years. In the post-war period the industry was 'protected' by the fact that it was virtually the only alternative source of supply to the American motor industry, the latter being restricted in its overseas sales effort for various reasons. Consequently the post-war British market was starved of cars, with as much as 77% of production being sold abroad (*Table 11.1*).

Table 11.1

PERCENTAGE OF BRITISH CAR PRODUCTION EXPORTED

Year	%	Year	%
1946	38·5	1951	77·3
1947	49·0	1952	69·0
1948	67·0	1953	51·3
1949	62·4	1954	48·4
1950	76·1	1955	43·3

As the supply situation began to ease in the early 1950s the way should have been open to continued and increased dominance of the world's export markets by U.K. cars. However, as early as 1955 it was obvious that this was not going to occur. In 1950★ the U.K. was the world's largest car exporter, selling overseas three times as many cars as the U.S.A. and six times as many as Germany, but by 1956 Germany had overtaken Britain as regards both production and exports.

The export of British cars in 1955 was a near record at over 388 000. Despite the fact that the industry retained its position as the world's largest exporter there were, however, a number of ominous signs. The rapid growth of German exports evident since 1953 continued unabated. West German salesmen were particularly successful in Western Europe and the United States, both markets being of high growth potential. Various transport difficulties led to broken promises on the part of British suppliers concerning delivery dates. While the U.K. was a monopoly supplier this was not disastrous, but in 1955 new foreign competition in the shape of West Germany was ready to step in. In the middle of 1955 large import cuts occurred in Australia

★ The post-1949 period was influenced by devaluation in 1949.

and New Zealand; this was particularly serious as these were by far the industry's largest markets, taking one in six of all cars produced. Together with South Africa they were the only major car outlets in the Southern hemisphere, where the peak selling season came during the British winter and therefore helped to offset sales fluctuations in the northern half of the globe.

Up to 1954 the major car exporters served different areas. West Germany, Italy and France concentrated on Continental Europe, and France also supplied her colonies; the U.S.A. served the Americas; the U.K. concentrated on the Commonwealth and made good sales to the U.S.A. and Europe. As West Germany re-entered trade from 1950 and Italy and France recovered, the European market grew sufficiently to allow each others sales to expand without harming the exports of its rivals. However, in 1955 West Germany began a vigorous sales campaign on a world wide basis, in many instances at the U.K.'s expense. In Europe the U.K. lost ground to Germany, who also sold more cars in the U.S.A. in 1955 than did the British. Further German headway was made in Asian and African Commonwealth countries as well as in New Zealand and Australia. As a result Germany displaced the U.S.A. as the world's second largest exporter, and then promptly displaced the U.K. from first place in 1956. The German efforts to export were prompted by similar reasons as were the British; the need to earn foreign exchange in order to foster economic recovery. In some ways the German task was easier in that their car producers did not have to contend with the same high degree of domestic excess demand as the British. Up to the mid-1950s the British producer could take comfort in the fact that his home market was potentially considerably larger than the German. In effect after 1955 the domestic sale of German cars exceeded that of the British but this still did not mean that the effective demand for cars in the U.K. had become less. For one thing, excess demand in the U.K. in the mid-1950s was still a feature, and secondly much of the German demand was for small cheap 'Bubble' cars. In terms of vehicles measured by a standard unit, domestic demand in the U.K. was higher than in Germany until the first years of the 1960s. By 1956 the penetration of the working class market by British car makers was well under way, whereas this process had not yet begun in West Germany. Consequently the growth of the German industry depended more on exports than did the British over the decade 1950–1960.

The U.K.'s share of the world export market in cars in 1950 was 54·6%; this had declined to 33% by 1955, and to 30% by 1957. The U.K. continued to lose ground during the rest of the decade, with the export share falling to under 20% by 1961. Between 1955 and 1961 West Germany's share increased from just over 30% to 43·4%. During the period 1961–1965 the U.K.'s share remained fairly constant at around 20%, but in the latter part of the decade it fell from just under 20% in 1965 to 15·7% in 1968. The position since 1964 is summarised in *Table 11.2*.

Table 11.2

PERCENTAGE SHARE OF CAR EXPORTS BY LEADING PRODUCING COUNTRIES

Country	1959	1964	1965	1966	1967	1968	1970
U.K.	26·1	21·7	19·9	17·1	15·6	15·7	13·4
France	23·7	14·2	15·5	15·3	17·0	14·6	18·2
W. Germany	33·9	43·4	45·5	45·1	41·9	41·9	34·5
Italy	10·0	10·0	9·8	11·4	12·5	13·0	11·5
Sweden	2·0	2·3	2·7	3·2	3·8	3·2	3·3
Japan	0·2	2·2	3·2	4·7	6·9	9·4	13·9
U.S.A./Canada	4·1	6·2	3·4	3·2	2·3	2·2	5·2
Total (%)	100	100	100	100	100	100	100
Total (1000s)	2 178	3 124	3 150	3 269	3 226	4 304	5 578

Sources: NEDO Data Book, *Motor Industry Statistics 1959–1968* and SMMT.

Between 1959 and 1964 the growth in world trade in cars was almost 50%, then between 1964 and 1967 trade virtually stagnated, only to increase rapidly again in 1968. Since 1956 West Germany has been the leading exporter, tending to account for nearly two-fifths of all exports. It is only fair to point out that German exports are highly skewed to one model in one market. Of total German exports of 1 802 000 in 1968, almost one million units were accounted for by the export of the Volkswagen Beetle, 570 000 of which were sold in the U.S.A. This fact in no way suggests that the German export performance is spurious or a statistical freak; the fact of the matter is simply that VW is able to find export markets for almost 70% of its output which is of overall benefit to the West German export drive. If the U.K., or France, or any other country, could come up with a product which was as easily marketable abroad then everyone would be delighted. Obviously the fact that Bedford exports around 70% of output in no way detracts from the significance of the U.K.'s figure for CV exports. In one way however the fantastic success of the VW Beetle in export markets is a source of weakness. If the foreign customer, and especially the American one, should turn against the Beetle, then the heavy weight of this model in total German exports would lead to a serious fall in total German exports and in their share of world car trade. If the VW effort in the U.S.A. is subtracted from the total German picture, Germany's share of world exports in 1967 and 1968 fall to 26% and 30% respectively. Although such a reduction is significant it still leaves West Germany clearly ahead of the field. Apart from 1967 and 1970 Britain had retained second place in the world export league although her market share had fallen while those of West Germany, Italy, and Japan had increased. In fact, the latter part of the 1960s had seen the market shares of both the U.K. and West Germany fall in the face of an extremely vigorous export drive on the part of Italy and Japan. If present trends continue it is evident that whereas 1946–1953 was the British period of export dominance, and 1954–1970 the West German, the next decade will belong to Italy and Japan as they erode the market shares held by the present leaders.

In terms of the percentage of British car output exported, the freak figures for the late 1940s and early 1950s tended to decline, reaching 44% in 1962 and a post-war low of 32% in 1967. By 1969, due to the continued domestic squeeze and the devaluation-led export boom*, provisional estimates put the export percentage as being in excess of 45%. The export position in the main car producing countries in 1969 is shown in *Table 11.3*.

Table 11.3

PERCENTAGE OF CAR PRODUCTION
EXPORTED (1969)

Country	%
U.S.A.	4·0
France	35·0
Italy	37·0
West Germany	62·0
Japan	22·0

The American motor industry exported over 330 000 vehicles in 1968, but such is the huge production volume on the one hand, and the general unsuitability of traditional American cars in export markets on the other, that the export percentage is very low. France's present total production and exports are very similar to the U.K.'s, whereas West Germany's total output and export percentage is considerably greater. Hence the fact that in 1968 Germany's car exports were almost three times those of the U.K. Italy's total production still tends to be

* In November 1967.

lower than the U.K.'s, but the gap during the late 1960s tended to
close rapidly. Japan's total production exceeded the U.K.'s but as the
industry's export drive was still in its infancy the difference between
the two countries' export percentages was relatively greater than the
difference between their production totals (*Table 11.4*).

Table 11.4

CAR PRODUCTION AND EXPORTS IN 1968 (1000s)

Country	Production	Exports	%
U.K.	1 816	677	37
U.S.A.	8 849	330	3·7
France	1 833	629	34
Italy	1 545	558	36
West Germany	2 862	1 786	62
Japan	2 056	406	20

So although the U.K.'s relative export position changed significantly
during the post-war period, apart from West Germany and its Volkswagen, the U.K. continued to hold its own in foreign markets.
Obviously in a very competitive trade new threats and new changes
in world market shares were to be expected. However, the U.K.
should be able to retain its position in the face of new competition,
whereas obviously it could not have been expected to do so after
1950 when room had to be found for new competitors. In 1971 the
situation was such that the main sufferer could be West Germany as it
had so much more to lose. If, however, the Germans, by exploring
new markets and introducing new products, were able to maintain
their position, and the U.K.'s position was further eroded, then one
could only conclude that the U.K. was less efficient than it should have
been.

THE PATTERN OF EXPORTS

THE QUEST FOR NEW MARKETS

The changing pattern of car exports since 1946 has been as drastic as
the change in the U.K.'s relative share of world exports. The industry
has faced three major changes in the direction of exports since 1946.
Between 1947 and 1956 the major market was Australia and New
Zealand. The sharp reduction in total exports, the export ratio, and

the share of world markets, which occurred in 1952 was partly due to larger deliveries to the home market and the rise of German competition, but was mainly due to import restrictions in the crucial Australian market in late 1951. At the end of 1955 the recovery in total exports, which was mainly due to the recovery of the Australian and New Zealand market was again halted in its tracks when total sales to New Zealand and Australia were halved in 1956. This was a result of the growth in the Australian car industry, which had been aided by a severe quota restriction imposed to discourage imports, and a rise in the sales tax. Manufacturers had to come to terms with the situation where direct sales to Australia would be more and more difficult, and could only be offset by expanding their Australian plants from assembly shops to centres for the manufacture of cars, parts, and components. In 1956 it was obvious that new markets had to be found quickly.

The obvious target was the American market, especially that for second cars. Exports to the U.S.A. increased from 74 000 in 1956 to 310 000 in 1959, British cars capturing almost 50% of the imported car market and displacing Germany from first place. This assault provoked a reaction by Detroit and American firms countered by producing compact cars to meet the challenge of European small cars. The smaller American firms attempting to find new market niches away from the 'style-change' competition of the Big Three (GMC, Ford and Chrysler) were the first to produce compacts; AMC's Rambler and Studebaker's Lark appeared early in 1959. In 1959 the U.K.'s share of American imports was 31·2% and in 1960 the figure was 28·6%, but by 1961 this was down to only 10·5%. After 1959 VW made great inroads into the British market in the U.S.A., and by the mid-1960s controlled over 80% of the American foreign car market. In absolute terms, U.K. sales to the U.S.A. in 1960 were 135 000 and only 30 500 in 1961. Although the U.K. position in the U.S.A. had tended to recover after 1961 with exports reaching over 97 000 in 1968, the industry had not been able to match its successes of the late 1950s in this market. In some ways the industry's failure to match its former American export performance—and therefore its dependence on the American market—was a good thing. Any new move on the part of the American car industry to counter imports would not be very harmful to the British industry when less than 12% of all car exports were sold in this market*. The appearance of new sub-compact and even smaller 'European-size' cars in 1969 and 1970 may have the same

* Although in value terms one fifth of all exports are sold in the U.S.A.

impact on importers as the 1959 compacts, even if the downturn is not so sudden and dramatic as in 1959.

Since the debacle of 1959 the British motor industry has turned increasingly to European markets and by 1971 they displayed the most vigorous growth. The creation of EFTA in 1960 which gradually led to the removal of all tariffs on industrial goods* in 1968 had been beneficial, but sales to the EEC had also increased substantially despite the common external tariff which put the British motor industry at a competitive disadvantage. Between 1959 and 1960 exports to Europe increased from 100 000 cars to almost 250 000, but between 1960 and 1961 a decline to just over 110 000 reinforced the disaster in the U.S. market. After 1961, however, the European market has been the scene of the British motor industry's main export drive (*Table 11.5*).

Table 11.5

MAIN BRITISH EXPORT MARKETS IN 1968

Country	Numerical value	Monetary value (£ million)	(%)	(1959 value) (£ million)	(%)
U.S.A.	97 069	58·8	21·0	86·7	39·0
Canada	43 354	21·5	7·7	31·7	14·2
EFTA	134 000*	52·8	18·9	17·0	7·6
EEC	145 000†	44·7	15·9	13·6	6·1
Australia	51 717	14·9	5·3	12·2	5·5
New Zealand	27 079	10·6	3·8	7·3	3·3
South Africa	35 685	12·9	4·6	9·3	4·2
Others	143 096	63·9	22·8	44·7	20·1
Totals	677 000	280·1	100·0	222·5	100·0

* Switzerland, Denmark and Irish Republic *only*.
† Belgium and France *only*.

By the end of the 1960s the pattern of U.K. exports was superior to that of previous years. Up to 1956 the effort was concentrated on two countries, and from 1956 to 1959 on just one. This specialisation by market made the industry vulnerable to fluctuations in those markets. By the end of the sixties, although Europe was the largest market this was in turn split into two main blocks, EFTA and EEC, and these in turn covered 13 full members. Presumably as integration in the EEC continued, the economic conditions in one country would be reflected elsewhere, but this was not necessarily so. Increased integra-

* Sometimes replaced by 'Revenue Raising' as distinct from 'Protective' duties however.

tion will probably see different areas expanding at different rates so that 'regional' development will emerge. So a downturn in demand in France will not necessarily mean a fall in German demand, even when the EEC is fully integrated. Community-wide decisions on activity and tariffs would, however, be more serious. Even then the European market is not dominant in the way that the American or Australian markets were. Hence the 'spreading of risks' should allow exports to develop gradually without the tremendous booms and slumps in exports which were provoked by changed conditions in overseas markets in the past.

COMPETITION IN WORLD MARKETS

FACTORS AFFECTING BRITISH COMPETITIVENESS

Now a brief word concerning why the U.K.'s export position in the world's car markets has commonly been regarded as one of decline. With a share of the world market equivalent to 54·6% in 1950 when other European countries had hardly begun to trade, it was inevitable that once new entrants appeared the U.K.'s market share would have to fall. What was not inevitable was the extent of the decline and the way the U.K. was overhauled so quickly by West Germany. Part of the answer lies in the rapid, almost too rapid, growth of the motor industry's car export market between 1946 and 1951. This 'production race' left little time either to control quality or establish sales and service networks which would back-up the original sales and therefore retain most of the new business. Instead a whole host of dissatisfied customers appeared and the reputation of British cars became one of poor quality, poor design, and poor service. Consequently many existing buyers of British cars, and people buying cars or imported cars for the first time, switched their allegiance to other products. As we have suggested earlier, the motor industry was not entirely to blame for this state of affairs, being the victim of the Crippsian 'export at all costs' policy.

Another reason for the relative and sometimes absolute decline in the export performance was due to the market specialisation of the British industry. First the Australia-New Zealand market and then the American-Canadian market became dominant. In the early 1950s the first market took almost 40% of all car exports whereas the latter in 1959 accounted for almost 55% of total car exports. Consequently any factor adversely affecting the U.K.'s sales in these markets would severely harm the total export drive. Having all the eggs in one basket proved disastrous both in 1956 and 1959.

Greater economic nationalism through protection and trade discrimination tended to hit the British industry's overseas sales efforts, particularly as exports were so narrowly based. At the end of the 1940s the Commonwealth market took over 60% of all car exports but during the 1950s many of these markets became virtually closed to direct exports, either because of tariffs—as in the case of Australia, or quotas—as in the case of India and Ceylon. As the decade progressed the direct import of cars into many markets was totally prohibited. So as tariff barriers were replaced by quotas, import licences, and other physical controls, the importance of Imperial Preference declined, even if the U.K. was sometimes given favourable treatment where quotas were concerned.

It is also true that the British family-car of the 1950s was technically conventional and unexciting. This was in marked contrast to the Volkswagen from Germany or the Fiat from Italy. Renault also introduced new ideas, although the poor quality of some of their cars led to a decline in overseas sales during the 1950s and early 1960s.

The reliability and low maintenance costs of the VW made it a good seller in all types of market including the U.S.A. In America sales were made to second-car owners and to people on lower incomes unable to afford the running costs of a new American car. In contrast to popular mythology, large VW sales came before the establishment of a large sales and service network, especially in the U.S.A. In the U.S.A. when the sales volume was noted the VW franchise became a valuable asset and the German firm was able to pick and choose from the best. Many other importers, including the British, often tended to pick up 'the dregs' or had to work through non-exclusive outlets. As VW sales increased further so the sales franchise became even more lucrative; hence initial sales followed by the establishment of a first-class sales and service network led to further export growth.

As the U.K. was the only non-American source of cars in the early post-war period, the sellers' market provoked a state of mind where it became accepted practice for the buyer to come to the seller. The new conditions of the mid-1950s, where firms could no longer sit back and expect buyers to come knocking at their doors, required a new sales approach. However, this was not appreciated soon enough and in fact it was only by about 1970 that the British marketing effort in scope and attitude, was beginning to rival that of its competitors. The 'Workshop of the World' mentality where the U.K. was the only source of supply conditioned the 'production orientated' firms to operate without an efficient marketing side.

Further problems during the 1960s were caused by the over-valuation of sterling*. Attempts to sell in third-markets in competition with other countries, some of whose currencies were undervalued, meant that profit margins to both the producer and to the dealer had to be reduced if prices were to remain competitive. This meant that the U.K. car producers' franchise was less prized both on grounds of profit margins and in terms of total turnover. If we accept the view that the 1960s saw a technical revolution in U.K. car design and the late 1960s an awareness that the marketing department was as important as those concerned with production, then one of the main constraints on successful exporting was the overvaluation of sterling. The devaluation of sterling in 1967 and the revaluation of the West German Deutschmark in 1969 tended to correct this fundamental imbalance. The devaluation of sterling was taken as an opportunity not so much to reduce export prices but to improve profit margins for both dealer and manufacturer. As a result dealers would be more prepared to put considerable effort and capital into marketing British cars.

The importance of overvalued and undervalued currencies is easily shown. Let us assume that the exchange rate is two Deutschmarks to one pound sterling. In Germany and the U.K. identical cars are made but because their colours differ trade occurs. In Germany, due to lower money costs, but the same real costs as in the U.K., the car costs £500 or 1000 Deutschmarks to make but in the U.K. it costs £600 or 1200 Deutschmarks to make. Assuming no tariffs or transport costs the German car is sold in the U.K. for a competitive price of £600 or 1200 DM and 'excess' profits of 200 DM are made. The U.K. car is sold in Germany for 1000 DM, or a loss of £100. So for the Germans 'exporting is fun' but for the U.K. firm, due to the general price level being too high—which means that sterling is overvalued—exports are expensive. From this the U.K. producer, unlike his German competitor, says that he needs a solid home market in order to bring costs down to a minimum; but if the basic problem is one where the British long-run average cost curve measured in terms of sterling is higher than the German the latter does not need a solid home market (*Figure 11.1*).

German costs at 50% of capacity equal the U.K.'s at 100%. At 100% of capacity German costs are lower than those in the U.K. by

* In turn caused by inflationary pressures and also by basic inefficiencies in the U.K. economy.

Figure 11.1

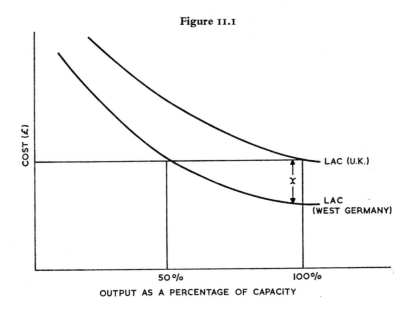

amount *x*. Here we assume that both firms are equally efficient and the cost differences are caused by higher capital and labour costs in the U.K. due to higher rates of inflation in the past. A devaluation of the £ or a revaluation of the DM so that 1·66 DM = £1 would equalise the long run average costs in both markets. So in terms of price or profits, devaluation was necessary for the U.K. car firms to compete with their German rivals, for little evidence of great differences in German or British productivity in the car plants is now evident*. In the mid-1960s this was not so, for instance in 1966 the number of cars produced per man per year at BMC, Ford, Vauxhall, and VW, was 8·5, 9·7, 10·6 and 16·0 respectively! As wage rates were not commensurate with these differences, unit costs (because of greater efficiency) were lower in Germany. So much for the possible reasons for the relative decline of U.K. car exports. Now would be a good point to turn to a discussion of competition in export markets.

Turnover taxes and Value Added Taxes in France, Germany and Italy have worked as an export incentive, for on export sales previously paid tax is refunded. For instance, VAT is paid on all home market sales less purchases of goods and services from registered suppliers. This avoids the double taxation which exists with a straight turnover

* Although as shown in the previous chapters, some differences still existed in 1970–1971.

tax. Each firm pays VAT only on the value added by itself or on purchases from overseas. When a firm exports it would not pay VAT on that sale, and is in fact 'rebated' with the VAT that its suppliers had paid on components and materials that finish up in the export good. VAT is claimed back on the total value of the export, not just on the value added by the exporter. This rebate goes wholly to the final exporter and can therefore act as an export incentive. Sweden and France have traditionally used the VAT system whereas Germany replaced its 'cascade' turnover tax by a VAT in 1968. The U.K. purchase tax levied at the wholesale stage cannot be rebated to the manufacturer of the item exported. Hence no export incentive is built into the tax system.

PRICING POLICIES

Due to the larger number of competitors and perhaps a lower degree of customer loyalty for imports, the degree of competition in export markets tends to be greater than in a producer's domestic market. Over the relevant ranges both demand and supply curves are more elastic in foreign markets than at home. The combination of a high degree of competition plus the sale of a large proportion of a firm's output in a protected home market, leads to more active short-run price competition in export markets than is usual in the home market. All firms engaged in international competition engage in price discrimination between home and export markets. In many instances export prices are below full average costs at scheduled capacity. This is evident when import duties and local taxes on car sales are deducted from the foreign retail price, and the higher selling, distribution, and administration costs, incurred abroad are added to full costs. Other costs include modifications to the product to suit local needs, the extra capital tied-up in extra stocks and the extended credit given in view of the longer time scale involved in delivery. In some markets at certain times, export sales are made at prices below marginal costs. Clearly this should not occur even in the short run if profits are to be maximised and should certainly lead to changes in long-run policy. However, if in the long-run prices covered marginal cost but failed to cover average costs, firms still tend to be reluctant to abandon export markets. It is possible that a firm taking a long-term view expects profits to be made eventually, or if local manufacture is contemplated then initial sales will serve to bring a firm's products to the attention of both potential customers and the local government which may control the number of local plants allowed; or the home government may impose sanctions if a firm's exports are not maintained.

The prices at which export sales can be made tend to be determined by the degree of international competition and not by a firm's own costs. These prices vary from market to market depending on its size, importance, and the degree of competition met locally. Generally they are below home market prices especially when additional export costs are included[*]. As we said in an earlier chapter, 84% of ex-works costs at scheduled output are variable. So if a firm is to make some contribution to overheads, prices must not fall below 84% of average costs at scheduled output volumes. If they do, then home sales subsidise exports and the domestic consumer is worse off as domestic prices are set so that total costs including profits equal total revenue. If cars sold abroad cover variable costs then at least some contribution to fixed costs is made. Therefore domestic prices can be that much lower compared with the situation where no export sales were made at all (always supposing that exports are not made at the expense of domestic sales).

Clearly prices set by the state of demand rather than by costs need not be harmful. If we remember that home market prices are always set above average costs (excluding profits) at scheduled output, and then allow for import duties and local taxes abroad it would seem that most export prices are above marginal cost. However, this is by no means universally so. For instance, it was reported[†] that many importers into the U.K. no longer set U.K. prices on the basis of manufacturing costs plus duty, transport and tax, but selected prices which were closely equivalent to the nearest U.K. car. There was nothing new in this but then it was stated that in some instances this meant reducing the cost-based price by some 15–20%. So if foreign massproducers had the same cost structure as the British, and indeed evidence suggested that at standard output their fixed cost proportion of total ex-works costs was as low as 10–12%, then prices were below marginal cost. If marginal cost was inflated by variable transport and selling costs then this was almost certainly the case. This policy was followed in order to build up U.K. sales and to establish a strong dealer network in advance of the time when tariffs between the U.K. and EEC disappeared. It was more than likely that some U.K. firms had followed a similar policy in sales to the EEC. Some actual examples are shown in *Table 11.6*.

[*] *The Effect of Government Economic Policy on the Motor Industry*, NEDO, p. 35 (1968).
[†] *Financial Times*, p. 17 (11 February 1970).

Table 11.6

CAR PRICES IN SELECTED MARKETS IN 1966 (£)*

Model	Home market	U.S.A.	Switzerland	Japan	France
U.K.					
Mini	515	526 (102%)	490 (95%)	887 (172%)	639 (124%)
Cortina	648	526 (81%)	535 (96%)	—	532 (96%)
Viva	579	—	569 (98%)	1 118 (172%)	575 (99%)
France					
Citroen DS21	1 243	1 327 (107%)	1 450 (117%)	2 770 (223%)	—
Renault 10	571	699 (122%)	619 (108%)	1 138 (199%)	—
Germany					
VW 1300	466	568 (123%)	561 (122%)	964 (210%)	508 (110%)
Opel Kadett	478	594 (124%)	581 (122%)	—	564 (118%)
Others					
Mustang (U.S.A.)	1 027		1 487 (172%)	2 750 (319%)	2 209 (215%)
Volvo (Sweden)	1 252	955 (76%)	1 013 (81%)	1 484 (119%)	1 222 (98%)
Toyota (Japan)	558	670 (120%)	—	—	596 (33%)
Moskvitch (U.S.S.R.)	1 786	—	636 (36%)	—	
Alfa Romeo (Italy)	1 310	1 900 (145%)	1 404 (107%)	2 285 (174%)	1 506 (115%)
Fiat 600 (Italy)	368	451 (122%)	445 (121%)	—	410 (111%)

Adapted from: *The Economist*, (p. 30. 9 July 1966,) * Prices include duties and taxes. The percentage of the home retail price is shown in parenthesis.

Pricing policy abroad depends on three main points: the acceptability of the product in a market, the urgency with which firms need to make sales and the degree of domestic protection. Firms such as Alfa Romeo, for instance, can charge relatively more for their products as their overseas customers are not influenced by price alone. In the case of Ford, Renault, or Moskvitch, the product is not unusual therefore competition with the home based product must be on a price basis. Given local sales and excise duties plus transport costs, this often means a degree of price cutting when the wholesale prices net of all duties at home and abroad are compared. Secondly, if a country really needs foreign exchange, as does the U.S.S.R., then foreign sales will be made at any price. Even if the profit margin on home sales was 100% the Moskvitch was clearly being 'dumped' abroad at below marginal cost. Finally and crucially, the degree of home protection determines the amount of overheads a firm can load onto domestic sales. If protection is great then most overheads are covered by domestic prices, and if dumping occurs home sales have to cover the difference between price and the marginal cost of exports. Clearly a protected home market allows a firm to be very competitive abroad. The smaller the degree of protection the closer must become the home and foreign wholesale prices. On the one hand excess domestic margins over marginal costs would leave a firm open to being undercut, and on the other the smaller the surplus over marginal cost earned domestically the higher the level of overhead recovery that must be earned abroad if the firm is to be profitable.

From *Table 11.6* we can deduce that abroad British and Continental cars were broadly comparable in price in third markets such as the U.S.A. and Switzerland, indeed, British prices tended to be somewhat lower type for type. In Switzerland the Opel was undercut by the almost identical Viva, and both the Viva and Cortina considerably undercut the Renault 10. If prices are taken as a guide to comparative production costs then it would appear that British cars are at no disadvantage compared with their Continental rivals. However, no such conclusion can be made from the data involved. We have already said that export prices are set to compete with those of one's rivals and are not determined by costs. Obviously export prices therefore need not reflect costs if one country's producer decides to follow the price leadership of another, or if different firms recoup more overheads in one market than in another. Clearly British Ford was pricing the Cortina to engage in short-run price competition with its rivals in order to build-up export markets. In the U.S.A. the relative prices between the Cortina and the Mini bore no relationship to their relative prices in the U.K., nor presumably to their relative production costs if domestic prices were largely governed by average total costs per unit at scheduled output. The extent to which the Cortina undercut the Kadett, Renault 10 and Volkswagen 1300, in Switzerland was partly due to EFTA preferences but mainly a result of short-run price competition. This was especially so when one noted that the Cortina was almost £70 more expensive than the Viva in the U.K. but almost £35 less in Switzerland. Comparing home-market prices may be more fruitful if we look at the wholesale price of broadly similar cars (*Table 11.7*).

From the table it would appear that the firms involved had somewhat dissimilar cost structures, with the German firms' costs being perhaps

Table 11.7

Model	Estimated ex-works price in the home country	U.S.A.	France	Percentage of price in France to home price
Cortina	£432	£374	£315	75·2
Viva	£387	—	£334	86·2
Mini	£358	£374	£370	103·0
Renault	£388	£498	—	—
VW 1300	£350	£400	£340	97·0
Opel Kadett	£357	£423	£373	105·0
Fiat 600	£256	£297	£270	105·4

the lowest. (Although if we take the effects of the British devaluation and the German revaluation, into account then German prices increase to around £420.)

In addition, the examples utilised show that the wholesale prices in export markets are often lower than domestically. In the case of the Cortina the difference is quite remarkable. The U.K. firms had to lower prices more than the German or Italian in order to counteract the discriminating effect of the tariff reductions within the EEC. However, even the German and Italian firms sold at ex-works prices below those prevailing at home. It may have been that the Cortina was being sold at less than marginal cost although the Viva appeared to be covering variable costs as of course was the Mini.

This clearly was only a tiny sample of cars in just two export markets and therefore no general rule could be deduced. All one could say was that wholesale prices in foreign markets may well have been below those in the domestic market but this was not necessarily so, even where the highly competitive market for mass produced cars was involved. Also export sales may sometimes have been made at prices below marginal cost, especially when a firm was engaged on a vigorous export drive.

The creation of trading blocks and the removal of tariff barriers within those blocks had increased export difficulties for a firm which was outside the block, and increased a firm's opportunities when it was inside. Although the U.K. had increased its EFTA car trade, the trade creation within the EEC car market had been greater than in the case of EFTA. In addition, the growth in incomes within the EEC plus a concerted sales drive, helped by devaluation and the Kennedy Round of tariff reductions, had increased the U.K.'s car exports to the EEC.

This was at a time when the tariffs within the EEC had been gradually reduced to zero (*Table 11.8*).

Table 11.8

	1964	1968
EFTA	104 100	118 100
EEC	115 800	144 700
All	672 500	676 500

So at a time of general export stagnation the U.K.'s European export drive especially to the EEC had been very marked. This major shift towards tackling the EEC market had been accompanied by a market push in unexplored areas. This change of markets had increased the sales of components, many were in kits for car assembly within the EEC. The British industry's assembly plants in Holland and Belgium have been expanded in order that U.K. cars would escape some of the penalties imposed by the common external tariff.

Increased competition could also come from the new generation of American small cars. Whereas the traditional American car did not have suitable roadholding for much less than perfect road conditions and was expensive to run, European cars had quite the opposite characteristics, offering economy and good performance and road-holding. A car like the VW size AMC Gremlin priced at £770, or the Ford Pinto costing under £800, could prove to be the start of a new export drive direct from the American car factories. The scope for price cutting may be small, however, due to the high wage structure in Detroit leaving little over for profits on a car of £800 which costs as much in labour charges to build as a car of £1200 or more. This and the low degree of protection in the American market meant that overheads had to be allocated evenly if profitable volumes were to be sold. Even so the American motor industry may become a new factor in the highly competitive export market for cars.

Over the last decade it would appear that, given the overall imbalance in domestic costs in the U.K. which caused the overvaluation of sterling, U.K. car firms had only been able to compete in the highly competitive car trade by cutting prices more than their competitors. In other words, to compete on price while having a higher level of costs inevitably meant a reduction in profits. This was at a time when the squeeze on domestic demand had reduced total output to a level which increased total unit costs by 2%. This was extremely serious if, for instance, overall profit margins were as low as 5% per unit. As a result of all these pressures, Continental car firms had shown a much higher rate of return on capital than the British producers. This gave them a larger cushion against which to cut prices in new overseas markets (*Table 11.9*).

Table 11.9

RETURN ON CAPITAL BEFORE TAX (1967)

Firm	Return (%)		(1961)
Fiat	10·7		
BMW	11·7 ⎫		
Daimler-Benz	10·6 ⎬ German Firms		9·5%
VW	10·0 ⎭		
Peugeot	10·5		
Seven U.K. Car Firms	1·8	U.K. Firms	12·6%

Following devaluation in 1967 and a round of domestic car-price increases in 1967–1968 both the foreign and domestic business of British car firms was put on a more profitable footing, with the result that in 1968 the net return on capital for the industry's main firms increased to 10·4%—commensurate with that of the industry's main European competitors. However, between 1969 and 1970 only Ford of the British producers made significant profits, BLMC did little better than break-even, and Vauxhall and Rootes made losses.

Other forms of competition as well as price competition are used, and used rather more aggressively than in the domestic market. For instance advertising 'knocking the opposition' had long been a feature of export sales techniques. Turning now from the positive side of competition to attempts to restrict the sale of foreign cars.

RESTRAINTS ON TRADE

Normal trade restrictions such as prohibitive tariffs, import quotas, and licences, are a feature of such policies. Other less obvious methods are used such as the system whereby a purchaser of a foreign car could only obtain inferior or non-existent credit arrangements, a system much beloved by the Japanese authorities in the 1960s. The establishment of various 'custom and use' regulations, safety and pollution ordinances can be used which would require expensive modifications to be made to imported models. It could be that the numbers sold would not justify the cost of trying to meet these regulations and the market would be effectively closed to many producers. Taxes based on size, horse-power, or even country of origin, can discriminate in favour of some car firms and against others. The most blatant restrictions on foreign sales are trade controls, either tariff or physical. Physical controls could take the form of quotas which are given to certain countries or to certain manufacturers; in some instances zero import quotas have been introduced*. On other occasions quotas are used in conjunction with tariffs. In Australia† importers could bring in 7500 units of a particular model but beyond that level the import tariff increased sharply. If however the firm involved is producing cars of 85% local content then the tariff on imported parts was very small. Many countries wishing to establish their own motor industry used variants of this system. Shrewd importers nevertheless could circumvent some of these schemes. In Australia the Japanese have often imported 7500 units of a model then altered the specifications very slightly and then called it a separate model. This has allowed efficiently made imports to enter the market in large numbers, and to undercut the models produced by low volume but high cost firms that have agreed to establish expensive manufacturing arrangements in Australia. Some trade, especially with Eastern Europe, is conducted on a bilateral basis with quotas for U.K. cars being given in exchange for a British quota on say a Czech or Rumanian product. No free system of vehicle import by the final customer buying from the producer exists. In some instances where quotas are removed tariffs are at such high levels as to preclude foreign makers from a particular market. In Japan from 1953 to 1960 the tariff on cars was 40%, reinforced by quota and other restrictions. In the 1960s quotas were abolished, but tariffs remained at between 35% and 40% depending on the wheelbase of the car. The Kennedy Round reduced the Japanese tariff on small and medium cars from 36% in 1968 to 30% in 1972, and from 28% to 17·5% for larger models. Where the main trading nations are concerned trade is becoming freer. Within EFTA and EEC tariffs are zero while the Kennedy round is reducing tariff protection on cars, by as much as 50% in the case of the EEC and U.K. Countries with existing low tariff barriers such as the U.S.A. and Sweden are introducing smaller reductions, as are the less developed European nations.

Although the previously mentioned VAT is levied at manufacturing stages as well as at the final retail stage cars manufactured in other countries (i.e. imported) do not escape this tax. In other words, the

* As in Ceylon in the 1960s, for instance.
† *The Times*, Business News (13 January 1970).

effect of the common external tariff is not offset by U.K. firms avoiding local taxation. In West Germany for instance an Import Turnover tax is levied on the duty-inflated price of imports at a rate of 11% which is the same as the domestic VAT. Similar special or additional taxes are levied on imports by all EEC countries* insuring that foreign cars carry the same internal tax burden as home produced units. Because many of these countries operate a VAT system their exporters are favourably placed because of the export rebate, compared with countries with purchase-taxes levied at wholesale or retail stages only.

THE RELATIONSHIP BETWEEN THE HOME AND EXPORT MARKETS

Turning now to the relationship between domestic demand and the car industry's export performance. In general terms the factors affecting export demand are: the levels of demand for cars in overseas markets; the availability of capacity to meet demand; the relative profitability of home and export sales; and the efficiency or competitive strength of the motor industry in relation to its export rivals which include competition by price, design, marketing, and sales and service networks.

OVERSEAS DEMAND

Overseas demand is affected by basic factors such as the economic climate or growth in incomes, and by structural factors such as the protection of a market to develop a domestic industry, the emergence of new domestic competition, and the shift in domestic demand to or from imported models. Changes in overseas aggregate demand are basically independent of the state of the domestic market except where the overseas country is dependent on exports to the domestic country for much of its income. However, a structural fall in the demand for U.K. exports in an important market could be due to neglecting the type of product required, or to a failure to improve the sales network due to too much attention being paid to the requirements of the home market.

* Many of the systems used being highly technical and detailed.

CAPACITY FOR EXPORTS

When considering the availability of capacity for exports it is implied that restriction of domestic demand will divert production abroad. If this means that the home market had been satisfied at the expense of exports, because total demand is greater than supply and exports have been sacrificed to home sales, then it does not square with the facts. In no year during the 1960s did output approach the limits set by standard capacity (*Table 11.10*).

Table 11.10

CAR OUTPUT AS A PERCENTAGE OF CAPACITY*

1960	1963	1965	1967
93%	83%	78%	64%

* BMC, Ford, Vauxhall, Rootes, Standard-Triumph, Jaguar and Rover.

The nearest approach to full capacity* was in 1960 when ample spare capacity still existed. Obviously, though temporary shortages for certain models can be a usual occurrence, this is often caused by a labour shortage in relation to plant capacity and also by instances of excess demand at the capacity output for a particular model. Due to common components being used a shortage of a particular model cannot always be divorced from a capacity constraint on the production of particular items such as body panels, engines or gearboxes. However, 100% capacity is taken to mean normal plant operation*, so overtime or extra shifts could increase output in the short run even if it meant increasing short-run marginal and average cost. So this allied to the fact that absolute capacity utilisation is well below the maximum has meant no long term shortages for any models, except perhaps for Jaguars.

On the other hand, the restriction of home demand would force a firm if it wished to maintain output at *near* capacity to seek larger export sales. So in this sense the domestic squeeze allied to the availability of capacity may be a factor in increasing exports. This point, however, cannot be really discussed in isolation from considerations of export profitability.

* Total capacity means standard capacity which is normally equivalent to 80% of absolute capacity.

PROFITABILITY OF EXPORTS

In most instances exports are made at a higher marginal cost than domestic sales because of a net increase in selling costs in comparison to domestic ones. These include higher distribution and transport charges, model modifications required to meet local conditions and regulations, and higher costs incurred from having more capital tied up for longer periods. But with prices determined by the degree of competition rather than by costs it has been seen that profit margins on exports are lower than those on domestic sales. Devaluation in 1967 helped to restore profit margins at the same time as it corrected the overvaluation of sterling. Kennedy Round tariff reductions also helped profit margins by reducing the amount by which foreign wholesale prices had to be lowered to offset the tariff barrier; this was true in all markets where the U.K. met tariff-free competitors. Because of these factors, arguments concerning the need for a large home market became less valid, especially when the protection around that market was being reduced. When sterling was overvalued, tariffs were higher, and the domestic use of labour wasteful and inefficient, a stronger home market was needed in order to give the U.K. industry a chance to cover most of its overheads on domestic sales, thereby allowing foreign price cutting to be undertaken without affecting overall profits. As we have seen, a domestic squeeze allied to highly competitive export markets meant that in the late 1960s European firms showed a higher return on capital than British firms. They were able to establish overseas markets through aggressive pricing policies without running the same risk of reducing total profits to almost zero. It must be remembered that on a marginal cost basis exports are profitable in the short-run if they contribute to fixed costs and enable plant capacity to be fully utilised. This is true of existing plant even if marginal cost is below the average cost of making cars for export. If, however, as a result of this export pricing policy, total average costs exceed average revenue, then in the long-run a change in policy would be justified. With new capacity the firm should either set a larger proportion of output aside for sale domestically or reduce the size of its total operation, thereby insuring the overall profitability of the new investment*. Total exports may still increase of course, but the low

* Reducing the size of the operation may of course mean a loss of scale economies and an increase in prices. This in turn could lead to domestic car firms being undercut even in their home market.

rate of return earned* could discourage the aggressive search for new business, unless taking a long view of the market persuaded the firm that investment devoted to further exports would eventually pay-off.

If sales are made abroad at prices below domestic prices and below average total costs, then a prosperous home market may be needed. With domestic prosperity a sufficient volume of sales will be forth-coming to enable the vast proportion of fixed costs to be covered domestically. This allows foreign sales to be made at very competitive prices without harming overall profits. This is especially needed if domestic costs are out of line, so that if unit margins are low a sufficient sales volume is generated and unit margins multiplied by output give a sufficient surplus. However, if home and foreign costs are comparable, or if the currency is undervalued, the large domestic market argument loses a great deal of its validity. A sufficient volume of export sales should be forthcoming at a price which is at the same time both fully competitive with the competition and profitable. This leads us to consider the general competitiveness of the U.K. industry.

In the short-run, no relationship between home demand and export performance is likely if the latter requires the creation of an overseas sales and service network. This means heavy investment and the use of this investment will not be affected by temporary reduction in home demand or in profits. However, the better use of an existing network can clearly increase exports in the short-run. In the long-run, a decline in overall profits may undermine a company's ability to compete in export markets as the ability to absorb temporary losses in a market, in the hope of future profits, will be lessened. Any reduction in home and foreign investment caused by a decline in profits will tend to reduce international competitiveness.

BUT WILL A DECLINE IN PROFITS CAUSED BY A DOMESTIC SQUEEZE TEND TO REDUCE INTERNATIONAL COMPETITIVENESS?

If the domestic market had reached saturation or if a secular downturn in car ownership occurred because of an increased demand for, say, helicopters, then the car firm must invest in exports or gradually go out of business. Furthermore, money could perhaps be raised on foreign capital markets, such as Australia, in order to finance the international sales network which, for instance, would take the firm's

---

* In 1962 the manufacturers' profit on sales to the EEC was perhaps 15s. compared with £20 at home (*The Sunday Times*, 11 November 1962).

Australian and British products. In short, the motor industry could be faced with a situation where the growth in profits was a function of exports and not the other way around. In other instances the home market may not be large enough to utilise all the capacity available. Therefore competitive domestic prices would depend on a strong export industry. This can be true in the long-run as well as the short-run. As we have seen earlier, short-run exports made at above marginal cost but below average cost could lead to reduced exports in the long-run. If however a home market is too small to provide the volume of sales which is needed for a firm to operate under conditions of long-run optimality, then the firm *must* find export outlets or perish.

In other words, export sales are needed to allow the firm to profitably use an optimum-sized plant; a sub-optimum plant fully used would lead to uncompetitive price and cost levels. Furthermore, an imperfectly competitive firm which practises price discrimination, but makes normal profits, must also increase exports. That is, if only normal profits are made, a squeezing of the home market means that average cost exceeds average revenue. To increase average revenue a concerted export drive is needed to shift the foreign demand curve to the right in order to restore the aggregate average revenue curve to its original position under the given price structure. That is, foreign sales must increase not because export prices are reduced but because the overall marketing of exports improves.

DOES A SUCCESSFUL EXPORT DRIVE DEPEND ON A STRONG HOME MARKET?

It is possible that long-term export success depends on this type of 'policy' but we have pointed out that it is not necessarily so. In addition, increased exports in the short-run *can* follow from the second type of 'policy', that is, a restriction of domestic demand. We can perhaps justify the latter viewpoint for the following reasons.

Although an examination of the statistical series for home sales and exports between 1955 and 1969 fails to show an inverse relationship, a comparison of home sales in year t and exports in $t+1$ suggests on the surface that a domestic squeeze does favourably affect exports. The recovery of exports in the year following the 'low point' is greater than the recovery in domestic sales. In year $t+2$, that the recovery in domestic demand is greater than the recovery in exports, held true in the recovery period following the low point in 1956 and

1961*. In 1967 the recovery in home sales compared with the 1966 low point was only marginal and exports only recovered in year $t+2$, that is after the recovery in home sales. However, in year $t+2$ (1968) the improvement in exports was significantly greater than the improvement in home sales in 1966 and 1967 taken together. Here the influence of devaluation was probably more important than the squeeze in domestic demand. In 1969 exports continued to increase whereas domestic demand turned downwards. So perhaps the reduction in the home market in year t made producers fight more vigorously than they would otherwise have done in export markets in year $t+1$. The domestic curbs may have been a significant jolt to producers to get out and win export orders. This is summarised in *Table 11.11*.

Table 11.11

RELATIONSHIP BETWEEN CAR EXPORTS AND HOME REGISTRATIONS

Year	Car exports (1000s)	Change (%)	Home registrations (1000s)	Change (%)
1950	397·7		134·4	
1951	368·1	−8·0	138·4	2·9
1952	308·9	−16·3	191·0	38·3
1953	307·3	−0·5	301·3	57·7
1954	372·0	21·0	394·3	30·8
1955	388·6	4·4	511·4	29·6
1956	335·4	−13·7	407·3	−20·4
1957	424·3	26·5	433·1	6·3
1958	484·0	14·1	566·3	30·7
1959	569·0	17·5	657·3	16·1
1960	569·9	0·2	820·1	24·8
1961	370·7	−35·0	756·0	−7·8
1962	544·9	47·0	800·2	5·8
1963	615·8	13·0	1 031·0	28·7
1964	679·3	10·3	1 216·0	18·0
1965	627·6	−7·6	1 149·0	−5·6
1966	556·0	−11·4	1 091·2	−5·0
1967	502·6	−9·7	1 143·0	4·7
1968	677·0	34·6	1 145·0	0·2
1969	771·6	14·0	1 013·0	−11·5
1970	690·3	−11·7		

Although these time-series appear to give a good relationship between the state of the home market and export sales, the application

* The decline in total production in 1951 and 1952 was caused by a decline in the demand for exports and not by domestic restriction. Home registrations continued to climb between 1948 and 1955.

of simple statistical tests to the regressions involved do not suggest that the state of home demand is a good explanation of changes in exports. The T statistic (the test of hypotheses and significance) tended to be less than 1·5 and the correlation coefficient was of the order of 0·225. A better explanation for changes in U.K. car exports was in fact provided by the state of world car-demand*. So although in theory squeezing the home market could increase exports in practice the relationship does not appear to be significant. On the other hand statistical analysis produces the correct sign, a downturn in home demand produces an upturn in exports with a lag of one year.

The decline in the U.K.'s share of world markets from 33·3% in 1955 to 15·7% in 1968 cannot really be blamed on Government 'stop-go' policies. We have seen that the reasons were more fundamental than this: the decline in traditional Commonwealth markets, the benefits which European firms had from trade-creation within the EEC, the high growth in incomes in the EEC plus the already higher level of car ownership in the U.K., all led to a higher 'natural' rate of growth of domestic car demand. Finally, European producers have in general produced at any one time fewer models on a large scale, with fewer model changes, than U.K. firms. This must have helped reduce their costs in comparison with those of British firms and thereby improved their competitive strength. Given these factors, the U.K. motor industry had in fact done well to be as successful as it was in the world's markets. But were these 'special' factors grounds for saying that the U.K. industry needed a strong guaranteed home market in order to export successfully?

We have seen the claim that a fall in profits due to a reduction in home sales will reduce the industry's desire and ability to invest in plant, equipment, and the export drive. If we accept that a reduction in home sales reduces profits, and have suggested that this is not *necessarily* so, then does investment fall? If we look at the data for profits and gross fixed investment, and lag the latter by one year, then there is a positive relationship between changes in profits and changes in investment†. If investment is lagged for two years the relationship is not so good and for three years an inverse relationship is general. So if we take a one year time-lag between profits and investment, not-

---

* For example, where Y is car exports, X the state of the domestic market and T the state of world demand,

$$\Delta Y_t = 5 \cdot 267 - 0 \cdot 031 \Delta X_{t-1} + 0 \cdot 2989 \Delta T_{t-1}$$
$$\quad\quad\quad\quad\quad (0 \cdot 13) \quad\quad\quad (1 \cdot 44)$$

The figure in parenthesis is the T statistic.

† See Chapter Nine, p. 365.

o

withstanding substantial investment grants given by the state, the relationship is positive.

The industry's claim that the introduction of new models can be hampered by a weak home market does not appear to be consistent with the facts. There is no statistically significant relationship between the state of home demand and the number of new models introduced*. Anyway too many model changes tend to inflate costs as mentioned previously.

The fall in the utilisation of capacity between 1963 and 1968 from 83% to 61% had affected total unit costs. But from our previous analysis it is likely that the total increase in unit costs was little more than 2%. Although the effect on profits does tend to be magnified, for instance, if profits are 5% of total unit costs and costs increase by 2%, then profits fall by 40%. On the other hand, Government action to curb the inflation which could have originally caused the squeeze may have prevented other costs increasing by as much as they would have without the squeeze. What evidence there is on this suggests that the effect would not be much greater than 1%. Therefore 'stop-go' does not have a significant effect on unit costs although the influence on profits can be considerable. Furthermore, a movement along a given cost curve rarely provokes a price-reaction whereas a shift in the curve does.

But what of the contention that without a profitable home market it is not worthwhile exporting as exports contribute little to profits? One answer to this would be that it would pay in the long-run to make exporting more profitable by producing and selling more efficiently, rather than rely on a home market which itself is likely to become more competitive if we enter the EEC and because of the 'Kennedy Round'. Exporting can be very profitable if the product and the marketing arrangements are suitable. From the few examples we showed earlier not all firms cut prices in foreign markets. These are strong enough on the side of marketing and in their range of models to expand export sales without needing to cut prices to the minimum. This is certainly true of Volkswagen in the U.S.A. where sales are made on the basis of an excellent dealership system, reliability of the product, and low maintenance and running costs. It was quite possible in the late 1960s that the American market was more profitable than the German one for VW paradoxically faced greater competition in Germany from the likes of Opel and Ford than it did in the U.S.A.

---

* In trying to relate changes in models to changes in home sales the T statistic was equally low (less than 0·72) during times of prosperity and depression. As it takes up to five years to plan a new model this is not surprising.

So if VW felt threatened by the new small American cars, it could have a margin in hand to allow the company some profitable price-cutting.

EXPORT SUCCESS DOES NOT FUNDAMENTALLY DEPEND ON A STRONG
HOME MARKET

The U.K. industry needs to rationalise and improve its product range, perhaps by producing fewer basic models on a larger scale and more efficiently. For instance, the difference in size between Daimler-Benz and Jaguar is not a function of 'stop-go', as excess demand for Jaguar's products was and is usual. Rather it was caused by a refusal to tap the stock market for sufficient finance to expand. Jaguar relied instead on self-financing out of a small cash stream, which *was* small because of the low volume of production and not because of low profit margins. Rationalised production and model ranges, economies in organisation and sales facilities would make British firms vigorous international competitors. These changes have tended to occur slowly between 1964 and 1970, not despite the squeeze in home sales, but perhaps because of the squeeze, which made change imperative and forced management to become receptive to new ideas. The structural changes which occurred after 1964, allied to devaluation, gradually made the industry better suited to face international competition. Between 1963 and 1967 the increase in labour productivity was zero whereas between 1967 and 1968 productivity in the motor industry increased by 9%. Although there was more growth to come in the domestic market, such was the density of car ownership and the density of cars per mile that the future growth rate would tend to decline. Even the growth of two-car families could be largely offset by the reduced mileage and wear and tear per car, which could result in increases in the average age of the car stock and a decline in the replacement rate. So future growth in the long-run may well be in the export sector. Clearly any short-run improvements in exports caused by domestic restrictions should ideally be followed up by an improved domestic market which would increase the cash flow available for investment. This in turn would provide the wherewithal for a long-run push in the export market where much of the industry's future growth lies. Furthermore, the motor industry of the future will be supranational and international, and arguments about home markets would tend to become irrelevant.

THE FUTURE OF BRITISH EXPORTS

The future of the British export drive has already been touched upon
but a few more points can be made. Most of the burden for increased
sales could fall on Leyland's shoulders. The American owned firms
are controlled from Detroit and whether or not they aggressively
pursue foreign sales is not a purely British decision. For instance,
Vauxhall has rarely sold in the U.S.A. and by the late 1960s was
virtually out of the EEC; both markets were left to the larger Opel
subsidiary of GMC, and U.K. Ford had also withdrawn from these
areas. In 1965 the company had been the most aggressive foreign
marketer in France and Italy, but by 1970 it had withdrawn completely.
In the event, Ford had more than made up for these losses by seeking
out new markets, especially in South America and the Far East.
However, the high growth markets have been left to German Ford
which had expanded much faster than its British counterpart during
the late 1960s. Rootes has been freer to pursue its own markets, but
one could expect a 'rationalisation' by Chrysler of the export drives of
Rootes, Simca, and Barrieros. Only British Leyland is truly free to
sell the world over, and only if this company is successful can a continued and successful British export drive be guaranteed.

Future developments will see increased sales of components for
foreign assembly. The export industry of the future could be one of
largely ferrying components around the globe rather than the sale of
complete cars. It is here then the real growth will come as more and
more countries will desire to establish their own car assembly, and
eventually car manufacturing facilities. In the very long run, countries
which now restrict imports to components may feel secure in allowing
completed cars in again to compete with domestic production, part of
which would itself be exported. So the export growth could be
erratic in terms of complete cars but steady in terms of the value of
exported items, such as cars plus parts and components*. As always,
marketing allied to price will be the main variables determining the
success or otherwise of a country's export drive.

The devaluation of sterling in 1967 had given the British car industry
an export boost and brought British costs, prices, and therefore profits
into line with the main European and Japanese firms. The long decline

---

* This trend can be to the benefit of the British motor industry. For instance
U.S. Ford did not deem it economic to tool-up to produce 1·6 litre to 2 litre
engines for its small car the Pinto. Instead it purchased these items from its
European subsidiaries which were expert in making engines of this size.

in the U.K.'s share of world trade in manufactures appeared to have been checked. The decline in the U.K.'s share of car exports was arrested for the first time since 1962, increasing marginally from 15·6% in 1967 to 15·7% in 1968. Rationalisation and increased technological change had been a feature of the U.K. economy since 1967. Any advantage given by devaluation should, however, not be eroded by cost increases otherwise the car industry would again find itself at a cost disadvantage. Unfortunately the signs were not good. In 1969 the increase in average wages in the U.K. of 8–9% was no greater than in most competing countries but it was much greater in relation to the increase in real output. In 1969 unit labour costs increased by 4–5%*, whereas elsewhere in industrial Europe (including West Germany) there was no significant increase. At that rate the advantages given by devaluation would soon disappear. Nevertheless, rationalisation, technological change, and a new 'export orientation' in British industry as a whole, could still remain.

British entry into the EEC would be another significant development. Although Imperial Preference would be lost this is of minor significance anyway where the car industry is concerned. The loss of EFTA preferences would be minimal as most EFTA countries would join the EEC at the same time as the U.K. Any adverse effect on the cost of living would be partly passed on in new wage increases, and these in turn would partly affect the prices of finished goods for domestic and overseas consumption. The cost of entering the EEC could in itself increase car prices by around 1–2%. This could lead to a decline in overseas sales, although this effect of price elasticity of demand could be offset by a price reduction for British cars in the EEC and the influence of the income elasticity of demand in other markets. Entry into the EEC is unlikely of itself to reduce exports for in terms of the price and quality of products, U.K. car firms are generally speaking on a par with their foreign competitors. However, whether Britain enters the EEC or not, the volume of imports into the U.K. and their percentage of the U.K. market is likely to increase.

THE BRITISH MARKET AND FOREIGN IMPORTS

One argument why the volume of imports into the U.K. is likely to increase is that the loss of a stable home market reduces the cost competitiveness of domestic firms and makes the home market more

* Annual Survey of the United Nations Economic Commission for Europe, Geneva (1970).

vulnerable to penetration by foreign producers. The increase in imports from 67 340 in 1966 to over 102 000 in 1969 occurred at a time when total U.K. production and sales to the home market had been falling or stagnant. If the cost structure of the car industry became uncompetitive at a time (1968–1972) when tariff barriers were being reduced progressively to 11%, it could lead to a switch in home demand to foreign products. Up to the present time the U.K. has had one of the most favourable net trade balances in motor vehicles both in relation to other producing countries and in relation to U.K. trade in general. The ratio of car exports to imports being typically of the order of in excess of 10:1. In addition, the imported content of the British motor industry's products has also been low, perhaps lying between 5% and 10% of total ex-works cost*.

It is certainly valid to say that if U.K. costs moved out of line with foreign ones, the domestic car market could be vulnerable to imports, although this is not the same thing as saying that domestic restriction will inevitably lead to this. After all, a 20% reduction in output may only increase total average costs of production by some 2% which on a cost plus basis would add about £25 to a £800 car after including the effects of *ad valorem* taxes and dealer margins. This may induce some customers at the margin to switch to foreign cars; but the elasticity of demand for cars being what it is, such an increase in relative prices is unlikely to cause more than a $3\frac{1}{2}$% change in demand. This is assuming that all the cost increase is passed-on; in fact, only changes in variable costs are likely to produce this reaction. Indeed, a general increase in U.K. costs would arise not so much from sub-optimum working, as from an increase in unit variable costs which produced an upward shift in the cost-curve. If a squeeze was used to restructure the economy, so that economic growth was sufficient to absorb most increases in factor remuneration, then the temporary loss of a strong home market would not of itself increase imports in either the short-run or the long-run. In 1970 a 10% increase in steel prices was likely to produce a final increase in car prices of the order of £25 to £30. As the steel industry was working to capacity, it meant that the strong home market for steel did not prevent inflationary cost increases within the industry, which in turn led to increases in car prices of the order of 2%.

The main reason why imports into the U.K. are likely to increase

* *The Effect of Government Economic Policy on the Motor Industry*, NEDO, p. 37 (1968).
With the 'internationalising' of car firms this could increase sharply, for instance Ford (U.K.) could buy engines from Germany. Equally the U.K. could export more components leaving the net position little changed.

is due to reasons other than the home market being weak. In all the main car producing nations engaged in free-trade, the import percentage in terms of domestic production, or domestic car sales, or domestic exports, is higher than in the U.K. In France 25% of all cars sold on the domestic market in 1969 were imported, in the U.S.A. the figure was over 12%, and this picture was repeated in other main producing nations such as Italy (19%) and Germany (23%). Minor producers with insufficient capacity either to meet all domestic requirements or demand, such as Sweden or Holland, have much higher import ratios. Typically, over 60% of cars are imported. The U.K. had been the exception, with imports traditionally accounting for less than 5% of the market. Clearly a weak home market did not explain the growth in imports, as Germany with a very strong and stable home market imported a larger proportion of its requirements from abroad, mainly from the rest of the EEC.

The U.K. car market had been protected by high tariff barriers on imported cars from the kind of import boom experienced abroad. However, as tariff barriers were reduced and as foreign firms sought new markets they increased their British sales effort. Prices were placed below domestic levels and often below variable costs in an effort to establish a strong dealer network in readiness for the time when the U.K. entered the EEC. As a result, the previous import peak of 1960, when imports took 7% of domestic sales, was exceeded in 1969 when imports reached almost 10% of sales. However, the two peaks 1960 and 1969 were caused by different factors and show the danger of generalising on the relationship between the state of the domestic market and imports.

In 1960 both domestic production and demand reached a peak and the boom led to shortages of a number of British models. Consequently imports were sucked into the economy on the crest of the boom. So here it was an excessively strong home market which increased imports, and not a weak one. Importers utilised the boom in overall demand and especially the demand for particular types of car, to increase sales, often without investing in proper sales and service facilities. This did not harm initial sales until the imported car purchaser wanted either to trade-in his car or required it servicing. Many importers damaged their image in the British market in 1960 by failing to follow-up sales with adequate dealership networks, in much the same way as did the U.K. industry in the early 1950s. Many importers found that they could find a reasonable number of retail outlets by using firms specialising in foreign cars or through small dealers, but few were able to persuade large well-equipped enterprises to sell their cars. A lack of a good network can, like uncompetitive prices, inhibit sales. Although many importers in 1960 were able to succeed because they sold in sectors where price was less important than either quality or variety, the main sales were made in the popular market. In 1960 this was in the £500 to £700 retail-price bracket. In 1960, of the 57 800 cars imported into the U.K. 28 000 were Renault Dauphine saloons sold in the medium size market. Less than 10 000 were expensive models or cheap models with no U.K. equivalent, such as the Fiat 600. In 1961 imports fell by over 50% to 22 759, mainly as a result of the general downturn in the U.K. market. The fall in imports was greater than the proportionate fall in total demand. This was probably because imports had been supplying the marginal market which disappeared when demand fell. In addition, new British cars heralding a new technical breakthrough in British car design came onto the market in large numbers, models such as the Mini, Triumph Herald, and Ford Anglia. The lack of adequate dealer networks plus the poor quality of some of the cars imported also adversely affected further imports. Only in the post-1968 period did Renault begin to erase the poor reputation for quality and maintenance it had acquired with the boom in Dauphine sales in 1960. With the recovery in the domestic market in 1962 came a recovery in the sale of imports and this continued until the setback in 1965 when total U.K. demand and production fell again. However between 1966 and 1971 the increased demand for imports was in marked contrast to the stagnant level of overall domestic demand and production. Until 1965 the volume of imports followed the booms and slumps of domestic demand, a strong home market leading to strong imports and vice versa. Since 1966 the weak home market was associated with booming imports which was a reversal of pre-1965 events. Was the reason for this any uncompetitiveness of U.K. firms which may have been caused by a weak home market?

The answer was almost certainly in the negative. For one thing the post-1967 import campaign was basically due to two firms, Fiat and Renault. In addition, Volkswagen maintained its position as the largest importer but between 1965 and 1969 its growth of sales was small, whereas the new dynamic executives at Fiat and Renault were embarked upon a vigorous world-wide export drive*. These three firms had gradually established a sales network equal to that used by domestic manufacturers. The imported car dealer was no longer necessarily the undercapitalised back-street trader that was typical prior to the mid-

* In 1970 VW retaliated to the threat to its import leadership by embarking on a vigorous sales campaign backed by increased supplies of cars from Germany.

1960s. Imported car owners on average still had further to travel in order to find a service point. Indeed in 1971 only Volkswagen, Renault, and Fiat, had more than 250 dealers each compared with 1500 Ford dealers. The strong dealer chains established by these firms allowed the sale of imported cars to increase significantly. Perhaps the basic reason for the increased demand for imported cars was the desire for greater variety and performance, a requirement which was being tapped and reinforced by the sound marketing approach introduced by the main importers. The type of import sold in the U.K. market had changed between 1961 and 1966. After the 1960 boom imports consisted mainly of economy cars such as the small Fiats and cheap Skodas which had no direct U.K. equivalent, or of relatively expensive models like Mercedes-Benz. Since 1966 the growth in imports was for cars which were closely competitive in performance and specification with existing British models. The market leader was the VW Beetle sold on the basis of a reputation for reliability and ruggedness which had built up a very loyal clientele. Over 72% of VW owners replaced their existing Beetle with another Beetle. At the same time the relatively slow growth in VW sales in the later 1960s appeared to suggest that relatively few new customers were found. Only in 1970 after an invigorating shake-up of the dealer network did net sales grow significantly. The largest net increases in terms of absolute numbers had been by Fiat, Renault, and Volvo (*Table 11.12*).

Table 11.12

IMPORTED CARS IN THE U.K.

Model	1964	1969	1970
Volkswagen	23 000	21 200	37 371
Fiat	10 500	21 000	23 476
Renault	8 500	20 000	31 159
Volvo	2 900	7 500	10 471
Others	21 460	32 300	51 332
Total	66 360	102 000	153 809

Fiat and Renault had been marketing cars deliberately priced in relation to the British competition in the mass market. Volvo, which had the advantage of tariff free import from Sweden, based its export campaign on sound marketing. From 1959 the Volvo name had been promoted in relation to quality and longevity to such good effect that the company was able to compete quite successfully in the Rover 2000 market. Other firms such as Mercedes, BMW, and Alfa Romeo, found particular niches in the British market away from direct U.K. competition.

The home market squeeze in the late 1960s was accompanied by a sales and marketing effort designed to solidly establish foreign firms in the U.K. market, and thereby allow them to sell cars of similar specifications to domestic types in direct competition with British makes. Buyers wanting to find variety and distinctiveness may be sympathetic to the sales-talk of the foreign car dealer, in turn a solidly based dealership induces a customer to actually make the decision to buy foreign. After the initial sales effort in 1960 importers consolidated their positions and put their marketing effort on a more solid basis. As a result a gradual improvement in their total market share occurred allowing them to reach 10% in 1969 and 14% in 1970. The quality of the sales network in terms of coverage, trained personnel, and equipment, was perhaps the crucial factor in establishing a large export market. As the very success of models like the Cortina and 1100 insure that large numbers appear on the British roads, then the desire for something different intensifies. The quality of both the product and the sales network governs whether the customer is held when he decides to replace his car. The importer, through vigorous marketing, may gain about 15% of the U.K. market permanently for when the home market is reflated the sale of imports could increase with the general increase in prosperity. Given further tariff reductions and possible entry into the EEC, imports could then take a larger proportion of U.K. sales.

It must be remembered that the large increase in imports came after the tariff reductions in the early 1960s and after the commencement of the Kennedy Round reductions in 1968. It was noteworthy that the Kennedy Round reductions were not accompanied by price reductions but by importers utilising the tariff cut to improve the return on British sales. Alternatively the tariff cut absorbed the inflationary cost increases experienced by all European car producers since the late 1960s. It was factors such as these, rather than any decline in the competitive strength of U.K. firms, which led to the post-1965 growth in imports. Further tariff reductions would reinforce these factors with imports growing to a more 'normal' level. So again such an increase in imports will not reflect a decline in the cost-competitiveness of U.K. firms any more than 23% of the German market being in the hands of importers reflects the inefficiency or the cost disadvantage of German firms. Turning now very briefly to the export of commercial vehicles.

COMMERCIAL VEHICLES

As in the case of cars, the export orientation of the British commercial vehicle industry is a purely post-war feature. In the late 1930s only about one in five cars and one in six commercial vehicles were exported (*Table 11.13*).

Table 11.13

U.K. EXPORTS IN THE IMMEDIATE PRE-WAR YEARS

Year	Cars			Commercial vehicles		
	Total Prod.	Exports	%	Total Prod.	Exports	%
1936	367 237	64 765	17·6	114 305	17 571	15·4
1937	379 310	78 113	20·6	113 946	21 072	18·5
1938	341 028	68 257	20·0	103 849	15 466	14·9
1939	305 000	n.a.	—	97 000	n.a.	—

Source: SMMT.

Of the mass-producers, only Ford and Bedford were serious exporters, the American parents using their U.K. subsidiaries mainly to supply the Imperial Preference market. In the 1930s Bedford accounted for about 50% of all CV exports, exporting something like one-third of total production. Of the many CV specialists, most were either too new or too small to attempt making significant export sales, the main effort coming from Leyland, AEC, Guy and Albion. These firms sold over one-third of total output abroad and in the process established a good name and reputation in foreign markets.

After 1945 the export drive brought more firms into the export market, but the main effort again came from firms which had always exported. These were the firms with established sales outlets and a good reputation in a number of foreign countries. Most of these established markets were in the Commonwealth although whereas 85% of all car exports in value terms in 1929 and 1937 were sold in Commonwealth countries, the figure for CVs was 73%. One of the main reasons for this relatively slight difference was that whereas New Zealand absorbed nearly 25% of all car exports it only provided a market for 7% of CV exports. Consequently the industry was slightly less orientated to the Imperial market and slightly less dependent on a small number of key markets. In the immediate post-war period this situation tended to persist although both sides of the motor industry sought new markets (*Table 11.14*).

At the same time as attempts were made to find new markets,

Table 11.14

U.K. EXPORTS TO THE COMMONWEALTH

	1937	1947	1948	1949
Value (%)				
Cars	85	58	62	69
Commercial vehicles	73	44	59	61
Value (£ million)				
Cars	8 315	38 047	60 169	64 314
Commercial vehicles	3 830	23 433	36 765	40 548

the value of CV exports increased by over six-fold compared with pre-war. This was an impressive performance considering that in 1945 the export-orientation of the CV industry was even less than that of the car industry, despite the activities of firms like Bedford and Leyland. Why should the pre- and post-war performances be so different?

One reason was the wartime activities of CV producers. Whereas car production virtually ceased, the military demand for trucks, buses, and other vehicles, meant a great increase in manufacturing capacity. Consequently as early as 1946, CV output at 148 000 units was 30% greater than the best pre-war level. Although this output was negligible compared with the unprecedented home demand, it did give the industry the capacity by which to abide by the Government's wishes regarding the need to export. War-time experience had produced improved designs, whereas car production in 1946 consisted of pre-war models; CV output consisted largely of designs developed either during the war or in the immediate post-war period. The improved products may have increased the already heavy foreign demand. In addition, U.K. manufacturers did not suffer from the severe post-war strikes that hit their U.S. rivals. The dollar shortage also helped U.K. CV exporters, but not by as much as it did the car men, as dollars were freed more readily for the purchase of investment goods such as CVs. Even so, U.S. production was four times that of the U.K. in 1946, but in 1950 the U.K. temporarily passed the U.S.A. as the world's largest CV exporter. Until the early 1950s the U.K. and the U.S.A. were virtually the only sources of CV supplies for customers in third markets as the period was marked by the absence of French, Italian and German makers.

Some problems remained of course as factories had to be re-equipped and changed back to CV production. Furthermore, 'Construction and Use' regulations differed at home and abroad and hence two distinct vehicle ranges had to be produced, which imposed costs because of duplication and the hindering of large-scale production runs. However, the larger producers were affected more than the specialists as the latter's survival depended upon their ability to produce non-standard vehicles. Material shortages were severe, but as vehicles tended to use less sheet-steel than cars production was not so badly affected except in the bus and van field where severe problems existed.

The CV industry was subject to a greater pressure of home demand than cars. For instance, purchase tax was not imposed until July 1950, and tended to be at a much lower rate than that levied on cars. The need for investment goods to aid post-war reconstruction meant that too much emphasis on exports to the detriment of home sales may have helped the balance of payments but perhaps only at the cost of long-term harm to economic growth. Hence although the official targets for exports were rarely achieved, no penalties in the shape of official direction or reduced steel allocations occurred. This tacit official recognition that home sales were crucial meant that the CV industry used proportionately more resources to satisfy the home market than did the car side.

Home demand was virtually unaffected either by the threat or the actuality of road transport nationalisation in 1947. It was true that the home registrations of goods vehicles fell from 134 700 in 1947 to 112 530 in 1948, but buses increased from 9800 to 12 350. In other words, it would appear that nationalisation or its threat led to very little in the way of cancelled orders or uncertainty in the transport sector. Of greater significance were the measures taken in 1947 to combat the balance of payments crisis, which included cuts in capital expenditure and increased profits tax. The emergence of a large state-buyer did not and does not affect the freedom of action and enterprise of the vehicle producers. On the contrary, much fruitful technical collaboration has occurred, as well as the emergence of a powerful state-owned transport sector able to combat the political lobbying of railway interests aimed to bias the transport sector in their favour. The partial denationalisation of road haulage in 1953, the continued freedom of 'C' licence operators, and the fact that between 1950 and 1968 only about one-quarter of the bus stock was state owned, meant that monopsony was not a feature of the CV market. Consequently the industry was able to produce and design vehicles in complete freedom but took into account the 'consumer sovereignty' of foreign as well as domestic customers. The devaluation of sterling in

1949 may have helped exports a little; however, as the main problem
was one of supply the imposition of purchase tax in 1950 was much
more significant from the point of view of improving the industry's
export percentage. Even so, during the post-war period the export
percentage of the car industry tended to be superior to that of the CV
industry (*Table 11.15*).

Table 11.15

PERCENTAGE OF OUTPUT EXPORTED

	1946	1949	1952	1955	1958	1060	1962	1964	1966	1968
Commercial vehicles	31	38	53	47	35	32	35	36	38	35
Cars	38	62	60	42	46	42	44	36	35	37

A number of reasons can explain this state of affairs, many of which
have been mentioned before. In the early post-war period the Government tended to be more strict concerning the car industry's domestic
quotas and often imposed higher levels of purchase tax on cars. The car
industry's greater use of very scarce sheet steel may have induced it to
strive harder in the export field in order to earn bonus allocations.
The Government looked favourably upon the efforts to replace and
expand worn out CV fleets especially where buses were concerned.
The excess demand for buses was satisfied by 1950 and by 1952 in the
case of trucks and vans, this was some three to four years before the
back-log in car demand was satisfied and indeed some traces of excess
demand lasted until 1959. The official view was that a balance was to
be struck between home and foreign demand, whereas where cars
were concerned the viewpoint was one of exports at all costs. On the
one hand vehicles were needed for post-war reconstruction and the
facilitating of economic growth in general. On the other hand there
was the need to earn foreign exchange through satisfying as many
customers as possible in the minimum possible time.

As mentioned before there was in practice no official discrimination
against firms failing to meet export quotas and this, allied to the fact
that the establishment of overseas sales networks was expensive, meant
that the firms exporting most vehicles after 1945 were those that had
always done so. However, the export quota system cannot be regarded
as a complete failure for without it exports would probably have
been lower. All firms made some effort to sell abroad, but more success
may have been achieved, especially on the CV side, if the Government

had used the powers it had available instead of wishing to avoid the stigma of being unfair. The 'push' on the car side to export more was greater than that on the CV side, the amount of 'pull' from abroad being comparable in both cases.

After 1952 the sellers' market started to disappear rapidly, mainly as a result of import restrictions in Australia and New Zealand which together took almost 25% of all CV exports in the period 1950–1952. The impact of this on CVs, however, was not as great as that on cars as the restrictions imposed on CV imports into these markets were less severe, and because the industry was very quick in diverting supplies to other markets. By 1953 the material shortages had largely disappeared as well. So whereas between 1946 and 1951 production was the main problem between 1951 and 1953 new patterns emerged with many export markets being restricted in one way or another. Between 1953 and 1956 the competition from European countries increased, and between 1956 and 1958 a slow down in the growth of world consumption and incomes occurred. All of this reduced the level of U.K. exports and then tended to prevent any marked recovery until 1959 and 1960. The political consequences of Suez and the political upheavals in different important markets all added to the export problems of the U.K. CV industry (*Table 11.16*).

Table 11.16

CAR AND COMMERCIAL VEHICLE EXPORTS 1950–1960

Year	CVs	Cars
1950	144 251	397 688
1951	136 880	368 101
1952	128 203	308 942
1953	104 696	307 368
1954	118 796	372 029
1955	104 048	388 564
1956	126 671	335 397
1957	122 957	424 320
1958	112 205	484 034
1959	128 055	568 971
1960	146 128	569 889

After reaching a peak in 1950 CV exports did very badly during the decade 1950–1960, only reaching a new peak in 1960. Similarly, car exports in the 1950s were generally below the level reached in 1950, but a new peak was reached in 1957 which heralded a boom in exports which did not burst until 1961. The worst export year compared with the *previous* best meant that CV exports had fallen by 28% compared with a 23% fall in car exports. The same erratic performance is evident on an annual basis with CV exports being more erratic than cars (*Table 11.17*).

Table 11.17

CHANGE IN EXPORTS COMPARED WITH PREVIOUS YEAR

Year	CVs	Cars
1951	−5·6%	−7·3%
1952	−6·3%	−16·1%
1953	−18·3%	−0·5%
1954	+13·4%	+21·0%
1955	−12·4%	+4·4%
1956	+21·7%	−13·7%
1957	−2·9%	+26·5%
1958	−8·7%	+14·0%
1959	+14·1%	+17·0%
1960	+14·1%	+0·2%

This position was reflected by a reduction in the export ratio for cars and commercial vehicles, and by the fall in the share of world exports accounted for by British producers. The share held by CVs fell to 25% in 1957 compared with 40% in 1950 but by 1962 this had increased to over 30% again. In fact the 1960s as a whole was a far better decade for CV exports than the 1950s, and the commercial vehicle producers did relatively better than the car producers. In terms of the percentage of output exported for the first time, the CV producers did as well as the car manufacturers, always remembering that it was often the same firms which were involved in both markets (*Table 11.18*).

Table 11.18

WORLD EXPORTS ACCOUNTED FOR BY THE U.K.

	1957	1959	1960	1961	1962	1963	1964	1965	1966	1967	1968
Percentage											
Cars	30	26·1	25·2	18·6	21·9	21·3	21·7	19·9	17·1	15·6	15·7
CVs	25	27·4	25·9	31·6	31·5	30·2	28·4	33·2	31·6	25·8	21·8
Numerical Value (1000s)											
Cars	424	569	570	371	545	616	679	628	556	503	677
CVs	123	128	146	168	150	159	169	166	166	135	142

The volume of world car exports increased steadily and rapidly between 1959 and 1964, then stagnated until 1968, when another rapid increase occurred. Similarly, world CV exports rose to a new peak in 1968 but over the whole period world export totals had moved in a very erratic way compared with car exports. In addition, there was little sign of the same underlying growth trend—world CV exports in 1968 were 38% greater than in 1959 compared with 97% for cars. It would appear that between 1957 and 1967 the British CV industry had improved its relative position *vis-à-vis* its main competitors, whereas the car industry's position remained one of relative decline. From this it can be deduced that the CV industry had been relatively successful in combating foreign competition, whereas the U.K. car industry has been unsuccessful. The CV industry had been able to maintain its position partly because it did not have so far to fall.

In terms of the percentage of output exported and the industry's share of world markets, the U.K. CV industry never achieved the same dominance in the early post-war period* as the car industry. As a result the industry did not over-extend itself by making sales beyond the capabilities of its sales and service network, nor in terms of sacrificing quality to quantity. In 1948 the U.K. car industry became the world's export leader only to lose its position to Germany in 1956. In 1950 the U.K. CV industry briefly displaced the U.S.A. as the world's largest exporter. However, in 1961 the U.K. became the dominant exporter in unit terms and in 1962 in value terms as well, until displaced from first place by Japan in 1967 and from second place by Germany in 1968.

Between 1950 and 1962 the number of commercial vehicles exported remained fairly constant at between 144 000 and 149 000 units. On the other hand, American exports fell from over 200 000 in 1960 to just over 100 000 in 1962. At the same time, the total world market increased from just over 340 000 units in 1950 to 476 000 in 1962, an increase of just 40% in 12 years; consequently the slight increase in U.K. exports meant that between 1950 and 1962 the British share of world CV markets only fell from 40% to 35%; compared with a fall of from 55% to 21·9% for cars. So the CV industry was partly able to maintain its position simply because it was easier to do so. At the same time, the car industry is still one of the world's largest exporters. However, following the difficult time faced by CV exports between 1950 and 1959 there is no doubt that the 1960s saw the CV industry being relatively more successful than the car industry in meeting foreign competition. Only the rapid growth of Japanese exports had

* 1946–1952.

proved too strong, and here a very large number of very light vehicles were involved.

In terms of unit sales, the car industry often sells over four times as many vehicles abroad as the CV industry, but in value terms the ratio is usually less than 2:1. This reflects the higher average value of medium and heavy CVs compared with that of a family car; in 1968 the average value of each car exported was £413 compared with £879 for each CV.

Table 11.19

U.K. CAR AND COMMERCIAL VEHICLE EXPORTS 1959–1968

	1959	1960	1961	1962	1963	1964	1965	1966	1967	1968
Volume (1000s)										
Cars	569	570	371	545	616	679	628	556	503	677
Commercial vehicles	128	146	168	150	159	170	166	166	135	142
Value (£ million)										
Cars	222·5	224·6	147·9	215·5	237·2	256·7	250·9	234·4	211·4	280·1
Commercial vehicles	89·0	104·3	121·9	114·0	121·4	126·5	137·1	142·1	116·8	124·9

In terms of total production over four times as many commercial vehicles as cars are produced, but in value terms the relationship is again about 2:1. This shows that in terms of total production and total exports the CV industry's importance is far greater than a simple comparison of the volumes involved would suggest. The success of the industry in overseas markets, especially where heavy and medium vehicles are involved, is underestimated by these value figures. As more and more countries close their markets to complete imports of cars and vehicles in order to establish their own manufacturing and assembly facilities, the export of components becomes much more important (*Table 11.20*).

Table 11.20

THE VALUE OF COMPONENT SALES (£ MILLION)

1959	1960	1961	1962	1963	1964	1965	1966	1967	1968
123·9	151·8	158·0	162·7	173·4	191·3	217·6	234·7	233·6	285·1

Increasing from 28·5% of the total value of motor industry exports in 1959, to 41·3% in 1968, exemplifies the growing importance of the sale of unassembled vehicles and individual items such as engines or gearboxes intended for use in overseas assembly plants. A large proportion of this is accounted for by CV parts. This adds to the success of the industry in foreign markets during the 1960s. Now briefly what are the reasons for this success?

The quality and design of British commercial vehicles allied to first class sales and service networks established by the main exporters have been important factors. The CV exporters also tended to spread their sales effort more widely than was usual on the car side, consequently any collapse of sales in one important market did not have the same catastrophic result as risks were spread. Even in 1968, for instance, almost 63% of all car exports went to the 10 most important markets compared with 49% in the case of CVs; the two most important markets took 20% and 21% respectively. So although the CV and car industries are equally dependent on their main markets, nevertheless the CV industry's efforts are more widely spread. Underdeveloped and developed countries have often given import licences for CVs even when the markets were closed to cars. In the case of Australia and South Africa there are fewer restrictions on the import of medium and heavy CVs than are placed on cars. In many instances it was easier to successfully establish assembly facilities for CV manufacture than for cars because of the much lower optimum for the output of medium and heavy CVs. Often indigenous bodybuilding facilities existed with local producers utilising wood, glass-fibre, or metal panels on a wood or metal framework. The methods of production and the materials used did not require a large capital outlay.

As we have seen previously, the demand for medium-weight vehicles developed early in the U.K. and provided a market which made it economic to mass produce simple trucks and buses. In the event this meant that the U.K. became the non-American CV production centre for the American owned firms. The CV operations of Ford, GMC and Chrysler, in contrast to the situation on the car side, are more developed in the U.K. than in their other main vehicle producing centres in Germany or France. Consequently whereas Germany may become the main centre for Ford's and GMC's car producing activities, the U.K. has strengthened its position as their CV producing centre. The large volume of output leads to significant internal and external economies of scale, giving the U.K. CV maker a considerable price advantage over his Continental rivals. For instance, the ex-works price of a Berliet five ton lorry was about £2400 compared with

£1100 for a British mass-produced unit of the same size. In addition the heavy vehicle producers in the U.K., if they produce their own major components, utilise cheap and ingenious production and assembly methods.

In Europe the heavy vehicle producers tend to use the most up-to-date machine tools, transfer equipment, and processes which tend to have an optimum capacity far in excess of the output levels at which they are actually used. Consequently Leyland trucks sold in France at a similar ex-works price to that prevailing in the U.K. were priced 25% above French equivalents despite tariffs adding 60% to landed costs*. This suggests a cost difference of 20% to 25% in favour of the U.K. firm. A British heavy vehicle assembled in France paying 22% duty is comparable in price to equivalent French models. The policy of firms like Bedford and Leyland is to surmount tariff barriers in order to compete in their competitors' domestic markets. They are helped by the fact that foreign producers inflate prices in their own markets in order that sales may be made at lower prices elsewhere. In general, U.K. firms charge the same or higher ex-works prices in foreign markets, and such is the reputation and sales efforts of British firms that they are able to do this. However, in Germany a vehicle costing £4500 ex-works is equivalent to British models costing £4000, but in the U.K. the German ex-works price is around £4100†. In foreign markets customers are very price conscious when faced with a range of alternative vehicles of similar quality; however, in the medium-weight sector, British costs and prices are unbeatable‡. As regards car derivatives, U.K. and foreign prices are comparable, and similarly in the medium-weight van sector, although the U.K. appears to have a slight advantage. As regards heavy vehicles, the U.K. industry is fully competitive with its foreign rivals, and the combination of price and quality often appears to tilt the balance in the U.K.'s favour.

Due to the relatively large output of heavy and medium vehicles in the U.K., the industry is stronger than that in many competing countries for a variety of reasons. No other CV industry in Europe is able to supply the range of vehicles and components which exists in the U.K. In France and Germany the CV industry does not make mass-produced medium-weight vehicles, and furthermore, the French producers of heavy vehicles have to rely on German or British diesel engines to supplement their ranges. Large and small French makers

* *The Economist* (11 May 1963).
† *Motor Transport* (27 August and 21 May 1965).
‡ A 7 ton Mercedes is about £1500 ex-works; a U.K. mass-produced unit about £1000–£1150.

alike also assemble foreign vehicles in order to widen the limited range of their own vehicles. The U.K. industry produces a wide variety of vehicles and components which cover most of the different requirements and weight brackets between 5 cwts. and 32 tons gross.

The relatively high labour content embodied in each heavy vehicle which is assembled by skilled labour, rather than by high volume methods, tends to price the American specialists out of third markets. The approximate ex-works costs of different vehicles from different sources are shown in *Table 11.21*.

Table 11.21

APPROXIMATE EX-WORKS COSTS IN DOMESTIC MARKETS*

	Typical heavy (24 tons gross +)	Typical medium–heavy (16 tons gross)
U.S.A. (Specialist)	£6 000	—
U.S.A. (GMC, etc.)	£4 800	—
U.K.	£4 000	£2 000
Germany	£4 200	—
Sweden	£4 600	—
Holland	£4 000	£2 400

* Derived from data on price, company turnover, dealer and producer profit margins.

The high price of labour, of non-standard components, and of labour-intensive components, tend to price American heavy vehicle producers out of world markets. Even firms like Ford or GMC's Truck and Coach Division find that although their output levels may justify the use of capital intensive manufacturing and assembly techniques, their heavy vehicle production by its nature still requires the use of more labour than is needed in car production. This is especially so in final assembly and in the assembly and manufacture of complex items such as diesel engines. Cummins, for instance, supplies its export markets from non-American sources, even finding it cheaper to ship engines to Mexico from Europe. Consequently although GMC is able to undercut specialists like Mack in the U.S.A., both types of firm are at a price disadvantage in world markets. Hence the vast majority of American CV exports are in the form of unassembled vehicles which entails a lower labour content. In the heavy vehicle market where hand-built quality vehicles predominate, small countries with small markets are able to support thriving CV producers. This is possible because the optimum production level for 'bespoke' producers is probably less than 10 000 units a year, and for quality producers like

Leyland around 25 000 a year. The production of major components on expensive transfer machines or automatically linked machine tools pushes the optimum to in excess of 100 000 a year, but as the size of the heavy vehicle market is limited this would probably result in sub-optimal working. The slowing down of production lines to build-in specialised features would also have the same result. Consequently a firm producing at levels below 25 000 units a year need not be at a significant cost disadvantage.

Often 'quality' is used to mask 'high costs' but Sweden and Holland are able to produce vehicles which customers regard as being value for money. The Swedes and Dutch purchase suitable expertise, capital equipment, components, and materials from the cheapest world sources. And although wages are high, especially in Sweden, product-ivity is high also. Excellent research and development facilities exist and this, allied to a concentration of sales efforts on a few selected markets, enabled a good export trade to be established. With a small and unprotected home market, Swedish and Dutch producers realised that exports of quality heavy vehicles was the only way to long-term survival. Arguments concerning a strong home market were irrelevant, as only export sales could supply the demand needed to allow a volume of output which was optimum for a highly integrated heavy vehicle producer. Of the 20 584 units made in Sweden in 1967, over 15 000 were exported. Without these export sales any firm producing its own diesel engines, as well as other major components, could not profitably keep its prices within £600 of those charged by U.K. firms. The Dutch, by buying-in more units than the Swedes, were able to match U.K. prices.

The Germans, however, use more capital-intensive production methods and, given their current output volumes, there may be some cost disadvantage in relation to the costs experienced by U.K. heavy vehicle producers (*Table 11.21* may overstate the penalty, as the domestic prices from which the cost estimates are derived are above their export prices). In the case of medium-weight vehicles, the small scale producer is at a greater price disadvantage, and where lighter vehicles of between 5 and 12 tons are concerned, U.K. producers are able to undercut the prices of their Continental rivals by almost 25% in many cases.

The external economies passed on by component makers and the internal economies reaped by the vehicle producers enable U.K. producers to offer a wide range of vehicles and components at com-petitive costs and prices. In the market for heavy vehicles, small countries are able to compete in the CV industry by concentrating on quality and exports. As a result the heavy vehicle export market is extremely competitive, with products being sold through a combination of price and quality. In the medium-weight sector U.K. producers tend to dominate world trade, the strongest competition coming from the Japanese.

A further factor helping the U.K. industry in comparison to the situation abroad has been the fact that the domestic market has been less restricted by rail-biased legislation. This has not been the case in Germany, France, or Italy. In the U.K.'s case, the strong export orientation of the industry, especially where medium and heavy CVs are concerned, has meant that the industry has been less dependent on the home market to provide a strong base. This has not been so evident in the case of Italy or France, where respectively only one in four and one in five CVs produced are exported. In the U.K.'s case over one in three are sold abroad. Hence a restriction of home demand may be relatively more serious to the overall prosperity of the CV industry abroad than in the U.K. The traditionally highly protected and inefficient French industry has been unable to offset any restriction of home demand by expanding exports, whereas the more efficient Italian and German industries were more successful. The German export percentage has been typically in the region of 30%, whereas the U.K.'s has been normally between 33% and 38%.

In relation to its main European and American competitors the U.K. has a comparative advantage in CV production. This could mean that, in terms of domestic costs in the supply of components and in the development of design and production expertise, the U.K. finds it easier and more efficient to expand CV output than does its rivals.

Table 11.22

MEAN RATIO OF U.K. TO FOREIGN PRODUCTION*

Country	Cars		Commercial vehicles	
U.S.A.	0·22:1	(0·21:1)	0·30:1	(0·22:1)
Germany	0·65:1	(0·63:1)	1·8:1	(1·7:1)
France	1·03:1	(0·99:1)	2·0:1	(1·7:1)
Italy	1·5:1	(1·2:1)	5·9:1	(3·4:1)
Japan	2·2:1	(0·88:1)	0·42:1	(0·20:1)

* Taken for period 1959–1968.

From *Table 11.22* it can be seen that although the U.S.A. produces more cars and commercial vehicles than the U.K. its comparative advantage in cars is greater. If these ratios are related to differences in productivity, then the U.S.A. has a greater comparative advantage—in the use of resources—over the U.K. in the production of cars. Hence it pays the U.S.A. to concentrate on car production and the U.K. on truck production. In a perfect world the U.S.A. would reduce CV production and, similarly, the U.K. would reduce car production. However, these ratios cannot really be taken to reflect differences in productivity as factor inputs are not constant in different countries, but with economies of scale up to at least two million units a year, the larger the output the more efficient the production method. Thus as a rough guide these ratios may point towards some difference in productivity. Where cars are concerned the U.K., France, Italy and Japan are in a similar position, whereas Germany and the U.S.A. may have a productivity advantage*. Where trucks are concerned, the U.K. could have a considerable advantage over its European rivals, a comparative advantage in relation to the U.S.A., but a disadvantage in relation to Japan. For instance, if wage rates in the U.S.A. are based on its comparative advantage in cars over the Europeans, then American wages could be almost five times the U.K.'s. But if CV wages in the U.S.A. are equivalent to car wages, then American CV output at only just over $3\frac{1}{3}$ times the U.K.'s would place the U.S. firms at a wage cost disadvantage. Although this is an oversimplification it may be nevertheless a rough guide to what actually occurs.

Where Japan is concerned the position is reversed. Light-to medium-weight vehicles are cheaper than the U.K. equivalents and their quality is comparable. Since the Japanese motor industry was based on commercial vehicles, many of the components made were originally tailor-made for CV production and then later adapted for use in cars; in the U.K. the opposite often occurred. Many items, such as electrical components, were therefore better adapted to CV use than some British items. In *Table 11.22*, the figures in parenthesis show the incremental ratio for 1968 alone. These figures continue to reflect the overall situation, except that the U.K.'s relative position declined in both the car and CV sector. So the picture presented is one where the U.K. CV industry has a price advantage *vis-à-vis* its European and American rivals, notably where medium and heavy vehicles are concerned, but it experiences a price disadvantage in relation to Japanese light and medium trucks. In the case of heavy vehicles the Japanese were not yet a force to be reckoned with in the late 1960s. Add this to the expertise gained on the marketing side and the strength of the U.K. industry becomes evident. However, the Japanese appear to be equal to this and the main threat to future British exports will

* See Chapters 10 and 12 for comparisons in productivity.

come from this quarter. By 1970 the Japanese industry was not yet export orientated as only 10% of production was exported, but such was the total volume that this alone was sufficient to make the Japanese CV exports the world's largest. Nevertheless, in the market for medium and heavy vehicles the U.K. was still able to hold its own against Japanese penetration and it would appear that the excellent commercial acumen evident in both the Japanese and British industries will largely determine future developments.

The U.K. industry is particularly strong in the export of expertise and 'bits and pieces'. As the export of complete vehicles becomes more difficult then the export of 'components' will become increasingly important. The flexible approach of U.K. firms in dealing with foreign markets means that they are prepared to substitute the export of parts for complete vehicles when the necessity arises, and this policy serves it well in the developing world. The British industry still appears to be superior in this respect to its European rivals. Furthermore, since the immediate growth market for vehicles is, unlike cars, in the under-developed world, then the British producers could easily improve their long-run position relative to that of their overseas competitors.

This concentration on the non-European market by the U.K. industry in turn points to the opportunities open to it within the EEC, especially now that the U.K. has become a member. The threat posed to foreign producers by British medium-weight producers is clearly illustrated by their desire to exclude commercial vehicles from Kennedy Round tariff reductions. A reduction of tariffs from 22% to 11% would have allowed British low-cost producers to increase their market penetration significantly, much to the discomfiture of existing German, French and Italian producers.

Table 11.23

U.K. EXPORTS OF COMMERCIAL VEHICLES (1966)

Region	Volume (1000s)	Percentage of total production	Value (£ million)
EFTA	34·2	8·0	24·2
EEC	11·6	3·0	8·4
Commonwealth	68·6	16·0	59·3
Total CV exports	165·9	38·0	142·1

The above picture excludes parts used in assembly abroad or sold to foreign producers. Due to the traditional concentration on 'other' world markets the industry's European effort has been limited. To break the German domination in Europe much effort in both time and finance will have to be spent on establishing adequate dealer networks, and especially in the EEC. Competitive prices will in themselves do much to increase the sale of medium-sized vehicles, but as regards vans and heavy vehicles, where Continental prices are more comparable, a dealer network will be one of the main factors governing the level of sales.

The net balance of trade in vehicles has been even more favourable than it has been in the case of cars. This situation is likely to continue, for whereas the American-owned firms may in the future concentrate component production in different centres, thereby importing car components presently made in the U.K., the U.K. is their only significant centre for CV production. The position for 1967 and 1968 is shown in *Table 11.24*.

Table 11.24

BALANCE OF TRADE ($£$ MILLION)

| | Exports | | Imports | | Ratio of Exports:Imports | | |
	1967	*1968*	*1967*	*1968*	*1959*	*1967*	*1968*
Cars	211	262	39	45	25:1	5·4:1	5·8:1
Vehicles	114	120	5	6	148:1	22·8:1	20·0:1
Components*	175	208	21	28	18·8:1	8·3:1	7·4:1

* During the 1960s Volvo of Sweden typically purchased £25 million of British components each year, so approximately 10% of the costs of a Volvo vehicle are accounted for by British components.

The import of foreign components for both the service of foreign cars and for use in British cars may already be on a significant upward trend. Despite the growth in the import of complete cars the ratio is still very much in the U.K.'s favour and in the case of commercial vehicles this is even more so. This latter reflects the efficiency of the home industry as well as the import duty burden on imported full-size CVs*, and the difficulty experienced in establishing an adequate dealership network. However, in all cases the ratio of export value to import value has fallen, and the fall for vehicles was more pronounced than that for cars.

In excess of 60% of all CV imports in unit terms are accounted for by Volkswagen; however the most significant increase in value terms occurred after 1967. This was mainly due to the boom in demand for heavy vehicles which had followed from (1) customers 'trading-up',

* Except those from EFTA.

(2) the increase in permitted sizes and in speed limits, and (3) the spread of motorways. Heavy vehicle producers have tended to have rather conservative investment policies although most of the small specialists doubled capacity from about 600 units a year in 1956 to 1200 a year by 1966. This, however, was insufficient to meet the surge in demand after 1964 and long waiting lists appeared, together with a thriving black market in stolen heavy vehicles. Further expansion occurred after 1966 with unit capacity increasing from around 1200 units a year to almost 2000 by 1970 on the part of some CV specialists and over 3000 units by others. However, Leyland's capacity had remained almost static throughout the 1960s. This shortage of capacity allowed some foreign heavy vehicle producers to enter the U.K. market and Mercedes, Magirus Deutz, Volvo, and Scania, were the most prominent.

In all cases British concessionaires are responsible for U.K. sales, and where Deutz is concerned the British dealership is run by Seddon Diesel following a disastrous effort on the part of another organisation*. Volvo and Scania are helped by the existence of tariff-free importation from Sweden, and although tariffs finally disappeared in 1968 they were so low in 1967 (6%) that both firms made their initial push in that year. In 1970 the Swedish firms were clearly suppliers of the most significant imports of heavy vehicles, and although their products retail at between £5000 and £5500 in the U.K. (which is above comparable U.K. types at between £4500 and £5000) both Volvo and Scania rapidly increased their sales. In other words, the customers felt that the extra payment represented value for money in terms of quality, reliability and performance.

The small specialists only export between 10% and 20% of total production, the main effort coming from traditional exporters such as Bedford and Leyland. Although some problems exist, such as problems concerning the quality of certain components and the poor export effort of some firms, by and large the CV industry's export position and performance is excellent. Although its export-import ratio has fallen, the absolute gap between the two has continued to widen and by maintaining its past performance in terms of marketing, design, quality, cost and price, the industry should remain one of the major forces in the world's CV markets. Perhaps its export spread has been inferior to that of some of its competitors with a significant lack of penetration in the EEC which cannot be solely explained by tariffs and other barriers. Consequently a new attack on certain markets is probably called for. However, the industry's strength in the export

* In 1971 Deutz assumed responsibility for its marketing effort.

field is formidable, and the advantages it has acquired should reinforce its position in the future.

The growth available in foreign markets and the necessity to take exporting seriously was recognised by companies like Leyland Motors and individuals like Sir Henry Spurrier at an early date. In the 1940s Spurrier was determined to see Leyland grow and survive in the world's motor industry. This meant the expansion of the firm from a small-scale CV producer in 1946 to an integrated mass-producer by 1970. The initial growth was firmly laid on the CV base, a base wedded to exports. Spurrier saw exports as the industry's lifeblood, as domestic expansion for heavy vehicles was strictly limited. The expanding markets were overseas where growing industrialisation meant an increasing demand for either complete CVs or for parts. The need to maintain the quality of the product, the efficiency and speed of the after sales network, was recognised as paramount. On the spot investigations were made by executives to insure that the firm's products were giving value for money and were equal to the competition. These were the ingredients for the success of Leyland, and the other CV producers. Such policies are still part and parcel of the industry's export efforts.

EXPORTS: SOME GENERAL CONCLUSIONS

In conclusion then we can say that the world demand for cars is likely to continue unabated in the foreseeable future. From a market of 19 million new registrations in 1968 demand is expected to grow to 26 million world-wide registrations in 1972.

The U.K. industry has a good export performance currently contributing about 17% of all U.K. exports in value terms. The industry continues to have a high export growth potential as the demand for cars increases in both under-developed and developed countries alike. Whether the industry translates this potential into actuality depends upon its overall export competitiveness. The industry makes a substantial net contribution to the balance of payments with a ratio of exports to imports of about 10:1. In addition, the import content in each car (at ex-works prices) is between 7% and 8% and in each vehicle between $8\frac{1}{2}$% and 10%. This is a lower figure than is general for British industry, and illustrates the large net contribution which the motor industry makes to the balance of payments.

Any expansion of home demand means a relatively small addition to imports. The improved marketing arrangements on the part of

importers, the demand for variety, and the reduction in tariffs, must
see a continued increase in the demand for imported cars and components. CV imports may also increase although remaining at a
relatively low level. Imported components for U.K. cars may also
increase, especially if the American firms concentrate the production of
particular items in single countries. More serious may be the inability
of the machine tool industry to satisfy all the motor industry's investment needs in the event of an investment boom; if past performances
are a guide, almost 50% of the machine tools installed in U.K. industry
at the top of a boom are imported. A successful export drive does not
depend on a strong home market but it does depend upon an industry
fully competitive in terms of design, manufacturing techniques,
quality, and marketing. A steady home market would of course
help by generating investment funds but it is not a necessary or
sufficient factor governing export growth.

Although a short-term restriction of home demand could reduce
profits it is unlikely that this would affect either the firm's willingness
to expand or its ability to do so[*]. The long-run growth in home and
export demand would induce manufacturers to expand and outside
investors to supply it with funds. Any long-run restriction on home
demand may be another matter. Expansion could then be limited with
the possibility that economies of scale would be lost resulting in higher
costs. This could affect competitiveness by making both home and
foreign prices higher than they need be, and/or any attempt to charge
lower prices abroad would lead to overall losses as insufficient home
sales exist to compensate for export prices set below average costs. On
the other hand, a firm with a small home market, for example Volvo
in Sweden, may have to export to keep down costs anyway. Alternatively, a large but artificially restricted home market could be offset
by a firm increasing its export sales sufficiently to bring the overall
financial position into surplus. With export orientation a firm may
become dependent for the majority of its sales and profits from overseas sales. Hence a strong home market, which was often interpreted to
mean a protected home market, need not be a *necessary* condition for
profits to be made in either the long-run or the short-run.

Another important point will be the continued growth of component
sales abroad; from £123·9 million or 28·5% of motor industry
exports in 1959, to £285·1 million or 41·3% of total exports in 1968,

[*] Our contention that export sales will vary inversely with the level of home
demand is borne out by recent empirical work by Ball, Eaton and Steiner,
'The Relationship between U.K. Export Performance in Manufactures & Internal
Demand', *Economic Journal*, pp. 501–518 (September 1966).

shows the trend of the future. Until the 'new' manufacturing centres feel strong enough, the export of increasing numbers of complete vehicles will become more difficult.

THE PATTERN OF WORLD TRADE IN MOTOR VEHICLES

To conclude this chapter a look is taken at the general pattern of trade in cars and commercial vehicles. The destinations of vehicles exported by the main vehicle producers (the U.K., U.S.A., Canada, France, Japan, West Germany, Italy and Sweden) are aggregated into the main world-wide geographical groupings of Europe, the Americas, Asia, Oceania and Africa. In the foreseeable future most imports of vehicles into the Americas will continue to be accounted for by the U.S.A. and Canada. Therefore we split-up the world regions in terms of their degree of commercial and industrial development. Europe is described as 'developed', the U.S.A. as 'highly developed', and the other three regions as 'developing'.

The pattern of the world trade in cars emanating from these three regions is shown in *Table 11.25*.

Table 11.25

PERCENTAGE OF TOTAL CAR EXPORTS
TO THE THREE WORLD REGIONS

Year	Highly developed	Developed	Developing
1960	34·2	42·8	23·0
1961	28·9	52·8	28·3
1962	26·6	56·3	23·1
1963	22·7	57·7	19·6
1964	26·6	53·8	19·6
1965	27·7	55·0	17·3
1966	35·1	50·2	14·7
1967	39·6	46·7	13·7
1968	34·9	44·1	21·0
1969	38·5	45·0	16·5

Typically, over 80% of imports into the Americas from outside is accounted for by imports into the U.S.A. and Canada★. Also, over 90%

★ In 1967 this figure was down to 66%.

of American and Canadian exports to the Americas were exports to each other. This means that the vast majority of car imports into the Americas is accounted for by the European countries and Japan, and over 63% of car imports into the Americas came from these sources.

Japan is included in the list of 'developed' countries in this analysis. Furthermore, as Japanese imports were very small over this period, the total volume of Asian car imports was virtually unaffected by whether Japanese imports were included or not.

About 50% of world trade in cars is accounted for by the developed countries. Virtually all car imports into developed countries have been from other developed countries; only a tiny proportion of imports have been from countries at a different stage of economic development, mainly from the U.S.A. and Canada. In contrast, about 38% of developed countries' car exports has been with highly developed and with developing economies.

The same approach was taken in examining the overall direction of commercial vehicle exports (*Table 11.26*).

Table 11.26

PERCENTAGE OF TOTAL COMMERCIAL VEHICLE EXPORTS
TO THE THREE WORLD REGIONS

Year	Highly developed	Developed	Developing
1960	27·0	36·1	26·9
1961	33·0	29·9	57·1
1962	38·4	23·1	38·5
1963	32·5	19·7	47·8
1964	30·0	22·5	47·5
1965	33·1	17·4	49·5
1966	29·7	28·3	42·0
1967	24·2	34·6	41·2
1968	24·1	28·1	47·8
1969	30·0	25·4	44·6

To all intents and purposes all CV imports into Europe were from other developed countries, but in this instance, intra-developed trade is much less significant as a proportion of total trade than it was in the case of cars. This is explained by the role of the CV as a capital good which helps to facilitate trade and industry in general and economic development in particular. In the case of intra-trade in the highly-developed part of the world, American and Canadian exports to each other typically accounted for 60% of all imports into American countries from outside, compared with around 37% in the case of cars★. A priori it may have been expected that America south of the Rio Grande would have accounted for a larger proportion of CV imports into the Americas than where car imports were concerned. It may appear that instead these countries were more ready to spend resources and reserves on consumption items than on developmental tools. The introduction of locally assembled cars and vehicles does not significantly change this conclusion; indeed the proportion of imported units to domestically produced ones was smaller in the case of cars than it was in the case of vehicles. However, the trade between the U.S.A. and Canada accounted for 79% of their total CV exports to the Americas. In other words 21% of American–Canadian CV exports to the Americas were sold south of the Rio Grande, compared with 10% in the case of cars. This implied that this part of the Americas supplemented its CV imports from the rest of the world by purchasing considerable numbers from the U.S.A. and Canada; indeed, 50% of their total CV imports came from this source compared with 20% in the case of cars. Typically, in the 1960s total cars imported into the Americas, apart from Canada and the U.S.A., exceeded 165 000 units and over 70 000 in the case of vehicles. In value terms CV imports often exceeded those of cars. Consequently the countries involved were spending a considerable part of their resources on transport equipment designed to help economic development.

In 1967, of 225 464 commercial vehicles exported to the Americas, 121 919 were bought by the U.S.A., 35 329 by Canada and the remaining 68 216 were sold on the rest of the Continent. In the same year, of 1 496 925 cars exported to the Americas from outside sources, 1 016 628 were sold in the U.S.A. and 35 329 in Canada. In short, some 30% of CV imports into the Americas from outside sources were sold in areas outside the U.S.A. and Canada compared with 34% of all car imports. However, most CV trade is with countries at different stages of economic development. In 1967, if intra Canadian–American trade is omitted, then over 55% of CV exports and 39% of car exports are between countries at different stages of economic development.

The more widely publicised theories of international trade explained the existence of trading in terms of the different factor endowments enjoyed by different countries. For instance, countries with a large capital:labour ratio would be more efficient in producing

---

★ The 90% of U.S. and Canadian exports to the Americas which are to each other accounts for almost 37% of all imports into American countries. In the case of commercial vehicles the figures are 79% and 57%.

capital intensive goods than those with a high labour:capital ratio. If we assume that the factor endowments of the three main categories of nation vary from a high capital:output ratio through a lower capital: output ratio, to a high labour:capital ratio, we can hazard a guess as to how well trade in motor vehicles is explained by theories which cite different factor endowments as the basis for international trade. As only some 55% of CV exports and 39% of car exports are traded between areas at different stages of development it would appear that theorems such as the Hecksher–Ohlin analysis are not a complete explanation of the causes of international trade, although it has provoked considerable debate and controversy embodied in a whole host of literature. The Leontief 'Paradox', for instance, suggested that most of the U.S.A.'s exports were *labour* intensive and her imports capital intensive. However, imported goods may have been made by capital intensive methods in the U.S.A. but they were made by *labour* intensive methods in their countries of origin. In other words, the analysis concerning the causes of trade has long been in a state of flux. Linder's interpretation of the basis of international trade was that trade was greatest between countries, not with different factor endowments, but with similar demand patterns★. Trade occurred if the traded good could be produced under conditions where substantial scale economies were possible and if the general economic conditions in export markets were similar to those at home.

In conclusion then, trade with the U.S.A. could exist because her labour costs would make American small cars either very expensive or unprofitable to produce†. Under-developed countries cannot produce cars as cheaply as the more developed areas. In practice the price of locally assembled or manufactured cars suggests a substantial cost penalty. All this could be interpreted to support Hecksher–Ohlin type analysis, but the large trade between directly comparable and competing nations tend more to the Linder type explanation.

★ S. B. Linder, *An Essay on Trade and Transformation*, J. Wiley, New York (1961).

† Nevertheless, all American firms have embarked on producing such vehicles partly as a strategic move aimed at imports.

12

LABOUR RELATIONS

Although the motor industry is mainly associated with the utilisation of vast amounts of capital, it is also one of the largest employers of labour in the U.K. Consequently the smooth operation of the industry depends upon a smooth inflow of labour as well as capital inputs. Any interruption of this flow at any point will lead to the immediate or eventual disruption of the output flow. As a result, labour relations, or the maintenance of good worker to employer relations, is of crucial importance. Before looking at this question more fully, let us have a brief look at the numbers employed in the industry.

EMPLOYMENT IN THE MOTOR INDUSTRY

EMPLOYMENT STATISTICS

The Ministry of Labour* and Department of Employment and Productivity (DEP) figures give the picture shown in *Table 12.1* regarding the numbers employed in the different regions in the U.K. motor industry.

As mentioned during an earlier brief look at location,† the establishment of plants in 'new' areas has meant the relative decline of the traditional centres of production in the Midlands and South East.

---

* Minimum List Heading 381 of the 1958 Standard Industrial Classification. These include motor vehicle manufacture and assembly plus the activities of most independent suppliers. The main category omitted is electrical components.

† Chapter 2, pp. 41–49.

Table 12.1

EMPLOYMENT IN THE U.K. MOTOR INDUSTRY (1000s)

Region	1959	1966*	1968
South East	150·6	188·4	165·5
South West	9·3	14·1	13·7
Midlands and Yorkshire	176·9	199·9	188·5
North West	29·4	56·7	68·3
Northern	2·1	5·0	5·5
Scotland	7·3	21·4	18·0
Wales	6·4	14·3	14·2
Total U.K.	382·1	499·8	473·8
As % of all employees in manufacturing	4·6	5·6	5·5

* A slight change in the classification of establishments covered.

At the same time, a strong upward trend in employment has been evident during the period 1959–1968, although sharp deviations about the trend occurred year by year. Indeed, the strong upward trend is evident for the entire post-war period when it is realised that total employment in the industry in 1947 was just some 306 000. Estimates by the SMMT put total employment in 1935 at 150 000, in 1930 at around 120 000, and in 1924 at around 100 000. A straight comparison of all these estimates is inadmissible due to the different methods and basis of calculation but they do point to a five-fold increase in employment between 1924 and 1968. Over the same period vehicle output increased by over fourteen-fold, illustrating the growth of labour productivity.

In terms of occupation and sex the data suggests that the growth in employment has mainly added to the demand for male labour (*Table 12.2*) whereas by occupation the proportion of non-manual to manual has varied in inverse proportion to total employment. In other words,

Table 12.2*

MALE AND FEMALE EMPLOYMENT (1000s)

Employees	1959	1966	1968
Males	329·8	431·6	409·0
Females	52·0	61·5	56·8

* The figures differ from the totals given in *Table 12.1* as the surveys were taken at different times of the year.

as demand falls it is easier to lay-off production workers quickly but more difficult to cut-down on the 'fixed' labour content such as managerial and technical staff. Clerical and administrative grades are more highly connected with current output and vary in proportion to current employment.

The occupational surveys by the then Ministry of Labour (now the DEP) only commenced in 1963. Since 1963 the proportion of manual employees has fallen from 79·4% to 77·0%, most of the reduction in employment falling on the non-staff grades (*Table 12.3*).

Table 12.3

MANUAL AND NON–MANUAL EMPLOYMENT (1000s)

Employees	1963	1966	1968
Manual	347·4	385·0	358·9
Non-manual	90·1	108·0	107·2

Of the total numbers employed in the motor industry the author estimates that over 340 000 are employed by the vehicle producers themselves. Approximate totals for the various manufacturers in 1970 are shown in *Table 12.4*

Table 12.4*

EMPLOYMENT BY THE MAJOR U.K. PRODUCERS IN 1970

Producer	No. manual workers employed	Total no. employed
BLMC	135 000	180 000+
Ford	55 000	70 000+
Rootes	26 000	40 000
Vauxhall	30 000	38 000
Others	10 000	16 000+

* These figures show the typical picture although in recession and boom the precise figures for individual firms can of course alter.

Of this number the vast majority are engaged in the manufacture and assembly of motor cars, perhaps fewer than 75 000 being employed on the CV side. In addition to this, the majority of people employed by outside suppliers are engaged in activities concerned with motor cars rather than vehicles.

These numbers are employed in a variety of different plants in different locations and of different sizes (*Table 12.5*).

Table 12.5

Producer	No. of plants
BLMC	60
Ford	22
Vauxhall–Bedford	3
Rootes	5

The two smallest producers each concentrate their output at two main car plants and one CV plant. These are integrated units engaged in manufacturing as well as assembly work. Rootes has two smaller plants engaged on component production. BLMC and Ford have eight and three large car and CV plants respectively; the rest are smaller units employing anything from a few hundred to around 5000 people. The vast majority are employed in the huge integrated plants at Longbridge, Cowley, Leyland, Coventry, Swindon, Dagenham and Halewood. In terms of labour relations the smaller the plant the more intimate these should be, but in the car industry small plants appear as strike prone as large ones,[*] although small firms are less strike prone than large ones. Why this should be will be explained later.

THE GROWTH OF INDUSTRIAL STRIFE

During the inter-war period the growth of large car plants took place at a time of less than full employment, when firms also tended to be smaller and less impersonal. After 1945 the economy was fully employed and a new phenomenon arose in the industry: labour militancy. Labour was less afraid to invoke industrial action in support of what they regarded to be a 'just grievance'. Before World War II, Ford and Vauxhall did not recognise and therefore did not negotiate with trade unions. It was only in 1944, for instance, that Ford reluctantly recognised the trade unions. Consequently after 1945 the labour force was better organised and better able to 'fight for its rights'. During the war, new negotiating machinery was established geared to manage-

[*] H. A. Turner, G. Clack and G. Roberts, *Labour Relations in the Motor Industry*, Allen and Unwin, London, pp. 167, 179, 328, etc. (1967).

ment–worker consultation; after 1945 the labour force was used to being consulted on matters, including those of pay and conditions. In the peacetime conditions prevailing, any manufacturer attempting to impose his will on the rank and file would have been flying in the face of a changed environment. So the post-war world where labour was in short supply led to a greater feeling of independence amongst workers where bargaining strength was increased by the opportunity to obtain alternative employment without difficulty. Compared with pre-war, 'workshop discipline' deteriorated and managements' motives came under critical scrutiny. The picture of the car plants as manned by grateful escapees of unemployment, especially from the Celtic fringes and the North of England, was replaced by one of a self-confident and assertive labour force. In the field of industrial relations the post-war situation has not been good.

Between 1959 and 1968 the number of industrial disputes in the British motor industry has been on a rising trend. However, the number of workers involved and the working days lost have fluctuated wildly. In terms of days lost per 1000 employees during each year between 1959 and 1970 the motor industry has a much worse record than industry in general (*Table 12.6*).

Table 12.6

	1960	*1964*	*1968*	*1970*
No. of stoppages	129	165	233	336
No. of workers involved	186 300	150 000	402 500	271 400
Working days lost	515 000	429 000	898 000	1 105 000
Days lost per 1 000 employees	1 000–1 500	500–1 000	1 800	2 000
Days lost per 1 000 employees in industry in general	100–250	50–100	200	300

Source: Department of Employment and Productivity figures.

Taking total employment, the motor industry accounts for 2·1% of the employed labour force, but over the period 1959–1968 it had on average provided 15·8% of the working days lost through strikes. Strikes cost BLMC over £70 million in lost saleable output in 1969 and strikes may also have been largely responsible for Vauxhall's post-tax loss in the same year. Comfort has been taken in the fact that the U.K.'s overall picture regarding days lost through strikes is superior to that in other industrial countries. But the motor industry's performance tends to be worse than its main rivals.

Even when the U.S.A.'s figures show a worse strike record in the motor industry these gross figures do not reflect the true position as regards overall industrial unrest and disruption to production. In the U.S.A. the United Automobile Workers Union signs a three-yearly contract with the car firms. At the time the contract is being negotiated a number of strikes occur, the main one being in one of the Big Three car firms. This official strike is part of the contract bargaining ritual; the bargain struck with the firm involved is then accepted by the other main U.S. producers. The firm chosen for 'the treatment' is the one with a reasonably healthy trading position, but if possible not GMC as the amount of strike-pay incurred on bringing Ford out on strike is considerably less than that involved in GMC's case*. The firm 'chosen' has time to increase pre-strike production and fill the showrooms with its cars and during the strike the annual face-lift would occur. Hence disruption is kept to a minimum. In addition, industrial peace reigns for three years until the next ritual.

In the U.K. strikes may be small scale but highly disruptive; 50 strikers in a component works can bring the entire industry to a halt without warning. No provisions can be made as strikes are unofficial, spontaneous and instantaneous and therefore highly disruptive to production. Obviously strikes can cause lost production but what causes the strike? In other words the weakness in any 'strike-breaking' legislation is that it attacks the symptom and not the cause of disruption, a cause which may be management's fault as much as or more so than labour's. It is to the particular causes and proneness of car workers to strike that we now turn.

THE CAUSES OF INDUSTRIAL STRIFE

LABOUR ORGANISATION

Unlike the American or German car industries the British industry faces not one trade union but a multitude—in BLMC's case 36 and in Ford's case 22 unions. Agreement and progress on industrial matters such as wages, conditions or productivity therefore is slow. The need is always for a speedy decision, but the lengthy inter-union negotiations have meant that trade union influence has become diffuse and decisions are reached only slowly. More power has been won by the shop-floor in general and shop stewards in particular. Being on the shop-floor has meant that shop stewards can take quick decisions and obtain

---

* In 1970 the UAW brought GMC to a standstill for 8 weeks when 380 000 manual workers were on strike.

results. Often the various managements have found it worthwhile to buy-off trouble at the local level regardless of the impact of such concessions on wage rates and working conditions elsewhere in the industry. Under these circumstances militancy equals results and this in turn equals new members for the trade union represented by the more successful shop stewards. Consequently rival trade union organisations have felt constrained in denouncing or suppressing zealous shop stewards even in the interests of the wider economic well-being of their members throughout the industry. As a result members are often thrown-out of work by a shop-floor strike in a very small section of the industry.

An attempt by the trade union leadership to regain control in the late 1960s was based on the view that power did indeed rest with union members and shop stewards. Consequently they must be consulted on matters that affect them. If negotiations between unions and management occur on the basis that the union side must consult and be given a mandate by shop stewards, then negotiators became delegates and not representatives. If negotiators reflect the members' wishes then bargaining can return to the centre without the shop floor feeling that their negotiators are out of touch or do not consult them enough. Official negotiations would therefore bind members as it was their wishes that were being carried out.

The thesis is that power returns to the centre as 'grass roots' democracy makes the rank and file more responsible. However, even this may not prevent unions fighting for members by trying to outbid each other in militancy. A case in point occurred in February 1970. A mass meeting of all Ford workers decided to return to work on the basis of an agreed pay settlement. Only the company's Swansea plant refused, and a shortage of Swansea components would have soon closed Ford's operations. Unfortunately the leaders of the Transport and General Workers Union and Amalgamated Engineering and Foundryworkers did not give the necessary leadership because of a fear of being outbid in militancy. Here *plant* democracy was irrelevant, that is, Ford's *national* wage bargain was not a plant by plant bargain, and therefore democracy in Swansea appeared as irresponsibility in Dagenham or Langley. A refusal by the unions to condemn the Swansea strike meant that 'grass roots democracy' was shown to be meaningless in practice as the majority were coerced by a tiny minority. To a certain extent then the militancy at plant level and the militancy shown by union leaders has stemmed from the large number of unions and the constraint this often places on really effective bargaining and leadership.

METHODS OF PAYMENT

Another factor leading to friction is bound up with the method of payment. Traditionally the Midland car factories paid workers on the basis of piece-work, each different job being priced at a particular rate so that each group of workers was watchful that all the other groups did not narrow or widen the pay differentials. The maintenance or the closing of differentials became tendentious and explosive issues. So as well as causing 'wage inflation', piece-rates build-in and intensify tensions. Working patterns become hard to change because of their possible effects on piece-rates, and any attempt to alter these or the product itself can be the source of acrimonious bargaining and spontaneous strikes. The four main motor firms are therefore moving in the direction of time-rates which keep differentials under close control and avoid the contentious bargaining and inflexibility built into individual piece-rates.

Ford, in its locations outside the West Midlands, has always paid time-rates, and Vauxhall consolidated its piece-rate system into time-rates in 1956. Standard-Triumph introduced a time-rate system, plus bonuses paid to production teams on a time-rate basis*, in 1948; piece-rates were not eliminated completely though—indeed, a strike of 400 engine fitters over piece-rates for a new model (the Triumph Dolomite) postponed its introduction in 1971. In 1970 Rootes changed from a piece-rate system to time-rates when the long-term advantages were deemed to justify the short-term expense. Rootes' Midland rates rose on average by 1s. 2d. an hour to 15s. 6d. with the top rate being 17s. 4d. Only the former British Motor Corporation retained piece-rates in their entirety in its Midlands factories. BMC hoped to improve the situation by the full use of job evaluation. This puts workers in wage grades according to systematically applied standards of skill, responsibility and experience. This could replace the hundreds of piecemeal agreements by as few as five grades†. This could lead to greater labour flexibility by avoiding demarcation disputes or changes in job 'prices', and the increased flexibility could conceivably reduce tension and the number of disputes. It could also avoid the

* Between 1948 and 1970 the Standard-Triumph payments system reverted, almost in its entirety, to piece-rates. These were fixed at such a level that during the 1950s the company's employees became probably the country's highest paid car workers.

† In 1971 BLMC's offer to consolidate the Cowley factories' piece-rate system into an hourly rate—initially at a rate of £1 an hour—was accepted by the assembly workers, and marked the beginning of the end of the BMC piece-rate system.

system of 'leap frogging' wage claims endemic in a piece-rate system.

Significantly, no CV producer pays by results as the lack of a homogeneous product makes piece-rates unworkable. Quality rather than speed is required here, and as one man can do a multitude of tasks, the bargaining endemic in a piece-rate system would be misplaced and time consuming. Another significant point is that whereas Vauxhall and Ford took their wage rates and wage systems with them to their new locations in the development areas, when the Midland firms moved to the Celtic fringes and the North of England, they left their piece-work systems behind them*. Time-rates of one sort or another were introduced into their new factories. Over time, different areas and different firms have tended to pay their workers more than others and it is here that one comes to the problem of differentials and the fight for parity.

Before World War II the Ford company paid its workers the highest wage rates in the industry. In 1938 the best Ford time-rate was 2s. 7d. an hour, generating earnings slightly better than those generated by incentive payment systems in Coventry. By 1968 the best Dagenham rate was 11s. 3½d. an hour compared with an average of 14s. 10½d. an hour in Coventry. The 480% increase in Coventry was only just sufficient to keep ahead of the increased cost of living, although the Ford workers had fallen behind†. So over time the car worker had just maintained his standard of living, and differentials had appeared between different firms. This latter point is illustrated in *Table 12.7*.

Table 12.7

NET RATE PER HOUR FOR AN IDENTICAL TASK*

Germany		France		Sweden	U.K.	
VW	13s. 1d.	Renault	8s. 4d.		BMC	
Ford	12s. 1d.	Citroen	7s. 4d.	Volvo 18s. 9d.	(Longbridge)	15s. 8d.
Opel	13s. 4d.	Peugeot	9s. 0d.		Ford	10s. 6d.
Mercedes	13s. 3d.				Vauxhall	9s. 10d.
BMW	12s. 5d.				Rootes (Ryton)	17s. 4d.

Source: *The Sunday Times*, p. 25 (21 December 1969).

* Installation of door lock with door handle and connecting rods (in 1969).

* There were a few exceptions to this. However, as piece-rates are bought out in the Midlands' plants by firms paying hourly rates in excess of £1, the regional workers will become more insistent in their demands for parity.

† Taking the purchasing power of the pound as 20s. in 1938, it was just over 5s. in 1968.

The differential and parity problem arises in three particular ways: within a plant; within a firm; and between firms. Within a plant the worker's aim is to maintain the differential between his pay and that of other groups of workers doing different jobs. As the jobs undertaken are so obviously varied there is no serious demand that all workers within a plant should achieve parity. When differentials between plants in the same firm are discussed, however, then parity is an important issue, especially after 1969 when workers in the 'new' areas became more aware of their inferior position following the publicity given to the Rootes–Ryton pay agreement*.

Regional differentials show evidence of replacing in-plant differentials as the major source of grievances within a given firm. Car workers have always been paid more in the Midlands than elsewhere, as it has been generally accepted within the motor industry—often erroneously† —that their productivity is higher and the labour supply is tighter. Ford and Vauxhall, however, pay the same rates in all their different plants, although differences in productivity exist. Rootes and BLMC pay different rates and in the latter's case the differentials have become extremely noticeable following the creation of British Leyland out of its constituent parts. Whereas BMC and Rootes tended to pay the equivalent of 5s. an hour less in the 'new' locations, the gap between the Leyland truck plants in Lancashire and the BMC car factories in the Midlands was of a similar order. This was the immediate cause of a severe strike at Leyland's in 1969. The average weekly wage in the Leyland truck plants was £21 compared with £30 for BMC in the Midlands. As will be shown later, other reasons existed for the strike, but parity with the Midlands was both an issue and a rallying call. On the basis of productivity Ford should perhaps differentiate between its Halewood workers and its Dagenham ones but its policy has been one of company-wide bargains and parity. Again, can parity between a truck plant and a car plant be justified? If we have two different products then it would appear that parity is irrelevant on objective grounds. However, if both the car and CV side were equally efficient then the marginal revenue product should be the same in each case and parity would be justified, although possibly at the expense of higher CV prices.

An equally contentious issue is parity between firms and again this

---

* In 1969 Rootes agreed to pay workers at its Ryton-on-Dunsmore plant in Coventry 17s. 4d. an hour to 'buy-out' the piece-work system in favour of a measured day-work system in which a fixed rate is paid in return for a n accepted output level.

† For instance, in 1968 Ford workers each produced 11·7 vehicles a year compared with 5·6 vehicles at British Leyland.

was brought to a head after the Rootes–Ryton agreement. The high wages paid in the Midland car plants have always influenced the wages in the component firms clustered around the car makers and sent ripples as far as Luton and Dagenham where unions had only tended to pay lip service to the need for inter-firm parity. The Ryton agreement, however, concentrated the minds of the Ford workers on the difference between their hourly earnings and those in the Midlands. Here it was felt that in the battle for parity the rank and file could not place any reliance on national trade union officials as they were held responsible for the workers' inferior position. This was not altogether fair, as the piece-work system did allow increased earnings from intensive work which time-rates did not. The type of payment system had been seen as a management prerogative and in addition, the Ford shop stewards were in favour of the Ford company-wide wage-structure as distinct from BMC's plant-by-plant bargaining. As Ford paid the same wages in all plants the company did not see why it should match its competitors highest wage any more than its lowest. One way out would have been to abandon the company wage system and to have given higher wages in plants in high wage areas and lower wages elsewhere. This would have given parity within areas, but again union leaders would have strenuously opposed giving-up the Ford company-wage. Also, the question of inter-firm parity would have only been solved at the expense of creating the BLMC problem, where the demand is for inter-plant parity with the Midlands.

So although the demand for parity has tended to exist on two levels (excluding intra-plant parity), with Ford and Vauxhall workers wanting parity between companies and BLMC workers wanting parity within the single company, in the end these demands amounted to the same thing. Workers wanted the same rates as those paid to the men in the Midlands. BLMC and Rootes were prepared to move towards wage rates related to parity of productivity; this of course meant that differences in productivity meant differences in wages. On this point union leaders tended to accept intellectually the basis of the argument, but the actual wage earner may have been less patient whilst his productivity was gradually brought up to Midland levels. The increased inter-change of views between shop stewards from different regions has given force to the parity movement as did another significant move. This was the growing alliance between British and Continental trade unionists, so the parity problem may shift to yet another plane with demands for international parity in Europe. If such an alliance becomes real any threat to transfer work from, say British to German factories would become hollow in the face of union 'blacking'. The parity movement may eventually become one of parity with the U.S.A., an eventuality fully endorsed by the UAW fearful of more work being transferred to foreign cheap-labour centres. Of course parity with the U.S.A. without commensurate productivity improvements would price European cars out of world markets*.

Another variant of the parity problem was the Coventry 'Toolroom Agreement'. Introduced as a war time measure to boost toolworkers earnings, to induce them not to move from crucial war time tasks to more lucrative assembly-line jobs, this tied toolroom wages to the average earnings of specified highly-paid production workers in the Coventry area. The system was retained after the war and led to 'wage drift' in the skilled-worker sector in Coventry. In 1971 the Coventry Engineering Workers Association unilaterally abolished the agreement, provoking a rash of unofficial strikes in the process. It would appear, however, that a system of payments based entirely on what other highly paid operatives earned and not on the productivity of the work force involved was questionable, and it made it difficult for motor manufacturers among others, to control unit costs of production.

The parity movement could be perhaps one of the most contentious and fractious issues of the 1970s. Clearly by the end of the 1960s it had led to 'grass roots democracy' a manifestation of which was the Ford workers' rejection in 1969 of a 30s. to 35s. pay increase agreed by the union negotiators. This lack of consultation tends to be a source of friction in itself. The shop stewards additional weapon could be the cry for parity with the Midlands. Indeed, the 1969 Ford strike led to a 'parity' strike and to a parity movement which first emerged as a serious force in 1970. This led to the highest pay award in the history of U.K. Ford of between £4 and £5 15s. a week. The cry for parity within a firm led (in 1969) to the first strike at Leylands since 1926. Again parity led to one of BMC's highest pay awards when the BMC Bathgate workers received an award of £4 10s. This award was partly related to productivity but the size of it was due to the parity movement.

If the parity movement becomes too successful there is the possibility of a clash between two incompatible shibboleths, parity versus differentials. Traditionally, since 1945 the hourly rate in the tight labour market of the Midlands has been higher, and tradition means a great deal where differentials are concerned. Hopefully inter-firm and

---

* Roughly speaking, each American worker is paid three times his European counterpart but produces over twice as much.

inter-area differentials are less entrenched than intra-plant ones; after all, in 1938 Ford paid the highest rates and it was only the immediate post-war labour shortage in the Midlands which gave rise to the present situation. In addition, Midland trade unionists have supported the new areas in their cry for parity for reasons of self interest. If wages are the same everywhere then there is less incentive to switch work away from the Midlands.

STRIKES IN KEY PLANTS

Another source of discontent is the disruption caused throughout a firm by strikes in a key plant. Many components, whether bought-out or manufactured within the combine, are purchased from a single source. Such a situation can lead to a relatively small strike crippling an entire complex. In 1970 a strike involving a few hundred men at Scottish Stampings Ayr closed the Bedford works, and a strike of just 117 component inspectors gradually threw all 27 000 Vauxhall-Bedford workers out of work. Thus the single source may cover not only parts and components but a specific task. Where division of labour is taken to a high degree, with each group of workers dependent on another, a strike by a small group responsible for one task can halt the entire operation. This is certainly the case in the motor industry. This brings home to car workers the idea that huge impersonal forces appear to be at work with their jobs threatened by factors completely beyond their control. In these cases it is usually the management and not the other workers who are blamed, all of which sours industrial relations. Where the small car and CV specialists are concerned, if suppliers are to find it worthwhile supplying their requirements, the assemblers must purchase components in volumes equivalent to between one month and six months supply. Consequently production is rarely interrupted by strikes in outside plants, which all goes to help industrial relations. Here the analysis comes near to one of the most important causes of strikes in the car industry.

PSYCHOLOGICAL FACTORS

An important factor governing labour relations is bound up in purely psychological reasons. Work in the car plants especially on the final trim, paint and assembly lines is monotonous, impersonal and anonymous. The monotony leads to weariness and frustration for which

strike action is often the safety valve. People subject to the pressures
of a moving assembly line can feel subordinate to and governed by
machinery. Under such pressures and conditions people can become
brittle and subject to 'wildcat' behaviour in an attempt to break the
frustrations built up by monotony. Frustration can come from other
factors arising from pressure of work. The impersonal factors, such as
strikes in other parts of the industry or the impersonal and mechanical
assembly track, can be important. The speed of the track may prevent a
man doing a job to his own satisfaction and lack of pride in one's work
can lead to dissatisfaction. The assembly track and its speed is regarded
as less of an ogre in piece-rate factories or where generous bonuses are
tied to time-rates* but the Ford track appears to lead to tremendous
animosity†. Perhaps Ford's problem was one of attempting to attain
BMC output figures on a Vauxhall wage structure.

Being a mere cog in the wheel and responsible for very little in the
way of creative output means that the assembly line generally can be a
very monotonous, impersonal and anonymous place to work. In the
engine plants workers tend to feel that they are creating something
which is technically and mechanically superior to past products and
this may give a sense of pride in one's work. Similarly in the CV
plants men feel a greater sense of identity with the product even in the
mass-producers' factories. This, together with a higher proportion of
skilled and older men than is usual where car production is concerned,
may mean a steadier work force and perhaps a happier one. The
assembly tracks in the mass-producing and quantity producing factories are faster moving than in the case of factories where specialist
cars and vehicles are produced. Hence the workers are under less
pressure and are able to take pride in producing a quality product.

Further resentment is often produced by the increasing size of the
firm‡ or trade union. Lack of consultation on the part of management
and union can cause strikes because the worker may feel more anonymous and less significant than ever. The deterioration of labour relations at Leyland's plant can be traced back to 1966 when some members
of the management team, who had close and long-standing ties with
the work-force, retired. The traditional close relationship between
management and men seemed to get less strong. The larger scale of

* Commentators dismissing the problems posed by 'track work' base their
evidence on experience in piece-rate factories. For instance, see G. Clack, *Industrial
Relations in a British Car Factory*, C.U.P., p. 90 (1967).
† See: G. Turner, *The Car Makers*, Penguin (1964), also *the Sunday Times*,
1 February 1970.
‡ This is only a tendency, for some large firms have good labour relations and
some small firms poor labour relations measured in terms of strike proneness.

Leyland's activities diverted management's attention from the crucial task of promoting and maintaining the personnel side of management. The increasing remoteness of top management from Lancashire meant that power resided elsewhere and the speed by which decisions were taken, which affected labour relations, tended to fall.

The car worker in the U.K. has become conditioned to seeing much of his earnings or even his job itself disappear overnight. At the same time his traditional conspicious consumption has led him to spend up to and beyond the limits of his current income by taking on numerous hire-purchase and other credit commitments*. Consequently earnings may be high but uncertain at a time when commitments are high and has led to much general uncertainty and worry on the part of the operative. This strengthens demands for higher immediate earnings and the car worker is often prepared to strike to achieve them if need be. Trade fluctuations or strikes in key plants lead to lay-offs of varying duration which in turn leads to ill-will, additional insecurity, and a feeling of general helplessness on the part of the worker. On the CV side, where output fluctuates less and larger component stocks are held, less uncertainty is attached to jobs and this increases workers' good will and general happiness. Strikes are therefore rare. For instance, ERF has never been on short-time, Leyland last experienced this in 1956, and Foden only in 1956, 1960 and 1971. Significantly, Foden has a slightly worse record of labour relations than the other CV specialists, although even here strikes are very few and far between.

Insecurity is therefore endemic in the car plants partly because of the fluctuations in earnings set against constant commitments but partly for historical reasons. Dagenham, for instance, 'grew out of misery' in the sense that much of the original labour force fled from unemployment and poverty in the depressed areas of the 1930s. The same is true of many people employed in Luton and the Midland car plants. The prosperity of the post-war period has meant many new jobs in the former depressed areas but significant migration to the South East and the Midlands still occurs. In addition, the expansion of the industry into areas of traditional militancy such as South Wales, Merseyside and Glasgow has meant that the labour force is still inhibited with the feeling of uncertainty. Any threat, real or imaginary, to a person's job can therefore lead to instant and massive strike action.

The type of 'manning-pattern' can also be important here. The U.K. system has been to have enough men to produce at maximum capacity throughout the year and any fall in demand means short-time working. The U.S. system is to gear manning to minimum yearly production

* See: G. Turner, *The Car Makers*, Penguin (1964).

levels. If demand increases or falls then overtime or sacking occurs. There is little 'short-time' in Detroit. BMC moved towards the U.S. system in 1966 by sacking 12 000 men but the short-term effects were disastrous. The U.S. system means greater security for the labour force in that consumption patterns geared to permanent income are not threatened by short-time working. In the U.K. the attempt to introduce U.S. manning scales had a disastrous impact on morale and BMC's productivity slumped because of the restrictive practices and strikes caused by uncertainty. Only by guaranteeing to halt the factory closures envisaged in the rationalisation scheme was BMC able to reassure the remaining labour force and restore productivity. However, in the long-run the movement to U.S. manning patterns should reduce uncertainty by avoiding short-time working. In a very severe slump the reintroduction of short-time may be preferable to sacking, but as such occurrences should be less frequent than formerly, uncertainty should be reduced and labour relations improved.

POLITICAL FACTORS

Political factors may play a minor role where strikes are concerned but are unlikely to be the overriding cause. An existing issue may be complicated by the desire of union leaders to establish themselves in the public eye or in the trade union movement generally. This could lead to increased militancy with rival unions attempting to 'deliver the goods'. Again politically motivated shop stewards may fan the flames thereby complicating an existing issue, but the strike would be caused by the 'real' factors which have led to discontent; it is only in this atmosphere of frustration and distrust that the ideologically motivated or megalomaniacal shop steward can thrive. Few workers are going to sacrifice earnings to suit the political or personal ambitions of individuals or groups of individuals.

THE NEGOTIATING STRUCTURE

The negotiating structure in any particular motor firm can affect labour-management relations. Ford and Vauxhall have traditionally negotiated independently, only recognising the trade unions during the war; Standard-Triumph followed suit in 1945, as did Rootes in 1970. However, British Leyland still has its wage negotiations handled through the Engineering Employers' Federation (EEF). As Standard-Leyland negotiated independently and only British Motor Holdings

P*

worked through the EEF, it could be that British Leyland as a whole may eventually move out of the EEF. If this occurs then the motor employers as a whole could co-ordinate policy on pay and conditions. This would be especially necessary if U.K. unions copied the UAW by picking on one of the main motor companies to gain initial concessions and then waiting for matching concessions by other producers. Under these circumstances the 'victim' should co-ordinate its offer with what the others were prepared to offer.

From time to time suggestions have been mooted for a special body to study the motor industry's industrial relations to suggest improvements, and to investigate individual disputes. This body would include unions and management in both the car producing and component making sectors. The extent to which frank discussion would take place would, however, probably be constrained by the knowledge that both sides would also be negotiating with each other over pay and conditions at a later date. In addition, this type of procedure would be of little use in solving local disputes which because they occur without warning can be most damaging of all.

It is possible, however, that in the future all motor companies may be in a position to conduct their own pay negotiations together with their own disputes procedure, a procedure which could be on an industry-wide basis. This would reach down from top management through works committees to the shop floor and would mean that British Leyland would come into line with the other producers. The emphasis on company and plant level bargaining with revised pay systems and disputes procedures would improve the overall standard of industrial relations. It would mean the virtual end of the EEF in its present form, with British Leyland and the component makers taking charge of their own affairs. Consequently the tortuous 70 year old disputes procedure, which causes as many troubles as it solves through its slowness of action, would be abandoned. This would mean that individual managements are willing to face up to their own responsibilities and not to pass them off to a loosely knit and ineffective employers' association.

THE ROLE OF MANAGEMENT

This leads us on to one of the main factors influencing labour relations and the incidence of strikes; the role and quality of management★.

★ See also: G. Clack, *Industrial Relations in a British Car Factory*, C.U.P., pp. 96–97 (1967).

In too many cases the motor companies were run by men who saw themselves as running an engineering company for engineers by engineers. Consequently whatever management skills they had were the product not of training but of their own personality. In this situation actions became the overriding prerogative but thinking and planning became luxuries. For instance, BMC spent £1000 on training each technologist, £250 on each technician, £200 on each craftsman but only £25 per head on management training. This led to an almost total lack of product planning on the one hand and efficient marketing on the other. Added to this, labour relations were not regarded as of sufficient importance to warrant board-room representation. Consequently this important sector was left either to junior management unsure of their own powers or to a changing group of head-office administrators called in to deal with trouble when it occurred. Of course this system was totally inadequate to ensure good labour relations. The need was for trained personnel officers at plant level who were given considerable powers of discretion to bargain and who were given a high status within the motor company's organisation. The need has been for management trained in ways of preventing issues being exaggerated into strike action and in tracing sources of possible grievance before they occur.

Some motor companies have been better prepared in curing grievances than others but most have been weak on the 'prevention' side. The Management Advisory Scheme at Vauxhall, which brought management and workers together to discuss general company policy and particular matters affecting industrial relations, was a notable success from 1945 to about 1960. Subsequently, consultation deteriorated as the company became much bigger, with greater emphasis being placed on car production. This and the comparatively low hourly wage rates became sources of strife. Furthermore, the two unions represented in Vauxhall's factories* changed their own attitudes and structure within the plants, with the result that the Management Advisory Committee virtually lost its power to influence matters; the unions tended to believe that the MAC was intended to stem their influence in the company. The workers representatives wielded more shop floor power than the official shop stewards. However, in the early 1960s the stewards formed the majority of workers representatives on the MAC, and this, together with the revival of a joint union structure evolved along more normal lines, meant that the unions began to feel that the MAC had outlived its usefulness. The emergence

* The National Union of Vehicle Builders and the Amalgamated Engineering Union.

of a joint shop stewards committee virtually succeeded the MAC. Furthermore, in the mid-1960s Vauxhall became a victim of an inter-union power struggle when the ETU claimed negotiating rights in the firm's factories, whereas the NUVB and AEU felt negotiations would be quicker and more efficient if negotiating rights were confined to themselves.

Labour relations at Vauxhall's Luton plant were nevertheless still better than those experienced elsewhere in the large motor companies. The other firms placed a far greater emphasis on financial incentives than on management–worker consultation. This clearly was not sufficient as it did nothing to allay many of the underlying fears and grievances which caused strikes. A lack of 'personnel bias' and a single minded orientation to production in too many managements has obviously led to deep-rooted discontent despite the high wages paid. Consequently many strikes may have been due fundamentally to indifference towards staff relationships by management. For instance, many managers regarded high wages as a replacement for worker consultation. The extent to which many managements were prepared to substitute finance for good labour relations was shown by the need for job evaluation in many plants. The 'decay' of BMC's wage system where the system became one of piece-rates gone slightly mad led to inflexibility, wage inflation, and a lack of control by management over its own pay system. The hundreds of different jobs paid at different rates had meant that any change in the nature and pace of work led to renegotiations and further negotiations to preserve differentials which in turn pushed up the general wage level. Any change in the product meant that much negotiation and time-wasting was involved. So as standard times and prices of a job cannot be imposed by management but must be agreed between the rate fixers and the individual operative, it has meant that in practice management has lost control over its pay system.

Often management has given in to shop floor militancy when refusing to concede some point at national level. This has undermined official procedure and shown that militancy pays. Buying off trouble by paying more money did not solve anything; at BMC it led to constant haggling and strife between worker and management and at Ford it meant continuous attempts by management to suffocate the internal shop stewards movement. The attempt at Ford's to rule by 'prerogative'—by restricting internal union activities—only produced a significant anti-management feeling among the rank and file. Management did not attempt to create a spirit of co-operation; rather, it tried to obstruct the grass roots union organisation. Too many managements were all too ready to hide behind their dignity and claim that a particular problem was management's prerogative alone and were therefore completely insensitive to the worker's concern about his own prosperity.

Management has too often given poor leadership on the industrial relations side not only by shying away from consultation but often by its own incompetence. Sometimes the poor financial returns shown by a firm are blamed on disruptions to output caused by strike action. More often the true cause is the lack of a good range of vehicles, poor marketing, and the operation of small and inefficient plants. It is true that occasionally strikes can be the main reason for a poor financial performance but often the true cause is the underlying reason for strike action!

On other occasions strikes merely exacerbate an already shaky situation. The 1961 Rootes strike at British Light Steel Pressings 'caused' the company to make a loss in 1961–1962; however, the group's financial situation had been vulnerable since the end of World War II. The company made a loss in 1956–1957 due to the recession in car demand, and further losses were made in 1964–1965, 1966–1967, and 1968–1969, due to poor marketing, a poor product range, and the domestic recession.

Clearly factors other than strike action are the real causes of financial losses, among them being the quality and expertise of management. If management shows that it is competent and gives the impression of running the firm successfully then workers are confident about future employment and earnings. In these circumstances the environment allows good labour relations to flourish. Quite the opposite is the case where a firm's future is in jeopardy. It has been suggested that the dominant fact behind all the labour trouble at Rootes' Linwood plant in the 1960s was a straightforward management failure*. The plant and the product made there never lived up to the grandiose predictions made for them. The company's poor product range made it vulnerable to a credit squeeze. The disproportionate fall in Rootes' sales after 1966 appeared to the workers as another example of mis-management rather than the fault of government action. This, in addition to a poor chain of communication between managers and workers, produced misunderstanding and led to an aura of uncertainty which poisoned the Linwood atmosphere. A failure to find alternative markets rather than the effects of a government-induced recession at home could be pointed at as the main problem, a problem which may have been induced by poor management. Credit squeezes are not unknown in France or

* *The Sunday Times* (25 May 1969).

Italy but short-time working and sackings are much rarer. Partly this is due to U.S. manning patterns but also to a vigorous search for new markets when home demand falls. If continental management is able to do this why not British? Perhaps it was easier to wring hands and blame government than to find new markets. Clearly incompetent management can be a cause of poor labour relations if it results in a failure to find new markets or puts a company's future in jeopardy; either way, jobs and earnings are threatened.

With the growth in size of the firm too many managements have become remote from the work force. If the relationship becomes too impersonal then trust and respect is often lost on both sides. Clearly the need is for improved personnel departments which see their role as consulting labour, channelling information from work floor to board room and vice versa, seeking out points of grievance before they become contentious and creating an atmosphere of trust, co-operation, confidence and respect.

Often departments residing under the title of industrial relations merely act as high powered public relations offices for management, rather than as a means of worker–management consultation. Such a situation is worse than useless. Therefore merely appointing an industrial relations director may not be sufficient. For instance, Ford established such a post in 1962 but nevertheless a strong distrust of management remained. Little shop floor bargaining occurred, which meant that shop stewards were given little opportunity to operate some constructive authority. In the factories of the U.S. parent, matters such as seniority, manning scales, and work loads are subject to mutual agreements with the stewards who then feel that they are daily dealing with members' problems. In the U.K., Ford's management regard such matters as their fief, thereby creating an atmosphere where any issue can blow up into a trial of strength. Good industrial relations obviously mean more than creating an industrial relations director. It involves a change in attitude on the side of management as much as on the trade union side, the substitution of conflict by co-operation and consultation.

THE ROLE OF THE TRADE UNIONS

Obviously then management has a crucial part to play. However, it is true that the union side must also show itself alive to the problems underlying any industrial friction. Trade unions, for instance, must be sure that attempts to gain wage parity must not be taken as an excuse to take militant action to preserve inter-regional or inter-firm differentials. It must also be recognised that if men do work harder in the Midland car factories then they are entitled to a greater reward. Likewise if the productivity of car workers is different to that of men working in tractor, CV, or component factories then again wage parity is not always justified. Parity would be unfair to the more productive workers and could lead to discontent and could also affect incentives to work harder. At Ford in 1968, each worker produced 11·7 vehicles worth £8000 compared with 5·6 vehicles worth £5180 at British Leyland. Ford, however, valued the fixed assets per worker at £5285 compared with £2217 at British Leyland. In other words, was Ford's increased labour productivity basically due to the substitution of capital for labour? This type of question is difficult to resolve but it does illustrate the need to ask whether output allocated to labour is in fact due to capital. In addition, such figures say nothing concerning the incremental labour:output ratio. Again, trade unions must avoid facing both ways as in the 'grass roots democracy' versus Swansea workers case. Situations like these only increase workers' frustration.

For the future, proposals for an industry-wide negotiating machinery could improve labour relations by increasing the speed of negotiations and agreements. Job evaluation could reduce the complexity of payment schemes and reduce friction. Grass roots democracy could give the rank and file more responsibility and remove the feeling of lack of consultation. Worker's participation in company strategy and tactics could also be beneficial with management taking more account of labour's susceptibilities, aspirations and fears. Regular meetings between management and unions could also thrash out various problems to both sides' advantage, replacing generations of conflict by one of management-labour co-operation.

CONCLUSIONS

These then are the main factors influencing labour relations. Clearly there is no single cause for good relations, or conversely, for strikes. The payments system can be cited as a source of friction, but Ford, with a time-rates system, is far from strike free. In the latter's case the shop stewards' campaign for parity with the Midlands accelerated swiftly and smoothly. However, the disparity in earnings cannot in itself explain this. Probably the nature of the Ford shop floor, where Ford workers are under particular strain, is important. Not only are cars produced at a fast rate of one a minute along each line, Ford workers, unlike their Midland colleagues, have no control over the pace of their work. The pressure of monotony from doing the same task at a fast rate for long hours at comparatively low wages all contribute to Ford workers' militancy. Monotony and pressure cannot be the whole story either. The comparatively leisurely pace of production at Leyland (Lancashire) by men with pride in their work did not save the situation when parity with the Midlands became an issue. Also, insensitive management and bungling at the top can always sour labour relations.

Perhaps psychological reasons covering monotony, frustration, uncertainty, and above all, the impersonal nature of the work involved, the lack of consultation by management and unions alike, allied to serious shortcomings on the management side, are all key problems. If management is able to find new markets to offset a trade depression at home and link this with U.S. manning patterns, then uncertainty disappears and workers feel that they are employed by a management which knows its business. If management gives the impression of knowing what it is doing then jobs are secure and labour relations can be put on a better footing. It is no accident that the better-run firms, the more efficient firms, the dynamic firms, tend on average to have less strikes and better labour relations than less go ahead enterprises.

In an uncertain environment workers fight for the maximum present rewards as they fear that their future employment is in jeopardy. If the well-run firm opens up a secure future for the labour force then workers become amenable to improving productivity in order to maximise long-term benefits. Clearly a responsibility lies on the trade union side at national and shop floor level to work for efficiency and good labour relations but equally management must show itself able to provide secure employment and growth.

APPENDIX

The parity problem illustrates the ease with which identical data can be manipulated to support different viewpoints. Comparison of sales and output per employee, for instance, or wage and salary costs per vehicle or total pay as a proportion of sales for different firms, do not take into account the fact that there are variations between companies' bought-out contents. The *higher* the bought-out content the more flattering would the above measurements appear in terms of labour productivity. A trade union negotiating team could point to higher sales per employee, lower wage and salary costs per vehicle and a smaller proportion of sales being accounted for by wages. This can be used to justify a larger pay claim per worker, conveniently forgetting that the most important factor is the high bought-out content. A more meaningful figure would be the value added per worker; the higher this figure in comparison to those produced by workers in other car firms the greater the justification for a pay claim, always supposing that the workers producing the higher value added are paid less than those in other firms and also that these other workers are *not* being paid more than their marginal revenue product. Often a high value added per worker is a sign of high capital:labour and high capital:output ratios and vice versa. So a poor performance on the part of labour may be caused by a poor investment programme on the part of the employer.

Further complications arise if a union case is based on hourly rates but an employer's rebuttal is based on yearly earnings. A firm suffering from few strikes and a high level of demand for its products gives a high level of employment and significant overtime opportunities. If such a firm pays lower hourly rates than a firm experiencing tremendous dislocation or a falling market, the employees of the first firm may have higher annual earnings. Clearly, however, the employees of a firm paying lower hourly rates must work longer to earn a given amount. There are other factors such as methods of wage payment, conditions of employment, the ratio of men employees to women and the amount of shift work which make a realistic comparison of the fortunes of different companies' employees extremely difficult to assess. The data on which parity arguments are based can thus be used by both sides of the bargaining table to bolster conflicting standpoints.

There is one area, however, where the statistics are reasonably unambiguous. As already mentioned* the two acid tests for a company's efficiency are the capital assets per man and the value added per man per firm, the two of which are shown to be highly correlated. What this relationship shows is that it would be quite unfair, for instance, for Ford to compare the labour productivity of its German and British operations without qualification. The output per worker in Ford (U.K.) may be only 75% of those in Ford (Germany), but British Ford in 1969 employed less than 75% as much capital per worker as its German counterpart. So despite the worse strike record of the former (*Table 12.8*) if the Briton was given the same automated tools as his German counterpart the productivities would be very similar.

One final point. From the available data there does not appear to be a

* See Chapter 10.

Table 12.8

DISPUTES AT FORD (U.K.) AND FORD (GERMANY) IN 1969

Year	Ford (U.K.)		Ford (Germany)	
	Strikes	Overtime bans	Strikes	Overtime bans
1967	50	36	0	0
1968	90	59	1	0
1969	63	26	1	0
1970	155	11	1	0

significant relationship between an increased incidence of strikes and a fall in car exports in the British motor industry (*Table 12.9*).

Table 12.9

STRIKES AND CAR EXPORTS IN THE BRITISH MOTOR INDUSTRY

	1960	1961	1962	1963	1964	1965	1966	1967	1968	1969
Car Exports (1000s)	570	371	545	616	679	628	556	503	677	772
Working days lost through strikes (1000s)	515	475	747	315	429	862	344	504	898	980
Number of strikes	129	102	116	129	165	165	170	223	233	297

The equation derived from the data, with car exports (E) as the dependent variable and days lost through strikes (X) as the independent variable is:

$$E = 490 \cdot 2 + 0 \cdot 15 X$$

The R^2 was 0·11 and the T statistic was 0·95★. Using the logs of the data the R^2 was 0·07 and the T statistic was 0·74. Hence no significant relationship was discernible and therefore one would hesitate to suggest that fluctuations in exports were significantly affected by strikes, either immediately or given a one year time lag. More often than not the increase in the number of working days lost was accompanied by increased exports, therefore little connection appears to exist between the number of strikes and the volume of exports.

★ The R^2 is the coefficient of determination, which is the ratio of the explained variation to the total variation. If the ratio was one then the variation in the dependent variable (exports) is all explained by the independent variable (strikes). As the R^2 is nearer zero than one in this case, and as the T statistic the test of hypotheses and significance is so low, given the size of the sample, then variations in the independent variable are not a good explanation of changes in the dependent variable.

INDEX